D1601181

At the Heart of the Empire

At the Heart of
the Empire

Indians and the
Colonial Encounter in
Late-Victorian Britain

Antoinette Burton

University of California Press

Berkeley / Los Angeles / London

University of California Press
Berkeley and Los Angeles, California

University of California Press, Ltd.
London, England

©1998 by the Regents of the University of California

Library of Congress Cataloging-in-Publication Data

Burton, Antoinette, 1961–. At the heart of the empire: Indians and the
colonial encounter in late-Victorian Britain / Antoinette Burton.
    p.   cm.
Includes bibliographical references and index.
ISBN 0-520-20958-3 (alk. paper)
1. East Indians—Great Britain—History—19th century. 2. Malabari,
Behramji M. (Behramji Merwanji), 1853–1912—Journeys—Great
Britain. 3. Ramabai Sarasvati, Pandita, 1858–1922—Journeys—Great
Britain. 4. Sorabji, Cornelia—Journeys—Great Britain.
5. Imperialism—Great Britain—History—19th century. 6. Great
Britain—Social life and customs—19th century. 7. Great Britain—
History—Victoria, 1837–1901. 8. Great Britain—Relations—
India. 9. India—Relations—Great Britain. 10. Great Britain—
Ethnic relations. I. Title.
DA125.S57B87 1998
305.891'411041'09034—dc21
96-29617

Manufactured in the United States of America

9 8 7 6 5 4 3 2 1

*To my father and my mother
for whom there'll always be an England*

"England," said Christophine. . . . "You think there is such a place?"

Jean Rhys, *Wide Sargasso Sea* (1966)

Contents

Illustrations

Acknowledgments

This book began with my curiosity about why two of nineteenth-century India's most accomplished women came to Britain seeking a medical degree but did not obtain one. That curiosity has been encouraged, indulged, and nurtured by many people. Although my gratitude cannot be fully expressed here, I hope to acknowledge at least some of my indebtedness to them. The research for this project would not have been possible without institutional support of all kinds. Thanks are therefore due to Indiana State University, the American Council of Learned Societies, and the American Philosophical Society, all of which financed summer research grants in support of this study. I am grateful to the National Endowment for the Humanities for the opportunity to participate in Michael Levenson's summer seminar, "The Culture of London, 1850–1920," which enabled me to appreciate Indian travelers' encounters in the imperial capital and the camaraderie of my fellow "Londonists" as well. Thanks also to Lynn Amidon at the Royal Free Hospital Archives, David Doughan and Veronica Perkins at the Fawcett Library, and, not least, Nicolle Ciofalo, Zachary Jaffe, and Valorie Huynh at the Milton Eisenhower Library at Johns Hopkins University, each of whom facilitated my research and helped track down obscure sources and references with apparently inexhaustible goodwill. William Alspaugh of the South Asia Collection at the Regenstein Library (University of Chicago) also proved helpful in finding the citation for a photograph, for which I am grateful. Richard Sorabji generously shared his memories and his photographs of Cornelia Sorabji, without which my understanding of her would have been quite different. To Amar and Sally Singh I am also grateful for glimpses of Janaki Majumdar. I have enjoyed the hospitality of the Sorabjis in Oxford; all the Arroyos in Chicago; Anna and Charles Denchfield in London; Audrey and Eric Matkins at Mellow Oak; the de Silvas in Sri Lanka; the Ahluwalias in Delhi; Ann McGrath and family in Sydney; and David Goodman, Julie McLeod, and Clara in Melbourne. I cherish these memories and look forward to repaying their generosity in years to come.

As I was writing and revising pieces of this manuscript, I was lucky enough to receive feedback from many generous and thoughtful colleagues in a variety of venues. All of them have contributed in large and small ways to the book it has become. They include Sanjam Ahluwalia, Sally Alexander, Emie Aronson, Marc Baer, Kate Baldwin, Sara Berry, Barbara Black, Joanne Brown, Barbara Caine, Chris Cannon, Sara Castro-Klaren, Nupur Chaudhuri, Paul Walker Clarke, Gary Daily, Deirdre d'Albertis, Lisa Kim Davis, Joanna de Groot, Susan Dehler, Chandra de Silva, Toby Ditz, Karen Dubinsky, Nadja Durbach, Belinda Edmondson, Shelly Eversley, Mary Fissell, Alison Fletcher, Ian Fletcher, Yaël Fletcher, Durba Ghosh, Pamela Gilbert, Rosemary Gould, Rob Gregg, Pat Grimshaw, Catherine Hall, Ellen Handy, Darlene Hantzis, Elke Heckner, Dorothy Helly, Heidi Holder, Kumari Jayawardena, Steve Johnstone, Sanjay Joshi, Morris Kaplan, Dane Kennedy, Diane Kirkby, Ann Klotz, Seth Koven, Lara Kriegel, Mike Kugler, Marilyn Lake, Michael Levenson, Maria Lima, Devoney Looser, Joseph McLaughlin, Harry Marks, Saloni Mathur, Fiona Paisley, Pamela Corpron Parker, Chandrika Paul, Sonali Perera, David Pike, Richard Price, Sumathi Ramaswami, Sue Reed, Jane Rendall, Frances Rosenfeld, Dorothy Ross, Bill Rowe, Penny Russell, Mahua Sarkar, Joan Scott, Sudipta Sen, Nayan Shah, Amy Smiley, Faith Smith, Mary Spongberg, Heather Streets, Hsu-Ming Teo, Kamala Visweswaran, Chris Waters, and Susan Zlotnick. Students in Audrey Kobayasi's women's studies class at Queen's University in the spring of 1996 were among the most engaged critics I have encountered, and I appreciate having been able to share my work with them. Among my students at Hopkins, Kelly Abbett, Sally Adee, Ghida Aljuburi, Angelique Budaya, Laurel Clark, Gail Dave, Suma Dronavalli, Jennifer Eggers, Anjali Kaur, Karen LeBlanc, Bahar Niakan, and Aileen Tien are remembered for their willingness to engage, to argue, and (especially) to disagree. Sheila Levine, for her part, has been a warm and supportive editor whose confidence in this project has been much appreciated.

Geraldine Forbes, Philippa Levine, Laura Tabili, Susan Thorne, and Angela Woollacott each read the entire manuscript in draft. Their comments offered challenges I hope I have met. Meera Kosambi and Uma Chakravarti were kind enough to read sections of the work-in-progress; their insights and their suggestions made all the difference. Mrinalini Sinha gave me astute and unfailingly helpful criticism all along the way; her influence on my work is perhaps greater than she realizes. Mary Poovey's guidance, and her friendship too, have been deeply appreciated. Janaki Nair and Padma Anagol were also careful readers; I only regret that our meetings are so infrequent. Maura O'Connor's warmth and like-mindedness are always comforting; and I am ever glad of Deb Rossum's companionship in the struggle. I feel as well profoundly grateful to Gerry Forbes for her high standards and dedication to women's history; to Barbara Ramusack for giving me a glimpse of "her India," and so much more; to Susan Thorne for her integrity and her critical insight; and to Angela Woollacott for her collegiality and friendship. Peter Marshall's interest and support have never subsided, while Doug Peers has been characteristically generous. Robert Reid-Pharr's wit, work, and friendship are cherished more than perhaps he knows.

George Robb keeps me in Victoriana, which makes all that walking almost worth it. Madhavi Kale's passion for history and her uniquely discerning eye help remind me of why I'm in this to begin with. Laura Mayhall is that rare combination of critical reader and faithful friend; meanwhile, Michael and Miss Izzy P. have made me laugh in Jackson and beyond it. Ann Klotz is as dear a friend as one could wish for. Knowing that Hannah Rosen is in the world makes many things possible. Jennifer Morgan has long been a mainstay, in work and play and matters of the heart. To Herman Bennett I owe an immeasurable debt—for all those walks around the track, but perhaps most of all for his political commitments. Kathy Navajas's friendship—and her affirmations—promise always to nurture and sustain. Thanks to Jan Paxton for her support in matters big and small and to Ranice Crosby for being in and around Jenkins Hall. Judy Walkowitz has offered me opportunities and insights from which I continue to benefit and for which I am grateful. In Philippa Levine, I continue to find a daily supporter and a remarkable friend.

This book is dedicated to my father and my mother—for whom there'll always be an England—in recognition of what they have given me, London included. Thanks to Monica (who prefers Paris); Vicki (whose love and laughter are essential); and Winnie and Frank (who are ever in my heart). And finally for Paul, who never asks but surely knows the reasons why.

Mapping a Critical Geography of Late-Nineteenth-Century Imperial Britain

This book examines three discrete instances of the colonial encounter in Victorian society — Pandita Ramabai at Cheltenham and Wantage, Cornelia Sorabji at Oxford, and Behramji Malabari in London — in order to explore how imperial ideologies played themselves out in personal, political, social, and cultural relations in late-nineteenth-century Britain. The accounts that these three left of their experiences in the British Isles in the 1880s and 1890s suggest that the United Kingdom could be as much of a "contact zone" as the colonies themselves.[1] Their experiences also provide historical evidence of how imperial power was staged at home and how it was contested by colonial "natives" at the heart of the empire itself. By investigating Indians' negotiations of colonialism in metropolitan localities, students of Victorian culture can more fully understand how Britain itself has historically been an imperial terrain — a site productive not just of imperial policy or attitudes directed outward, but of colonial encounters within. And by engaging with some historically specific colonial encounters "at home," readers of British history can more fully appreciate some of the ways imperial power relations were challenged and remade by colonial subjects not just in the far-flung territories of the empire but more centrally, in the social spaces of "domestic" Victorian imperial culture itself.

As Edward Said observes in the first few pages of *Culture and Imperialism*, historians of the West can no longer ignore "empires and the imperial context" in their history-writing.[2] The enduring purchase of Said's work — its "irritative process of critique" — lies in its insistence that what is at risk from attention to orientalism is the integrity of the European "heartland" itself, because "the principal motifs and tropes of . . . European cultural tradition, far from being self-generated, were the product[s] of constant, intricate, but mostly unacknowledged traffic with the non-European world."[3] Recent scholarship in British history has documented the traces of empire that were everywhere to be found at home before World War I — in spaces as diverse as the Boy Scouts, Bovril advertisements, and biscuit tins; in productions as varied as novels, feminist pamphlets, and music halls; and in cartographies as particular as Oxbridge, London, and the Franco-British Exhibition.[4] If there is little consensus about the significance of empire's impact on Britain's domestic cultural formations, primary evidence of its constitutive role nonetheless abounds, and scholars of the Georgian, Victorian, and Edwardian periods are at work to remap Greater Britain as an imperial landscape, using a variety of evidentiary bases and techniques.[5] More attention needs to be paid, however, to the cultures of movement that brought a variety of colonial subjects — Indian, African, Caribbean, Chinese, and even Irish — to England's "green and pleasant land" and made them visible on the cultural landscape well before the immigration trends of the post-1945 period.[6] Mohandas K. Gandhi, who lived in London in the 1880s, is just the most famous of many "native" Indian subjects who lived and worked in England, walking the city streets and encountering "native" Britons along their pathways.[7] And yet although it was axiomatic from the eighteenth century onward that even slaves were free once they set foot onto British soil, Indians were not at liberty to wander Victorian Britain without facing barriers thrown up by the exigencies of Britain's role as an imperial power and, more specifically, by the dictates of the civilizing mission that a variety of Britons believed to be their special gift to colonial peoples. As Liz Stanley has suggested, the map of the British Isles was itself inscribed with the *colonial* power of Britain.[8] This power was consequential not only in terms of its economic and political impact but also in its effect on everyday relations between Britons and their colonial "fellow subjects" — and between Britons and Britons as well, since the status of former slaves and colonial peoples was crucial to debates about what constituted "British" citizenship in the nineteenth century and after.[9]

Thanks to Rozina Visram's invaluable work, *Ayahs, Lascars and Princes: The History of Indians in Britain, 1700–1947*, we know that by the 1880s, Indians had been a presence in the British Isles for a hundred and fifty years: at least as long, in fact, as the British Empire in India.[10] What is less well-known is how, as "colonial" subjects, they experienced imperial ideologies at work in the so-called motherland: what it was like to be the "Other" in the British Isles, to encounter English people and prejudices on English soil, and to confront the kinds of colonial stereotypes that were the stuff of imperial culture not just in India but in Great Britain proper and among native Britons. This study examines how ideologies of imperialism worked in the cultural practices of some English people at the epicenter of empire — that is, the southeast corner of Great Britain — and how the colonial subjects they encountered there engaged with those practices.[11] It suggests that many Britons, even those who never left Britain, were implicated in imperial power relations because Victorian culture at home sponsored a variety of possibilities for colonial encounters of the most casual and the most spectacular kind. And it treats the accounts that Ramabai, Sorabji, and Malabari left of their sojourns in Britain not simply as the return or even the refusal of the colonizing gaze but as complex and critical ethnographies of late-Victorian British culture and society. In their letters, newspaper articles, pamphlets, and travelogues, colonial travelers worked to transform themselves (variously, temporarily, and often unstably) from objects of metropolitan spectacle to exhibitors of Western mores, and displayed for audiences (both public and private, Indian and British) exactly how unmannered and coercive Western "civilization," could be, particularly where imperial benevolence was concerned. In doing so they left historical evidence of empire's local impact in Britain, especially on convictions about what Victorian "Englishness" was and ought to be. Ramabai's, Sorabji's, and Malabari's sojourns in Britain illustrate how the colonial encounter in the late nineteenth-century Western metropole could unsettle the boundaries of empire and remake power relations in imperial culture. They also provide a glimpse of some of the shrewd social and cultural strategies that "the voyage in" required.

Pandita Ramabai (1858–1922) was an educator and social reformer who came to England in 1883 seeking a medical education through the good offices of sympathetic English women. Her initial contacts were with the Anglican Sisters of Saint Mary the Virgin at Wantage, whose connections with the educator Dorothea Beale in turn enabled her to study at Cheltenham Ladies' College. Although deeply influenced by her relationships with English women, Ramabai's conversion to Christianity and her subsequent struggles with the Anglican Church hierarchy over doctrinal matters caused her ultimately to break with both of the women's communities, religious and educational, in which she had resided. When she left England in 1886 she had not fulfilled her intention of becoming a medical doctor and, indeed, had found more sympathy and financial support among American women reformers than among her British "sisters"—in large measure because she resisted her benefactors' attempts to make her an evangelical missionary for India. Ramabai returned to India, where she became a champion of the Hindu widows' cause whose reform work in western India was celebrated throughout the world. The letters she wrote to a variety of English patrons while in Britain contested the reach of ecclesiastical authority in determining the direction of her reform activities. They also document Ramabai's close, critical reading of the colonizing practices enacted in the domestic Christianizing mission for India — an ethnographic approach that was pedagogic in purpose, aiming as it did to educate her patrons about the orientalist presumptions of their evangelizing intentions.[12] Ramabai's travels to the metropole reveal some of the constraints that imperial power relationships placed on the possibilities of women's solidarity, as well as the courage and self-determination required by an Indian woman trying to negotiate a path for herself and her reform program at the intersection of imperial Christianity, women's philanthropy, and social reform.

Three years after Ramabai's departure, Cornelia Sorabji (1866–1954) arrived in Britain to take up the study of law at Somerville College, Oxford. Sorabji came into contact with some of the great minds of her time — A. V. Dicey, Max Muller, Benjamin Jowett — and despite considerable opposition to her pursuit of credentials in the law, she passed the Bachelor of Civil Law exam in 1892 and qualified for the bar in 1922.[13] She became a pleader in the Calcutta court of wards and was famous internationally by the 1930s, both for her work on behalf of *purdahnashin* and because of her defense of Katherine Mayo's *Mother India*.[14] As in Ramabai's case, Sorabji's original intention in coming to Britain was to train as a doctor. A Parsi born into a Christian family in Bombay presidency, she believed, as did many other women of her generation (whether Indian or British), that the practice of medicine was among the most culturally appropriate professions for women. But her English friends in Britain dissuaded her from this path, hoping instead that she would become a teacher and hence help to advance their own schemes for female education in India. Sorabji strenuously resisted her patrons' attempts to fix her as a secular missionary for India and, as her correspondence to her family in Poona during these years attests, she struggled to wrest control of her own destiny from those do-gooders in Britain who claimed to have her best interests at heart. Her letters furnish us with another close reading of how imperial ideologies were at work in and around the philanthropic world of Victorian Oxford. Sorabji's success in negotiating both her patrons and the Oxford examination system testifies not simply to her personal determination to succeed but to her canny discernment of, and at times her complicity with, the ways in which imperial priorities masqueraded as "civilizing" philanthropy in Victorian imperial culture, especially where Indian women were concerned.

Behramji Malabari (1853–1912) did not come to Britain to pursue an education; nor was he dependent on benefactors for his passage, his living arrangements, or his maintenance. Unlike either Ramabai or Sorabji, he was a well-established professional man, a Bombay poet and journalist of some renown, before he arrived in London in 1890. And yet he too had to negotiate the status of "colonial native" that was continually ascribed to him as he wandered the byways of the late-Victorian imperial metropolis. Also a Parsi, he thought of himself as a patriotic colonial citizen-subject, and he arrived in England in order to organize support among English reformers and politicians for Hindu child-wives and child-widows in India. Like his countrywomen he encountered all manner of Britons in public and private; his account of his London sojourn, *The Indian Eye on English Life*, is most remarkable for what it reveals about the kind of reception Indian men might expect on the streets of the empire's capital city. Malabari encountered challenge after challenge to his aspirations to be a flaneur and, in the chaos of the urban metropole, to his quest to be seen as a respectable Indian gentleman as well. If his trip to London did not diminish his anglophilia, it nonetheless prompted him to produce a more critical reading of English culture, Western sexual mores, and European modernity than he might have done from Bombay. Partly as a result of his lobbying efforts in Britain and of the campaign against child marriage he helped to wage in Bombay, the Government of India passed the Age of Consent Act of 1891, legislation that raised the age of consent for girls in India from ten to twelve years of age, making sexual intercourse illegal with a girl below the stipulated age.[15]

Like Ramabai's and Sorabji's correspondence, Malabari's narrative of his sojourn in the "motherland" of the empire is a kind of ethnographic text, offering yet another close reading of English civilization, and especially of London life, in the late-Victorian period. As Sherry Ortner has argued, an ethnographic stance is as much a process contingent on the location of the body in space and time as it is "an interpretive mode"— a mode that travel throws into particularly bold relief.[16] Just as it did for the others, travel to Britain and across its various landscapes enabled Malabari to evaluate the twin phenomena of "Englishness" and British imperialism from a different perspective than was available in India, where encounters between the "native" and the "Briton" were different in degree if not in kind. Janaki Agnes Penelope Majumdar (W. C. Bonnerjee's daughter) recalled the fin de siècle Raj as a time when "Anglo-Indians thoroughly despised 'natives' as a class, though they were friendly enough to those whom they thought had money and position." If Indians wished to gain access to European society in India they had to adapt themselves to English manners and culture, though this was not necessarily a guarantee of social intercourse.[17] While opportunities for personal interaction with Britons may have been more available in Britain than in India (where the regulation of space was a crucial technology of colonial rule), the relative intimacy of metropolitan social life was routinely intruded upon, and indeed already fully constituted by, the presumptions of British imperial power. What Ramabai, Sorabji, and Malabari all came to understand, through different experiences and with various degrees of critical appreciation, was how elusive the goal of feeling comfortably "at home" as a British colonial subject in domestic imperial culture could be.

During an extended historical moment like ours when much attention is being given to the ways in which empire and its Others shaped Euro-American consciousness and cultural practices, narratives of colonial travelers in Victorian Britain remind Westerners that the flow of ideas, commerce, and people was not just from Britain to the colonies. Either because they were part of permanent communities with long histories and traditions in the British Isles, or because they were travelers or temporary residents in various metropoles and regions throughout the United Kingdom, a variety of colonial "Others" circulated at the very heart of the British Empire before the twentieth century. They were, as Gretchen Gerzina has noted, a "continual and very English presence" from the Elizabethan settlement onward.[18] To draw attention to this phenomenon is no mere pluralizing gesture. Ramabai's, Sorabji's, and Malabari's accounts rematerialize the movement of colonial subjects from the so-called peripheries to the ostensible center of the late-Victorian empire. In examining their narratives I hope to contribute to the project of recovering the presence of nonwhite peoples in Victorian Britain, to conversations about empire's impact on metropolitan society, and to the mapping of a new critical geography of "national" history in imperial Britain.[19] An enterprise like this one, which is committed to moving current debates about British imperial culture into the physical spaces of "home," requires a recognition of the fact that the will of the Victorian age was conceived in spatial terms. Consequently, the story of Britain's insularity from empire remains one of the most enduring fictions produced by Victorian culture, even if some elites and historians (like J. R. Seeley) were astute enough to see through the "conceptual separation of metropole and colony" that was a common, though unspoken, Victorian cultural possession.[20] People, ideas and commerce flowed from West to East in the narratives that dominated the nineteenth-century cultural imagination, with the "voyage out" serving as a recurrent metaphor for the centrifugal pull of Britain's colonial possessions. The exotic and safely distant world that Victorians mapped as empire figured almost as another planet, far away from England's green and pleasant land, disconnected in time and space from the mother country — that stolid and basically static domestic referent. In fact, of course, metropolitan society had been both indissolubly linked to and continuously remade by Britain's colonial possessions since the sixteenth century, when merchant capitalists first brought products of the European slave trade — gold, ivory, pepper, as well as some slaves — to English and Scottish shores. One simple and stunning measure of the material and symbolic impact of empire on "domestic" British society is to be found in the word "guinea," which, by the eighteenth century, had become the popular name for the gold struck into coin in 1663 from the coast of Africa.[21] Evidence of Britain's imperial wealth and power continued to make its way to the heart of the empire in the form of both human and commercial capital, as the traffic in goods and people from the colonies became crucial to Britain's national prosperity and international preeminence down to the midtwentieth century and beyond. Even after the abolition of the slave trade, colonial peoples came to Britain, taking up permanent or semipermanent residence; manufactures based on the raw materials produced from colonial plantations filled the marketplaces of the "nation of shopkeepers"; and displays of Britain's colonial influence and power were everywhere on offer in Britain at home — whether it was through the medium of political debates, missionary activities, consumer capitalism, novels, children's books, regional exhibitions, the decorative arts, or popular entertainments. Especially because claims about the impact of the imperial enterprise in Britain "proper" are coming under assault at the very moment when they are becoming axiomatic, it bears repeating that empire was and is not just a phenomenon "out there" but a fundamental and constitutive part of English culture and national identity at home, where "the fact of empire was registered not only in political debate . . . but entered the social fabric, the intellectual discourse and the life of the imagination."[22] Confronting the "local" effects of imperialism requires, therefore, a new cultural geography and, more important, a radically different way of looking at those cartographies to which we have become accustomed. It means working to see and to read the domestic cultural landscape for the traces of imperialism that are there, unobtrusive and perhaps even invisible to the eye trained in thinking of empire as something remote, at one remove from the "motherland." Historicizing the presence of colonial peoples in Victorian Britain makes manifest, above all, the various ways in which imperial England itself was available for consumption, appropriation, and refiguration by its colonial subjects.

Despite historical evidence to the contrary, the persistent conviction that home and empire were separate spheres — to which the Victorians, and many historians after them, have been so deeply attached — cannot be dismissed as just any other fiction.[23] As with all accounts of cultural identity, this particular representation of Britain's past and of its present involves a contest over geography, over territorial integrity — over what Victorians themselves called "the Island Story."[24] Histories of the presence of colonial peoples in the British Isles before 1945 provide the most contentious challenge to the narrative of splendid isolation produced by nineteenth- and twentieth-century historians, and not simply because they suggest that the flow of people and ideas from East to West helped to create and sustain metropolitan society. As Paul Gilroy has argued with regard to the emergence of black history in Britain, such narratives themselves are perceived as "an illegitimate intrusion into a vision of authentic national life that, prior to their arrival, was as stable and peaceful as it was ethnically undifferentiated."[25] Twentieth-century British politicians no less than nineteenth-century British historians have been opposed to narratives of Britain "as a racially-mixed . . . painfully divided, class-ridden society . . . [because that is not] the image of Britain that others should be allowed to see."[26] There can be little doubt that history, as a representation of a culture's past to itself and to the world, is above all else a terrain of struggle — or that representation itself, as a technology of cultural meanings, is implicated in all struggles for power. Accusations by a British government minister in 1995 that the elevation of historical figures like Olaudah Equiano and Mary Seacole to the status of British heroes constituted a "betrayal" of true British history and "national identity" surely testifies to the political contests that representation has the power to set in motion.[27] In their capacity as critics of the legend of the rise of a homogeneous, consensual nation-state, historians of domestic imperial culture insist on this struggle: for they challenge the presumption, foundational to the very notion of "English" history, that Victorian Britain, at least, was either purely white or unproblematically English. In doing so, they question the legitimacy of a national history that views the nonwhite populations of the late twentieth century as fallout from the disintegration of empire rather than as the predictable outcome of centuries of imperial power and engagement — or, more subversively, as Britons with a history at once inseparable from and at odds with the Island Story. As David Dabydeen has observed, the historical meanings attached to English convictions of insularity must be grappled with since, with over half a million West Indians in late twentieth-century Britain, "England today is the largest West Indian island after Jamaica and Trinidad."[28]

The trajectories of Ramabai, Sorabji, and Malabari through late-Victorian Britain are part of these counternarratives, though not necessarily in any self-evident way. They were only three of hundreds, perhaps thousands, of colonial subjects who passed through the imperial metropole for travel, for study, or in search of support for their reform projects in India in the nineteenth century. They are hardly representative of nineteenth-century Indians, let alone of the wide variety of colonized peoples, the Irish included, who came to British shores seeking education, work, or escape from economic or political oppression in the lands of their birth. A Hindu woman converted to Christianity, a Parsi Christian woman training in the law, a Parsi male social reformer— none of them was even predictably "Indian" in Victorian cultural terms, where stereotypes of "the Hindu" and "the Muslim" were common despite the cultural heterogeneity of the colonial population, and at a time when the notion of any kind of "Indian" national unity or identity was considered impossible.[29] At the same time, differences of gender, class, caste, religion, and sociocultural location guaranteed that their experiences of Britain and their appropriations of "Indianness" could not be identical or even typical of what any or all Indians on the move experienced. Most significantly perhaps, none of them took up permanent residence in the British Isles. Malabari's 1890 voyage was one of at least two between Bombay and London, and Ramabai visited England only once after 1886. Cornelia Sorabji, for her part, returned again and again over the course of her lifetime, insisting in her autobiography that she was someone who had "warmed her hands at two fires" and had been "homed in two countries, England and India."[30] The ways in which their narratives are linked to revisionist histories of Britain are thus complex, especially since those histories have often been produced in the service of reclaiming a "black Britannia," where "black" can mean colonial (i.e., South Asian, East Asian, Arab) but can also signify exclusively African and Afro-Caribbean communities.[31]

And yet, just as the Salman Rushdie affair is, to quote Gilroy, part of "the convoluted history of black settlement in Britain," the traces left by Ramabai, Sorabji, and Malabari of their experiences in the United Kingdom also have something to contribute to new cultural geographies of the imperial metropolis.[32] Their deliberate migrations remind us that in addition to the flow of European troops, travelers, and settlers from home to empire, there was a smaller but nonetheless influential movement of colonial peoples moving through the United Kingdom, making Britain at home a multiethnic nation and a site of diasporic movement across the whole of the nineteenth century. Gandhi's passage from India to South Africa to London and back again during the late-Victorian and Edwardian periods is perhaps the most famous example of how significant such colonial migrancy could be, though his impact on world-historical events should not distract us from the influence Ramabai, Sorabji, and Malabari each had on regional Indian politics and with it, on "national" Indian history as well.[33] To insist upon the phenomenon of migrancy in the Victorian period is not simply a function of updating or otherwise modernizing a British historical tradition that willfully disavows its own imperial past. Rather, I am interested in rematerializing the movement of colonial subjects from the "peripheries" to the ostensible center of the late-Victorian empire in order to interrogate the distinctions between Home and Away that defined the imagined geography of empire in the nineteenth century and, in the process, to challenge the quintessentially Victorian conviction that "England possesses an unbroken history of cultural homogeneity and territorial integrity."[34] And I take as my point of departure Mrinalini Sinha's call to revision Britain's historically national frame of reference in order "to recognize its location in a larger imperial social formation."[35] Integral to these projects is a recognition of the ways in which colonial peoples on the move to and through the metropole helped to established some South Asians as "Indian" and in the process, worked to consolidate Britons as "British" (or, commonly, as "English") and Britain itself as "Britain" in the late nineteenth century. Although the mobility of colonial peoples and their embrace of travel as an anticolonial and modernizing possibility may be something of a truism in cultural studies, the fact that their encounters with Britons in a variety of social spaces helped to secure "Englishness" as a cultural practice is by no means axiomatic among students of British, and especially Victorian, history. Indeed, for the cultural episteme of the Victorian period, where fixity — geographical, social, political — was nothing less than an emblem of the modern, foregrounding the movements of colonial peoples between, across, and around a variety of "modern" Western landscapes poses a critical challenge to traditions of Western history-writing dependent on the progress of the territorially bounded nations out of which such narratives have been produced.[36]

All of the individuals figured here also traveled in India both before and after their trips abroad, suggesting that the British "colonial" border need not be read as the chief marker of urbanity, modernity, or identity.[37] Paris loomed as large as London in the imaginations of many Indian travelers in the nineteenth century, as a survey of colonial guidebooks reveals.[38] Nor was Britain the only Western country to which these three traveled. Ramabai went to the United States; both Sorabji and Malabari traveled in Europe as well. All of these experiences are important for understanding who they were and how they engaged with "the West" more generally. At the same time, travel to and through Britain was freighted with specific (if varied) symbolic meanings for Indians in the nineteenth century because it produced a series of encounters — and for some, a display of cosmopolitanism — peculiar to India's relationship to the Raj. Taken together, the accounts left by Ramabai and others underscore the fact that the Victorian empire produced cultures not just of travel but of perpetual movement from East to West, out of which contemporary diasporas have grown and have begun to make their impact felt on nation-states globally. And their testimonies require us to remember that during the same historical moment when Indian culture and society was the relentless object of colonial scrutiny, there were some admittedly privileged colonial subjects at work producing ethnographies of "native" British culture that Britons had to confront and contend with.[39]

My emphasis on individual figures notwithstanding, I am not attempting to write definitive biographies of Ramabai, Sorabji, or Malabari. Critical evaluations of Ramabai's life exist, many of them written by feminist historians in and outside India, upon whom I have drawn heavily in my focus on her time in Britain. Sorabji is beginning to be treated as a subject of feminist inquiry, though until now little attention has been paid to the letters she wrote to her parents from Oxford. And while Malabari's activity in the Age of Consent Act controversy has been well documented, his roles as flaneur and ethnographer have not been examined in depth. Although their time in Britain undoubtedly shaped their biographies, I want to read the accounts of these three more specifically as evidence of how movement to and through the colonial metropole might influence, without fully determining, the variegated experiences of colonial subjects at a specific historical moment.[40] My emphasis on specificity of time (the 1880s and early 1890s) and place (Cheltenham, Wantage, London, Oxford) marks out a commitment to cultural analysis that is nonetheless vested in a densely historicized reading rather than in either pastiche or change over the *longue durée*. This commitment to historical "thickness" has been identified as one of the characteristics of cultural history — an investment that highlights its ethnographic as well as its linguistic turn and allows for a vertical rather than an exclusively horizontal vision.[41] A close reading of the testimonies treated here allows us to appreciate not only the particularized experiences of these three individuals but also some of the structural conditions and contingencies of late-Victorian imperial benevolence, one of whose primary objects of reform was "the Indian woman"— a late-Victorian metropolitan trope with which Ramabai, Sorabji, and Malabari each engaged, albeit in different ways. The fact that all three left textual accounts behind highlights their elite status compared with that of many colonial peoples who traveled in Britain, as well as the structural privilege such travel itself conferred on their discursive productions. The preservation of Sorabji's letters in the India Office Library in London through the influence of her friend, Lady Elena Richmond, effectively demonstrates how deeply archival collections are implicated in systems of socioeconomic power.[42] That many of her papers are housed in Britain and not in India may be a lasting testimony to Sorabji's anglophilia, but it is also evidence of the enduring power of colonial knowledge systems (like archives) to shape history-writing as well.

Significantly perhaps, the women wrote private letters, while Malabari published a book in two editions, in Bombay and London. Although I have focused on the writing each one did in the 1880s and 1890s for the sake of underscoring their contemporaneity as well as the significance of the fin de siècle for colonial cultures of movement, all of them wrote in a variety of genres during their lifetimes, a fact to which I have alluded in their respective chapters. In addition to being an acclaimed Gujerati poet, Malabari wrote for newspapers both in India and in Britain. Sorabji wrote journal articles and a number of books in English, including a 1934 autobiography. Ramabai, for her part, wrote books in English and Marathi, including a travelogue, *Pandita Ramabai yancha Englandcha Pravas* (1883) that details her time in England.[43] In this sense, the genres that shaped their ethnographies were neither singular nor categorizable as simply "gendered." The publication of Malabari's *Indian Eye* undoubtedly had much to do with the colonial sexual politics of the Age of Consent Act of 1891 which gave him such visibility in Britain as a spokesman for Indian women. Ramabai's and Sorabji's financial and emotional dependence on their benefactors and their families, who form the audiences for their correspondence, surely structured their letter-writing habits no less than their self-representations — circumstances that were as much the product of colonialism in all its complex dynamics as of their situations "as women." As with all primary sources, the experiences these materials give us access to are partial representations of complex historical realities, and the voices they permit us to hear require us to ask under what material conditions they have been made available, and for what purposes.[44]

Engaging critically with the temporarily diasporic voices such as those dealt with in this book calls for not just a reappraisal of the parameters and permeability of the nineteenth-century imperial nation-state, but an interrogation of what — and who — has traditionally been considered a legitimate subject of "British" history.[45] And because the politics of space and of territoriality is at the heart of historiography in the West, asking where imperial culture begins, where it ends, and how it is transported across boundaries must be part of that interrogation as well. Any struggle to reconstitute power relations is undoubtedly a struggle "to reorganize their spatial bases."[46] Few can escape the struggle over geography, and British history in an age of postcoloniality is no exception.[47] If narratives of geography are at stake in narratives of history,[48] then in the end making colonial people in Victorian England subjects of history may mean displacing nation-states like Britain and even India from center stage. It may call for an analytic frame, as Carol Breckenridge has argued, that recognizes that "the imperium at the heart of the nation-state" was "not an entity *sui generis*."[49] It may even require a cultural map that is "all border" as well — especially since the nation itself has historically functioned as "the ideological alibi of the territorial state."[50] "Who needs the nation?" is, therefore, not simply a rhetorical question.[51] It represents a call for history-writing that does not take the nation-state for granted, and may even question its imaginative centrality for some historical actors operating under specific material circumstances. In the case of Indian travelers to the Victorian metropole, at any rate, Britain was merely a temporary theater where colonial encounters occurred and certain kinds of cultural responses could be enacted. Resistance to the operations of colonial power at home was both possible and effective, even if it was not always chosen as a strategy of negotiation. It is worth underscoring that for Ramabai, Sorabji, and Malabari, as for many colonial peoples who traveled through the British Isles in this period, late-nineteenth-century Britain was in many respects just a passageway, one staging ground in a lifetime of professional commitments, political identifications, and social action. To those who doubted this, Ramabai and the others would likely have replied that the nature of their engagements with imperial culture in Britain had as much to do with the exigencies of contemporary Maharashtrian cultural politics as they did with concerns about British metropolitan perceptions. Indeed, as Kumkum Sangari has argued, "the colonial states and cultural formations established under the aegis of imperialism . . . produced specifiable ideological configurations which loop and spread across 'national' boundaries"—so that empire, nation, and colony were not necessarily always imaginatively distinct for these particular "Indian fellow-subjects."[52] The movements of colonial travelers across a variety of borders, and back again, suggest not that the transient inevitably becomes permanent but that " 'permanence' itself is an ongoing fabrication" upon which national histories no less than nation-states evidently depend. To echo Catherine Hall's evocative phrase, "unpacking imperial histories" means recognizing the insufficiency of core-periphery models and calls for analysis of the ways in which colonial subjects, goods, and ideas "criss-crossed" the globe.[53] The narratives examined here may, finally, be said to exemplify the claim that colonialism was not a process that began in the metropole and expanded outward but was, rather, an historical moment "when new encounters within the world facilitated the formation of the categories of metropole and colony in the first place."[54]

The project of historicizing the action—and the agency—of such ambiguously "national" subjects as the three people under consideration here presents exciting and unsettling challenges to the historian. Because critically engaged historical work aims to trouble conventional narratives and exhilarates in the shifting ground of historical production itself, it is important, and indeed essential, to embrace the challenges and offer interpretive frameworks against which evidence can be tested and new categories of analysis can be measured. This book attempts to take the question of cultural identity seriously because it has been and remains an extremely powerful discourse in the West, and because it provides important clues as to how subjects of history are simultaneously made and make themselves. Critical interest in identity is arguably a late-twentieth-century phenomenon, though as Himani Bannerji observes, "[T]here has been throughout colonization, slavery and after, an identity politics already in place — though not acknowledged as such." Indeed, one of the questions generated by the colonial encounter on the subcontinent and outside it was precisely how "Indians" were to acquire markers of cultural, regional, and religious identity that did not betray their "origins" but that were also intelligible — and instructive — to Western interlocutors.[55] *At the Heart of the Empire* presumes that colonial identities have not historically been unified but have instead been fragmented across a variety of cultural axes, and that they have been determined in part in the social relations of the everyday — at the intersection, in other words, of the public and the private, the personal and the historical, the social and the political.[56] The question of "determination" is undoubtedly a vexed one. Working out the connections between social determination and individual subjectivity is, as Ania Loomba remarks, an ongoing political struggle for students of power interested in understanding how culture operates and how people work within and against it.[57] With Aijaz Ahmad, Judith Walkowitz, and others, I define culture not as "entrapment," but as "the givenness of circumstances within which individuals *make* their choices, their lives, their histories."[58] The field of culture, in other words, is a terrain of ongoing struggle and practice, a "realm where one engages with and elaborates a politics."[59] As we shall see, in domestic Victorian imperial culture the fact of colonialism shaped the terrains through which Indians walked and the spaces where they were required to elaborate the politics of their location(s) as colonial subjects. Most significantly, even the "givenness" of these terrains was in flux, negotiable, contestable — so that they were able to act as agents even while they were interpolated in particular ways by colonial discourses.[60]

The case of Ramabai is instructive here. As chapter 3 illustrates, her experience of imperial culture at Cheltenham and Wantage brought her into dialogue not with a monolithic colonial Christian culture but with a variety of individuals and institutions who were differently implicated in the colonial projects of the Anglican Church. The bishops with whom she corresponded had an unmistakably evangelical agenda in mind: they wanted Ramabai for the mission field. So did the sisters of Saint Mary the Virgin — but at stake for them as an order and for Sister Geraldine as Ramabai's spiritual mother was their authority over a recalcitrant Christian convert from Hinduism. For them as for Dorothea Beale of the Cheltenham Ladies' College, fears about what the impact would be for the reputations of their all-female institutions should Ramabai not fulfill the wishes of their male superiors and benefactors contributed to their "colonial" attitudes toward Ramabai. Their personal and social locations, in other words, helped to determine their actions. Nor can English women's attitudes be judged the same simply by virtue of shared national and gender identities. Beale's own religious doubts made her more sympathetic to Ramabai than Sister Geraldine was, though perhaps no less colonial in her evaluations — an important reminder that Britons' relationships to empire were as differentiated as those of colonial travelers.[61] As for Ramabai, the theological arguments she advanced about the true nature of Christianity reveal the dangers of imagining identity as pure, homogenized, or unaffected by personal history and ever-shifting cultural locations. As shall be evident, her conversion to Christianity did not make her a Christian in any "given" or self-evident sense of the word: she fought the orthodoxies of Anglicanism in order to synthesize her own particular definition of the term and with it, her own pathway out of the constraints of imperial culture in Britain toward the reform of Indian women's condition in India. The convert is surely inescapably hybrid, especially where, as Sangari has suggested, to be hybrid means "to represent the pressure of . . . historical placement."[62] Ramabai's hybridity was neither predictable nor static, but radically contingent on time and place, as her contests with orthodox Hindus in India in the 1890s illustrate.[63]

If Ramabai's performances of cultural identity can be deemed resistant and even heroic, Sorabji's negotiations of imperial power and colonial relations in Britain provide an interesting contrast. They suggest in the first instance that the dynamics of "resistance" and "complicity" only partially capture the dialectics of the colonial encounter, regardless of what ground it occurs on.[64] Sorabji's letters moreover demonstrate that the behavior and attitudes of "the Indian woman" are never predictable, and that without a carefully historicized account of her "contexts of utterance," the category of "the Indian woman"— like the trope of "woman" itself — cannot stand.[65] I want to be clear here that my purpose is not to find the "authentic Indian woman" or to make "the native" speak — in part because I recognize, with Lata Mani and Rey

Chow, that speaking itself always already "belongs to a . . . well-defined structure and history of domination."⁶⁶ The task at hand is to resist interpretive regimes that require homogeneous selves by grounding an analysis of identities in the materiality of historical circumstances — by trying to match Sorabji's narratives, in other words, "to the occasion of their telling."⁶⁷ In scrutinizing the complex of cultural meanings that a figure like Sorabji engaged with as she struggled to speak "as 'the' Indian woman," I hope "to make available for political critique the network of meanings, assumptions, and images that constitute the background and the stuff of intentional action." Rather than representing a threat to agency, this kind of analysis helps to explain how agency is possible while recognizing at the same time the constraints imposed upon it by structural determinants.⁶⁸

Chapter 3 therefore looks at Sorabji's circulation around Victorian Oxford and London, using her weekly letters home to examine the kinds of strategic identifications she mobilized so that she could survive the pressures of being "the Indian woman" at Somerville College. As a Parsi "by nationality," the daughter of Christian converts well-known in the mission community in India and Britain, and an Indian woman studying for a degree in the law (when few women, whether English or Indian, pursued such a course), Sorabji was also a profoundly hybrid subject, laying claim to several interlocking identities at once. This point about the simultaneity of identities cannot be overemphasized: for her Parsiness and her Christianity were not serially related, as in laid side by side, but mutually constitutive. Nor were they the effects of an historically objective condition ("Indian womanhood"). They were, as we shall see, "very much a matter of narrative production"— with Sorabji as well as her English friends and patrons constructing her identity to suit their own purposes.⁶⁹ Deeply influenced by her parents' evangelical and reform activities, Sorabji was invested in a sense of ethnic authenticity vis-à-vis other Indians, especially Hindus, and indeed came to pathologize Hindu women in the same terms as many Britons did — all this while calling herself, and practicing as, a Christian. She was at times a resistant subject, as when she refused to be "placarded about" by the Church Missionary Society or when she opted for law rather than teacher training, against the wishes of one of her supporters. She was also resolutely anglophilic, antinationalist, and anti–women's suffrage — positions she first articulated at Oxford and that would continue to characterize her politics later in life. Nor was gender "extractable" from Sorabji's status as an Indian, a Parsi Christian, and a colonial subject — either in her eyes or those of the Britons she encountered.[70] It is worth underscoring here that Sorabji's time in Oxford was preceded by Ramabai's at Cheltenham and Wantage, and that Sorabji therefore lived, in the Victorian public eye, partly in the shadow of Ramabai's reputation. The publicity given to Sorabji's Oxford education was also preceded somewhat more sensationally by the reputation of another Hindu woman, Rukhmabai, whose Bombay divorce case filled the metropolitan and provincial newspapers in Britain between 1884 and 1888. Sorabji's quest to represent herself as "the" authentic Indian woman in Britain must thus be read against these and other floating signifiers of "Indian womanhood" that circulated throughout Victorian culture at home.[71] Her story is, therefore, important historical evidence of the instability and contingency of Victorian colonial identities not just at the level of macrohistorical circumstances but, as Vinay Lal has suggested in a different context, "at the micro-level of colonial practices in their minutiae."[72] The point is not that nothing can be generalized from an account of Sorabji's experiences, but that generalizations are often insufficient for understanding how multiple, contradictory, partial, and strategic identities can be in certain historical circumstances. Her identities were not, in other words, "an historically accomplished fact" but an ongoing, productive process.[73] What Sorabji's narrative suggests is that they were not only situated individually, but that she was continually producing them through recourse to what Frances Gouda calls a variety of "cultural grammars" as well.[74]

If Western ideals of femininity were crucial to these cultural grammars, Victorian ideals of manliness were also critical to dynamics of the colonial encounter as it occurred on British soil. The story of Behramji Malabari's sojourn in London detailed in chapter 4 illustrates how the presumptions of Victorian masculinity could shape an Indian man's "identity project" in a specific cultural context — that is, in the "mother" city of the kingdom and the empire.[75] *The Indian Eye* was part of a genre of travel literature written by Indian men in the 1880s and after for an English-speaking Indian audience; it also participated in the literature of investigative journalism in Britain initiated by Henry Mayhew and carried out by Henry Gavin, John Shaw, and Jack London well into the twentieth century. Malabari not only mediated both traditions, but his text demonstrates the facility with which a colonial subject could work the connections and inhabit the discursive domains between the two. Mediation was a cultural strategy perhaps uniquely available to Parsis, who in the nineteenth century acted as cultural negotiators between the English in India and other "native populations." It was a liminal position Malabari took up with great vigor in his campaign against child marriage, in which he chastised antireform Hindus for failing to protect vulnerable child brides with many of the same arguments English reformers had used against sati and child marriage. Indeed, his anglophilia matched Sorabji's and derived from the same sense of Parsi ethnic superiority to "other" Indians that she articulated.[76] Dressed in Indian "costume" and wandering around London in the company of an English woman, an Indian servant, or an Indian friend, Malabari was constantly assaulted by "street arabs" and other evidently well-meaning but curious native onlookers — as an object of fun, of ridicule, and of unwelcome solicitation. He was not much more free to walk the streets of empire than Sorabji was, although the terms upon which they were interpolated were perhaps gender specific: like a number of Indian men passing through English cities in this period, he was approached by a London prostitute, while Cornelia was accosted by an English woman who pronounced her to be "look[ing] so very heathen."[77] Malabari's intensified chivalry toward Hindu women in the wake of his trip suggests that like femininity, masculinity is not an exclusive or stable identity, that it is always mediated by race, class, and historical context, and that it is called into question variously, depending on specific, situational asymmetries of power.[78] Given the tremendous weight that Britons placed on the performance of "English" masculinity as evidence of colonial men's capacity for self-government, its confident display was considered necessary in order to prove that Indians were able to reform, if not rule, themselves. At stake, then, in the micropolitics of gentlemanliness for Malabari, as well as for a variety of members of the Indian National Congress who traveled to Britain in the late-Victorian period, was nothing less than the future and direction of British rule in India.

Implicit in each of these readings is the presumption that "the terms of cultural engagement, whether antagonistic or affiliative, are produced performatively"— and that there is no authentic or originary "Indianness" to be (re)captured.[79] In fact, each of the three colonial subjects here was engaged in performing "the" colonial as "the Indian" either willingly or resistantly — or in some less binary way, depending on the specific context and the stakes involved.[80] In many respects, "being Indian" was something to be learned by travel to Britain — a performance to be tested, a habitus to be tried out and reinvented on a regular basis, especially given the fact that "India" was not considered to be a coherent national political entity in the late-Victorian period.[81] Also implied here is a particular notion of hybridity. In contrast to some interpretations, from which I have certainly gained insight, the examples excavated here suggest that hybridity is not necessarily only about "mixed" biological or even cultural origins, but manifestly about movement through space and through time.[82] Sorabji's experiences and representations were not identical to Ramabai's, and their differences cannot be understood either in terms of their personal idiosyncrasies or the most obvious distinctions (i.e., Sorabji's Parsi Christianness versus Ramabai's conversion) between them.[83] Each woman operated within and against different "territorial imperatives"— different contexts of utterance that, although finally both Victorian and colonial, interpolated each woman in local and specific ways.[84] Malabari's experiences were both similar and different from those of his countrywomen, not just because he was a man but, again, because his masculinity had specific signification in the sexual-cultural economy of imperial London — signs that at once enabled him to make certain choices and worked to prevent him, in domestic imperial culture, from making others. These kinds of readings recognize that cultural identities are grounded in place[85] even as they self-consciously attempt to deracinate identity from its potentially static geographical moorings — at a moment when any theoretical engagement with identity, especially colonial identities, risks being dismissed as either fetishism or as an unreflected "romance of the indigene."[86]

Such readings give historical purchase to the concept of identity as performance and offer a possible way out of both the trap of essentialism and the vise of agency-versus-determination alluded to above — in large part because they presume that identity has historically always been "compromised." As shall become clear below, the travel accounts dealt with here suggest that identity may be, as Vera Kutzinski argues, "at best an open question, something to be negotiated and renegotiated across all kinds of divides on an almost-daily basis."[87] This approach furnishes a flexible and usable method for historians and other practitioners who wish to ground their work in the radical contingency of both history and culture because they see the two as fundamentally interdependent. The space of the everyday, of social relations, is a place where "the 'unspeakable' stories of subjectivity meet the narratives of history, [and] of culture."[88] The everyday is, in other words, one place where the work of historicizing cultural identities can profitably be undertaken, especially when the kinds of historical voices "recovered" here are not viewed as transparent, but are treated themselves as representations in a field of struggle and on a terrain of power.[89] The fact that Britain was itself an imperialized terrain arguably transformed even the "everyday" passage of Ramabai, Sorabji, and Malabari through it into a set of spectacular events, and it raises questions about how the fabric of imperial culture in Britain lends a particular kind of political dimension to the problem of the "domestic" subject.[90]

A place on the map is indeed a place in history and in culture — in imperial culture in Victorian Britain as well as in many other contemporary and historical locations.[91] And although this is an insight being produced and worked out at the margins of several disciplines and in the spaces in between — history, literature, African American studies, cultural studies, postcolonialism and women's studies — I acknowledge my intellectual debts to feminists, for whom the "dismantling of received geography," to borrow from Carole Boyce Davies, has been a preoccupation for a century and longer.[92] It is no accident that some of the most innovative and challenging work in British history, in diaspora and cultural studies, and in postcolonialism is being undertaken by feminist women and men for whom the politics of identity and of their own implication in it is key to revisioning history, culture, and power. Indeed, feminist scholars, by virtue of their interdisciplinarity and their reliance on real and imagined communities outside conventionally institutional frameworks, may be said to work in something like a diasporic relationship to the academy.[93] The kinds of rethinking and remapping that they have done, in dialogic tension with the lived realities of race, class, and postcolonial politics, under a plurality of signs and affiliations and for an equally diverse set of audiences and purposes, has been foundational to if not constitutive of the struggle for power inside the academy and out in the twentieth century. Feminist challenges have also been critical to contests about the politics of representation, of culture, and of history-writing. In aligning myself and this project with feminist work, I wish to make clearer the contributions that feminist practices can make to national histories, postcolonial projects, and gender studies.

Primary among these contributions is the conviction that "the recesses of domestic space," whether familial or national, are valid sites of historical excavation.[94] As Nell Painter has argued, if feminist history has taught us anything, it is that the private and the historical are not segregated domains of intellectual inquiry. Or, to put it another way, "inti-mate and social domains" are one.[95] Despite the insistence of some re-cent critiques to the contrary, feminist engagement with social position-ality and cultural identities need not substitute the personal for the po-litical, the "ludic" for the material, or representation for "reality." Especially if it is grounded in the material and respectful of context, feminist historiography at least can illuminate how inaccurately these polarities reflect the untidy complex of even marginal identities at work in culture — sometimes in the interest of social transformation, some-times in the service of conformism and tradition.[96] Insisting on the in-tersection of racial and class systems with the intimately historical lives of women and men is crucial to the politics of this conviction. So is the emphasis on identities as multiple attachments, as contingent on time and space and, above all, as the products of struggle.[97] As Meaghan Morris so succinctly puts it, "[T]here *is* now no way back from relational thinking about gender, race and class" to a simpler identity fundamen-talism — along *any* single axis.[98] Although this commitment is by now a commonplace of feminist theory, historical evidence that permits us to observe it in practice has been rare enough, especially outside the North American context. The colonial ethnographies examined here are exceedingly rich in this regard, and attention to them may help refine methodological approaches to the variously co-implicated systems of race, class, and gender — especially by challenging the facile use of race as a category of analysis, by insisting that it works not as a receptacle of meaning but rather as a crucible out of which gender and other identities are formed.[99] At the same time, of course, the ideological work and material realities of race and ethnicity do not always displace other cri-teria of social status, cultural power, or historical agency; and, as Susan Thorne and Madhavi Kale have argued, one discourse may, under cer-tain historical conditions, manage and even discipline another.[100] For this reason I am committed to questioning approaches to colonialism that insist on a binary axis between colonizer and colonized because they do not do justice to the complexity of colonial relations in situ. Again, although this is not a uniquely feminist insight, it has drawn much of its theoretical power from the work of feminist historians in the West and outside it.[101] Gender, class, caste, ethnicity, and religion complicated the apparently oppositional relations of colonial power in ways that are readily discernible — and like all historical interpretation, eminently con-testable — in the narratives offered here. Taken separately or together, they may not tell the whole truth about Victorian imperial culture, but they nevertheless attest to the fact that "we can no longer tell history as a single story"— or tell that story inside a single, national frame.[102] Most important, they remind us how critical it is for historians to acknowledge the need for multiple pasts and to embrace what Ann Stoler calls "the scrambled categories in which people lived," not just under colonial regimes but in the postcolonial present as well.[103]

CHAPTER I

The Voyage In

English social life is still English social life, and trying to enter it is like trying to enter a club.

Nirad C. Chaudhuri, *A Passage to England* (1972)

When Doctor Thorndike, the late-nineteenth-century forensic scientist and rival to Sherlock Holmes, walked at a leisurely pace along Upper Bedford Place, he observed that "the Asiatic and African faces that one sees at the windows of these Bloomsbury boarding-houses almost suggest an overflow from the ethnological galleries of the adjacent British Museum."[1] Thorndike's casual observation is one among many traces of evidence testifying to the nature of the encounter between Victorian Britons and colonial peoples on British soil. It illustrates the ways in which that encounter, however impersonal and apparently nonchalant, was startling and could prompt English men and women to articulate some revealing presumptions. Here Doctor Thorndike, with all the detachment of a scientist, classified contemporary Africans and "Asiatics" as fit for exhibition: he could only imagine them behind glass, as curiosities overflowing from the storehouse of Britain's "national collection." And, as most museum-goers are encouraged to do, he evinced no interest in how these artifacts of British imperial rule got to Upper Bedford Place or what they might be doing there. As such they remained a decorative backdrop to the larger narrative — a micro-museum of "collectibles" in and of themselves — thereby ensuring for the reader that Bloomsbury, like the British Museum itself, would be seen as "a storehouse of consumable goods that could be brought back to England" and as evidence of the aestheticizing influence of British colonialism at home.[2]

The people Thorndike saw at the window were most likely African, Caribbean, and South Asian men who had come to Britain seeking either employment or educational opportunities. Although colonial students tended to live all over London in the Victorian period and often moved from one lodging house to another during their educational course, Bloomsbury was as popular a location then as it is now because of its proximity to the British Library, the Inns of Court, and Temple Bar. The National Indian Association estimated in 1885 that there were upward of 160 Indian students at British universities; by 1910 the number was 700 and climbing.[3] Looking back on his student days in England the Indian nationalist Surendranath Banerjea remembered a thriving "Indian colony" in London, while another contemporary recorded that "the Bar [was] thronged with native Barristers-at-law" in the late-Victorian period.[4] Among the men who studied for the bar in fin de siècle London was Mohandas K. Gandhi, whose autobiography details his impressions of Britain, his encounters with the "natives," and his ongoing attempts to dress as an English man.[5] Although this book focuses chiefly on Indians in the south of England, it is worth underscoring that candidates for the Indian Civil Service and other degrees from India took up not just the life of English students but also their vacation culture as well, traveling all over the British Isles between terms and recording their impressions of rural and provincial life in addition to their encounters with the urban West. Thus even as images of and commodities from India populated Victorian culture at home, Indians themselves were traversing English, Irish, Welsh, and Scottish landscapes, making their way into the most localized of metropolitan spaces, seeing and being seen by a variety of native Britons.

Before proceeding, I wish to make explicit the parameters of the kind of "voyage in" I am tracking in this chapter. First and foremost, I am concerned with the later nineteenth century, which for heuristic purposes I will periodize as 1880–1914. I do so in order to combat the presumption that if historians want to talk about people of color in Britain they must talk exclusively about post-1945 population displacement; I want to resist the notion, in other words, that the phenomenon of colonial "natives" in the metropole is a twentieth-century phenomenon from which the Victorian period can be hermetically sealed off. There is detailed historical work available — as well as more work yet to be done — on colonial peoples, slave and free, who traveled to, lived, and worked in the United Kingdom in the centuries before the *Empire Windrush* brought immigrants and especially West Indian labor to Britain in a highly publicized wave of post-World War II emigration. According to Peter Fryer, "Black people — by whom I mean Africans and Asians and their descendants — have been living in Britain for close on 500 years."[6] Folarin Shyllon puts it ever more bluntly: "[B]y the middle of the seventeenth century at least, a thriving black community had been established, and Britain ceased to be a white man's country."[7]

Despite recent monographic attention to the question, scholarship on the multiracial, multicultural makeup of Britain has yet to make its way into the grand narratives of British history.[8] This disjuncture persists despite the fact that, as Kim Hall has argued, blacks were coming to the metropole and blackness was being consolidated as a cultural category at the very same moment that the term "Great Britain" was first being articulated in the early modern period.[9] And yet English men and women of the modern era ("Britain's white natives," to borrow from Roger Ballard) could not have been totally unaware that people of color circulated in the metropole, at least in urban areas.[10] With the triangular slave trade serving as the "spinal cord" of commercial capitalism, the traffic in slaves "was carried out before the full gaze of the public" into the early nineteenth century. People of color, slave and free, were everywhere to be seen on the streets, in the docks, and even on evangelical hustings, as the career of the mulatto Methodist minister Robert Wedderburn attests. Even when they were not actually present, images of slaves were everywhere inscribed — on the Liverpool Town Hall or in electoral placards and on all manner of ephemeral materials both before abolition and after. At the general election of 1831, "the abolitionists dragged Negroes to elections with golden chains and, where they could find no Negroes, chimney sweeps."[11] Refugees from Madagascar, "native converts" from China and Malaya, "colored" visitors to the Great Exhibition, held in 1851, and the occasional tour of colonial royals represent some of the more spectacular evidence of colonial peoples that Britons might have witnessed before the 1870s.[12] Nor was the figure of the metropolitan "black" limited to slaves or Africans. Well into mid-century and beyond, Britons would have been able to remember "when in the streets of London, Liverpool, Southampton and other ports, there was no more familiar spectacle than of Indian beggars, dancing and rapping their tom-toms under the windows," as one late-Victorian observer recalled. "Many were seamen, who had been robbed of their wages in the purlieus of the docks," he remembered, while "others were brought from various lands by speculators, to be exhibited at shows and theaters, and then likewise turned adrift."[13]

If British historians are alert to the demographic effects of Victorian and pre-Victorian imperialism, they cite them rarely enough. Until quite recently, when Victorianists have addressed empire they have tended to construe it as a rather abstract phenomenon "out there"—to be recaptured either through analyses of English men's and women's travel writings or through the high political discourses of government proclamations and official policies. Empire has also been viewed as a sporadically manifest phenomenon "at home," embodied in eruptions like the Crimean War, the Mutiny or the Governor Eyre controversy—events that intruded on a domestic culture that is presumed to be otherwise oblivious to the fact of empire. Christine Bolt's pioneering monograph, *Victorian Attitudes to Race*, is one of the few comprehensive studies to examine how racial discourses shaped nineteenth-century British culture, even as it firmly locates those discourses as exterior to Britain proper. "During the middle years of the nineteenth century," she writes, " 'race,' like 'civilization,' became one of the great catchwords of those Victorians who concerned themselves with events *outside Britain*."[14] The work of Lorimer, Rich, Walvin, Shyllon, Fryer, Visram, Killingray, Tabili, Hall, McClintock, and others has been an important intervention in this regard, even while as a corpus of scholarship it remains as yet underutilized by historians concerned with plotting the "national" histories of modern Britain.[15] When empire *has* had a face in domestic Victorian historiography, it has been that of the primitive and geographically distant savage or, even more telling, of the overburdened, cheerfully civilizing English man or woman who is equally far-removed from the comforts of "Home." Spatial remoteness—itself historically an indicator of backwardness and civilizability—has been a kind of unspoken requirement for defining an event, a discourse, or a physical site as properly "imperial" in Victorian culture. Despite the availability of primary evidence and secondary sources that point to the preoccupying presence of colonial peoples in nineteenth-century Britain, "the colonial encounter"—like empire itself—is presumed to have occurred out of sight, off-center, definitively "over there."[16]

The question of visibility inevitably raises the problem of numbers as well as of descriptors. In empirical terms, populations "of color" (a designation Kathleen Wilson argues was an eighteenth-century phrase) were both small and elusive of measurement in the Victorian period.[17]

Africans in the United Kingdom numbered 30,000 in the eighteenth century, though as Dorothy George remarked over fifty years ago, "their great number . . . has been little commented on."[18] Statistics are hard to come by, and categories are even more slippery. Peter Fryer estimates that there were 10,000 "black people" in Britain at the beginning of the nineteenth century; David Killingray puts the number of "Africans" at 4,540 in 1911 and 11,000 in 1951; Visram quotes sources testifying that there were almost 4,000 "lascars" alone in London in 1873–74 — a figure that included Indians, Africans, Malaysians, Chinese, Arabs, Turks, and South Sea Islanders. Nor do these kinds of numbers necessarily account for diasporic movement.[19] While statistics are scarce for the early nineteenth century, scholars agree that the 1850s witnessed a drop in numbers for the nonwhite community that rose again at the end of the century — a drop in keeping with the city's overall population decline in the 1860s and after.[20] In comparative as well as in absolute terms the "black population" — by which is meant, after Fryer and others, Afro-Caribbeans, South Asians, and their descendants — was a minority. Clearly the racialized nomenclature used to define these groups itself prevents, or at the very least problematizes, a cultural reading of their presence because it forces us back to skin color as the determinant of "Otherness," when in fact some "whites" (the Irish, the Jews) occupied the same socioeconomic status and discursive position as migrants from the Caribbean, India, and "the East."[21] Such facile categorizations also do little to account for the even more statistically elusive Eurasian population in Victorian Britain. Olive Christian Malvery, an Anglo-Indian Christian woman who captivated turn-of-the-century metropolitan audiences with her photojournalist investigations of the "dark" side of London life, has been recently "rediscovered" by James Winter and Judith R. Walkowitz. Like Ramabai, Sorabji, and Malabari, Malvery represents just one of the more spectacular, and in her case, mixed-race, "Britons" available for historians' scrutiny. Her canny manipulations of images of the Indian, the Jew, and the Cockney suggest how precarious these identity categories could be and how contingent their production was on recognition by an urban middle-class audience.[22]

The "voyage in" of Jewish and Irish immigrants, in addition to a variety of European nationals, Arabs, and Chinese toward the end of the century, meant that black Britons were one of many "non-English," "nonwhite" groups inhabiting the British Isles, with the vast majority of them living in cities. From Mayhew's "Hindoo tract sellers" to the "lascar's room" in *Edwin Drood* to the mysterious Indian jugglers in

Wilkie Collins's *The Moonstone*, colonial figures crossed the Victorian field of vision, representing themselves in fiction, protoethnography, journalism, and a variety of more ephemeral locations.[23] Late twentieth-century race relations experts, surveying the migration trends of five centuries, commented in 1970 that although a diversity of people had come to settle in Britain since the early modern period, "their variety pales to the sameness of a monochrome print when they are compared with the immigrants of the tropical Commonwealth who have arrived here in the last twenty years."[24] The late twentieth-century "scopic feast" notwithstanding, there was a mosaic of communities in the British Isles well before the First World War. George Sims's *Edwardian London* provides incontrovertible textual and visual evidence that while they may have numbered only in the thousands, by the end of the nineteenth century immigrants to the United Kingdom had created a kaleidoscopic effect across the landscape that caught — and held — the metropolitan eye.[25] By 1901, journalists referred to the "Indian and Colonial side of London" as part of a terrain routinely "inundated" by "representatives" from "the utmost frontiers of the Empire."[26]

There will be some for whom these demographics signify a negligible presence at best and, indeed, the relative statistical fewness of colonial "natives" in the metropole may help explain the historiographical invisibility of colonial encounters in Victorian Britain until the crop of work on "coloured minorities" appeared in the 1970s and 1980s. This brings me to my second point. For although I am not unmindful of population statistics, mine is not an argument about the ratio of white English to black Britons in the nineteenth century; nor is it contingent on the number of Africans or Indians that we can count as having lived in the British Isles before World War I. I am less interested in patterns of residence or even communities per se than I am in the fact of colonial peoples' travel to and movement through a variety of British landscapes in the Victorian period — what Paul Gilroy calls "traditions of ceaseless motion" that are particular to, though perhaps not exclusively identical with, the "black Atlantic" experience.[27] I believe with Toni Morrison that the habit of ignoring the presence of even these continuously mobile colonial subjects in and across Britain may be "understood to be a graceful, even generous, liberal gesture" but that "it requires hard work" and "willed scholarly indifference" *not* to see nonwhite peoples on the Victorian landscape, however numerically few they may have been.[28] For there is abundant evidence that they were everywhere — on street corners, in West End theaters and lodging houses, in traveling road shows and exhibitions, in slums and working-class neighborhoods, in university lecture courses and medical school laboratories, speaking from public platforms and on the floor of the House of Commons. In all these spaces they encountered Britons who also encountered them, even if, as Ruth Frankenberg has observed, "the Other [has been] more palatable [when] confined within the white imaginary than in person."[29] Taking notice of these encounters puts Edward Said's insights about the centrality of empire to work in the context of a "national" metropolitan history like Britain's, thereby challenging historians of western European modernity to face some of the limitations inherent in writing domestic histories as if empire had left no trace of itself in either human or commercial capital "at home." Said and those who dialogue with him are thereby compelled to acknowledge that the colonial periphery can be found at the metropolitan center not just contemporaneously but historically as well.[30]

My third and final preliminary point is this: while there has been a tremendous amount of work done on the Afro-Caribbean diaspora by an international congeries of scholars, less attention has been paid to the South Asian diaspora in historical terms. In fact, despite a growing body of work around this subject — both in terms of academic books and novels and shorter fiction — the concept of a "South Asian diaspora" has to compete for legitimacy in academic circles with the African and Jewish diasporas and has, by implication, to prove its own historical viability.[31] One result of this phenomenon is that scholarly work on peoples of African descent in Britain has been carried on not only in isolation from the mainstream of British social and cultural history, but also without benefit of the insights to be gained by historical work on the Indian diaspora in the United Kingdom and elsewhere. Historically as today, minorities in Britain have not necessarily been political allies, partly because of racism within communities of color and partly because of the ways in which the dominant culture depends on, and even requires, divisive stereotypes and intranational apartheid in order to exercise what hegemonies it does.[32] One notable exception to this was the Indian-Irish alliance in parliamentary circles in the 1880s.[33] Another was Dusé Mohammed Ali, a Pan-Africanist who endeavored to create ties with the Asian community and to forge Afro-Asian solidarity among displaced colonial peoples in imperial Britain in the decade before World War I and after its outbreak. Ian Duffield's work on Ali and on the communities surrounding the *African Times and Orient Review* in particular suggests possibilities for alliances between a variety of "black Britons" that have not for the most part been realized since. And there is some evidence to suggest that Indians in the Victorian period exhibited the same kind of racism toward Africans as "native" Britons did.[34] Nonetheless, Indians did participate in the creation of a particular kind of diasporic corridor between South Asia and the Victorian metropole, compelling white Britons to meet them on equal ground in the motherland and to take them seriously as British imperial subjects instead of viewing them simply as the exotic objects of the domestic, civilizing gaze. As we shall see, Indians used their experiences in imperial Britain to strengthen their various personal and political commitments to professional advancement, to reform, and in some cases to Indian nationalism on the world stage. Neither the imperial cultural politics of daily life in the late-nineteenth-century metropole nor indeed the fate of the British Empire itself can properly be understood without reference to their presence in Britain at home in the Victorian period.

Although Ramabai, Malabari, and Sorabji were exceptional in many respects, they were part of a continuous stream of colonial travelers, students, and reformers who made their way to and through the British Isles in the nineteenth century. Indian students and Indian princes are among the colonial people most visible to historians of Victorian Britain because of the texts they left behind and the kinds of middle- and upper-class cultural spaces many of them traveled through. The arrivals and departures of well-heeled Indian visitors were regularly noted in the *Indian Magazine and Review*, the journal of the National Indian Association. Papers like the London *Times* and periodicals like the *Illustrated London News* and the *Saturday Review* gave regular attention to Indians resident in the United Kingdom and their activities. Indians of all castes, classes, religions, and ethnic communities had been a presence in the British Isles for a century and a half by the time Ramabai, Malabari, and Sorabji took up temporary residence in southeast England in the late-nineteenth century. Ayahs, lascars, and princes, students and reformers, politicians and maharanis — all traveled to the heart of the empire in the Victorian period. Some remained; others were just passing through. Still others — like seamen who jumped ship — were forcibly returned to India through the combined efforts of the India Office, elite Indians, and metropolitan reformers.[35] Dadhabai Naoroji, known as "the Grand Old Man of India," was elected a member of Parliament for Central Finsbury in 1892. His election, together with that of M. Bhownaggree to the House of Commons in 1895, marked the high tide of Indians' visibility at the national political level in late-Victorian Britain.[36] In addition to these men in high places, there were other colonials in London with a different but equally revealing relationship to the corridors of power who caught the public eye. As Joseph Salter, a member of the London City Mission who took a special interest in the Indian poor at home, told his audience in 1873, "[W]ithin a short distance of the Houses of Parliament some twenty Asiatic vagrants are living."[37]

Salter continued to do work for the mission into the 1890s, recording the sites around the city where destitute and working-class Indians lived and chronicling the comings and goings of Indian elites like the Queen of Oude and the fate of dozens of lascars as well.[38] Indian women were less frequent travelers to Britain than Indian men were, though some of the most famous Indian women of the nineteenth century — Pandita Ramabai, Cornelia Sorabji, Rukhmabai, and Sarojini Naidu, among others — came to England in the 1880s and 1890s in search of educational, professional, and reform opportunities. Sunity Devi, the Maharani of Cooch Behar and the daughter of Keshub Chunder Sen, was one of a number of dignitaries' wives who traveled to Britain for ceremonial occasions like the Queen's Jubilee celebrations.[39] Wives of lascars and destitute Indian women are much less visible in traditional archives, but a variety of popular sources suggest that they too were scattered across the domestic, and perhaps especially the urban, landscape. Many seamen and presumably impoverished women too died of diseases contracted during the passage to Britain, of cold and starvation on the docks and on the streets of London, or else by violence in the byways of the city. Salter's two treatises, *The Asiatic in England* and *The East in the West*, provide evidence that for every Indian who ended up on the floor of the House of Commons or returned to India as a barrister there were several at least who either died or lived out their lives in poverty in the urban neighborhoods of Britain's port cities.[40] Indian beggars were also a common sight on the streets of Victorian London, and "colonial natives" were to be observed as woodworkers, dancers, "villagers," and visitors in 1886, when the Indian and Colonial Exhibition made a huge and successful spectacle of empire in the capital city.[41]

It is worth emphasizing that the flow of Indians to England and back again was just one dimension of diasporic movement out of South Asia into the rest of the world and that not all Indians who came to Britain did so out of unconstrained choice. The end of slavery and the Africa slave trade in the 1830s provoked a crisis of labor in British colonies, and efforts to recruit workers were directed toward India; in addition to settling in the United Kingdom, Indians ended up in the West Indies, South Africa, Fiji, Burma, and elsewhere, often as indentured workers. The ostensibly "free" labor they provided served the postemancipation imperial economy extremely well, guaranteeing as it did that the production of colonial commodities could continue uninterrupted and that the myth of Britain's leadership in fostering economic progress through the mobilization of a "self"-governing "colored" workforce would be consolidated in new historical forms.[42] In fact the problem of Indians abroad was an important topic for the early Indian National Congress, as for example when the British government tried to regulate labor practices or, as in the 1890s, to oust "free" Indians through literacy tests because they were threatening the commercial viability of white traders in South Africa.[43] Gandhi's own formative experiences and his agitation on behalf of expatriate Indians there is powerful evidence of the far-reaching political impact of South Asians in diaspora worldwide. As Hugh Tinker has observed, Indians have always been a "people on the move." Even in India itself, "population mobility was inherent in the social order and the peasantry lived in a state of flux." The great diversity of motives and circumstances that have prompted this diaspora notwithstanding, Western stereotypes have emphasized Indian emigrants as impoverished laborers — with Gandhi himself typically referred to as "the Coolie lawyer."[44]

Determining with certainty how Britons, in all their social complexity and variation, received Indians who crossed their paths in the United Kingdom is a difficult proposition. A *Times* correspondent reporting on the visit of a Muslim dignitary in May of 1884 remarked that "the individuality of a Asiatic makes but little impression on the mind of a European observer, who is apt to consider him as a type of his race and creed, and not as a man with some personal qualities and feelings which make him different from his neighbors."[45] As Kim Hall has observed with regard to Africans in Jacobean England, "[T]he status of black people as curiosities or oddities meant that they were considered both as individual 'cases' and as emblematic of a larger group."[46] How interchangeable one "Asiatic" might be with another in early Victorian Britain may be evidenced from reports that when Rammohun Roy, the Indian theist who visited England in the late 1820s, appeared on the streets of London, he was greeted by cries of "Tippoo! Tippoo!" For English people well versed in the history of British conquest in India, Tipu Sultan — a powerful late-eighteenth-century Indian leader based in Mysore who repeatedly tried to thwart British attempts to consolidate colonial rule under Cornwallis and Wellesley — was perhaps the most recognizable embodiment of an Indian man they could conjure.[47] In fact, Roy's impact on public perceptions of India and Indian people was ultimately enormous, in part because he died while in Britain and was buried at Stapleton Grove near Bristol. That he was a theist and was willing and able to converse with contemporary English evangelicals about the possibilities of reconciling Hinduism and Christianity made him all the more celebrated as a martyr to Indian reform among a certain segment of the British public. One reviewer of his memoirs described him as "a vigorous opponent of Hindu superstition" and "a subtle disputant with Christian ministers" — two qualities that led to some interesting encounters with English men and women.[48]

While in London, Roy was the guest of families living in Bedford Square and Regent Street, and he met a wide variety of people at dinner parties and At Homes given in his honor.[49] After his death, Mary Carpenter, who had hosted him in Bristol and was present at his death, organized a volume of memoirs to commemorate his passing as well as his impact on the English people he encountered. Matthew Hill recalled as follows: "I only met the Rajah Rammohun Roy once in my life. It was at a dinner party given by Dr. Arnott. One of the guests was Robert Owen, who evinced a strong desire to bring the Rajah over to his socialistic opinions. He persevered with great earnestness; but the Rajah, who seemed well acquainted with the subject, and who spoke our language in marvelous perfection, answered his arguments with consummate skill, until Robert somewhat lost his temper, a very rare occurrence which I had never witnessed before. The defeat of the kindhearted philanthropist was accomplished with great suavity on the part of his opponent."[50] English women who met Roy "in public" were often eager to do so because they believed that he was either on the verge of converting to Christianity or that he all but embraced it. Religion provided a respectable cover for the kind of social intercourse with a man of color on British soil that would have been otherwise unthinkable at the time and, for that matter, for some years to come in India.[51] The following anecdote, supplied by an unnamed "estimable lady," gives some inkling of the sensation Roy caused "in society," not just to those women who spoke with him but to those who observed such exchanges as well.

At a small evening party at my house in Grenville Street, [organized] principally to meet the Rajah, he referred to the doctrine of original sin, in a way that startled a lady of low church, a very charming and amiable woman, who had brought her daughter. "But surely, sir," she exclaimed, "you don't believe in original sin?" He looked at her, and she blushed deeply. After a minute, he seemed to comprehend the whole, and very gently inclining, he said, "I believe it is a doctrine, which, in many well-regulated minds has tended to promote humility, the first of Christian virtues; for my own part, I have never been able to see evidence of it."

The next morning my sweet friend called to apologise for what she said, and added that she had never seen or heard anything so beautiful as this in society.[52]

Whether on the city streets of London when taken for "Tippoo" or in the more privatized space of the London drawing room, Roy was made into something of a spectacle by onlookers, many of whom were invested in representing him as a "manly figure," not to be confused with the portly "Baboos who babble." One contemporary, who left an account of Roy's sojourn in Britain, assured readers that "in the prime of manhood his figure was beyond the common height, and was stout and muscular in proportion."[53] The traditionally Western feminine qualities of "gentleness" and "sweetness" through which he was constructed by middle-class English women legitimated their interactions with him at the same time that it enabled them to feel a part of the British civilizing mission. "Who knows," wrote one of Mary Carpenter's correspondents, "but this man may be one of the many instruments by which God, in his mysterious providence, may accomplish the overthrow of idolatry?"[54] As the above passage indicates, Roy was no pawn in these imperial parlor games. While he pursued discussions about the relationship of Christianity to Hinduism both in private and in the public forums of the British periodical press, he steadfastly, if politely, resisted attempts to brand him as a convert — and no doubt vexed many acquaintances by proffering the view that "Jesus was an oriental."[55] He attended several different Unitarian chapels, but as one observer remarked, "it was his system to avoid . . . identifying himself with any religious body." And he remained until his death puzzled and somewhat bemused by his own popularity in Britain. "I must confess I have done very little to entitle me to your . . . admiration of my conduct," he told a Unitarian meeting in 1831. "What have I done? — I do not know what I have done! — If I have ever rendered you any services they must be very trifling — very trifling I am sure."[56]

As with a number of Indians visiting Britain in the Victorian period, Roy was made into a celebrity by well-meaning Britons interested in shaping his work, his image, and above all his Indianness to their own ends. Despite the fact that he had traveled to the United Kingdom as a political observer and consultant — he was interested in the Reform Bill and had business with the East India Company — he was lionized as "the Apostle of the East" and cast before the public primarily if not exclusively as a religious reformer.[57] His commentaries questioning the Shastric origins of sati were used to transform him into an authority on social questions and, posthumously, to justify English women's intervention in women's condition in India.[58] The celebrity that British social and political reformers afforded him in Britain, and particularly his ties with Mary Carpenter, helped attract Indians to Britain, not least because he was buried near her Red Lodge home in Bristol. His mausoleum was an important pilgrimage site for Indians in the nineteenth century, and few who came to Britain to study did not make the journey to pay their respects. More often than not in the 1860s and 1870s they also visited Mary Carpenter and were thus drawn into the ever-growing circle of social reformers and feminists in Britain interested in and organizationally committed to Indian reform.[59]

It would be an exaggeration to say that Roy alone precipitated or even prompted the flow of Indians to Britain. But the publicity given to his visit in Britain and in turn in India made travel to the British Isles a mark of progressive social commitment and reform leadership — especially for a certain class of Indian men. In the 1870s, Roy's image as the quintessentially cosmopolitan Indian was briefly overshadowed for the next generation of metropolitan social reformers by Keshub Chunder Sen, who toured the British Isles in 1870. Like Roy before him, Keshub Chunder Sen was a theist who had been instrumental in the formation of the Brahmo Samaj, a reformist Hindu organization in Bengal. Brahmoism has been described as a "halfway house" between Christianity and Hinduism. Its members were theists who opposed idol worship and believed that "personal religious adaptation and wider social reform could take place within the embrace of Hindu tradition."[60] The Brahmo Covenant established by Debendranath Tagore in 1845, with its call for the worship of a Supreme Being and the doing of good works, would seem to ratify this definition, though the split between Tagore and Keshub Chunder Sen over doctrinal issues as well as the ramifications of conversion for caste status suggests how contested it could be.[61] Why Keshub decided to visit England in the first place is not entirely certain. His seven-month sojourn (March to September) followed on the heels of his rise to prominence as the leader of the Brahmo Samaj.

The consolidation of a variety of smaller sects he carried out under its umbrella in the 1860s came at the expense of old friendships and some supporters in Bengal, and he may have felt the need to escape organizational and sectarian-political pressures for a while. He told Frances Power Cobbe that he wished "to study the social institutions and customs of the country" and to spread "knowledge of the social and moral condition of India" among Britons.[62] In any event, Keshub Chunder Sen's trip was a tremendous success insofar as publicity was concerned, and it confirmed in the minds of many Britons the possibility that there was great scope for English social reform schemes in India.

"English cities sometimes take strange fancies to . . . certain individuals for a season, and London specially suffers from such fits of sporadic hero-worship. . . . [Keshub Chunder Sen] became the rage of the day. There was no newspaper that did not chronicle his doings, and there was no English town to which his fame did not spread." So wrote Pratap Chandra Majumdar, a young disciple of Keshub Chunder Sen's who was one of several attendants to accompany him on his first and only trip to Britain.[63] As Keshub's biographer, Majumdar was invested in proclaiming the success of the trip. And yet it would be difficult even now to gainsay the accuracy of his account. Sen was mobbed by an English public for whom the memory of Roy was fading and the cause of India was becoming extraordinarily popular— due in part to the publication of Mary Carpenter's *Six Months in India*, which narrated her first trip to the subcontinent in two volumes. In it she described what she viewed as the lamentable condition of women's and girls' education and called for English women especially to throw themselves into the work of colonial reform.[64] Keshub's diary records the whirlwind of visits, talks, dinners, services, and tea parties he attended not just in London but all over the United Kingdom. He was so busy and so exhausted by all the demands made on him by an eager British public that he had a breakdown two months after arriving.[65] Given Roy's fate under similar circumstances he could not but be alarmed and after his collapse he undertook a more measured routine.[66]

Like his celebrated countryman before him, Keshub Chunder Sen was introduced to a variety of prominent English men and women from all walks of life. He met with Lord Lawrence, the former viceroy, conversed with John Stuart Mill, and was presented to the Queen at Osborne. He visited Frances Power Cobbe, a well-known theist and women's rights supporter who commented that he was the only Indian she knew "who could enjoy a joke thoroughly, like one of ourselves."[67] He mixed socially

with Max Muller, the orientalist at Oxford, met the historian J. R. Seeley, breakfasted with William Gladstone, attended soirees organized by
Elizabeth Adelaide Manning, and participated in a Female Reform Society meeting where Millicent Fawcett, John Bright, and Harriet Taylor
were all in attendance.[68] For recreation he watched the university boat
races, toured Westminster Abbey, and sampled the paintings at the
Royal Academy of Arts. In addition to the social whirl, Keshub gave
literally dozens of talks at Unitarian chapels, temperance societies, city
halls, theistic and philosophical societies, and private meetings all over
England and Scotland, many of which have been reprinted with his diary
by The Writers' Workshop in India. These documents, together with
contemporary newspaper accounts of his visit, lend credence to both
Meredith Borthwick's estimate that Keshub Chunder Sen was seen by
as many as forty thousand Britons and Max Muller's claim that he was
a "household name" in Victorian Britain.[69]

Keshub's popularity among the British bordered on obsession, and
this tells us something about how ready a certain stratum of English
people was to recast what they "saw" in Keshub Chunder Sen according
to their own scruples and prejudices. His eating habits (he was a vegetarian) were such a source of fascination that the Reverend Robert
Spears of the Foreign Unitarian Association "drew up a routine of his
daily habits which were published in handbills" and circulated all over
the south of England.[70] Newspapers reported on his lectures, tours, and
receptions, and not always in flattering terms, as *Punch*'s sarcastic little
ditty "Baboo Keshub Chunder Sen" testifies. "Have *you* heard — if so
where and when — / of Baboo Keshub Chunder Sen? / The name sur-
passes human ken — / Baboo Keshub Chunder Sen! / Big as an ox, or
small as wren / . . . Let's beard this 'lion' in his den. / So come to tea
and muffins, then, / With Baboo Keshub Chunder Sen."[71] Commentators routinely dwelled on his physical appearance, which the *Pall Mall
Budget* reported as "striking." He had, the author continued, "a certain
quiet dignity, in harmony with the simplicity of his dress and the absence
of any formal gesticulation. His features are well cut, and combine a
certain sweetness with an expression of marked decision."[72] This was
very much in keeping with the tensions inherent in descriptions of Roy
some forty years earlier: there is a process of effeminizing going on here
that was apparently necessary to reconcile Keshub's Indian "simplicity"
with his reformist intellect and his appeal to British women. Sen was
lionized by the latter, many of whom commented on his physical appeal.
Frances Power Cobbe, for example, thought he was "the ideal of a great

teacher." "He had a tall, manly figure, always clothed in a black robe of some light cloth like French *soutane*, a very handsome square face with [a] powerful jaw; the complexion and eyes of a Southern Italian; and all the Eastern gentle dignity of manner."[73] Cobbe also commented on how well he and Majumdar spoke English; Keshub in particular spoke "without error of any kind, or a single betrayal of foreign accent." Although the Unitarian chapels would appear to have been chiefly responsible for his wide circulation around London, in her autobiography Cobbe recalls that it was she who "gathered many influential men to meet him and they were impressed by him as much as I was."[74]

Keshub, for his part, professed to be as baffled as Roy had been by the attention, especially from "the ladies." "Is it because they are more kind and hospitable to strangers or are they more hearty in their sympathy with Theists?" he wondered in his diary. By no means were all of his encounters with women easy ones. In the middle of April he recorded receiving a letter from a Mrs. Bevan, whom he had never met, "saying she had something very important to communicate to me and that she would be very glad to see me at lunch someday. . . . With great curiosity I drive down to see her. But how bitter and sad is my disappointment when I find that after giving me a somewhat cold reception she begins to preach and catechises me as to what my difficulties are in accepting Christ in an orthodox way. It shows her warm and firm faith indeed, but to me it is anything but agreeable after the trouble and expense incurred in coming all this way."[75]

His dealings with Mary Carpenter were even more discomfiting. Although he did not record any of it in his England diary, Keshub Chunder Sen's attendant Majumdar gave the following account of what he witnessed his master experiencing at Carpenter's home in Bristol: "[She] took in hand her oriental guest most completely and, with her well-known discipline, gave him incessant direction about the usages and etiquettes of English society. Her restless spirit of reform criticised his dress, his diet, even the manner of combing his hair; in fact she hemmed him in with so many warnings, injunctions and engagements that the mild Hindu reformer felt inconveniently straitened. We are afraid Miss Carpenter at times found Keshub an intractable pupil, and in the end something like a coolness sprang up between them, but Keshub bravely pulled through the crisis at Red Lodge."[76] Keshub proved intractable in matters other than his personal grooming habits. He resisted embracing Christianity "in an orthodox way," and while he preached extensively in chapels, on Sundays, on subjects like "God Is Love," "Whom Have I in

Heaven but Thee" and "Christ and Christianity," he rejected all attempts
at proselytizing and finally (possibly because of other unrecorded instances like his tea with Mrs. Bevan) decried many of the tenets and
cultural forms of British Christianity at his lecture for the Swedenborg
Society in June.[77]

What's more, although he approved of English women's schemes to
help Indian women's education and suggested that Carpenter found
what was to become the National Indian Association for this purpose,
Keshub Chunder Sen was not as supportive of women's rights issues as
some in Britain might have hoped. These expectations were in any event
somewhat misplaced, since although he had supported widow remarriage as part of the Brahmo program, he had not declared himself in
favor of women's emancipation before coming to Britain. His biographer, Meredith Borthwick, argues that he believed in women's equal
access to religion but never saw emancipation as an end in itself.[78] At
his lecture "Female Education in India," given in conjunction with the
East India Association at the Society of Fine Arts in London in May of
1870, Keshub Chunder Sen condemned child marriage as "pernicious"
and recommended zenana (secluded, single-sex) instruction for Indian
women. This in itself was not at odds with what English women envi-
sioned for Indian girls, but Sen's later reversal on child marriage was.
At least one of his English female correspondents, Sophia Dobson Col-
lett, broke with him when he allowed his underage daughter Sunity to
be married to the Maharaja of Cooch Behar—this, after he had helped
to ensure the passage of the Native Marriage Bill in 1872, which conferred legality on Brahmo marriages, set an age minimum of sixteen for
boys and fourteen for girls, and sanctioned both intercaste marriage and
widow remarriage.[79] Sen, for his part, was undaunted by what his English friends thought of him. In his last public address in Southampton
in the fall of 1870 he declared to the listening crowd that "as I came here
an Indian, I go back a confirmed Indian . . . [F]arewell, dear England;
with all thy faults, I love thee still."[80]

Keshub's position on his daughter's early marriage effectively retarded
the momentum his reputation had gained after over half a year in England. It was "the most controversial event" in the history of the Brahmo
Samaj as well, and Sen's reputation in India never really recovered from
it either.[81] Although he and Roy were conventionally paired in British
imperial discourse as models of progressive Indian manhood and social
reform leadership, Roy underwent something of a revival as a cult figure
and a model in Britain in the aftermath of the Cooch Behar controversy.

By the 1880s he was being compared not just to Keshub Chunder Sen but to a new generation of Indian men coming to Britain in greater numbers to plead the case of Indian nationalism before the British public. The *Saturday Review* held Roy up as an exemplary figure in 1888 — calling him a masterful orator and a dispassionate advocate of reform and change — in explicit contrast to the "Bhoses and Ghoses," who were nothing but "bombastic," "turgid," and capable of repeating nothing but "stale arguments" from public platforms.[82] The markedly hostile response that the British press exhibited toward these later reformers is something I will return to. For now it bears reiterating how foundational the images that the British constructed of Roy and to a lesser degree of Keshub Chunder Sen remained to notions of what an Indian gentleman should look like and how he should behave in the imperial metropole — and how crucial these images were in shaping a variety of other colonial encounters in Victorian Britain.

The Victorian, and particularly the London public's, preoccupation with Rammohun Roy and Keshub Chunder Sen, as significant as it was, should not prevent us from seeing how far beyond the capital city these men traveled, or that there were other Indians, mostly men and some women, who made their way across the British landscape and hence were there to be seen and observed by native Britons. As I have noted, both Brahmos not only toured England but traveled all over the British Isles. Although most Indians who came to the United Kingdom had business of one kind or another in London, they often combined schoolwork or official duties with more leisurely tours of the countryside. Two naval architects from Bombay, Jehangeer Nowrojee and Hirjeebhoy Merwanjee, lived and worked for two years in England between 1839 and 1841 and are good examples of how mobile colonial natives in Britain could be. Their almost five hundred–page journal details the hundreds of places they went in and around London and beyond — from Madame Tussaud's to Windsor Castle to Maidstone to Bristol to Gloucester to Glasgow. Everywhere they went they drew crowds of local people, large and small, eager to catch a glimpse of them and their retinue of three servants. When they arrived at London Bridge "an immense number of persons flocked round us to view our costumes . . . [We] five persons in the Parsee costume collected quite a mob . . . [W]e think a thousand persons congregated."[83] They may have overestimated the number, but they also repeatedly testified that people gathered as they traveled, and not always unobtrusively. On one occasion people called out to ask them whether they were Chinese, Spanish, or Turkish.

The two men did not record an explicit objection to this, but they understood that they were being scrutinized and exoticized. On their visit to the Zoological Gardens, they remarked that they attracted "a very great number around us for the peculiarity of our dress, and we were objects of very great curiosity to the visitors — as much so perhaps as the winged and four footed animals of the place."[84] Even in small towns they were mobbed by curiosity-seekers: "[In] all the little places through which we passed, poured forth nearly their whole population to gaze upon us in our foreign costume." So great were the numbers in one town that Nowrojee and Merwanjee had trouble getting back into their carriage.[85]

It might well be argued that country people traveling to London or city folk walking Victorian English country lanes would have attracted as much attention as Indians in either place. Like the more famous Roy and Sen, the Bombay architects were nonetheless made a spectacle of in the streets — an experience that prompted them to comment on the apparent precariousness of British imperial power. As if to dwarf the imperial metropole in return, they observed in passing that "we thought it a great wonder that such a small and insignificant speck as England appears [to be] on the map of the world, can . . . attract so many nations . . . to her."[86] Remarking on and grappling with the experience of being made a spectacle of in the imperial metropole was in fact one of the chief preoccupations of Indians writing about their experiences in Victorian Britain. Indeed, there is hardly an account written in English by an eastern traveler to England in the nineteenth century that does not mention the public scrutiny to which Indians were subject, due mostly, they believed, to their "Oriental" clothing but also to their "dark" visages in a sea of white faces.[87] Some, like the Persian dignitaries visiting Bath in the 1830s, surely exaggerated when they claimed that "over ten thousand men and women" gathered outside the window of the house they were staying in. Such hyperbole was no doubt designed to convey that oppressive sense of being watched which other colonial travelers would echo down the century. What began as amusement ended in annoyance, and they were "obliged to leave the windows and conceal our caps."[88] Lesser personages did not perhaps attract the same kind of attention, but walking about unhindered by an obtrusive public gaze was difficult even for the average Indian traveler. Behramji Malabari, whose *Indian Eye on English Life* was published in 1893, was accosted by "street arabs" and well-meaning English ladies wanting to take his photograph. Nor was he alone in believing that on several occasions he was the object of solicitation from streetwalkers — or that he had been singled out because he "looked" Indian.[89] If Indian men were subject to commodification and aggressive consumption as they walked the streets of the mother country, the relatively few Indian women who aspired to be flaneurs experienced the constraints imposed on them by the simultaneous burden of being female and colonial in public. As Cornelia Sorabji, who studied at Oxford in the 1880s, recalled in her autobiography, she was stopped on the street by a passerby who, unsolicited, exclaimed that she looked "so very heathen."[90] Negotiating what Michael Levenson calls the many "interior spaces" of urban life produced its own kind of spectacle as well.[91] T. N. Mukharji, who came to London in an official capacity for the Indian and Colonial Exhibition in 1886, recounted what a stir he caused by sitting down to eat in one of the refreshment areas inside the exhibition hall. He was particularly aware of the curiosity of one family, who spent the better part of ten minutes pointing to and whispering about him, until the father finally approached and engaged him in conversation about the Indian wares on display. He obliged, and even pulled up a chair to sit with them. But he was not unaware of the spectacular effects of this rather intimate, albeit public, colonial encounter. "I went on chattering for a quarter of an hour," he reported, furnishing the daughter of the family "with sufficient means . . . to brag among her less fortunate relations for six months to come of her having actually seen and talked to a genuine 'Blackie.' "[92]

The fact that the culture and artifacts of India were everywhere on display — both formally and informally — throughout Britain in the Victorian period shaped the social and cultural terrain through which Indian travelers walked and complicated the terms upon which they were obliged to negotiate their own spectacularity in the eyes of native Britons. Dr. Thorndike's casual observation, quoted at the beginning of the chapter, suggests some of the stereotypical representations produced at the intersection of commodity capitalism, museum culture, and imperialism at home with which Indians in the metropole had to reckon. The Great Exhibition of 1851, which displayed the raw materials and the wares of Britain's most celebrated "possession," also brought a number of colonial people under the gaze of the British public.[93] As Annie Coombes has so skillfully demonstrated, by the end of the century a wide spectrum of the British public was quite used to consuming colonial Others in exactly the same fashion; for many who had been school children in the 1890s and after, to do so was a regular and unremarkable feature of school outings and later of childhood memory.[94] In addition to the British Museum, there was the Museum at South Kensington, which by the 1870s housed a celebrated collection of Indian artifacts, some belonging to the former East India Company, some the leftovers from the 1851 exhibition; Madame Tussaud's, which had displays of the Indian Mutiny and a variety of Indian princes in wax; and finally, the Indian and Colonial Exhibition, whose lavish Jeypore, Bombay, Punjab, and other Indian courts drew over five million visitors in the several months it was open to the public.[95] Indians traveling to Britain in the late-Victorian period made the rounds to these sites as well as to other more ephemeral exhibitions.

Their reactions to "India on display" varied from nonchalance to bemusement to sadness and satire. Rakhal Haldar Das, who studied at University College, London, in the early 1860s and later became a civil servant in Bengal, recorded his disappointment with the India Museum (in South Kensington): "It was painful to see the state chair of gold of the late Lion of the Punjab with a mere picture upon it; shawls without Babus; musical instruments without a Hindu player; *jezails* and swords without *sipahis* and *sawars* . . . and above all, hookahs without the fume of fantastic shapes!"[96] Where Thorndike smirked at the spillover of colonial "collectibles" into London streets, Das mourned the absence of "real" Indians and hence, for him, the fundamental inauthenticity of Western curatorial inventions of "the Indian way of life." His lament might be read as a contestation of what Donna Haraway calls "the effective truth of manhood, the state conferred on the visitor who effectively passes through the trial of the Museum." In this case, Das seems to be challenging the possibility that the colonial body could successfully be (re)produced or made permanent through exhibition.[97] That Das visited the exhibit six or seven times in the course of his year and a half in Britain gives some indication of the contradictory responses temporary exile at the heart of the empire could evoke.[98] P. J. Ragaviah professed to be frightened by what she saw of the Indian Mutiny in Madame Tussaud's Chamber of Horrors: "[T]he illustration is so very exact that I thought I was on the battlefield, and so did not stay long for fear of swooning." Significantly, she did not record the slaughter scenes but claimed that all that she could recall in the end was the rather noble figure of the Nana, "whose model is placed in a sitting posture, of pale dark colour, with a brahminical thread across his shoulder."[99]

Such organized spectacles were not, in other words, passively consumed. R. C. Dutt, for example, thought that the Indian and Colonial Exhibition proved that "backward as India is in machinery and in practical and useful products, her ancient arts, her exquisite workmanship in gold, silver and ivory, and her fabrics of fine texture and unsurpassed beauty, are still the wonder of the modern world, and were the themes of unbounded admiration among hundreds of thousands of English ladies who visited these Courts."[100] Spectacles like the exhibition of 1886 were quite purposefully reproduced by Indian observers both as critiques of how the British saw India as well as evidence of Indians' capacity to consume British (imperial) culture like any other "native" Britons. At times the didacticism of museum display worked in interesting ways. Nowhere was this more powerfully evident than at the British Museum, which Inderpal Grewal has aptly termed "an embodiment of aesthetic classifications."[101] Jhinda Ram waxed eloquent about the Egyptian galleries in the British Museum in his 1893 travelogue, *My Trip to Europe*, identifying apparently quite effortlessly with the orientalist readings of Egypt as a classical but finally primitive culture ripe for collection at the imperial center.[102] Differentiating India as not just any colony but a special and culturally superior British possession was constitutive of the late-Victorian exhibitionary impulse, and it was a message appreciated by a number of Indian visitors to Britain.[103] Even so, such distinctions were neither uniform nor predictable: India was at times displayed in "ethnological galleries" alongside African materials, and "West" Indian performers could be read by naive Britons as "South Asian" *Indians*, as Mukharji discovered to his distress when talking to some English visitors to the 1886 Exhibition.[104] He did his best to disabuse them of this misapprehension, thus revealing his own investments in appearing as a certain kind of colonial person: closer to a citizen perhaps than to a subject, if citizenship meant the capacity to distinguish a subject from an object — the capacity, that is, to recognize and to appreciate the "real" colonial.

It could be argued that Indians exhibited aspirations to both Englishness and British citizenship by embarking on a kind of Grand Tour and producing narratives of that tour for consumption at home in India. Significantly, a number of the travelogues written in the 1880s and after were entitled some variation of "My Trip to Europe," of which an account of Britain might be proportionally the largest part, with the majority of that in turn devoted to London. The resulting guidebooks were written to be of general use to Indian travelers and students and, one has the impression, to satisfy a middle-class, English-educated or-speaking Indian public eager to devour a commodified Britain as armchair tourists as well. Westminster Abbey, Saint Paul's, the Inns of Court,

Buckingham Palace — all these attractions were displayed in fairly for-mulaic terms, with appropriate digests of English history rehearsed in order to contextualize in both space and time the map of London that inevitably emerged. As Jhinda Ram wrote enthusiastically of London, the entire city was a "living museum."[105] If this is a return of the imperial gaze, an objectification of the imperial metropole in response to the kinds of relentless scrutiny to which Indians were subject in Britain in public, it is also of course a shrewd and canny advertisement for the consuma-bility of Britain by an Indian reading public. Given the fact that crossing the ocean threatened to violate caste proscriptions, the proliferation of guidebooks and similar texts suggests the secularization of a certain stra-tum of Hindu society that orthodox reformers in India feared; their end-of-century rhetoric may even have been in part a response to this phe-nomenon. The popularity of such productions may in any event be gauged by a remark made by R. C. Dutt in the preface to his 1890 book, *Three Years in Europe*. His publisher had been pressing him for a long time "to bring out my travels to Europe," but he had been skeptical. " 'It is an old story now,' I said, 'many of my countrymen have traveled in Europe, and all know about Europe.' 'It may be an old story,' [the pub-lisher] rejoined, 'but [it is] none the less interesting to us.' "[106]

The 1886 exhibition undoubtedly helped to galvanize this literature. It was advertised in the *Bombay Gazette* as well as in other Anglo-Indian newspapers in India from the moment of its inception in 1884 until its dismantling in the fall of 1886. Thomas Cook and Sons offered special tours from India designed to reassure Indians worried about fulfilling caste requirements on the sea voyage over, and a number of Indian men wrote travelogues occasioned by their visit in 1886 which had originated as columns in Indian newspapers about their experiences.[107] The exhi-bition also provided a spectacular opportunity for a number of Indians to articulate their relationships to empire and, most important, to en-gage that overdetermined signifier of civilization, English culture. Eigh-teen eighty-six was crucial, therefore, not just because it displayed so much Indian cultural material, and not simply because it brought so many Indian and other colonial visitors to London, but because it pro-vided an opportunity for Indian men to reveal the failure of the will to imperial power intended by the exhibition, as well as to articulate their own views about what such an abortive bid meant for the future of India. R. C. Dutt's account is significant here. Like other such travel-ogues, it is full of the sights and sounds of London, of amazement at the traffic, the shops, the sheer vastness of the city — all the conventions, in short, of the London guidebook. Although he happened to be in London at the time of the exhibition, he made it clear in his narrative that he was dragooned by the reception committee into being put on display, along with other "colonial visitors," at various parties, fetes, and ceremonies connected with the exhibition. His insistence that they pursued him, in spite of the fact that he had not registered his name anywhere, suggests not just how conspicuous he felt he was, but how many controls, albeit unofficial, were in place to monitor the mobility of Indians in Britain.[108]

One of the exhibition excursions was to Bristol, where the "colonials" were given a tour of local manufacturing concerns — but not before being paraded with flags and banners all through the city streets.[109] Dutt recounted how he struck up a conversation with one of the owners, who warned him not to be misled by the apparent prosperity of London and, by implication, by the confidence displayed by the exhibition. "Times were never harder," Dutt was told. "Our ships remain in our harbors, our manufactures find no markets, our men are unemployed . . . all the markets are glutted, all nations are competing." At the dinner that followed, one of the organizers made a speech in which he hinted that the white settler colonies like Australia might repeal their import duties on English goods, and there was a spirited debate on the notion of imperial federation — an idea that the "colonials from Australia spiritedly reject, arguing that colonies should be given 'permission to manage their *own* affairs their *own* way.' "[110] What happened next is a telling rhetorical maneuver on Dutt's part. He segued almost immediately into a discussion of the 1886 election, in which debates about Irish Home Rule rocked the country, and in which Gladstone's Home Rule proposal was roundly defeated. Dutt did not miss a beat:

But one need not be a prophet to see that Ireland *shall* have some kind of a home rule before long . . . and is it a bold prophecy to make that the time is not so far distant — that some of our young men may live to see it — when it will be considered unwise to govern any country or any people without consulting the people's wishes, without some kind of representative institutions? Men in power at the present day will laugh at the idea — but nevertheless, the wave of liberal opinions in England is advancing with a rapidity which is remarkable and significant. Measures which were considered radical 15 years ago are now considered practicable or even not advanced enough, and conservatives in the present day are, it is a well-known fact, purloining and adopting one by one those measures which 20 years ago one could only broach as ideas. The conservatives cannot help themselves — they must either do this or go to the wall — for the nation wants these measures. And in no respect is the advance of these liberal ideas more conspicuous than in . . . the relation of England with her dependencies. Many of us who are young and even many of us now in our middle age will probably live to see the day when the people of India will have a constitutional means of expressing their views on the administration of their country, when their views will to a large extent shape that administration, and when their hands will to a great extent manage that administration. The divine right of conquerors will be as obsolete a phrase in the political dictionary of the twentieth century as the divine right of kings is in the nineteenth, and the people of India will be [as] proud of their connection with England as the sons of Englishmen in Australia and Canada.[111]

Here, Dutt moved from a critique of the exhibition to a critical reading of another quintessential product of English culture: the parliamentary election. He argued that the political system that had just turned out the liberals did not know the true desires of "the nation" and suggested that if the Liberal-Whig interpretation of history was correct, home rule for India was inevitable. Not least, he implied that the passage of Indian colonial administration into the hands of Indians was a foregone conclusion. And finally, because it was after all the exhibition that had originated this narrative, he referred back to the conversation over free trade at Bristol with no small irony; for if Indians proved to be as "proud" of their connections to the motherland as the Australians at the Bristol banquet, the continuation of Britain's economic stability in this brave new world was by no means guaranteed.

When Indians traveled to the heart of the empire, then, they discovered themselves as "colonial subjects" *and* worked to remake that very category by reappropriating the imperial gaze and, in some cases, explicitly challenging the aim and direction of British imperial politics at the highest level. Others ostensibly less concerned with returning the imperial gaze have nonetheless left evidence behind to show that they were neither contained by London nor constrained by being exoticized in the ostensible motherland. Rabindranath Tagore, who studied at University College, London, in the late 1870s, rode the omnibuses and railways all over the city and into the suburbs. He also spent time in Brighton and at Torquay where his brother's wife lived with her children.[112] Indians studying for the bar or for medicine were often buttonholed as speakers for local temperance, education, or female reform gatherings. The National Indian Association, which had branches all over England in the 1870s, would have been one such venue.[113] Indians took holidays

like any other university students and they would have been seen traversing the lake region, the Scottish highlands, and even Ireland in in-
creasing numbers after the 1880s. University towns like Cambridge, Oxford, Glasgow, and Edinburgh had their share of colonial migrants and
immigrants as well. How they were received in these diffuse spaces is
difficult to know; their memoirs are not usually detailed on this score,
and the nature of their encounters was no doubt peculiar to time, place,
and context. Das, for example, commented obliquely after his return
from a visit to Brighton that "I can afford to bear the ridicule of men
who are dazzled by mere appearances"— suggesting that he might have
been accosted either verbally or physically on the street.[114] This kind of
direct physical assault was not uncommon. Gandhi mentioned it, but
only in passing, as having happened to an Indian friend of his in London, while for Behramji Malabari, it was an unwelcome, an unpleasant
and, finally, a bewildering experience.[115]

Indians recording such experiences in Britain did so with various
degrees of criticism as they looked back on "the voyage in." Nellie Blair
(née Bonnerjee, daughter of W. C. Bonnerjee) spent much of her childhood in Croydon boarding with an English family, where "it was always
impressed upon us that we being Indians were inferior, that our parents
paid too little for us in return for what we got, that our hands could
not be clean being dark-skinned, etc., etc."[116] Tagore, for his part, waxed
eloquent about the English family he lived with and praised the mother
of the household for embodying the "ideal of the Indian wife." At the
same time he remembered that the headmaster at the public school he
briefly attended remarked, "What a splendid head you have!" a characteristic of which he was acutely conscious for the rest of his life.[117] And
his account of being made to sing upon command for one elderly English female acquaintance was an experience whose embarrassment Tagore could scarcely contain in his memoirs.[118] On the other hand, Syed
Ameer Ali, a Muslim student in London in the early 1870s, recalled that
when asked what he thought of Britain at the time, he had replied, "I
love it," and in his memoirs he insisted that English society was more
open to "foreigners" then than it was to become in later years. He was
not alone in this opinion.[119] Das was amused at being "salaamed by
rustics" in the early 1860s, while Sasipada Banerji's son remembered his
father being "kindly received by everyone from the Secretary of State
for India down to the common English working men and women" on
a visit in 1871.[120] Regardless of their reception, what remains certain is
that colonial natives were to be found both upstairs and downstairs in

Victorian society. It would have been difficult not to notice their presence, if only fleetingly, at least in the capital city of the empire: for "natives of the east" could be seen from the West End to Whitechapel, "clad gaily in attire of many colors, or in peerless white."[121] Even Britons who were otherwise unaware of Indians in their midst would probably have known that the Queen herself had two Indian servants, Abdul Karim and Mohamet, whom she took on in the year of her jubilee (1887). Victoria was reported to be "as excited about them as a child would be with a new toy," and she tried to learn Hindustani in order to be better able to communicate with them. Abdul eventually advanced to the position of secretary, and the Queen had a special cottage built for him; both Indians remained in her service until the end of her reign and could be seen posed with her in a variety of photographs and other representations in the Victorian period.[122]

The majority of Victorians who met Indians personally or saw them from afar seldom fully appreciated the risks they took in crossing "the black waters" to come to Britain.[123] Nearly every account of the sojourn of a Hindu in the United Kingdom begins with a discussion of the family, friends, and community leaders who had to be persuaded to let the would-be traveler depart. Gandhi's mother's fear that he would be breaking caste by going to London and that once there he would not be able to keep up with Hindu dietary regulations was not untypical. The promise he made to her to adhere to his vegetarianism proved a greater challenge than he had anticipated; his search for acceptable food and his personal battle to justify his eating choices to Indians and Britons alike structured much of his time in Britain. Among other things, it made attending the requisite Temple Bar dinners very awkward and drew attention to his Hinduism among his fellows, who hesitated in any event "to mix on terms of social equality with a[n] . . . [Indian] gentleman."[124] P. M. Majumdar, who was later W. C. Bonnerjee's son-in-law, "learnt to be very clever at pretending to drink without really doing so . . . quietly disposing of his glass of whiskey in some convenient receptacle."[125] Disapprobation at home could have serious consequences: having taken the decision to study abroad, Gandhi was treated like an outcast, while Sasipada Banerji and his wife were stoned as they paid a visit to his ancestral home before leaving India for Britain.[126] Surendranath Banerjea made all his preparations in secret and although he was not stoned, crowds flocked to watch him set sail fearing he would not return alive. As it turned out, his father died before he could return, a twist of fate that remained, even fifty years later, "one of the saddest moments of my life."[127] R. C. Dutt had the same tragic experience, made even more difficult because his father had strenuously opposed his going to study in Britain and even cut him off financially while he was there.[128] Muslims had no such caste proscriptions, though as in the case of Syed Ameer Ali, they might have had to negotiate other kinds of disapproval before they set out for Britain. Ali, who was called to the bar in 1873, recounted how he went to see Sir William Grey, then-Lieutenant Governor of Bengal, before setting sail. Grey was "a stiff man, quite typically bureaucratic" who made it clear that he "did not see *why* I was going to England." In the end Lord Mayo, the viceroy, was more helpful and gave Ali letters of introduction that connected him to Henry and Millicent Fawcett and other politicians and reformers in Victorian London.[129]

If the voyage in brought with it the potential for disgracing and outcasting Hindu men, it was all the more culturally and socially perilous for women — with the result that until the 1880s, and even after, relatively few high-caste Hindu women traveled to the British Isles. Some who came were the wives of Indian social reformers or would-be barristers. Sasipada Banerji, who was invited to come to Britain by Mary Carpenter after Carpenter's third visit to India, was anxious about bringing his wife with him. He wrote the following letter to Carpenter in anticipation of his visit: "I accept your invitation with some hesitation. [My wife] does not know English. Your friends must not expect much from her visit. You know how difficult it is for a Hindu lady to give up idolatry and various superstitious notions of her country. I accept your kind invitation to take her with me, not that she will be able to do anything to satisfy your friends, but only to show to my country women that they could have their due position in Society."[130] Having his wife with him in England may have been intended as a display of his progressiveness either by him or Carpenter or both. At the same time, Banerji's protectiveness of his wife and his warning to Carpenter that her sensibilities must be considered demonstrates a shrewdness about the possibilities for spectacle that their togetherness might provide in Britain. As it was, the *Asiatic of London* for 1872 proudly declared Mrs. Banerji "the first Hindu lady who has ever visited England," and the couple named their first child, a son born in England, Albion.[131] It was rare enough for law students to bring their wives to London while they were studying for the bar; most left their young families at home and some kept their marital status ambiguous if not hidden when they circulated in public. Gandhi was later ashamed at having done just this, though it did not prevent him from confessing at some length how he lived the life of a carefree English bachelor, walking out with his landlady's daughter and allowing himself to be lured by various unspecified sexual temptations during a vegetarian conference at Portsmouth.[132]

Not all Indian women came as wives. Toru Dutt, the Bengali poetess later acclaimed by Edmund Gosse, came as a teenager to Britain with her family. She and her sister attended lectures for women at Cambridge in 1869, and her poem "Near Hastings" describes how conspicuous she and her sister felt as Indians outside London.[133] All of W. C. Bonnerjee's daughters (and sons) were educated in England; his wife Hemangini was often left to run the household in Croydon alone when Bonnerjee returned to Calcutta to attend to Indian National Congress business as well as to his law practice at the Calcutta High Court.[134] Sarojini Naidu, the poet and Indian nationalist, was sent by her parents to Britain to study in order to put off a marriage decision. She spent three years in England, studying at King's College, London, and Girton College, Cambridge.[135] Among the best known women to leave India was Anandibai Joshi, who went to the United States to train as a doctor at the Philadelphia Medical College for Women. Her premature death while in America made her a martyr and an object lesson about the dangers of travel abroad among many Indian reformers, men and women.[136] Pandita Ramabai and Cornelia Sorabji were just two of the most prominent Indian women of the nineteenth century to try to follow in her footsteps. They both came to Britain in the 1880s to become doctors, though each was dissuaded by English benefactors who had other plans for them.[137] For Hindu women, getting to Britain might require the defiance of norms that brought different though equally perilous consequences from those that followed on a Hindu man's departure: Anasuya Sarabhai, for example, came secretly to England to study medicine to escape a child marriage and prevent her husband from exercising his conjugal rights.[138] As an interesting sidelight, Gandhi also wanted originally to become a doctor, but he had decided in favor of the law at the suggestion of family advisors well before he arrived in Britain.[139]

Because Indian women who came to Britain tended to be more dependent on the financial support of English reformers and philanthropists (Sorabji competed for but was denied the Government of India scholarship in 1887 on the grounds that it was reserved for men), they had less structural control over their movements, career plans, and encounters than did most Indian men. All the same, as the cases of Ramabai and Sorabji both demonstrate, Indian women did not necessarily allow well-meaning Britons to control their destinies. While those two did not end up becoming medical doctors as they had initially wished, their contributions to reform along the paths they had chosen after they returned to India were virtually unmatched in the late nineteenth and early twentieth century. And Indian women did become doctors in the Victorian period, despite all odds. Rukhmabai, who had gained publicity in Britain in the mid-1880s because she refused to remain the child bride of an unsuitable husband, trained as a physician at the London School of Medicine for Women, qualifying at Edinburgh in 1893. She was made famous in Britain not just by the British newspapers' attention to her divorce case, which was considerable, but by Rudyard Kipling's 1887 ditty, "In the Case of Rukhmibhaio" as well.[140] Kadambini Ganguly also traveled west to train as a doctor.[141] Increasingly after 1885, Indian women were eligible for medical training in Britain under the auspices of the Dufferin Fund for Supplying Female Medical Aid to Indian Women.[142] Sorabji, living perhaps vicariously and in any event determined that at least one member of her family should succeed where she had not, arranged for her sister Alice to come to Britain to study at the London School of Medicine, where she qualified as a doctor in the early twentieth century.

If colonial natives were wandering all over the map of Britain, there arose in the Victorian period a number of institutions concerned with regulating their movements, assaying their numbers, and supervising their encounters with native-born Britons. The earliest such institution was the Strangers' Home for Asiatics, Africans and South Sea Islanders, which was established in 1856–57 by Henry Venn, the secretary of the Church Missionary Society, in West India Road, near the Church of Saint Andrews, Limehouse. According to Rozina Visram, the Strangers' Home served three purposes: it was a lodging house for a variety of foreign sailors (at a cost of about eight shillings a week); a repatriation center for Asian sailors who wanted employment on ships returning to the East; and finally, a center for propagating the Christian gospel among "heathen" sailors.[143] Significantly, some of the initial monies had been contributed by the Maharajah of Duleep Singh, and the scheme was supported in principle as well by some Indian gentlemen traveling to Britain during this period who were distressed and even annoyed to find Indian beggars approaching them on the streets of London.[144] The India Office had a more official interest in keeping tabs on the colonial destitute, in part because complaints about wayward Indian seamen in the London streets were often in the news. It contributed £200 a year to the home.[145] Joseph Salter, who did evangelical work at the home and among Indian, Chinese, and African seamen and their families all over London, claimed that its philosophy was to "give rest to the bodies of travelers who have reached us from the distant East"— by which he meant especially "spiritual rest."[146] Like others who supported the home, he argued that "our Christianity is our fairest jewel" and that by ignoring this particular colonial population, England was failing to do her Christian duty by them.[147] And he took great delight in detailing the visual effects of this failure, reminding his readers that "Westminster has always had its contingent of Asiatic mendicants, with the usual undergrowth of half-castes" and highlighting one pub in east London called the Royal Sovereign, which "stood in the midst of an Asiatic jungle of courts and alleys."[148] But the directors of the Strangers' Home were not concerned simply with lodging and converting lascars. As Visram details, they used the 1823 Merchant Shipping Act to try to coerce servants and others who were found destitute in England onto ships sailing back east.[149] According to one source, over a period of twelve years approximately five thousand "Asiatics, Africans and Polynesians" were "received" into the home.[150] Thus although the Strangers' Home was committed to dealing with the colonials in their midst, ensuring the voyage out rather than encouraging the voyage in was actually its raison d'être.

At the other end of the social spectrum was the Northbrook Indian Club (later, Society), founded in 1879 through the efforts of Lord Northbrook, the former viceroy, and British civil servants returned from India. According to a statement issued by Northbrook himself, the club was "intended to be a common centre of social community for English gentlemen interested in India, and Indian gentlemen who may be in England, either as students or travelers." He added that "the want had long been greatly felt of some club in London where Indian gentlemen coming to this country might find a place to mix with European gentlemen interested in or connected with India."[151] During the first few years of its existence, the club attracted more Indians than Britons, leading its organizers to move it in 1883 from Bedford Row to Whitehall Gardens — which was considered both a more "central . . . and a more suitable situation." It was also a more expensive location and the club's officers, in an attempt to drum up support in India, circulated an appeal for funds that raised £12,000 from Indian subscribers alone. Northbrook felt justified in this tack: "[A]s the society was intended for the benefit of natives of India, [we] have relied on the necessary funds being supplied in India."[152] Among the contributors was the Maharajah Rawal

Shree Takhtsingjee, who, along with M. Bhownaggree, attended the reopening of the club in Whitehall Gardens in May of 1883.[153]

The *Times* heralded the Northbrook Club as a welcome and much-needed effort to bring Indians and Britons together "on a footing of social equality." "Natives who come to this country have hitherto been at a certain disadvantage," the editorial continued.

To the majority of Englishmen India is distant, and unknown, and though Englishmen are rarely slow to offer hospitality to foreigners entitled to claim their acquaintance, yet it must be admitted that the opportunities afforded to Indians of entering English society have hitherto been less frequent than is desirable. The reason is to be sought not so much in any lack of good-will on the part of Englishmen as in the great want which has hitherto existed of those common facilities of inter-course which other foreign visitors enjoy in various forms . . . [T]he Northbrook Club will tend to abate that supposed air of superciliousness which natives in India often attribute to Europeans, and it will convince native Indians of culture and refinement that there is no barrier between themselves and English gentlemen which cannot be surmounted by a better knowledge of each other and by the intercourse which such knowledge engenders.[154]

To this end, the newly furnished club had a billiards room, a library, and a dining room that looked out over the Thames Embankment. Lest native Indian gentlemen forget where they were or the world-historical circumstances that had brought them there, the reading room was decorated with portraits of viceroys and engravings "illustrative of notable events in the history of India."[155]

For all its uptown appointments and clubland atmosphere, the Northbrook establishment had at least one feature in common with the Strangers' Home: it aimed to oversee as well as accommodate Indians in Britain, albeit those in different circumstances than their compatriots in the East End. The original object of the club was "to provide a proper system of guardianship for persons of good family in India sent to England for education." The promotion of "social intercourse" was, in other words, a secondary aim. "The evils which resulted from young men from India being sent to this country to study for the Bar, the Indian Civil Service, and . . . medicine, without being placed under proper guardianship," the London *Times* intoned, "were of the gravest character, and had been frequently brought to public notice."[156] We can only speculate on what these "evils" were. No doubt London society was as disapproving of young Gandhis walking the streets with the daughters of English landladies as Gandhi was ashamed of that kind of conduct many years later. At least one late-Victorian novelist cruelly mocked the behavior of Indian "Baboos" who courted their landlady's daughters while hiding the fact that they were already married in India.[157] By the 1880s Indian gentlemen "on the loose" in London were enough of a concern among former Indian officials and their set to warrant the creation of a special space for "intercourse" between British and "colonial" gentlemen at the heart of the empire. With its emphasis both on guardianship and the careful screening of natives of acceptable "culture and refinement" for mixing with English gentlemen, the Northbrook Club, like the Strangers' Home at the opposite end of the city, did as much to manage the colonial encounter at home as it did to promote it.[158]

Occupying the middle ground between the West End clubs and the East End docks — figuratively if not exactly literally — was the National Indian Association, located at the home of Elizabeth Adelaide Manning at Bloomfield Road, Maida Vale. The NIA had been founded by Mary Carpenter in Bristol in 1870 in the wake of Sen's visit and the interest in Indian female education his tour of the British Isles stimulated. It came under the capable supervision of Manning, who had been the treasurer of the London branch since the early 1870s. She moved the association to London after Carpenter's death in 1877, where it continued to serve as the primary clearinghouse for Indian students until World War I. Its monthly journal, entitled the *Indian Magazine and Review* from the mid-1880s onward, provided a unique public space in Britain for debates on Indian women's education and colonial social reform more generally in which Indians and Britons, both in India and at home, vigorously participated. Several organizations involved in Indian affairs were affiliated with it, including the Northbrook Club, which had originated as an NIA subcommittee, and the Dufferin Fund, which had ties to the NIA through female physicians at the London School of Medicine for Women.[159] There were few Indian students or travelers who came to Britain in the nineteenth century who did not attend the At Homes, soirees, or lectures sponsored by the association. Several Indian women, including Sorabji and Rukhmabai, lived temporarily with Manning or visited her home, which doubled as the NIA office. Manning was keen not just on bringing English people together with Indians — which was among the purposes of the association — but on linking up expatriate colonials with each other for the duration of their stay in the United Kingdom as well. Sorabji, who privately told her parents she did not enjoy Rukhmabai's company, was nonetheless thrown together with her at Miss Manning's during their term breaks and had to make the best of it.[160] Even Gandhi could be found at Miss Manning's events during his student days in London. He recalled in his autobiography that whenever he went to NIA gatherings at her home he "used to sit tongue-tied, never speaking except when spoken to." She introduced him to Narayan Hemchandra, a Bengali writer, at an NIA function, and their friendship helped sustain Gandhi during the rest of his time in England, not least because Hemchandra was also a practicing vegetarian.[161] There were, to be sure, other informal social settings where expatriate Indians could meet, among them W. C. Bonnerjee's home in Croydon, dubbed "Kidderpore Croydon" in honor of the family's Indian residence. As Mrs. Arthur Alexander recalled many years later, "[O]n Sunday afternoons . . . all the servants were set free and in the evening Mrs. Bonnerjee prepared an Indian meal for family and guests. What an oasis Kidderpore must have been to the dozens of young Indian students in London who came there on Sundays and were transported in spirit to their own country!"[162]

The NIA soirees at Miss Manning's were, however, the most regular public functions where Indians and Britons could mix in southeast England. The objects of the association were, at least originally, rather general: "to extend a knowledge of India" throughout the United Kingdom and "to promote by voluntary effort the enlightenment and improvement of our Hindu fellow-subjects."[163] Because of its founder's commitment to Indian female education, the NIA always had a vested interest in promoting the cause of Indian education in general and the careers of Indian students in particular. Just before her death Carpenter had, together with Lady Anna Gore-Langton, developed a scheme for female teacher training. Elizabeth Manning carried on that tradition, linking the NIA with the Froebel Society and other metropolitan training schools and trying to interest Indian women in considering education as a career. As debates about English women entering the medical profession gained publicity in the 1870s and early 1880s, the NIA also provided a forum for the free exchange of ideas on the subject. It was at an NIA meeting in December of 1882 that Elizabeth Beilby, a former missionary in India, first brought before the British public her conviction that British women needed credentialed medical training before they could go to India in a healing capacity. In this sense the NIA anticipated the creation of the Countess of Dufferin's fund (1885), though relations were friendly and the association remained an enabler for women seeking a medical education with a view to practicing in India.[164]

It helped advertise women's educational successes, bring Indian women's writing before the British public, and sponsor speakers, gallery talks, and other public forums having to do with colonial conditions and reform, all over Britain. In the wake of Carpenter's death it also raised money for scholarships in her name and regularly reported on events sponsored by its regional branches in the United Kingdom and throughout India. The NIA was, together with the British feminist community, the lifeblood of domestic Victorian reform interest in India. As the *Indian Magazine and Review* phrased it, the association served as "the needed link" between Indians and Britons in the empire and at home.[165]

Theoretically, the NIA was committed "to co-operat[ing] with enlightened natives of India in their efforts for the improvement of their countrymen."[166] But although Sen took credit for founding it and Syed Ameer Ali for suggesting its name, in practice Manning ran the London-based association virtually single-handedly.[167] And, at least in the case of Sorabji, she tried to override one young Indian woman's desires to study medicine, so that Sorabji could fulfill Manning's dream of obtaining a native female head for a teacher-training school in India.[168] In fact, as more and more Indian students came to Britain in the 1880s to pursue courses of study at London, Oxbridge, and Edinburgh, the business of "superintendence" began to emerge as a preoccupying function of the NIA. To be sure, Indians already in Britain contributed to this effort, writing articles for the *Indian Magazine and Review* detailing what life in a British university was like, for readers in India who were either considering studying in the United Kingdom or who were, as the parents of potential students, worried about sending their children into unknown cultural waters thousands of miles away.[169] As one correspondent remarked, "[T]en or twenty years ago the visit of a Hindu in London was a thing almost unknown." Thanks in part to the influence of the NIA, "the advantages of a stay in this country are [now] more and more appreciated in India every day."[170] Sorabji's arrival in Somerville prompted an article by the college principal and a collaborator specifically aimed at Indian women interested in coming west for higher education, though the majority of the information the NIA broadcast applied to men.[171]

The NIA was not the only institution in late-Victorian Britain concerned expressly with Indian students. Since the 1870s, the health, both physical and mental, of Indian students in Britain had been of some concern, in large part because a number of them who had come to study had committed suicide.[172] The Oriental Institute at Woking, founded in 1884, was established partly to address the pressures facing Indian students who were away from home for the first time and found themselves under the stress of "the cram." Not only was it to be "a center for Oriental learning in England" but an establishment dedicated to providing "the special appliances that alone enable natives of the East of good family to preserve their religion or caste while residing in England for educational or official purposes."[173] Faced with this competition, the NIA's role grew to encompass more than just making information on the opportunities available in Britain to "hopeful travelers" coming from India.[174] In September of 1885 the Association announced that it was producing a circular advertising what the NIA was prepared to do to help Indian students who came to the United Kingdom. Among the services offered was help in securing lodgings, in gaining exposure to "English home life," and in choosing clothes and disbursing monies for fees, and so on. Indian students were advised to consult the association's *Handbook* before leaving India, to follow its recommendations, to make the kinds of housing arrangements it suggested, and to take seriously the precautions it offered — down to what kinds of clothes to wear and where to buy them:

Students are advised to bring only such clothes with them as are necessary for the voyage, which should include a thick overcoat and warm underclothing.

English clothing is procured better and at less cost in England. Indian costume, being unsuited to the climate, is not ordinarily worn by Indian students, but it is desirable that the student should provide himself with such dress, for use on special occasions.[175]

The "special occasions" mentioned were probably an allusion to the royal audience. Indians in Britain from "respectable" families were often presented to Queen Victoria, who insisted that they dress in their "native costume" on such occasions.

More broadly, the advice on clothing suggests how far some Britons were willing to go to shape the appearance of Indians in public, in an era when dress reform, as Himani Bannerji has shown, was a prominent feature of *bhadralok* culture in India.[176] It explains in part why Gandhi was so intent on procuring the outfit of an English gentleman while he was a student in London: whatever anxieties Indians might have experienced about their appearance were not just anticipated but intensified by the NIA — and by some anglophilic Indians as well. As Janaki Agnes

Penelope Majumdar recalled, her father, W. C. Bonnerjee, "always in-sisted upon our wearing English dress and would never allow us to put on saris, even for fun. This was, I imagine, because of the disrepute sari-wearing women had been in 40 years earlier if they went about, and he retained this early prejudice as long as he lived."[177] Not everyone con-formed. Sorabji often wore saris during her time at Somerville, even though she had worn more Westernized clothing growing up in Poona. And although she was quite anglophilic in other respects, she routinely used her dress as part of a defiant performance of a certain kind of Indian womanhood rather than submit to the kind of Anglicization that the NIA apparently encouraged.[178] Significantly, Indians who contributed pieces to the *Indian Magazine and Review* on life in the metropole or at British universities were all but silent on the dress question, focusing instead on what courses students were advised to take, what sights they should be sure to see or, most tellingly, the kinds of money problems they were likely to have.[179]

The "Superintendence Committee" of the National Indian Associa-tion saw itself as promoting "friendly guidance" to Indian students whom it believed were disinclined to live "under supervision" while in Britain.[180] The association's concern, however genuine, was also pater-nalistic: an editorial in the *Indian Magazine and Review* of 1891 worried that Indian students were "frequently sent to England when they have scarcely passed boyhood," and that in these circumstances they were in danger of falling into bad company.[181] If the *Indian Magazine and Re-view*'s editor was prepared to be euphemistic, there were others ready and willing to declare the civilizing mission behind the whole notion of "superintendence." Mary Pinhey wrote a lengthy piece for the *Indian Magazine and Review* in May of 1891 in which she was quite candid about her concerns. "The astute Oriental mind rather delights in crooked ways," she wrote. She continued: "There is a certain lumpiness about the Oriental character, a want of pluck and backbone, and a general ignorance of what is expressed by the word 'honour,' which can only be got rid of, if at all, by a thorough immersion in the spirit of English life . . . [N]othing can be more dangerous than to send youths to England, at a most critical age, to live far away from their natural guardians; deprived of the sanctions of caste and of their religion; entirely free for the first time in their lives from all control; well supplied probably with money and exposed to all the temptations and seductions of a great city like London."[182]

Like the patrons of the Strangers' Home and the Northbrook Club,

Pinhey wanted to control not just Indians but their encounters with their fellow subjects in the metropole. Nothing less than the preservation of imperial rule and with it, the social-cultural hierarchies of colonialism in everyday life at home, was at stake. For "even where no serious evil comes of their sojourn in England, young men are tempted to forget here their real place in the social side of their own country." The average English man who encountered "Orientals" on his own soil, she concluded, "regards all . . . [of them] as of one class"—and this was clearly a mistake.[183] The ramifications of such a misreading were implicit, if unspoken. Failure to notice that Indian gentlemen were neither equivalent to the masses of India nor on a par with English men might lead to notions about the possibilities of political equality—possibilities that in the Victorian period, even among Britons sympathetic to the cause of Indian reform, were quite unthinkable.

Whether her opinions were the result of Pinhey's personal encounters with Indians—at NIA events, perhaps—is not known. Less than a decade earlier the debate over the Ilbert Bill (which proposed to grant Indian civil servants criminal jurisdiction over some European British subjects, among whom numbered white women) had polarized this kind of opinion in India and England. In the post-Mutiny period, British female reformers sympathetic to Indian women's education, like Annette Ackroyd Beveridge, had made it clear that there were certain boundaries that were to be maintained at all costs, the boundary between white women and Indian men being chief among them.[184] It should be noted that Indians were not necessarily always pleased when their children "married English": as Janaki Majumdar recalled, Sir Tarak Nath Palit drove his son out of the house in which they were living in Britain because the son wanted to marry an English girl, and "they were never reconciled in spite of all the efforts of their friends."[185] Even those Britons not offended by mixed marriages worried about social ostracism facing Indian men who took English wives—ostracism that at least one English female observer believed to be stronger in India than in England.[186] Pinhey may have been among those who agreed and who found it necessary to reiterate that position given the increase in Indians coming to Britain and making their way into London society in this period. In any event, her views did not go unchallenged. Angry and disheartened responses from Indian correspondents appeared in the June issue of the *Indian Magazine and Review*, and while the NIA appeared in its editorial to side with Pinhey, the weight of "colonial" opinion was against her. One contributor called her account "fiction," while another insisted that for every Indian student who foundered, there were plenty who succeeded and returned to India having achieved their educational goals. Another claimed that she had exaggerated "the dark picture of the life of an Indian student in London," while still another called her article "nothing but very painful reflections cast on the natives of India." "All pleasure must go," wrote one correspondent who signed himself or herself "S.A.M.S.," "if we are spoken of thus, or . . . [if] English people think of us in the way intimated in the article."[187]

This short-lived contretemps does not appear to have affected the operation or the direction of the NIA in any significant way. Indians continued to submit articles for the *Indian Magazine and Review* detailing their views of "the modes of living in England" and even occasionally waxing rhapsodic about the joys of imperial citizenship. Professions of loyalty sometimes bordered on the saccharine, but they should not necessarily be dismissed as such. They often had their own subtle political effects, if not their expressly political purposes. Syed A. M. Shah, who spent an afternoon at the Tower of London in the spring of 1893, for example, wrote enthusiastically about his afternoon out and expressed his pride at having been "born in the glorious reign of our noble Queen-Empress Victoria. Through her government we are protected from all sorts of dangers, and also our property and our sacred religions: this is the real blessing which we, the British subjects, enjoy under our good Queen-Empress, upon whose rule the sun never sets."[188] Shah's attitude may have been prompted by hearing about all those who had been subjected to execution at the Tower through the ages, and indeed, he expressed thanks that he had not been born under the reign of a medieval English monarch. But the historical function of the Tower and its message about the benefits of subjecthood — and the dangers of disloyalty — were not lost on him. As did other British visitors no doubt, Shah came away from the Tower feeling grateful for being a "British subject." And along with his delight at the many "wonders and curiosities" London had to offer, his essay for the *Indian Magazine* announced his confidence that his claim to that status was as sound as that of any other Briton.

It was this confidence that made would-be barristers and Indian Civil Service (ICS) applicants a potential threat to the cultural norms of national life in the imperial metropole no less than to the future of the empire itself. For more than one Indian student who came to Britain in order to obtain credentials in the law or the colonial bureaucracy in the 1860s and 1870s rose to prominence in the Indian nationalist movement and returned to the metropole in the late 1880s and 1890s to demand a measure of political equality and representation for his fellow subjects in India. As Visram notes, the list of those who studied in Britain reads like "a roll call of the Indian [political] elite," with Gandhi, Nehru, Jinnah, and, in the twentieth century, Indira Gandhi, representing just four of the names best known outside of India today.[189] For some if not many it was partly their experiences in Britain that honed their appreciation for the injustices of imperial rule and enabled them to see clearly and with personalized conviction that the promise of equality allegedly implicit in the civilizing mission was hollow indeed. Surendranath Banerjea, one of the founders of the Indian National Congress, is a case in point. He came to London in 1869 to study for the ICS exam. He traveled with R. C. Dutt and Behari Lal Gupta, both later involved in Indian nationalist politics, and was shepherded through London by W. C. Bonnerjee, another future INC leader who was on scholarship in the capital city at the time to prepare for the bar.[190] Banerjea lived variously in lodging houses and with an English family who, as he later recalled, "impressed me with the clean, orderly methodical lives of the English-middle class."[191] After studying hard, he passed the first competitive exam, but within a few weeks of his name being published among the list of successful examinees, the legitimacy of his candidacy was questioned because of an alleged discrepancy between his age at matriculation and the age required for examination. The removal of his name from the list of successful candidates sparked outrage in India, where the newspapers were full of articles condemning the decision of the Civil Service Commissioners. Banerjea recalled that "I was not prepared to take this decision lying down," and he hired two English lawyers to fight it in the courts. The judge ruled in favor of Banerjea and one other Indian who had been the subject of similar objections, and while the ICS contested the ruling, they were both ultimately reinstated.[192] Although Banerjea lost almost a year in fighting the case, he sat the final exam in 1870 and finally qualified. He remained remarkably free of bitterness about the incident years later and praised the English men who had helped him through the ordeal, confessing to "a genuine admiration for those great institutions which have helped to build up British life and the fabric of British constitutional freedom."[193] Like Shah at the Tower of London, Banerjea's professed identification with the hallmarks of British culture and civilization had a critical edge. His experiences as a student in Britain left him secure in the knowledge that "an Englishman, no matter what his station or calling may be, has a soft corner in his heart for a good fighter"—a maxim that leaders of the Indian National Congress put to the test for almost eight decades.[194]

In the late nineteenth century, reform of the colonial civil service was one of the first avenues through which ambitious and nationally minded Indians sought to equalize the structure of imperial power. Even the London *Times* recognized it as being among "the first rank of national problems."[195] Among the Indian leaders of this reform effort was Monmohun Ghose, who, along with his brother Lalmohun, was an English-educated barrister who had been supportive of Banerjea's court case as part of a larger campaign for bureaucratic reform. The Ghose brothers, who traveled back and forth between Britain and India from the 1860s (when Monmohun was among Carpenter's favorite visitors at the Red Lodge) were among the most active Indians in Britain in the last quarter of the nineteenth century. They made deputations to Gladstone and Ripon, promoted conferences on Indian questions, and, in 1883, Lalmohun ran unsuccessfully as a Liberal candidate for Deptford.[196] It was in his capacity as a delegate for the Indian National Congress that Monmohun traveled to England in 1885 in order to try to influence the parliamentary elections — and it was on this occasion that he was among those branded a poor imitation of Ram Roy on the public platform by the *Saturday Review*.[197] In response to this delegation and to the increasingly visible presence of Indian nationalists generally, the *Review* offered one of the most succinct and unguarded statements about the threat such Indian men posed to the fate of the British Empire to be articulated in the Victorian period: "[W]hen the question of admitting native Indians to civil employment was first raised, it can scarcely have occurred to the most zealous advocate of equality that they would claim seats in the House of Commons."[198]

As an example of understatement such a view is quite remarkable, especially when juxtaposed with the rather more impassioned responses to which Indian nationalists in Britain and, in the process, the British reading public, were treated. The 1885 delegates were cast as "a batch of young cuckoos" who "talk as men might whose fathers had defended the Star Chamber or lost their heads on Tower Hill." Not only had they failed to live up to Roy's example, they were "vapouring, gushing rhetoricians," and the Congress they represented, "an irresponsible association" peopled with "busy-bodies, notoriety-seekers and incendiaries." Congress's claims to government were nothing more than "pretensions" and their desire to "superintend the reconstruction of the Government of India can be regarded as a dull joke."[199] The vehemence of these reactions can hardly be surprising; indeed, it resonates with the kinds of ridicule and satire directed at suffrage women and working men seeking political inclusion in the Victorian imperial nation-state during this period as well.[200] As with these other groups, proof of masculinity was the test of political participation; and it was the capability of Indian men *qua men* to speak for, to represent, a nation, of which these Britons were contemptuous. To be sure, the very concept of India as a nation was unimaginable, if not reprehensible, to those who ruled the Victorian empire. As one journalist put it, "[T]he Nation of India is a pure fiction."[201] But it was at base the capacities of Indians — and their inadequacies as "English" men as evidenced by their behavior in Britain — that was at issue. Those who proposed self-government, wrote a contributor to the *Saturday Review*, "must have an amazing trust in their own impudence and in the credulity of Englishmen . . . [O]ur Empire was not built by the Baboo's oratory, but by Englishmen's force of character."[202] Resisting the nationalist onslaught thus became a test of the mettle of English manhood in the face of Indians who were pretenders by any other name. It also provided an opportunity to consolidate definitions of English manliness at a historical moment contemporaneous with the Criminal Law Amendment Act when challenges to "modern" Western modes of masculinity were being worked out and renegotiated in the Victorian public domain.[203] Attention to Indian nationalists in Britain did not just reflect metropolitan interest in empire, therefore, but helped reconstitute "national" interest as an imperial social and political concern. The INC's activities in Britain, in conjunction with the women's suffrage movement, the anti-Contagious Diseases Acts agitation, and other feminist campaigns, helped to remake the boundaries of colonial rule *and* to undermine the sovereignty of "Britain" proper by signaling that Indian reformers claimed that ostensibly "domestic" space as their own.

Eighteen eight-five was not of course the first moment when Indian men who had come up through the ranks of either business or professional training dared to criticize British rule on British soil. Dadhabai Naoroji and W. C. Bonnerjee, both of whom had been instrumental in organizing the East India Association in Britain, sponsored lectures and spoke out themselves from public platforms about the need for ICS reform and self-government in India. As early as 1867 Bonnerjee had called for "a representative Assembly, and a Senate sitting in India, with a power of veto to the Governor General, but under the same restriction as exists in America, with perhaps an absolute power of veto to the

Crown."[204] By 1889, Indian students with nationalist aspirations were publishing a newspaper from England designed "to give expression to the Bona Fide Opinions of the Native and Anglo-Indian Press on Indian National Politics, etc."[205] The *Indian Appeal* was short-lived, but it was quickly followed by *India: A Journal for the Discussion of Indian Affairs*, a paper published at Charing Cross Road and connected with the British Committee of the Indian National Congress.[206] It was perhaps in order to remain distinguishable from these kinds of platforms that the NIA disclaimed involvement in "political" as well as proselytizing matters, though its work could hardly be called apolitical, as at least one of its subscribers recognized.[207] But it was not until the mid-1880s, when the INC was organized and nationalist aspirations had a regular, if geographically mobile, yearly meeting that Indian men in Britain began to come under such intense public scrutiny and such fierce ridicule. Rudyard Kipling, who had satirized Lord Ripon and the Ilbert Bill the year before, now added a ballad called "The Indian Delegates" to the chorus of disapproval that greeted Ghose and his countrymen in 1885. It was a mockery of "platform men" who allegedly swallowed English education whole but who, despite all their learning, could not possibly represent the masses of India: "And we thought at the very least, / These gentlemen of the East, / Stood man by man as ally and as brother; / But we find it is not the case, / And one half of the civilized race / Objects to eating dinner with the other."[208] And if this were not enough, the lengthy poem was published with a subheading that read: "A farcical comedietta now running, with enormous success, in London."[209]

Indians in Britain were undaunted. In 1886 Dadhabai Naoroji canvassed for a parliamentary seat at Holborn on the Liberal ticket and lost. Lord Salisbury made a speech, which quickly became infamous, in which he attributed Naoroji's defeat to the fact that he was a "black man." He went on to declare that "however great the progress of mankind has been, and however far we have advanced in overcoming prejudices, I doubt if we have yet got to that point when a British constituency will take a black man to represent them . . . [A]t all events he was a man of another race who was very unlikely to represent an English community."[210] Roy had been dismissed as "a black man" by an East India Company official during his sojourn in Britain, but not as publicly as Naoroji was decried.[211] And Salisbury was not the only one. Sir Lepel Griffin, former chief secretary of the Punjab, attacked Naoroji's candidacy in the *Times* and in so doing revealed the racism and xenophobia that lay only just below the surface of English and late-Victorian manners and "civility" where the subjects of empire were concerned. Griffin argued that Naoroji "had nothing to recommend him to an English constituency except for a 'gift of fluency common to all Orientals.' " According to Griffin he was "an alien in race, in custom, in religion; destitute of local sympathy or local knowledge, no more unsuitable representative could be imagined or suggested. As to the people of India, Mr. Naoroji no more represents them, than a Polish Jew settled in Whitechapel represents the people of England. He is a Parsee, member of a small foreign colony, probably Semitic in origin, settled in the West of India. The Parsees are the Jews of India; intelligent, industrious, and wealthy . . . But they are quite as much aliens to the people of India as the English rulers can possibly be."[212] In addition to being an unwittingly persuasive indictment of British justifications of colonial rule — and a remarkable commentary on the complexities of multicultural community in Victorian Britain as well — Griffin's diatribe laid bare the realities at the heart of some colonial encounters at home in Britain. His public assault must have been particularly galling for Naoroji since Griffin was then the chairman of the East India Association, which Naoroji had patronized since the 1860s in an effort to bring Indians and Britons together in support of the economic and political reform of the Raj. Even Naoroji's supporters in the Liberal party were cautious, with some urging him to try a seat in Scotland instead, because Scots had a reputation for being "more liberal than English liberals." Recommendations that he play the proper part were also forthcoming. William Digby, founding member of the British Committee of the Indian National Congress in London and a friend of Indian political reform, advised that he exchange his Parsi headdress for an English hat, as it was "better to appear altogether like an Englishman." Visram argues that the fact that he was a light-skinned Indian who had lived in Britain for many years helped Naoroji's candidacy when he ran again in 1892 and was elected a member of Parliament for Central Finsbury. Given the hostility, intraparty politics, and unbridled racism that surrounded his second run, it is no inconsiderable achievement that he won at all. It is also a testament to the partial and contested nature of colonial hegemony, even and especially in Britain proper.

Former colonial officials like Griffin were partly responsible for encouraging hostility toward Indian nationalists and their claims to citizenship and belonging. Anglo-Indians and former India men were also crucial in circulating colonial knowledge around Britain through newspapers, museum displays, and other forms of popular culture and entertainment in the Victorian period. The Indian and Colonial Exhibition, for example, was largely a Government of India enterprise, as were both the plans for the Imperial Museum and the India collection that ended up in the Museum of South Kensington.[213] This is not to say that what was offered in newspapers or grand spectacle was passively consumed by English readers or exhibition-goers, who were undoubtedly as diverse in their responses to stereotypes produced in the metropole as Indians themselves. Interest in India was moreover diffused through British culture at home in a host of institutional and commercial sites as well, providing opportunities for engagement and contestation in a variety of milieus. Projects like the India Museum or the Queen's Jubilee began as instruments of high culture but they inevitably permeated other cultural spaces so that Indians, like India itself, came to be imagined as the "natural" possessions of public discourse and the national imaginary by different classes and under a variety of conditions at home. This was especially true of images of famous Indian men like Roy and Sen and the Maharaja of Duleep Singh, whose trajectory from India to England and France and back again was a regular feature of newspaper coverage in the 1880s, and not just in a metropolitan daily like the *Times*.[214] Snide remarks and toplofty criticisms directed at members of Congress by the domestic press may be read as declarations of ownership of Indian colonial subjects being articulated at the same historical moment that Indian nationalism emerged as a political force — again suggesting the precariousness of colonial power and the kinds of strategies used to shore it up at moments of crisis.

The sputtering contempt with which some prominent Britons at home met Indian nationalism and its representatives lasted for decades. Events took a murderous turn in 1909, when Sir William Curzon-Wyllie, the political aide-de-camp, was killed at an NIA soiree. His assassin, Madan Lal Dingra, together with a number of other Indians before World War I, embraced radical tactics in pursuit of their political goals. Not unlike the British suffragettes whom Gandhi admired so much on one of his return trips to London in the early twentieth century, these nationalists choose revolutionary politics over the reassurances of Whig historical progress offered to more than one group seeking a place at the table on the grounds of equality before the twentieth century.[215] In the Victorian period, before the hope of democratic inclusion had been exhausted, the British public's attention was fixed on India as spectacular evidence of the power of British civilization, while its inhabitants who ventured to the heart of the empire were routinely made spectacles of.

As the 1880s gave way to the 1890s, public attention became divided between Congressmen and the fate of Indian child wives, widows, and girls, as some Indian reformers sought an age-of-consent law to raise the legal age of marriage for girls and boys. Rukhmabai's trial, Malabari's agitation, and Ramabai's home for widows in Poona were considered by some to be the real story of reform in India, and the machinations of INC delegates and supporters took something of a backseat to these issues, at least in metropolitan public forums like the London *Times* and the *Saturday Review*.[216] With the exception of continued interest in the scheme to supply India with "lady doctors," both English and Indian, the focus was increasingly on social reform events in India rather than on Indians in Britain. And yet of course there were still colonial natives traveling back and forth between India and imperial metropole in search of education, professional training, or simply a tour of the motherland. There, for better or worse, they observed "the cosmopolitan character" of British society and negotiated the unique and complex colonial encounters that the fact of empire guaranteed.[217]

It is this diasporic movement that is important not to lose sight of. So many of the "colonial natives" who made their way to the United Kingdom in the nineteenth century were cultural migrants drawn to Britain in search of self-improvement and, with it, social and political regeneration for the motherland that ultimately claimed them — India itself. Like Ramabai, Sorabji, Malabari, Naoroji, Gandhi, Banerjea, and the Ghoses, all returned to India; and while each one's relationship to the nationalist movement was enacted differently, if at all, their commitment to India and to their countrymen and women was their motive purpose. As one historian has observed, Indians abroad may be said to have helped "pave the way . . . for Indian emancipation within the frontiers of India."[218] If they came to Britain with illusions about the politics of everyday life in the imperial metropole, they may have been ultimately disabused. Even when they were anglophiles, as Sorabji was, they left evidence of their struggle against the operations of imperial power, at both micro- and macrolevels, from which we can reconstruct a history of the colonial encounter at the metropolitan centers of empire.

As Edward Said argues at the very beginning of *Culture and Imperialism*,

The world has changed since Conrad and Dickens in ways that have surprised, and often alarmed, metropolitan Europeans and Americans, who now confront large nonwhite populations in their midst, and face an impressive roster of newly empowered voices asking for their narratives to be heard. The point of my book is that such populations and voices have been there for some time, thanks to the globalized processes set in motion by modern imperialism; to ignore or otherwise discount the overlapping experience of Westerners and Orientals, the interdependence of cultural terrains in which colonizer and colonized coexisted and battled each other through projections as well as rival geographies, narratives, and histories, is to miss what is essential about the world in the past century.[219]

It is also crucial, as I hope I have made clearer, for understanding what was foundational to British culture in the last century. The point is not to leave the nation in place simply by rematerializing heretofore underrepresented populations or even by noting the mobility of colonial peoples, but rather to interrogate the assumption that the nation has always been an a priori, coherent whole and that fragmented identities and cultures of movement are characteristic of contemporary postcolonial modernity exclusively. As Ann Stoler observes, such assumptions "not only buy into a foundational colonial script . . . they undermine any effort to identify the historical construction and subversions of those categories themselves."[220] By finding, seeing, and confronting the fragmentary evidence of "the voyage in" in the Victorian period, we can perhaps more fully appreciate the ways in which the United Kingdom itself was an imperial terrain upon which some of the earliest and most energetically contested struggles for cultural space, political self-representation, and colonial independence were waged before the twentieth century. Only then is it possible to countenance the historical fact that "the modern state did not have a pristinely metropolitan existence that *then* got transported . . . to the colonies."[221] In contrast to what Ann Stoler has persuasively argued for the Dutch East Indies context, rarely is the "precarious vulnerability" of imperial systems the starting point for histories of the British Empire, even among practitioners of the "new imperial history."[222] Indeed, the very concept of Britain, and of England within it, seems to have what Renata Salecl calls a "fantasy structure" that is more resilient and more resistant to its own displacement than almost any other "national" imaginary today.[223] If attention to colonial ethnographies destabilizes notions of the integrity — geographical and cultural — of "Britain" as it has been traditionally understood, then the critical geography they help illuminate must be counted as one of the lingering effects of Britain's nineteenth-century empire itself.

CHAPTER 2

"Restless Desire"

Pandita Ramabai at Cheltenham and Wantage,
1883–86

Nobody continues to remain in the same state forever. There is
nothing in this ever-changing world which stays in the same
condition from beginning to end.

Pandita Ramabai, *Stree Dharma-Neeti* (1882)

When Pandita Ramabai died in 1922, the *Times of India*
remembered her as one of the "makers of modern India." A. B. Shah,
who published her letters and correspondence under the auspices of the
Maharashtra State Board for Literacy and Culture in 1977, argued that
she was "the greatest woman produced by modern India and one of the
greatest Indians in all history." Her biographers, meanwhile, have called
her the "mother" and the "builder" of modern India.[1] Historians of
Indian women and feminist scholars interested in the origins and history
of women's movements in South Asia have been no less extravagant: as
Susie Tharu and K. Lalita put it in *Women Writing in India*, Ramabai
was "a legend in her own lifetime."[2] Ramabai's life story and her reform
work represent a particularly powerful strand in the many traditions of
Indian feminism, since she contested both indigenous patriarchy and
colonial rule through public discourse and institution-building—activities that received India-wide attention from the 1880s until her death
and beyond. In part because she devoted her life to the cause of Indian
women, she was at odds with nationalist discourse and with some nationalist leaders, especially in western India, who in turn used her reform
program as the basis for their critiques of the anglicization of "true"

Indian social reform.[3] Like the history of Indian women's social and political work in the modern period more generally, Ramabai's biography is at once parallel to and in collision with the trajectories of "the Indian nation" and Indian nationalism(s) as well.[4]

If Ramabai is a "national" subject of Indian history *and* an indisputably gendered subject of Indian nationalism, she is also the subject of an Indian diasporic movement whose contemporary manifestations have received some attention but whose histories have yet to be written. Gandhi's peripatetic youth, and the impact it had on creating, sustaining, and popularizing a nationalist consciousness, would seem to suggest that being a displaced subject of imperial rule was consequential to political action — that there was something about being in temporary or permanent exile that nurtured resistance by changing the terms, the very grounds, upon which the violence of colonialism was enacted. The fact that so many Indian men who came to London to train as barristers were among the founders and leaders of the Indian National Congress, and that a number of Indian women educated in the West were galvanized to take up social reform in India, may also bear out this speculation. Ramabai's time in Britain was certainly not uniquely responsible for the kind of resistant colonial subject she became. She was already well-known in India before 1883 as a woman willing to challenge Hindu custom by marrying outside of her caste, speaking in public, and holding Indian men accountable for what she viewed as the unfortunate condition of Indian women. And yet, the ground Ramabai covered and the distances she traveled as a young, and later widowed, high-caste woman makes her more radical than her conversion to Christianity, her confrontations with Hindu orthodox opponents over her widows' home, or even her opposition to the Government of India over famine relief in the 1890s — all of which gained her great notoriety in her lifetime. In some respects her trip to the United States was even more unconventional than travel to Britain in the nineteenth century.[5] Meera Kosambi has argued that it was in part "her life of unceasing pilgrimage" that enabled Ramabai to produce some of the most astutely gendered critiques of nationalist reform and the British imperial civilizing mission in the nineteenth century.[6] In an era when travel for high-caste Hindu women was considered unsexing and heretical, those who left India seeking support and education in the West were roundly condemned for defiling themselves, their families, and indeed the very category of "Indian womanhood" itself. They became "public women" in the most disrespectable sense, opening themselves up to physical violence, recrim-

Figure 1 Pandita Ramabai and daughter Manorama.

ination, and ridicule and thereby challenging some of the most basic cultural codes of nineteenth-century civil society.[7] Making Indian women's activities outside "South Asia proper" visible is, therefore, a constitutive part of what Radha Kumar has so aptly called "the history of doing"—the history of India's women's work since the early nineteenth century.[8]

The story of what Ramabai did during her travels both in India and outside it is, in other words, as much a part of Indian "nationalist" history as it is of Indian women's history, even though it may disrupt each of their nation-bounded narratives in different ways — and may belong finally to neither. Her sojourn in England is crucial for understanding how she discovered herself as a colonial subject and how she encountered Christianity as a terrain of imperial power. As Kosambi has suggested, Ramabai's feminist consciousness did not emerge fully formed but developed over time and as a result of a variety of influences, the simultaneous struggle "against church and colonialism" being a formative one.[9] This chapter argues that Ramabai's encounter with the domestic mission project in Britain prompted her to refine her understanding of the ways in which colonial social relations were being made through theological argument and evangelical institutional practice in Victorian Britain, and to contest the colonizing power of organized Christianity. Ramabai's engagement with and ultimately her refusal of the terms of Anglican orthodoxy in the metropole helped to shape her militance, her reform commitments, and with them, the history of feminism in its world-historical context. To her patrons, her battles offered a mirror of their own colonial investments and provided an opportunity for them to consolidate their particular versions of what "the English Christian mission to India" ought to be — models of "English" colonizing behavior that arguably depended on a recalcitrant "Indian" convert to shape them and give them cultural meaning. Ramabai's letters and correspondence may therefore be read as an ethnography of the colonial reform project as it was being imagined, carried out, resisted, and reformulated in late-Victorian Britain.

In an article in the *Cheltenham College Ladies Magazine* in the fall of 1884 called "Notes of Conversations with Ramabai," Pandita Ramabai gave an account of her early life in India, her struggles with Christianity, and her quest to come to Britain so that she could study medicine and help improve the lives of her countrywomen in India. This narrative, like the better known *Testimony* she was to write for a larger, Christian, and

female reform public in 1907, represents her search for spiritual fulfillment as the motivating purpose of her life. It also bears the marks of
her struggle with the variety of English people with whom she had been
corresponding and interacting over the terms of her conversion since
the fall of 1883. Ramabai emphasized to her English readers both the
comfort she had found in the theism of the Brahmo Samaj *and* her
continued dissatisfaction with the philosophical "truths" afforded by the
kind of Christianity on offer to potential Hindu converts in India. She
wrote that although some of the arguments made by Father Goreh (a
Christian convert and a Marathi scholar who resided at the Cowley Fathers' Mission House, next to the sisters' convent in Poona) "moved me
somewhat, I never showed that they did, and appeared by no means a
hopeful subject." She continued to ask "many questions." Even after she
began to be persuaded that "Christianity was the mother of Theism in
India," Ramabai could not let go of the "intellectual difficulties" posed
by Christian teachings — difficulties she confessed that the missionaries
she argued with in India could not help her resolve. "Unsettled as I was
in mind," she told readers of the college *Magazine*, "I felt a restless desire
to go to England."[10]

Ramabai's construction of her youth as a time of "restless desire" for
spiritual satisfaction was no doubt an attempt to understand and represent her trip to Britain as part of a providential trajectory in the early
months following her Christian conversion. Such a quest for theological
engagement and clarification may have been atypical for an Indian
woman of her generation, but it was true to the pattern of pilgrimage
that characterized much of her life. She was born into "a learned but
indigent Brahmin household."[11] Her father, Ananta Dongre (titled Shas-
tri), owned rice fields and coconut plantations in Maharashtra but lost
his property as a result of trying to maintain a pilgrimage site on the
borders of the princely state of Mysore. He and his family — including
Ramabai's paternal grandparents — took up a wandering life, moving
from place to place as Puranikas, or readers of the Puranic verses in
public.[12] This vocation, as Ramabai called it, was a means of earning a
living without begging. It was also a way of popularizing the stories,
gods, and goddesses of the sacred texts. It was thus a very basic liveli-
hood and a holy exercise as well, insofar as its spiritual purpose was the
attainment of Moksha, or "liberation from the everlasting trouble of
reincarnation, in millions and millions of animal species, and undergo-
ing the pains of suffering countless millions of diseases and deaths," as
Ramabai herself explained it.[13] The family's migration began when Ra-

mabai was six months old (ca. 1858): her mother later recounted to her that she had been placed in a cane box and carried around from place to place. "Thus my pilgrim life began when I was a little baby."[14]

Ramabai had a brother and a sister who lived until early adulthood; she had three additional siblings but they did not live that long; she was the youngest.[15] Her mother Lakshmibai, who was her father's second wife, had been encouraged by him to learn to read, and she became well versed in the Puranas as well as other sacred texts. In the early twentieth century, looking back on her parents' marriage, Ramabai was keen to stress that her mother's education had not interfered with her wifely obligations: "[S]he performed all her home duties, cooked, washed, and did all the housework, took care of her children, attended to guests, and did all that was required of a good religious wife and mother." In a culture where learning to read was believed to be enough to make women widows — and in light of her parents' tragic death — Ramabai's emphasis on her mother's respectability may be read as an attempt to protect Lakshmibai's reputation as well as her father's memory from orthodox criticism almost half a century after their demise.[16] Her mother's literacy brought the opprobrium of local village pundits on Ramabai's father's head during his lifetime. He was summoned to the chief seat of the Madhva Vaishnava sect and compelled to defend his insistence on teaching his wife "the sacred language of the gods."[17] According to Ramabai, "[H]is extensive studies in the Hindu sacred literature enabled him to quote chapter and verse of each sacred book, which gives authority to teach women and Shudras." Although such arguments might easily have been deemed heresy, he evidently managed to persuade the guru and the chief pundits before whom he was called that it was not wrong for women and lower-castes to be taught Sanskrit Puranic literature; in any event, they "did not put him out of caste, nor was he molested by anyone after this." That her parents were heroes in Ramabai's eyes there can be little doubt. Their pursuit of religious devotion at the expense of temporal possessions also undoubtedly helped to shape her own quest for a similar kind of spiritual purity and fulfillment. Nevertheless, she regretted that what little money her family had was not used "to advance our secular education [so that] we might have been able to earn our living in some way."[18] This was out of the question; the children were totally secluded from non-Hindu practices and people so that they would be "strictly religious and adhere to the old faith." But the wandering life to which Ramabai's father committed his family was a difficult one, plagued by poverty and, by the late 1870s, famine.

As Ramabai recalled in 1907, "[N]othing but starvation was before us." Her father, mother, and sister all succumbed to the famine within two years of each other, and she and her brother were orphaned by the time she was sixteen.[19]

Given the fact that famine claimed the lives of her parents and sister, it is particularly poignant that Ramabai often figured her own search for spiritual fulfillment as a hunger needing to be satisfied.[20] Indeed, she and her brother became "famine wanderers," as Ramabai was to refer to them in later years.[21] For some time after they had lost their parents, Ramabai and her brother, Shrinivas, continued to wander, "still visiting sacred places, bathing in rivers, and worshipping the gods and goddesses, in order to get our desire." In one of her autobiographical fragments, Ramabai claimed that they were on the move because they were persecuted by those opposed to her being unmarried, though this explanation drops out in later accounts of her life story.[22] What is consistent, however, is the fact that at this point, the faith of their parents began to fail them both. They continued to adhere to caste rules and to "the conditions laid down in the sacred books," but they began to doubt the efficacy of their prayers and practices and to question the possibility that they would be rewarded by the gods for their efforts to lead pure, devotional lives. "Our faith in our religion," wrote Ramabai, "had grown cold." Meanwhile they traveled everywhere on foot, covering much of the subcontinent in their travels. They went as far north as Kashmir and as far east as Calcutta, where they ended up in 1878. In the brief autobiographical narrative she produced for the sisters at Wantage in 1883, Ramabai claimed that she and her brother traveled for six to seven years and walked two thousand miles — making her, as Kosambi has noted, "perhaps the most well-traveled person among her contemporaries." In the *Testimony* Ramabai wrote in 1907, she remembered the distance as four thousand miles. The discrepancy is not significant except as an indication of how extensive, how unending, and how exhausting this trek was to become in her memory.[23]

It was in Calcutta that Ramabai and her brother first came into contact with Christianity. Although Christian missionaries had "mounted a frontal attack through educational institutions and public proselytization" across India during the nineteenth century, she had apparently had little personal contact with them.[24] When they attended a "Christian people's gathering" Ramabai and her brother were thus shocked to find Indian men ("whose names sounded like those of Brahmans but whose way of dressing showed that they had become 'Sahibs' ") drinking tea with English people. Ramabai's account of their first experience of a Christian service reads like a mini-ethnography — with a kind of clinical perspective on the practices of Christianity that was one of the hallmarks of her engagement with Western religion. "We looked upon the proceedings of the assembly with curiosity, but did not understand what they were about. After a little while one of them opened a book and read something out of it and then they knelt down before their chairs and some said something with closed eyes. We were told that was the way they prayed to God. We did not see any image to which they paid homage but it seemed as though they were paying homage to the chairs before which they knelt. Such was the crude idea of Christian worship that impressed itself on my mind."[25] She was given a Bible in Sanskrit but it was incomprehensible to her, not just because it was written in a form of Sanskrit that was different from the Sanskrit to which she was accustomed but because the teachings were so different. "I thought it quite a waste of time to read that Book, but I have never parted with it since."[26]

There were, however, many other books to read, and Ramabai spent much of her time in Calcutta studying books of Hindu law, the Dharma Shastras, and the Mahabharata. She had learned to read in the first place from her mother, with her father's approval and encouragement.[27] Ramabai was approached by pundits in Calcutta to speak to purdah women on the duties of women according to the Shastras. What began as self-education for the purpose of public lecturing became a series of lessons in the concurrence of all Hindu texts on the question of women's exclusion from Moksha — except through reincarnation as a high-caste Hindu man or, alternatively, through "utter abandonment of her will to that of her husband."[28] Nor were women allowed to study the Vedas and Vedanta, an exclusion that also had tremendous spiritual implications, since "without knowing them, no one can know the Brahma; without knowing Brahma, no one can get liberation."[29] Ramabai herself was reluctant to read the Vedas, until Keshub Chunder Sen (leader of the Brahmo Samaj) gave her a copy of them, implicitly challenging her conviction that to study them would be "breaking the rules of religion." Echoing the reform projects of Jotirao Phule (1827–90), "the father of the nonbrahman movement in Maharashtra," Ramabai insisted upon the link between exclusions based on sex and those based on caste, arguing that "these are the two things upon which all Shastras and others are agreed."[30] In retrospect, she claimed that this discovery was an awakening: "[M]y eyes were being gradually opened; I was waking up to my own hopeless condition as a woman, and it was becoming clearer and clearer to me that I had no place anywhere as far as religion was concerned." Her sense of restlessness continued: "I became quite dissatisfied with myself, I wanted something more than the Shastras could give me, but I did not know what it was that I wanted."[31]

Ramabai's brother died after their arrival in Calcutta; by 1880, as she told the sisters of Saint Mary the Virgin at Wantage, "I was alone in the world."[32] Six months thereafter she married "a Bengali gentleman of the Shudra caste" who had been a friend of her brother's.[33] She defended her late marriage (she was twenty-two) on the grounds that her father had seen how miserable her sister was made by early marriage; she defended choosing to marry outside her caste by declaring that she had "lost all faith in the religion of our ancestors." These were themes she took up later in *The High-Caste Hindu Woman*, where she held the Hindu marriage system, together with caste, responsible for girls' and women's low status and condition.[34] In fact, the question of early marriage had plagued her natal household: her progressive father tried to reverse the pattern of residence by keeping her sister at home when she married, but the son-in-law sued and the court upheld his right in accordance with Hindu law.[35] Ramabai's husband, Bipin Behari Das, was an educated man; he had degrees from Calcutta University and was a pleader in the court at Sylhet.[36] Because she was prohibited by Hindu law from marrying a Shudra, and because "neither my husband nor I believed in the Hindu religion," they were married under the Native Marriage Act III (1872) in a civil court in June of 1880.[37] They lived in Silchar (in Assam), and it was here that she had her first formal tutelage in the principles of Christian faith from a Baptist missionary, Isaac Allen. At this stage, Ramabai recalled, she had lost all faith in her "former religion," and "my heart [was] hungering after something better."[38] Her husband, who had studied in a mission school, was not supportive of her interest in Christianity; he did not like the idea of his wife "being publicly baptized and joining the despised Christian community." He actually forbade Allen from coming to the house, and, according to Ramabai, had he lived much longer, "I do not know just what would have happened." Her husband died of cholera within a year of their marriage (1881) and Ramabai was now a widow with a baby daughter, Manorama, at the age of twenty-four.[39] Undaunted, she moved to Poona, where she was first schooled in English by Miss Hurford, who was attached to the mission staff of the sisters of Saint Mary the Virgin. Here in Poona she also became involved with the leaders of the Prarthana Samaj, which had been founded in the wake of Keshub Chunder Sen's visit to Maharashtra in the 1860s.[40]

Poona was the center of Maratha Brahmanism as well as the site of social reform activity and controversy from the 1860s onwards. Questions of "womanhood" and especially of widow remarriage had been in the forefront of public discussion when Pandita Ramabai arrived in 1882. A society for the promotion of widow remarriage had been established there in 1866 and several prominent reformers, including M. G. Ranade, tried to put reformist ideas into practice by educating their child wives.[41] If some reformers welcomed her, however, the challenges she posed to late-nineteenth-century Hindu tradition, as a woman and as a widow who dared to read the sacred texts, were predictably unpopular among conservative Hindus. As the *Times of India* put it, "[S]he had before her marriage suffered much persecution on account of her advanced views about female emancipation, while the mere fact of her remaining un-married was calculated to shock the orthodox."[42] To be sure, it was because of their "unused" sexuality that widows had to be marked off culturally and physically; they also had to be "shut off from the male gaze and to shut themselves off from their own sexuality."[43] And yet it was not these facts alone that made Ramabai such "a startling and un-comfortable figure." As Rosalind O'Hanlon has noted, "[H]er very public condemnations of the consequences of 'respectable' domestic life for Hindu women caused fury most of all because they hit precisely against nationalist attempts to identify home as a sacrosanct domain for Hinduism's innermost spiritual values."[44]

Ramabai's reform convictions grew out of a deep personal commitment to improving the condition of Indian women. Her concerns about Indian women's "uplift" were shared by a growing number of late nineteenth-century Indian social reformers, some of whom were women — though few of these were as plain-speaking about either the problems confronting Hindu widows or the urgent need for institutional reform to ameliorate their situations.[45] Tarabai Shinde, the Maratha Brahman woman whose pamphlet, *A Comparison between Men and Women*, offered a blistering critique of gender relations in colonial India, was one among several women in western India contemporary with Ramabai who engaged with Hindu tradition in public before Rukhmabai's trial exploded onto the Indian newspaper scene in the mid-eighties and after.[46] Shinde's exposition had been prompted by the case of Vijaylakshmi, the widowed daughter of a Gujerati Brahman family, who was sentenced to hang for killing her newborn, illegitimate baby daughter.[47] Ramabai's public pronouncements were motivated by the less sensational but equally moving instances of Indian women's suffering that she had observed in her wanderings throughout the Indian subcontinent. She told the sisters at Wantage that while traveling with her brother she had had "a good opportunity of seeing the sufferings of Hindu women" and was "much touched by their sorrows . . . [T]his made us think of how much it was possible to improve the condition of women and raise them out of their degradation. We were able to do nothing directly to help them but in towns and villages we often addressed large audiences of people, and urged upon them the education of women and children. In order to be able to converse with the different races we were obliged to learn Hindi (as it is a general language in India) and Bengalee." After her husband's death, she spoke at various gatherings and meetings, giving publicity to the cause of female education throughout India.[48] Together with like-minded men and women in Poona, Ramabai also helped to found the Arya Mahila Samaj, or Aryan Women's Society, which was committed to Indian women's education and social reform. Ramabai was by no means alone in her concerns about widows. D. K. Karve, who was eleven years old when the first widow remarriage was publicly celebrated in Bombay in 1869, was considered by many to be the father of widow rehabilitation in western India. His widows' home project in Poona, which attracted attention in the closing years of the nineteenth century, did much to prepare Indian women for work, reform, and travel to worlds outside India as well.[49] In part because Ramabai was received as such a phenomenon on the Maharashtrian scene, it is worth pausing to remark on her accomplishments up to this point: in the midst of an impoverished and difficult childhood, she had become a Sanskrit scholar as a result of training by her mother, and was versed in a number of indigenous languages, with a smattering of English as well. By the age of twenty she was recognized by the titles "Pandita," meaning eminent scholar-teacher, and "Saraswati," a reference to the Hindu goddess of learning, and had commanded the attention of local and presidencywide reformers in western India.[50]

By the time she was asked to testify for the Government of India's Commission on Education in 1882 (referred to also as the Hunter Commission), Pandita Ramabai had gained considerable renown for her views on the need for reforms for women and children, not just in India but in Britain as well. She told the commission that India's women needed female teacher training and inspectresses of schools — the personnel and the bureaucratic structure, in other words, necessary to guarantee both the permanence of women's educational reform and the government's sustained commitment to it.[51] And no doubt to the chagrin of some Indian male reformers, she told the commission that 99 percent of the male population in India was opposed to female education.[52] Ramabai also spoke to the issue of "lady doctors" in India, advancing what was to become a central claim in English reformers' arguments about the need for female medical aid to Indian women: namely that native women refused to be attended by male doctors and hence required the services of trained female physicians.[53] According to Ramabai's testimony, this want of female doctors was the cause "of hundreds of thousands of women dying premature deaths," and she called on the government to make provision specifically for the medical education of Indian women.[54] Her concern for health conditions among Indian women undoubtedly prompted her own desire to become a doctor. In her travels throughout India she had been repeatedly moved by the sufferings of Hindu women; her goal, as she put it, was "to fit myself for a life of usefulness, in order to benefit my countrywomen."[55] Like several of her Indian women contemporaries, it was the quest for a medical education that brought Pandita Ramabai to England in the first place, since before the mid-1880s there were no facilities for would-be women doctors to study in India, except in Madras.[56] She knew the work of the sisters of the Community of Saint Mary the Virgin (CSMV) in Poona, whose efforts on behalf of Indian women had greatly impressed her, and arrangements were made from Poona for her to stay at Wantage.[57]

According to several sources, Ramabai wanted assistance but was wary of accepting charity.[58] Consequently, she undertook to write a book, *Stree Dharma-Neeti*, published in 1882, and used the proceeds from its sale to finance her passage to England.[59] Ramabai's determination to be self-supporting led Sister Geraldine of Wantage to characterize her as willful and proud, but it is clear from Ramabai's own testimonials that self-sufficiency was the only condition under which she was prepared to accept the generosity of communities like Saint Mary's and Cheltenham.[60] Characteristically, when she decided to make a trip to the United States in 1886, she wrote what remains her most famous book in the West, *The High-Caste Hindu Woman*, in order to underwrite the cost of her own expenses. Ten thousand copies of the book sold out before Ramabai left America in 1888, bringing her a profit of Rs. 25,000.[61] What's more, she came to Britain on the understanding that she would teach Marathi to the sisters at Wantage in exchange for being taught English, with her room and board provided.[62] The implication of Sister Geraldine's reading of Ramabai is something I shall return to, but it is worth remarking that her insistence upon financing herself enabled her to become "one of the few nineteenth-century women who were able to support themselves with their writing"—either in India or outside it.[63] Ramabai traveled to England in the spring of 1883 with her daughter and a female companion, Anandibai Bhagat, who came to England to do a course in teacher training. Ramabai was baptized with the name "Mary Rama" in the autumn of 1883 at Wantage, with Sister Geraldine of the CSMV acting as her spiritual guide and mother.[64]

This event evidently surprised the missionary community back in Poona, to whom Ramabai had made it clear that she did not intend to convert. Historians interested in Ramabai's life and in social reform for and by women in India more generally continue to speculate as to why she ended up embracing baptism. The sisters at Wantage believed that her conversion was prompted by the suicide of Anandibai in the fall of 1883, but it seems at least equally likely that her decision was motivated by her admiration for the work that the sisters at Wantage did for working-class and "fallen" women.[65] Of concern to us here is not determining with absolute certainty why she converted—which we cannot in any event ever know—but rather what kinds of narratives were produced to explain her conversion, by whom, and for what ends.[66] The sisters, for their part, were undoubtedly anxious to represent Ramabai's embrace of Christianity as legitimate and sincere, in addition to having been prompted by the need for emotional support in the wake of her friend's death. Her conversion certainly caused a sensation in India, and later provoked severe criticism of her by certain Indian reformers; as Meera Kosambi has noted, B. G. Tilak "started to openly accuse her of nationwide missionary designs."[67] Once she had established her own institutions, like the widows' home in Bombay (1889), Ramabai found herself trying continually to balance the competing claims of religious and secular education for Indian women, at odds with both the missionary and the Hindu communities in India—so much so that she came to refer to herself as a "Christian outcast."[68]

Shortly after her conversion (that is, by January of 1884), Ramabai was in residence at Cheltenham Ladies' College, under the care and guidance of its head, Dorothea Beale. Over thirty years later, looking back on Ramabai's time at the college, Sister Geraldine (1843–1918) explained that she sent Ramabai to Cheltenham because "I would say that intellectually I was not equipped for such work as instructing" her and because, although Sister Geraldine had spent time in India, "my work had almost wholly been in a European and Eurasian high school, and so I had had no experience in native work."[69] There is no evidence in the correspondence to suggest that the CSMV sisters sent Ramabai to Cheltenham for any other reason except that they wished her to pursue her education.[70] It was not theological differences, in other words, which prompted Sister Geraldine to send Ramabai to Cheltenham; these developed after Ramabai left for Cheltenham. Even in their most disputatious moments, Pandita Ramabai and Sister Geraldine kept up a vigorous correspondence that was virtually uninterrupted for several years.[71] Their letters, as well as those between Ramabai and Beale, Beale and Sister Geraldine, and each of the women with Anglican clergymen, provide firsthand evidence of how thoroughly grounded the rhetoric of social relations was in the language of colonial theology, as well as how imperial power relations invariably intruded on personal — even and especially "sisterly" — relationships at the imperial center.

At issue initially was the question of whether or not a cross should be displayed on the CSMV premises in Poona.[72] In spite of the fact that Father Goreh and Sister Eleanor of the Poona Mission House both wanted it, Ramabai appears to have been against it. Conceding to Sister Geraldine that a cross might be instructive, Ramabai insisted that it be inscribed in Sanskrit rather than in Latin. Her reasoning on this point was as follows: "Do you think that [the] Latin language has something better in it than our old Sanskrit or have you the same feeling for the Latin as the Brahmins have for Sanskrit (i.e. to think it to be the Sacred Language and spoken by God and Angels)? I stick fast to Sanskrit, not because I think it to be sacred or the language of the gods, but because it is the most beautiful, and the oldest language of my dear native land. And, therefore, if I must have a Cross, I should like to see Sanskrit words written upon it instead of the Latin words."[73] Ramabai's concern was for the successful transmission of Christianity to Indian soil, and her objection to the Latin inscription was, as she indicates, that most Indians, and Indian women in particular, would be mystified by its meaning. "I do not myself understand the Latin, neither (do) my countrywomen (with some exceptions). And even also Latin is not the mother tongue of the Marathi (people), so our Indian sisters will not find a single word in it that they know or is like to some word that is known to them. Then why should we be kept in ignorance of our professed text?"[74] For Ramabai it was a question of evangelical strategy, as well as a lesson in cultural literacy. She informed Sister Geraldine that she was going to write and tell Father Goreh that "in some things I cannot agree with him."[75] As she did in the case of other theological issues, Sister Geraldine interpreted Ramabai's stance as willful disobedience, telling her bishop that "I . . . tried to make the difficulty which arose an opportunity for showing her that she could not act independently but must defer in her judgment to those in authority."[76] Ramabai, in contrast, viewed the cross incident with the intellectual curiosity of an enthusiastic convert. She referred to her own discussion of the inscription as "my argument" and closed her letter to Sister Geraldine with the hope that "you will of course write to me what you think."[77]

As time went on the doctrinal conflicts became more detailed, more acrimonious, and more polarizing. Ramabai raised objections to the doctrine of the Trinity, the Thirty-Nine Articles, the Athanasian Creed, and the deity of Christ.[78] It is important to note that these were not concerns mentioned in passing; nor did they arise casually in the course of epistolary conversation. Both Ramabai and Sister Geraldine wrote pages and pages delineating their respective positions, quoting extensively from scriptural texts, and invoking contemporary theological authorities to reinforce or legitimate their points.[79] Their exchanges embody the kind of genuine spiritual anguish for which the Victorians are so well-known, and that at times seems inaccessible to modern sensibilities. For Sister Geraldine the difficulty was particularly acute, since it became clear that Ramabai had been baptized while still in doubt over the nature of the Trinity and (a related issue) the divinity of Jesus.[80] Such doctrinal doubts on Ramabai's part were perhaps fueled by her encounter with all kinds of Christian denominations in England — "such a Babel of religions," as she put it.[81] Sister Geraldine lectured Ramabai on the dangers of heresy, asking, "[I]s the Church wrong in not allowing into her Communion those whose teaching and practice is not in accordance with that given to us by our Lord?"[82] Ramabai's reply was equally direct. "Am I to submit to your teaching that your Anglican Church is the sole treasury of truth and that all other bodies are sinning against the Church and teaching false religion? But I think otherwise. And I cannot hold my peace."[83] She even produced her own version of the creed, which she claimed to "derive directly from Christ's teaching."[84] As A. B. Shah has written, Ramabai's interpretations struck at the heart of "the Church's insistence on unquestioning uniformity." It was a uniformity to which Sister Geraldine, for her part, unquestioningly adhered. In her capacity as Ramabai's spiritual mother in England, she felt responsibility for her charge's religious education. As she herself readily admitted, "I will not ask you to take this on my authority," since for Sister Geraldine it was the church and Holy Scripture who together dictated the conditions of faith.[85] Ramabai's own spiritual doubts notwithstanding, Sister Geraldine clearly wished to fashion Ramabai's Christianity in her own image.

As Ramabai was quickly to discover, Sister Geraldine was not the only one with an interest in developing Ramabai's religious life. Dorothea Beale was equally involved in shaping her spiritual direction, and she shared Sister Geraldine's concern that Ramabai was being unduly influenced by other religious viewpoints, most notably those of some local "ladies of the Unitarian interest."[86] Whether Ramabai's interest in contemporary nonconformity was the product of her own theological inquiries or of the influence of friends in Cheltenham and environs is not easily discernible from the correspondence. It was probably a combination of both. She read widely in nineteenth century theological literature, from Canon Westcott to Max Muller to Rammohun Roy, and she was extremely well versed in scriptural texts as well. What remains certain is that Beale saw herself as the one to step in and clarify Ramabai's views on Christianity. Writing to assuage Sister Geraldine's doubts, Beale assured her that Ramabai would in the end be "firmly established in the Christian faith" and fully able to preach conversion upon her return to India, but *only* if she could be persuaded to study Christianity "as a philosophy. She cannot," Beale continued, "receive it merely as an historical revelation, it must also commend itself to her conscience . . . If she does not find someone to whom she can speak freely, she will be silent, and might easily pass into Unitarianism . . . I cannot help thinking that God has given me some preparation of mind and heart to help her with."[87] Beale's allusion to her own spiritual crises (to which she made reference more than once in correspondence with Sister Geraldine) was intended to reassure the sisters about her capacity to help Ramabai. She had struggled with her own religious doubts in the 1870s — doubts that had temporarily plunged her into depression and a "fever" of the soul.[88] Needless to say, her view of Christianity as a "philosophy" can hardly have comforted Sister Geraldine. Beale later proffered her opinion that it was not prudent "to try to keep her away from people . . . who think differently. She has gone through so much already, and now she has got her feet on a Rock, these currents will not sweep her away, I am persuaded."[89] In fact, it was always Beale's position that Ramabai was eminently "teachable." "We must not be anxious," she wrote, "but really trust God with that wonderful mind and character that He has fashioned for her."[90]

Ramabai's spiritual education became something of a contest of authority between Beale and Sister Geraldine. Their triangular correspondence is evidence not just of Ramabai's contest of the colonial mission project but of the ways in which colonialism could and did bring colonizers into conflict with each other as well. In the wake of a letter from Ramabai in which she had detailed her difficulties in accepting the doctrine of the perfect nature of the Savior,[91] Sister Geraldine wrote anxiously to the Bishop of Lincoln about the effects of Ramabai's time at Cheltenham on the direction of her spiritual life:

Miss Beale hardly recognizes the position she is placing herself in. She is undoubtedly misunderstanding and mismanaging Ramabai — and when Ramabai has thrown us off [as] she is certain to do if Miss Beale continues the attitude she is at present taking with her, Ramabai will at the first rub with Miss Beale throw off her authority too.

This will cause an open scandal, and it will not reflect well on the part Miss Beale has played in the matter. She did distinctly say to me and others [that] she considered a year at Cheltenham enough, and now recalls her words.[92]

At one point both Ramabai and Beale believed that Sister Geraldine wanted Ramabai to leave Cheltenham on account of their differences,[93] despite Sister Geraldine's reassurance to Ramabai that "money is no consideration where your welfare is concerned. We wish only to do the *very best* for you."[94] Beale, for her part, apparently felt threatened enough by the insinuation that Ramabai's experiences at Cheltenham were responsible for her "straying," to write to Canon Butler to dissuade him from making a similar conclusion.[95] In any event both Beale and Sister Geraldine felt that their reputations were on the line. At stake in their determination to control and monitor Ramabai's spiritual progress according to their own lights was their authority as "professional" Christian women — as well as the professional reputation of the female-based institutions that they oversaw.

Neither Beale nor Sister Geraldine were, of course, able to act as free agents. Although the all-women communities that they supervised are both examples of what some enterprising English women were able to achieve under the constraints of late-Victorian social and political structures, each one was accountable ultimately to the patriarchal institutions that governed them.[96] It might be argued that given the basically secular character of Cheltenham, Beale was less vulnerable than Sister Geraldine was to her Anglican superiors. At the same time, however, Beale was not without her own worries. In August of 1885, when Ramabai declined an invitation to a retreat at Wantage, Beale regretfully endorsed Ramabai's choice, apparently to avoid a confrontation with her own superior. "I don't think the Dean will enter into her difficulties," she wrote to Sister Geraldine, "and if he expects her to bow down, and she will not, then the breach will be widened. I am *so* sorry."[97] Both women corresponded with superiors in the church, and each was concerned that she might be held responsible for what was considered by 1885 to be Ramabai's virtual apostasy. Their concerns were very real. For as Ramabai's ability to articulate her dissension — her determination to speak in "a voice of my own"[98] — became more and more evident, it appeared to those involved that the "eclipse" of her religious faith was endangering what the Anglican Church intended to be Ramabai's true purpose: namely, that she return to India in an evangelical capacity and convert natives in her homeland to Christianity. If the church officials with whom she corresponded understood that her original intention was to become a medical doctor, they had to be reminded of it.[99] According to Sister Geraldine, that plan seems to have been abandoned fairly early on in her stay because of Ramabai's deafness. In any event, from the point of view of the churchmen, Ramabai was to be schooled in the correct forms of Christianity. As Eric Hobsbawm has observed, the late nineteenth century was "the classic age of massive missionary endeavor."[100] She had to be set straight at least in part because she was intended to be a soldier in the vast missionary army that advanced the spread of Christianity in Britain's empire.[101]

By the mid-1880s, that army had a number of native converts in its ranks — though not so many that the Anglicans among them who had become missionaries couldn't be listed by name in the Church Missionary Society's history, written in 1899. The CMS's college at Islington had been training Indian, Chinese, African, and Turkish men, and even one Maori chief, since the 1850s; among its graduates was Father Goreh himself. Relatively few native missionaries were women, and many of those, like Cornelia Sorabji's mother, were married to local clergymen.[102] Ramabai's celebrity made her a potentially important ally for the CMS, one not to be lost through mismanagement. Hence the bishops of Lahore and Bombay, with whom Beale, Sister Geraldine, and Ramabai all corresponded, were extremely anxious to prevent Ramabai's religious "wanderings" from endangering her evangelical potential in the mission field.[103] Explanations about how Ramabai's "mission" might be placed at risk varied. There were some who from the beginning viewed Ramabai's very presence in England as itself deleterious to the success of evangelization. According to the Bishop of Lahore in England: "I fear there will be an end to her great work as a Reformer in India, if she remains on this side of the water. If she has not the heroic courage I take her to have, she will of course gladly settle down and become an English lady; but my impression is that the wail of her Indian sisters will not suffer her to rest, till she has mingled her tears with theirs, not in the way of sympathy at a distance, but where they can trickle from face to face."[104]

The Bishop of Bombay feared much the same, warning that too long in England would render Ramabai "spoilt" and "useless for all work in India." In response to news that Ramabai was considering taking up public lecturing on Indian subjects, he wrote the following to Dorothea Beale: "There is not a missionary or a Bishop in India who would not endorse what I say. A native Christian (Anglicised) is ruined for life as far as future usefulness is concerned. I consider that if Ramabai begins to lecture . . . the hope of her doing good work among her country-women is at an end . . . Ramabai owes herself to her countrywomen. English girls have not the shadow of a claim on her, and every moment that she gives to them means a fresh obstacle in the way of her discharging what is clearly the one function to which God has called her."[105] And, in a line that illustrates some of the institutional pressure Sister Geraldine may have been laboring under, he wrote, "Had I ever dreamt of the Sisters allowing such an arrangement to be made without asking the advice of those to whom it would have been natural that they should look in such a case, I should have warned them how fatal it might prove."[106]

The question of Ramabai's public lecturing animated much of her correspondence with both the bishops and her various English "sisters" in 1885. Given the radical political meanings attached to English women speaking in public during this period, the bishop may have been anxious about the scandal her publicity might bring upon the Anglican community. An equally likely explanation can be found in contemporary notions about the seclusion of women in India and the efficacy of separate-sphere ideologies for conversion in non-Western societies. In keeping with late-nineteenth-century Christian missionary ideology, Ramabai's usefulness was considered to be directly tied to her personal access, as an "authentic" Indian woman, to the masses of women in India —

"not in the way of sympathy at a distance," as the Bishop of Lahore had put it, "but where . . . [the tears] can trickle from face to face."[107] Concerns about Ramabai's "publicity" revolved around the scandal it would cause in India "even among the better sort of native men." Moreover, according to the Bishop of Bombay, "nothing would ever undo the harm it would do her among native women."[108] It therefore seemed critical to the Anglican clergy that "we must be careful not to advertise her, or to make too much of her in 'public' . . . it would not be well for her to have anything to do with any but her own sex."[109] "Public" here can be taken to mean outside of the all-women's communities of Wantage or Cheltenham. Eager to mould Ramabai into the most efficient instrument for evangelization possible, the Anglican hierarchy invoked the practices of purdah as they understood them as justification for secluding Ramabai from the public eye in England. Contamination of Ramabai by public exposure to mixed audiences would, it was believed, endanger her special access to Indian women — access not afforded to either male or female British missionaries nor even to male Indian converts. The prohibitions placed on her lecturing in public may well have been intended to discipline a willful convert, but they were also part of a set of strategies designed to maximize evangelical success. Furthermore, by dictating the terms of her experience in England, the bishops were intending to shape the methods of her future work in India.

Dorothea Beale, educator that she was, intervened with the Bishop of Bombay to explain the benefits of Ramabai's services to her immediate community. Beale told the bishop that English girls who "in the natural course of things, will go to India" were getting to know "the native mind" through informal sessions and Sanskrit lessons with Ramabai at Cheltenham.[110] "Her one desire," Beale reassured him, "is to see some institutions at work for the higher education of her countrywomen, and for delivering them from the evils and utter degradation of many a widow's life."[111] Ramabai, for her part, saw the Anglican clergy's objections as a misrepresentation of social practices in India and, ultimately, as an interference with her personal liberty. She railed at the insinuation that English bishops knew India better than she did, and that therefore she should submit to their judgment. To argue such a thing, she told Sister Geraldine frankly, "is plainly saying no less than that the people who are not of that country know India and its people far better than I do, who am born and brought up in it and that you or rather the people who are your advisors, do not trust me and my honour, that they have the authority to decide anything for me, and that I ought not to have a voice of my own to say anything against that decision . . . I know India and its people . . . better than any foreigners even if they have been staying in India from [a] long time before I was born. If you and your countrypeople do not trust the people of India, it matters little, but for my part, I do trust and love my country with all my heart."[112] Over the course of several letters, Ramabai informed Sister Geraldine that she had spoken publicly in India by the invitation of a variety of pundits, and that as far as teaching or lecturing to men or mixed audiences was concerned, her parents had fully approved. It was not, in other words, the break with cultural tradition that the bishops were trying to make it. "You can call some of my countrywomen 'hedged,' "she conceded, "but you cannot apply this adjective to Marathi Brahmin women." Referring to Sister Geraldine's own experiences in Poona, she reminded her that "you have seen yourself that Marathi ladies are neither hedged nor kept behind thick veiled curtains." In what was perhaps a slight against "enlightened" British rule in India, she pointed out that "even in the days of Mussulman rulers they never used to be so."[113]

In addition to defending her right to do as she chose in England, Ramabai was intent on defining her own concepts of reform in India and, more specifically, what shape her reform work there would take. She assured Sister Geraldine that she was not really particularly anxious to be giving lessons or lecturing to young men, "but I *am* anxious to do away with all kinds of prejudices which deprive a woman in India of her proper place in society."[114] She went on to ask: "Can I confine my work only to women in India and have nothing to do with men? I do not think so. To help women to come forward in the society I must first of all . . . teach men of poorer classes. Then when men are convinced of the necessity of elevating the condition of their women, I shall have access to their Zenanas. Unless I begin to have regular and pure intercourse with men, I shall in vain hope and try to help my countrywomen."[115] Ramabai's vision of how social reform should proceed was clearly at odds with the gender-specific, gender-targeted evangelical strategies articulated by the Anglican bishops — strategies that in fact underpinned the entire ideological apparatus of evangelization in the nineteenth century. What is more, in this passage at least, her reform concerns seem, in the absence of any explicitly evangelical language, to be quite secular.

Finally, Ramabai made it clear that while she would not act against Sister Geraldine's decision, "I do not want to ask or follow the opinion of the bishops before whom you are going again to put this matter." To

Sister Geraldine's accusation that she was abusing her liberty and was in danger of being labeled lawless, she responded fiercely and without equivocation. "I have not acted as a lawless woman," she told her, "and never want to do so. When people decide anything for me, without consulting me about it, I of course call it interfering with my liberty, and am not willing to let them do it. Suppose you were in my place and an unknown bishop were to advise your friends to decide a thing for you without telling you about it, and your friends did so, what would you think of it? Would you feel bound to accept every word or rule which comes from the bishop as the expression of the will of the Most High[?] Perhaps you would. I am not quite sure about it . . . ." As for her conscience, she assured Sister Geraldine that "it does not trouble me in this matter and that is quite enough. It will be impossible for me to follow others in every single act and to be always pleasing them and never think of myself."[116] Ramabai understood that this debate over her "publicity" was nothing less than a struggle for defining the terms of Indian women's emancipation, and she saw that struggle as intimately tied up with her own personal battle for self-determination. Here she confided to Beale what she could not say directly to Sister Geraldine: "In such a matter and in all other matters, I shall speak openly and plainly that they have no right to decide anything for me. And I shall not allow anyone to lay hand on my personal liberty. I have taken all matters concerning me in my own hand. Although I am poor and weak in body I have (thank God Who has given me it) a mind strong enough to resist all these meaningless social customs which deprive a woman of her proper place in society."[117] That woman was in this case Ramabai herself, and her "proper place" was as a social reformer of her own fashioning in India. In the end, Ramabai was true to her word, and the question of lecturing in England never came up again — though she lectured throughout her tour of the United States and became an influential speaker for the Women's Christian Temperance Union in India.[118]

Protecting Ramabai's reputation by controlling her movements in other, more intrusive ways had been of strategic concern to the English women involved in her life since the very beginning of her time in Britain. She was originally intended to come under the supervision of Sister Elizabeth, but that plan had to be scotched because Elizabeth was in charge of a rescue home for fallen women in Fulham and it was deemed inappropriate for Ramabai to be living there.[119] Limiting Ramabai's mobility was considered essential to safeguarding her respectability. Sister Geraldine worked hard to dissuade her from going by herself to London, even though she was hardly unchaperoned: she stayed with Mrs. Gilmore of the CMS — one of the "local ladies" whom Sister Geraldine so distrusted. Gilmore was a member of the Society and had traveled to India in the early 1880s; she would also play a role in Sorabji's experience of domestic missionary reform.[120] Ramabai was invited out by Dr. Frances Hoggan as well, a medical doctor who practiced in India and who asked her to see "an exhibition of women's work conducted by women" in Bristol.[121] Ramabai visited the memorial to Rammohun Roy while there and spent some time in the company of a single Indian man, a Mr. Rao, whom Ramabai had evidently invited to come to Britain as her escort after her friend Anandibai Bhagat's death. It was an outing that continued to distress Sister Geraldine some forty years after the fact.[122]

For someone who had been as mobile as Ramabai, these restrictions chafed, especially since her own relatives had not imposed any such limitations on her activities. Nor was she unaware of the importance of decorum for women, having devoted a whole section on the subject in *Stree Dharma-Neeti*, published in 1882 before her trip to England.[123] "It surprises me very much to think that neither my father nor my husband objected [to] my mother's or my teaching young men while some English people are doing so," she wrote spiritedly to Sister Geraldine in the spring of 1885. "It is true [that Hindu women] do not mix as a general rule with men as you do in England, but you cannot say now some of them do not [do] so. I am one of those 'some' and am not afraid of men."[124] Ramabai thereby signaled her rejection of any attempt by the Anglican patriarchs to usurp what they imagined, wrongly, to be the paternal authority of her father and husband in matters concerning her public self-representation. Nor did she fail to use this occasion as an opportunity to challenge directly the authority of the church and its representatives over her: "It seems to me that you are advising me . . . to accept the will of those who have authority, etc. This however I cannot accept. I have a conscience, a mind and judgment of my own, I must think [for] myself and so [do] everything which GOD has given me the power of doing . . . I am . . . not bound to accept every word that falls down from the lips of bishops or priests . . . I have just with great efforts freed myself from the yoke of the Indian priestly tribe, so I am not at present willing to place myself under a similar yoke by accepting everything which comes from the priests as [the] authorized command of the most high."[125]

Here Ramabai was instructing the metropolitan Christian establishment in the particular stakes and peculiar difficulties of becoming a

Christian convert under colonial rule, by unmasking how implicated the Anglican hierarchy was in the maintenance of imperial power relations through its disciplining of converts like herself. No doubt she understood that her conversion was a kind of "civil death," casting her out permanently from Hindu communities in India and making her an always recalcitrant subject of colonial Christian authority.[126] Ramabai's refusal to fall under the "yoke" of either Hindu or Christian orthodoxies may well represent a quest, to borrow from Gauri Viswanathan, for an "uncolonial" space where new forms of resistance could be imagined and articulated.[127] But it is equally a declaration of her determination not to be fixed in the space where British imperial power and colonial Christianity were not just contiguous, but completely coincidental. It also reflects her recognition that the challenges her presence represented to colonial reformers was not merely a question of imperial Christian authority or even gender relations, but a matter of how convictions about Indian racial and cultural inferiority could shape the colonial encounter in Britain. Ramabai used Sister Geraldine and Beale as sounding boards for these contests of ecclesiastical-imperial authority, but at the same time she was not shy about confronting the bishops themselves. As she told Canon Butler, "You have never gone through the same experience of choosing another religion for yourself, which was totally foreign to you, as I have. . . . You, wise and experienced and old as you are, cannot interpenetrate my poor feelings. You will, I trust, not be offended if I say so, for no man is omniscient . . . If a Hindoo theologian — however learned and holy and good he may be — comes and tells you your religion was a false one, and that you were to accept humbly everything that he taught, could you do it?"

If this is an assertion of the validity of personal experience over the dictates of the church's teachings, it is also an unabashed attempt to equalize relations between a church canon and a "native" convert. Although candid and confrontational, Ramabai remained eager to demonstrate that she retained no ill will toward her adversaries, typically signing her letters "your humble child in Christ" or "your loving pupil" and almost always using her baptismal name, "Mary Rama" — perhaps as a reminder of her attachment to and sincerity about her new faith. She also sometimes added a postscript, reassuring either Sister Geraldine or the bishops that she intended no disrespect and valued the opportunity to speak freely to them on such contentious issues. Butler, for his part, was unmoved; after receiving the letter in which Ramabai exhorted him to consider himself in her position, he wrote to Beale lamenting

Ramabai's "vanity" and reasserting that "the real danger to her lies in the *courting* she receives."[128]

As these exchanges indicate, Pandita Ramabai's very presence alarmed her correspondents because she was disturbing the natural order of things. In this context the "natural order" was not just the subordination of native willfulness to English wisdom or even of native Christians to British ecclesiastical authority, but potentially of the Anglican sisters' prescribed submission in clerical matters to the male hierarchy.[129] The Bishop of Lahore insisted that it was the fact of Ramabai in England that threatened to undermine her potential for missionary work. "*As a rule* I have protested," he wrote to Beale in May of 1884, "against young Christian Hindoos being sent over to England, as they have almost uniformly scorned work among their own country men, and become wholly denationalised."[130] In the same letter he suggested that Ramabai might be appropriate for his mission station. That he viewed her as a prize in terms of his personal missionary goals in India cannot be in doubt: "I do not wish to covet the advantage such an arrangement would give to the Mission work in my own Diocese," he assured Beale, "but would do my best to promote it, if the opening should occur, and the course of God's Providence should render it desirable."[131] His suggestion, however veiled, is that the cost of the English women's carelessness might be the removal of Pandita Ramabai herself from the communities at Cheltenham and Wantage sooner than expected. Ramabai was alternately viewed as damaged goods, as too valuable an investment to be lost, and as the best "native" commodity the Christian church had access to. In all three cases, the quality of her performance in the mission field was seen to depend on the orthodoxy of her religious education. It was this contingency that made control of her spiritual direction — one might also say, of her spiritual life — so essential. There were some who feared that it was already too late. George Hunter, the director of Indian medical work at Oxford, told Beale that "her influence as a fellow countrywoman with Indian natives is utterly at an end. She will have no more access than an English woman." His advice was to bring her up to be as English as may be, and then to "let her go as part of the staff of some English institution."[132] Canon Butler did not necessarily agree, and, in keeping with the contemporary belief that the conversion of women was the task of women, he told Beale that "I think Ramabai's knowledge of Indian ways, etc. will give her a power of influence which no English woman can have." What she badly needed, in his view, was "an English development of her Indian brains."[133] The fact that Ramabai was allowed to remain in England testifies to the power of the conviction that time spent in Britain had its inevitably civilizing effects, and that those effects were divinely ordained. As the Bishop of Bombay later clarified to Beale, "I did not mean to say that I regretted her having come to this country at all. That seems to have been God's providential way of bringing her to the truth."[134]

For the most part, Sister Geraldine concurred with the bishops' sentiments. She framed the problem as one of disobedience not simply to religious authority, but to imperial authority as well. Of Ramabai's frustration, she wrote to Beale: "She has to learn that as a Christian, she is bound to accept the authority of those over her in the Church. She is a little inclined to take too independent a line, and though this is but a temporal matter [the issue of public lecturing], yet she should be willing even in this, to accept the opinion of those, who from their position in India and from their experience had a right to speak." She moreover urged Beale to use the occasion to "give her a little teaching on submission to authority," in order that Ramabai might derive a "fruitful" lesson from the incident.[135] Ramabai's actual deafness may have seemed more than a little ironic to Sister Geraldine, symbolizing for her as it must have the Indian woman's apparent inability to hear the messages of the "true faith."[136]

Beale's reactions were on the whole more sympathetic. She wrote to Sister Geraldine that she could understand why Ramabai considered her right to public lecturing "a matter of principle." According to Beale, "It seems a matter in which we ought not to bind her conscience, indeed she feels she could not be bound." To Canon Butler however she wrote to apologize for Ramabai's angry tone and to try to present Ramabai's position in the best possible light: "She will never perhaps think exactly as we do, but if she did, she would not so well be a teacher for India. I am now beginning to see, for instance, why she does not so readily accept sacramental teaching as we do. She is afraid of its being confused by native thought with their own pantheism."[137] In what was perhaps her most welcome gesture to Ramabai, Beale wrote that "we can object to everything because we can fully understand nothing."[138] Ramabai took great comfort in Beale's willingness to engage her in constructive dialogue, and at one point called her "a fellow-labourer with me" for truth.[139]

Beale, it must be said, had her own priorities: she was as concerned as the Anglican clergy that Ramabai not be spoiled for work in India. Like many women reformers of her generation she believed that Indian women needed English women's direction; and, again, like many of her contemporaries, she hoped to contribute to enterprises that would help Indian women in India "to lead a life of usefulness . . . instead of the life of degradation and uselessness that makes them regret the times of Suttee."[140] She viewed Ramabai's residence at Cheltenham as an encouragement to young college girls interested in working on behalf of Indian women — an interest that Beale was eager to cultivate through the person of Ramabai herself. In a letter to Sister Geraldine in 1885 she said she hoped that Ramabai might eventually found "some sort of college for teaching the widows," presumably prompted by the example of Beale's own establishment at Cheltenham.[141] Moreover, gifts from the Royal Bounty Fund and from Prime Minister Gladstone toward Ramabai's stay at Cheltenham gave the college something of a public profile, connecting Cheltenham with the growing philanthropic commitment to Indian women's education, which was of special interest to Queen Victoria.[142] None of this suggests that Beale's sympathies with Ramabai's spiritual crises were anything but genuine, only that Beale anticipated that Ramabai's success and happiness in England might have some material benefits for Indian women and, not incidentally, for her own educational institution and its reputation as well. Her biographer Josephine Kamm discerned Beale's investment in Ramabai and represented their relationship as teacher-student, if not mistress/disciple — as when Kamm later recalled that when Ramabai returned to India, "she founded a mission school and a training college which faithfully reflected much of Dorothea's teaching."[143]

Beale and Sister Geraldine did not necessarily agree on the form of Christianity that Ramabai should adopt, on how to "manage" her, or, for that matter, on what the exact nature of her "mission" to India might be. And yet they both attributed what they perceived as her slippage from Christian orthodoxy to the fact that she was Indian and, more specifically, to her connections with the Brahmo Samaj. Beale felt that a residual Brahmoism had "developed [in her] a feeling against the miraculous element."[144] "A little impatience on our part," she feared, "might throw her back into the Unitarian teaching of the Brahmo Samaj."[145] This was a concern shared by Sister Geraldine and may account for their shared paranoia about Unitarian influences in and around Cheltenham. As Sister Geraldine wrote to Reverend Gore sometime in the summer of 1885: "From what I saw of Ramabai during the Easter vacation, I feel that her tendency was to take up an independent line . . . I fear the love of popularity is a very great snare to her, and that she has been of late in correspondence with some of her old Brahmo friends and has some idea of working with them in the future. A diluted Christianity without Christ is what I feel she is in danger of drifting in to."[146] Years later, Sister Geraldine attributed Ramabai's theological "drifting" to a "great want in the Hindu mind": its pantheism makes it "illogical and this lack of logical reasoning doubtless hinders the reception of the thought of the Kingdom of Heaven extending and embracing earth."[147] Sister Geraldine was by no means alone in this view. As Eugene Stock, a historian of the CMS and a contemporary of Sister Geraldine's, put it, "Hinduism has never satisfied the more thoughtful Hindus."[148] Although Sister Geraldine's mistrust of Ramabai, and her conviction that Ramabai's background was a perpetual threat to her Christian orthodoxy, should be read as concern for her charge's spiritual health, it is also true that Sister Geraldine harbored conventional Victorian notions of what Indian, and more specifically, Hindu, women were capable of.[149] As she wrote to Dorothea Beale in December of 1883, "[I]n committing her to your care, we desire to do so from the standpoint that a parent places a child with you for education."[150] And again later: "[W]e feel she needs as careful guarding and as much holding in as those who are much younger in point of age than herself."[151] As time went on, the twin characterizations of childishness and vanity dominated Sister Geraldine's explanations of why Ramabai failed to embrace certain orthodox precepts.[152] She had reason, one imagines, to emphasize Ramabai's essential "Indianness" over the apparent failure of her own spiritual influence. In any event, the more trenchant Ramabai's challenges to authority, the more "native" she became in Sister Geraldine's eyes. Applying her most savage characterization to Ramabai's criticisms of the Indian government's famine relief policies in the 1890s, she labeled her "disloyal,"[153] "childish, sensational and seditious."[154]

Such allusions to the childishness, untrustworthiness, and vanity of Indians are typical instances of late-nineteenth-century European orientalism and are thus perhaps not surprising in this context. That said, they clearly structured Sister Geraldine's entire relationship with Ramabai. Because she could only view Ramabai's informed resistance as prideful and vain — the tantrums of an ignorant child — she dismissed Ramabai's doctrinal quarrels as "fictions residing in the manifold recesses of . . . [her] fertile brain."[155] This was precisely the attitude that eventually alienated Ramabai from Wantage and, finally, from Sister Geraldine herself. Most significantly, these orientalist prejudices, reinforced by the belief that Hinduism constituted a continual temptation to Indian

Christian converts on their native soil, ultimately prevented Sister Geraldine from having much confidence in Ramabai's abilities to work at what the church intended to train her for—evangelization of one sort or another in colonial India. For a time, Sister Geraldine seemed to think Ramabai's willfulness in matters theological might be cured. Thus she wrote to the Reverend Gore in 1885: "I think England is better for Ramabai in her present state of mind. Were she now to return to India, Christianity would, I fear, lose its hold of her entirely."[156] Gradually, however, she began to have less faith in Ramabai's potential as an instrument of Christianity in India, possibly because she began to realize that Ramabai's tendency toward spiritual independence was not temporary. Ramabai's estimable reform career in India would compel Sister Geraldine later to admit that Ramabai's "independent mind has brought her into . . . prominence with the whole civilized world."[157] In the 1880s, however, she confided to Dorothea Beale that while Ramabai might be capable of organizing missionary efforts in India, she was not capable of running a mission herself.[158]

As Sister Geraldine's correspondence with Ramabai suggested time and again, she believed that willfulness in doctrinal matters presaged disaster in the mission field and might even endanger the whole British missionary enterprise. What is revealing here is not so much Sister Geraldine's convictions—they are what one might expect of a late-nineteenth-century Anglican nun—but rather the authority that she claimed, and that she attempted to exercise, over Ramabai herself. Though she readily ceded doctrinal authority to scripture, and her own authority to that of her ecclesiastical superiors, she was not willing to relinquish what she believed to be her final authority on what Ramabai's apostasy meant. The following passage, extracted from a letter to Ramabai, underlines precisely what Sister Geraldine believed to be at stake in Ramabai's challenges to Anglican orthodoxy:

You think the Church uncharitable because it does not allow that those who have broken away from her are still to be accounted as part of her. But look at the question from another point of view. Take for example a corporate body of any kind. It may be either a nation, a municipality, a regiment, school or anything you like to name. It must have its rules, officers and disciplines. If any member, or members, refuse to submit to its officers or otherwise set discipline at nought, they would be free to give up the rights and privileges of membership and go elsewhere. Now the Church is an indivisible Kingdom and delegated Government. Christ is its King, and the Government which He has ordained for His Kingdom is that of Apostles or Bishops. We as members of Christ's Kingdom's are not free to choose any other form of religious Government than this.[159]

As her choice of language indicates, Sister Geraldine saw in Ramabai's "heresies" a threat to the entire imperial order—a "corporate body" bound together by rules apparently agreed upon through a consensus that was both foreordained and legitimated by the church. For Sister Geraldine Christ's earthly kingdom was coterminous with British government worldwide; Ramabai's challenges to one signified disobedience to both. As such they were literally untenable — which is to say, Sister Geraldine invested so much time and energy in trying to refute Ramabai's arguments because she could not conceive of a world in which they might logically exist. For Ramabai, on the other hand, spiritual independence was never a matter of willfulness or pride, but rather a question of "the inner voice which is so strongly and loudly speaking to me." It was a voice that, in Ramabai's own words, "nothing can ever silence."[160] Despite Ramabai's protestations to the contrary — despite her attempts in fact to read her own resistance as respectful if tenacious difference rather than as rejection or disobedience — Sister Geraldine insisted until the end of her life that Ramabai had been wrongheaded and prideful and that consequently her time in England remained one of the most "painful episodes" in the conversion of India. Long after Ramabai's international reputation as social reformer was well-established, and in marked contrast to the hagiographic outpourings about her life by British, American, and Indian evangelicals, Sister Geraldine produced a critical view of her as a quasi-successful Christian missionary, insinuating that she remained vulnerable to "native" influences in India and was easily manipulated as a "cats-paw" by a variety of self-interested parties.[161]

To be sure, Ramabai's attitudes *did* imperil the imperial missionary cause as Sister Geraldine understood it, especially where the submission of native converts unquestioningly to ecclesiastical hierarchy was the defining requirement of evangelical work. She also offered to her benefactors an unflattering picture of their own religious authority — one that arguably depicted her as the truly engaged Christian struggling to reconcile her own doubts with scriptural teachings. There can be no clearer declaration of Ramabai's intention to make her own way — or of her determination to link her self-reliance to that inescapably Christian principle, conscience — than this passage: "I must be allowed to think for myself. God has given me a conscience, not to accept everything slavishly . . . but 'hear and see' for myself."[162] As she wrote to Beale over the public lecturing debate, "[O]ther people may call me an infidel if they like, but I trust in Him alone who is God, Father, and Guide, and [who] will surely show me His ways."[163] This was not mere argumentation for Ramabai; she believed that her very spiritual life was at stake. "Religion is such an awful matter," she wrote to Canon Butler, "that both parties are responsible for what they say or prove. It is not a rule of Arithmetic, Algebra or Chemistry that we may prove it by experiments." Like other "native" women who encountered the coercive power of British imperial rule, Ramabai was determined not to be the "experiment" upon which the success of colonial Christianity was tested.[164] Adherence to this conviction was indeed the condition upon which she agreed to stay in conversation, in dialogue with her superiors. "So if you agree not to be a lawyer but a searcher after truth in all your arguments," she continued, "I will most gladly bring my difficulties before you."[165]

Well might Sister Geraldine grieve, as she did in the fall of 1885, "that one of India's daughters whom we hoped God was training to carry a ray of light back to that benighted land should be returning to that darkness without the light of Truth."[166] Ramabai's unwillingness to conform was not simply the rebellion of an individual convert; her critiques threw the "Englishness" of the Anglican mission model into bold relief for metropolitan observers. But Sister Geraldine's real anguish stemmed from the fact that "you seem to be following a self-chosen path."[167] That choice, that autonomy upon which Ramabai insisted, struck at the heart of Sister Geraldine's authority to claim the universal truthfulness of Anglican Christian orthodoxy and, by implication, Britain's moral and cultural hegemony as well. In this sense, Ramabai's independence may also be read as an indication that the languages of English individualism were open to scrutiny, to co-optation and reformulation. It goes with out saying that Sister Geraldine's authority itself was one that depended entirely on cosmology of Christian imperialism, which she described above. To balk at it, for whatever reason, was to reject the spiritual authority of the Mother Church, of the Mother country, and, not least of course, of Mother Geraldine herself. It is in this context, the context of a church and an empire that were both conceived of as feminine, if not maternal ("those who have broken away from *her*," "the *Mother* country," etc.),[168] that Ramabai's experience of "sisterhood" during her time in England must be grounded. These are the terms that dictated — although in the case of Ramabai, they did not necessarily determine —

the contours of sisterhood between Indian women and English women in the late nineteenth century. If nothing else, Ramabai's insistence on following her own path helped to unmask the cultural presumptions of their ostensibly universal, providential mission — even as she compelled them to declare their investments in the "English" way of doing things. The relationship between Sister Geraldine and Ramabai, and to a lesser degree between Dorothea Beale and Ramabai, was, in short, less a question of sisterhood than a struggle for authority — authority over which version of female reform would prevail in India. It might be even more accurate to say that sisterhood itself in this historical particular instance became a contest for authority *because* of its imperial context. Solidarity between women of different nations, religions, and cultures was not given by virtue of a common gender but could be, as Ramabai's own eloquence attests, the product of self-determination, personal integrity, and negotiation.[169]

As time went on, and Ramabai felt her interpretations of India, of social reform, and of her role in it resisted in England, her doubts about the truths of Anglican doctrine multiplied. By 1885 she regretted that "I cannot induce myself entirely to believe the miracles of the Bible" or the Apostles' Creed.[170] She told Beale, "I have no doubt that Jesus is raised by God from the dead; but I doubt the resurrection of his earthly body."[171] Ramabai's challenges to Anglican dogma were no less forcefully articulated than her attitudes in the controversy over public speaking. As in that instance, these too were framed around the question of authority: Ramabai tended to privilege the word of scripture over the dicta of the church, a disposition that Sister Geraldine rightly viewed as a challenge to distinctively Anglican precepts. Ramabai's objection to the sacrament of confession is exemplary of the kinds of conflicts she had with orthodox Anglicanism:

I see and understand, you and Canon Butler are much displeased with me because I do not go to confession. I must tell you I shall in no way do anything which is not satisfactory to my mind; not that I shall say that every religious duty must be satisfactory to *me*, but I mean that it must be proved from [the] Bible that people cannot obtain salvation unless [they] do such and such [a] thing. From [the] Bible I can derive the necessity of confessing sins or faults to *one another* and to GOD, and not to a particular priest . . .

I do not like formalities as you know very well . . . I am bound to do things which are commanded by our Saviour as necessary for salvation and to please GOD, and these I will do by GOD's help, as I have promised on the occasion of my baptism, as much as it lies in my power, but I shall not do [anything] which is not necessary, and which it passes my power of doing . . .

It is very wrong of the Canon to say [I am under the Devil's influence] . . . only because I differ with . . . [him] in certain things . . . I am one of the least, but one of Christ's disciples. I shall hear him and others, when their advice agrees with His Own direction.[172]

What Sister Geraldine never fully comprehended was that Ramabai's suspicion of priests, like her opposition to the cross at the Poona mission, stemmed in part from her concern that the trappings of Christianity might be confused with those of Hinduism by recent Indian converts. In Ramabai's view, priests and "idols" were the hallmarks of Hindu religious tradition and as such she feared that an overemphasis on them in the Christian context might "lead my fellow (Indian) Christians into wrong ideas."[173] "It is all right with you, who are Christians from generations," she wrote Sister Geraldine, " . . . but I am just plucked down from (as Indians say) Hinduism and Brahmoism, so I know very well and sympathise with their feelings."[174] As her doctrinal doubts became more acute, she felt less and less comfortable confiding in Sister Geraldine. She experienced the sisters at Wantage as a community whose "whole tone is that they are right . . . and if I ask a question they are apt to say: 'You sin against such and such commandment of God.' "[175]

Debates about the basic sincerity of Ramabai's conversion or about her fundamental desire to understand and embrace the message of Christianity are not especially germane here. Her insistence on following her will and her instincts must be read in the context of her overarching belief that even and especially her own will was subject to the authority of God.[176] Contrary to Anglican teachings, however, she also believed that "yet we have the great gift from God, i.e., our own free will. By it we are to decide for ourselves what we are to do, and fulfill our intended work." For Ramabai it came down to a question of whose authority was to determine her spiritual direction. "Is Christianity the teaching of Christ or the teaching of a certain body of men?" she asked Beale in one of the last letters she wrote her in England. "I should like to know. If it is taken as the teaching of a certain party, I can with good conscience say that I have never believed in that teaching, and am not bound to accept it."[177] What her questions reveal is her sensitivity to the coercive aspects of Anglican (and for that matter, of any) orthodoxy. Given that such orthodoxy was considered to be the formula for the civilizing of

India, Ramabai's rejection of it was, as Sister Geraldine sensed, a challenge to the whole Christian imperial project. Let us be absolutely clear on the implications of this gesture. Ramabai did not merely question the rationale for Britain's imperial presence; her critique was much more radical than that. By articulating resistance to the authority of the church in matters doctrinal and matters Indian, she pointed to the orientalist basis of the church's social mission. And, by demonstrating that she was not prepared to work within its parameters, she contested the church's claim to exercise a monopoly on evangelical and social reform strategies in India. Pandita Ramabai recognized that, in the struggle for reform in India, evangelical orthodoxy was a metaphor for imperial authority. Her "apostasy" was, in a very real sense, the grounds for constructing an alternative female reform consciousness in the context of late-nineteenth-century imperial Britain.

As I have suggested, Sister Geraldine, Dorothea Beale, and the Anglican bishops were evidently correct when they discerned that Ramabai's experience in England was endangering their plans for her evangelical work in India. What they did not realize was the extent to which their own insistent exercise of authority prompted her doctrinal challenges and pushed her toward what was, in the end, an eloquently articulated critique of the liberal-imperial social reform program. This is not to say that Ramabai's critique was simply the product of her conflicts with the ecclesiastical hierarchy. Rather, it suggests that she used the clashes over religious orthodoxy as an opportunity to contest the terms of Western Christian colonial reform and to free herself from the authorities, both religious and cultural, through which her English friends were trying to discipline her. That she exploited the discourses of evangelical Christianity does not diminish the incisiveness of her critique. Significantly, Ramabai was not prepared to break with either the community at Wantage or at Cheltenham simply because she did not agree with the particular brand of orthodoxy that the Anglican Church required of her. Although she was troubled by the rifts that her own doubts caused, especially in her relationship with Sister Geraldine, she recognized that members of the clergy were as compelled by their own consciences as she was by hers, conceding to Beale that it was "quite natural" that the sisters at Wantage "should think anyone who questions the truthfulness of their beliefs is sinning."[178] What altered her relationship permanently with Sister Geraldine was not doctrinal differences per se but a conflict over the fate of her daughter, Manorama. Sometime in the fall of 1885,[179] Ramabai began to express concern that the sisters at

Wantage[180] were taking over Mano's religious education. As her letters indicate, she clearly feared that they were trying to instill in the daughter the orthodoxy that they had been unable to effect in the mother. In particular, Ramabai was wary of the Athanasian Creed, evidence of which she thought she could detect in Mano's prayers. Also of concern was the doctrine of the Trinity, with Ramabai making it quite clear to Sister Geraldine that since it was not a doctrine to be found in scripture, she did not want her child brought up a Trinitarian.[181]

Without minimizing the substantive theological import of these disputes too much, it is possible to interpret the dispute involving Mano as another clash over authority. This one was to prove final. For Ramabai's objection was not just to Sister Geraldine's teaching Mano how to pray; she also resented the nun's telling her daughter that her mother's prayer ways were not necessarily the best, since Ramabai herself was still in the process of learning them.[182] This was a clear breach of Ramabai's maternal authority, and it marks the turning point in her relationship with Sister Geraldine. Ramabai left Cheltenham and returned to Wantage to supervise Mano herself but not before, according to Sister Geraldine, she marked up Mano's books and requested that the sisters teach her daughter only "a theistic religion."[183] It was not long after this she left England for North America, wearied by her struggle with "professional missionaries" and eager to launch her own reform schemes for Indian women in India. To Sister Geraldine she wrote: "[A]s I know you are doing right according to your faith, I cannot blame you . . . And if I were to take my child with me to stay at Cheltenham, a great confusion would befall my study; besides there is a great scarcity of time and money. Then when I am caught between two impossibilities, there remains but one thing for me . . . and that is to leave Cheltenham. I shall be very sorry to do so, for it is my greatest happiness to study under Miss Beale. But my duty to my God and to my child is greater than any of my own happiness."[184] Sister Geraldine's response was equally uncompromising: she told Ramabai that she was "spiritually not in a condition to judge in spiritual matters for your own child." Her concern was real since in her view on this particular question of authority rode Mano's salvation. "You say Mano ought to obey you," she wrote to Ramabai. "God grant that you may never give her cause to feel that your authority is contrary to that of her Heavenly father."[185] Ramabai's concerns were of course equally real. She wanted Mano's final authority to be her own mother and her God, it is true, but she also wanted it to be India itself:

[M]y heart is full of gratitude to those who have been kind to us, but dear Ajeebai, I cannot make up my mind to leave Mano in England . . . I want her to be one of us, and love our countrypeople as one of them, and not as a strange or superior being. We are not as refined and lofty as the English people are, and if she is brought up in England, she will surely be an Englishwoman. Even if she comes to me in after days, she will be a foreigner and can never occupy the same place in our countrypeople's hearts as if she had been one of them. I do not want her to be too proud to acknowledge that she is one of India's daughters. I do not want her to blush when our name is mentioned, such being often the case with those who have made their homes in foreign lands.[186]

If this was an acknowledgment of the power that Sister Geraldine — together with English culture and evangelical Christianity — might have on Mano and her mother, it was also a statement about the power that Ramabai herself possessed to contest the reach of that authority, at least at this moment of crisis. And, given Mano's later role in her mother's reform projects in India, it may be taken as further indication of Ramabai's determination to control the agenda of female reform in India in the next generation.[187] Ramabai's correspondence suggests that she was already considering a trip to North America when the discussion about Mano occurred; and, as Meera Kosambi's translations of Ramabai's *Stree Dharma-Neeti* suggests, she had long considered motherhood one of women's most important duties.[188] I would not like to overstate the significance of the conflict over Mano, but it represents, I think, another expression of how theological, personal, and cultural tensions manifested themselves in Ramabai's encounters with her British benefactors. The realities of single motherhood in the nineteenth century meant that Ramabai continued to depend on the sisters at Wantage for Mano's education and care: though Ramabai took Mano to America she sent her back after a few months, in July 1886, while she traveled west in the United States.[189]

Ironically, for *both* Sister Geraldine and Ramabai the battle for Christ and for "civilization" was ultimately also a battle for personal authority.[190] As for many women reformers concerned about India in the late nineteenth century, it was a battle with gendered meanings, one that revealed that the "family" dynamics between English women and Indian women in the imperial context were shaped as much by maternal authority as sisterly solidarity, if not more so. Ramabai clearly recognized not just the stakes of authority, but also of authorship itself. Speaking of Christian apologists, she remarked that "they all more or less fall into the same mistake, namely when they want to establish the doctrine which *they think* is right, they will give any text a meaning which perhaps was not meant by the author."[191] Although she was here referring to scripture, this might be taken as a comment on Ramabai's own experience in England. She understood that experience as a story whose meanings she wished to interpret, against the various meanings that were being read onto it for her. Just as she fought to author the history of her time in England, so too she authored her own explanations about the methods and the purpose of women's reform for women in India. Hers was a useful ethnography of the conditions under which the conversion and reform of India were being carried out for any who cared to read it. "Missionaries who want to convert the Hindoo to their own religion," she wrote, "would do well to take care not to call themselves the only inheritors of truth, and all others 'the so-called false philosophers,' for the Hindoo as a rule will not be content to look at or hear only one side, and it is quite natural that they should not."[192] It was perhaps as didactic in its own way as the instruction sanctioned by the church, but it was nonetheless a reading that challenged the efficacy and the disinterestedness of the imperial power relationships in situ in India that Ramabai herself had resisted during her time in England.

She also, tellingly, worked to author her own resistant reading of international sisterhood. Despite the fact that after she left England in 1886 she only returned once, in 1898, she remained grateful to both Beale and Sister Geraldine for all they had taught her.[193] Among the convictions that were strengthened was that "the religious belief of each individual should be independent of anyone's teaching, and that no one has a right to load an infant mind with things that even the teacher cannot understand."[194] For Ramabai, the articulation of her differences with Sister Geraldine, although painful on both sides, did not signify either personal disobedience or the rejection of her person. For Ramabai it meant that differences could coexist, and that those who differed — over doctrine, creed, or life choices — might too. "We may more than a thousand times differ in our opinions and must be separated by unavoidable temporal difficulties," she wrote to Sister Geraldine, "but it does not in anyway follow that we must be enemies of or indifferent to each other."[195] In the end, as Ramabai's departure from England indicates, peaceful coexistence was not in her case possible at close proximity. That she chose to leave and seek support elsewhere is not evidence of failure, but rather of informed and critical resistance — a gesture remarkably free of bitterness or recrimination on her part. It is also arguably an example of what ethnographers call the refusal to be a subject, at least under the terms offered by colonial Christianity in Britain.[196]

Ramabai's attempts to negotiate sisterhood within the confines of imperial culture in Britain, to determine her personal role, and to respectfully differ with the terms outlined by Christian imperial and feminine authority constitute in no small measure a self-conscious reworking of an imaginative geography of the world of women. As Meera Kosambi has noted, Ramabai's motto was "self-reliance for women."[197] It was a maxim whose value she no doubt came to appreciate at least in part because of her struggles for autonomy at Cheltenham and Wantage — struggles that dramatized the tension between her desire to bear witness to God, on the one hand, and her determination to control her own destiny, on the other. Ramabai's time in England thus demonstrates that feminist consciousness can develop not only within the context of "sisterhood," but often does so in spite of it. Her particular history is equally compelling evidence that in the geopolitical context of imperialism, even and perhaps especially encounters between women could not, and indeed cannot, be totally free of its ideological effects. Although she may have initially believed herself to be free to wander "all over the map," she could not comfortably remain in the imperial metropole. Imperial England proved to be inhospitable ground for Ramabai's developing female reform consciousness. The United States, where she went after England to raise money for the widows' home she established in Bombay in 1889, was more hospitable, at least where financial support for her reform projects were concerned. Her travels from Philadelphia to San Francisco to Boston continued her pilgrimage and are a part of her biography yet to be fully historicized.[198] Meanwhile, this particular segment of her story is equally compelling evidence that the field of power laid out by imperial culture, whether in the metropole or in the colonial possessions, was historically and remains today an eminently contested and continually contestable terrain.

CHAPTER 3

Cornelia Sorabji
in Victorian Oxford

One cannot come away from Oxford the same as one goes there.
Cornelia Sorabji, Letters (1891)

Nowhere does the English temper show itself more clearly than in its relation to the universities.
M. Creighton,
Historical Lectures and Addresses (1903)

In a letter to the London *Times* of April 13, 1888, Lady Mary Hobhouse — the wife of a former law member of the Governor General's Council in India and a patron of Indian women's education in her own right — announced that Cornelia Sorabji of Poona would be coming to Britain to pursue a degree in medicine. The letter, which provided details of Sorabji's educational and family background, described her as a young woman "of pure Indian birth," and made public the fund that had been established by the Hobhouses to finance Sorabji's medical education.[1] A Parsi born into a Christian family in Bombay presidency in the 1860s, Sorabji was neither typical of Indians who traveled to Britain in the nineteenth century (the vast majority of whom were Hindu men) nor was she necessarily "purely" Indian, if such a purity of identity may be said to exist outside the fantasy of colonialism and its adherents.[2] Hobhouse's attempt to figure Cornelia Sorabji both as a kind of unalloyed colonial and incontrovertibly "national" subject represents one of the discursive means by which imperial Britons sought to consolidate the cultural contradictions and internal divisions that

were in part the effect of colonialism as irreducibly, coherently, and ineluctably Other. Hobhouse no doubt viewed it as her task to "sell" Cornelia Sorabji to an English metropolitan audience that was sympathetic
to the plight of Indian womanhood but not necessarily well versed in
the variety of local and regional differences that might be subsumed
under the overarching, homogenizing category of "the Indian woman."
For Hobhouse, as well as for a number the well-meaning British patrons
who helped to subsidize Sorabji's Oxford education, Cornelia's commodification under the sign of "the" authentic Indian woman was a
testimony to their own capacity to discern her essential difference, to
exoticize it, and not least, to make it available in the metropolitan mar-
ketplace — all ostensibly for Sorabji's own good.

In fact, Sorabji's experiences reveal how travel to and circulation
through the various domestic landscapes of imperial Britain could throw
the axis of *colonial* difference into bold relief and, indeed, could even
disclose the precariousness of the binaries upon which such difference
was predicated. This chapter treats Cornelia Sorabji's Somerville correspondence as an ethnography of late-Victorian Oxford in an attempt to
excavate the particular conditions under which an Indian woman sought
to speak in the voice of "the Indian woman" in late-Victorian Britain.[3]
Sorabji had much in common with Pandita Ramabai — both were from
western India, both came to Britain originally to be doctors, both experienced the intrusive benevolence of imperial Britons who believed
they had the best interests of their colonial charges at heart. And yet
their social locations were not exactly identical, and their strategies for
navigating imperial culture in the metropole differed significantly. Sorabji had been born to Christian parents. As a result, her family history
acquired a particular set of cultural meanings for her in Oxford — meanings that were to structure her apprehensions of Englishness and colonial culture from the 1880s until her death in 1954. Despite the fact that
her plans to study medicine were thwarted by well-meaning English
philanthropists, Sorabji remained an anglophile who returned to Britain
over and over again during the course of her lifetime. She considered
herself an "ardent . . . little Tory,"[4] opposed nationalist reformers' efforts,
and rejected both the vote for women and what she considered the
unfemininity of the few suffrage reformers she met in Britain. Her life's
work on behalf of purdah women — whom she represented in court,
thereby securing for them rights to property and inheritance that social
custom might otherwise have prevented them from claiming — did not
so much advance women's legal emancipation or social independence as

CORNELIA SORABJI.

Figure 2 Cornelia Sorabji, from *The Queen*, 1889.

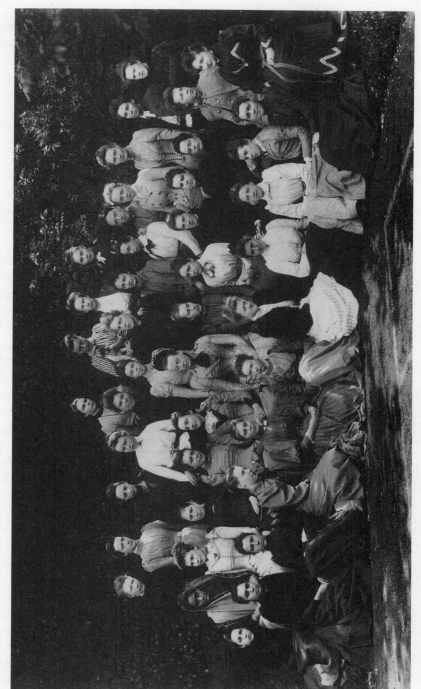

Figure 3 Somerville College, class of 1891. Cornelia Sorabji is first on the left, second row.

it preserved the gender segregation regulated by cultural norms and hence, one might argue, upheld the status quo. According to Susie Tharu and K. Lalita, she was "both a fighter and a victim of her times." In Vera Brittain's estimation she "chose the wrong direction at an important moment in history, and was repudiated by the currents of her time with a completeness which tends to withhold from her the status that is due her."[5] Although she was in many respects a "pioneering" Indian woman — transgressing gender boundaries in India and race and gender boundaries in Britain — like Pandita Ramabai, she cannot necessarily be understood by recourse to the analytical categories offered by either nationalist or feminist historiographies.[6]

An analysis of how Sorabji was shaped, without being fully determined, by her movement from Poona to Oxford — the heart of the heart of the Victorian empire, as it were — provides insight into the impact of colonial mentalities on a woman who was differently "Indian," in her mind and in the eyes of many who engaged with her, than Pandita Ramabai. Sorabji's Oxford experience illustrates the ways in which the category of "Indian," as well as that of "woman," is historically specific and culturally contingent — the product of complex negotiations between a subject and her contexts. Rather than rehabilitate Sorabji as an unsung feminist heroine — a project she would have abhorred, having no time for the "women's rights women" of her day — what I want to do is "restore her to appropriate memory"[7] by exploring the coexistence of her anglophilia with the oppositional attitudes toward British imperial ideologies she developed privately as she negotiated the very public social and colonial reform cultures of late-Victorian England. As with Ramabai's correspondence, Sorabji's offers us an opportunity to see how instrumental an Indian woman could be in consolidating Britons' convictions about what "Englishness" was and what the right and proper path to reform and celebrity should be — suggesting again that ideas about what it meant to be or act "English" were made and remade at the level of the local as well as the "national" sphere and were produced in relationship to colonial images and manifestations of empire at home. Sorabji's letters from Oxford, written to her parents in Poona between 1889 and 1894, offer a critical reading of middle- and upper-middle class Victorian culture, from Oxford to the Church Missionary Society to the female social reform movement in London. Like all ethnographies, they also tell us much about Sorabji herself. Her investments in the class status offered by Oxford, combined with a kind of Parsi nationalism and her strategic use of the celebrity surrounding her image as "the Indian woman" in Victorian Britain, complicate the traditional lens through which we tend to understand colonial subjectivities and, with them, history-writing on empire, "home," and women's particular negotiation of the sociopolitical spaces in between. For her story suggests that not all colonial subjects rejected the values of Victorian imperial culture, and that when they did it was accomplished unevenly and unpredictably. As it did for some other late-Victorian colonial subjects, an identification with "Englishness" functioned as a socially sanctioned means of becoming a citizen for Sorabji, albeit an imperial one.[8]

Between 1889 and 1892 Cornelia Sorabji resided at Somerville College, Oxford, where she studied law in anticipation of becoming a barrister. Unlike Pandita Ramabai, whose conversion to Christianity in England in 1883 had sent shock waves through the Indian social reform community in Bombay, Cornelia Sorabji had been a lifelong Christian when she arrived in London in August 1889 at the age of twenty-three.[9] Her father, the Reverend Sorabji Kharsedji, was a convert from Zoroastrianism; her mother Franscina was a tribal (possibly a Toda) woman raised as a Christian in India by an army officer and his wife, Lord Francis and Lady Cornelia Ford.[10] Kharsedji's conversion had provoked outrage not just in his family but in the Parsi community around Bombay more generally, an experience that Sorabji was to recount later in her memoir of her parents' lives.[11] Both Cornelia's parents were active in the Christian social reform community in Poona, where her father was an agent for the Church Missionary Society and her mother had run the Victoria High School for Girls (VHS) since 1876. Franscina herself had traveled to England in 1887 and extracts from the annual report of her school were featured in the *Indian Female Evangelist*, an English mission magazine, in the 1880s and 1890s.[12] The impact of her parents' religious devotion, their social work among the less fortunate in and around Poona, and, above all, their commitment to education, was enormous on their fifth daughter, Cornelia — not only for her own career path, but also in terms of the adoration for them it generated in her. "There is one circumstance . . . in my life, of which I may boast, unashamed," she wrote in her autobiography, *India Calling* (1934): "that is my inheritance, the fact that I am the child of my Parents. For there are no two people in all the world whom I would have chosen as my parents, if choice had been given me, save just my very own Father and Mother."[13] Sorabji admired her father's conversion (which had occurred, in her words, "in the manner of the Early Martyrs of the Christian Church, at peril of death") and her mother's "understanding in heart and mind" as well as her "gifts of construction and organization which were unknown among the Indians of her day." Cornelia's weekly letters home to them (always addressed to "Dearest Ones") during her time at Oxford and her memoir of them, *Therefore*, together attest to their centrality in her emotional world well beyond her adolescence. Indeed, she remained dependent on their approval well into her twenties. Her parents' hard work and their unselfish devotion to educational reform causes produced the same discipline and socially minded commitments in several of their children as in their most famous daughter. In addition to Cornelia's becoming a pleader in the Court of Wards, her sister Susie founded a girls' school; her brother, Dick, became a barrister; her sister Alice qualified as a medical doctor; her sister Pheroze was a professional singer; and her sisters Lena and Mary both worked in the VHS.[14] Individually and as a family, the Sorabjis of Poona were an influential presence in the social and cultural landscape of Bombay presidency from the late nineteenth century until the Second World War.

Despite the impact of her father's conversion on Sorabji's Christian convictions, it was her mother whom Cornelia chose to remember as the heart and soul of the Sorabji family, the very embodiment of its conviction that "we were in the world to serve others."[15] In Franscina's eyes, daughters were not the calamity most Indians considered them to be (she had seven in all).[16] She viewed them rather as "women that Indian wanted . . . for her service." Franscina Sorabji, whom the London *Times* called one of the "pioneers of progress and of education for women and children" in western India,[17] not only believed in the gospel of work through which such service might be accomplished, she lived it — both in the VHS and outside it. Throughout Cornelia's youth her mother traveled to local villages to visit the poor and sick and welcomed the same in the family house at Poona. "There were great excitements in store," Cornelia recalled in later years, "for the child who was allowed to accompany her on her visits to the villages, and to see how airless huts were cleaned and readjusted at her asking: how she dealt with child and woman, whatever the trouble, or with the whole village if an epidemic were afoot."[18]

In her autobiography, Cornelia credited her mother's encounters with local women in distress with directing her toward the law. When Cornelia was eight or nine, a Gujerati Hindu woman came to the Sorabji home to ask Franscina for help with a legal matter: she was a widow who had sought out a businessman to manage the property that had been left to her in accordance with Hindu law. She later discovered that he had swindled her out of her inheritance by making himself her legal guardian without her knowledge but with her (de jure) consent, since she was illiterate and had signed the necessary papers over to him in good faith. Cornelia did not record what advice, if any, Franscina gave to the woman. But she did recall the incident over fifty years later as a formative one for her future career choice. Franscina told her daughter that "there are many Indian women in trouble that way," and if she wished to be useful she should study the law: "that will show you the way to help in this kind of trouble." From that moment onward, according to her autobiography, Cornelia knew that she was going to be a lawyer; "and my little sister was equally determined to be a Doctor."[19]

Memory is highly selective, and Cornelia's reconstruction of her path toward the law represents an interesting and, for our purposes, a significant revisioning of events. She undertook this revision partly out of a sense of indebtedness to her mother, but also in an attempt to link her later work for *purdahnashin* with a family tradition of self-sacrificing outreach to Indian, and more specifically to Hindu, women. That a Hindu woman disenfranchised by a scheming Indian man should function as the explanation for Cornelia's choice of the law as a profession is extremely revealing, and not only because it was medical qualification, rather than the law, which she had initially sought when she headed for Britain to pursue higher education. Sorabji's relationships with other Hindu women — such as her prominent contemporaries, Ramabai and Rukhmabai — as well as with that highly charged Victorian category, "the Hindu woman," were fraught with an ambivalence that is in some measure attributable to her Christian upbringing. For proselytizing Indian converts no less than for European missionaries in India, Hindus were the object of evangelical instruction, reformist scrutiny and, inevitably, social and cultural "Othering." For Parsi Christians like the Sorabjis, to religious difference was added another dimension: a sense of ethnic difference and national feeling. As Cornelia put it bluntly in *India Calling*, "I am Parsee by nationality."[20] With that declaration, Sorabji announced what she had long adhered to as the defining differences between her community and that of the Hindus. What's more, she established herself as the interpreter of peculiarly Hindu religious customs and social practices to an audience that was presumed to be non-Indian and probably British — an audience that would also, she appears to have presumed, read her sympathies as similar to their own. Her descriptions of her childhood in *India Calling* are full of didactic examples of what differentiated her family from other Indians. Whereas the Sorabji children were " 'brought up English'—i.e., on English nursery tales with English discipline"—most Indian children were, in her view, spoilt and misbehaved. The treatment of women was for Cornelia the ultimate index of cultural difference: orthodox Hindu women "live[d] in subjection to their husbands"; "Moslem women remained in purdah"; "but our women have never been secluded."[21] The independence and careerist goals of the Sorabji women were an explicit contrast to what Sorabji saw as the slavish lives of women in the Hindu community, from whom Parsis sought and maintained an "apartness" that their Persian "origin, temperament, and habits of life . . . made inevitable."[22] Dress—a cultural marker that preoccupied Sorabji throughout her time in Britain—represented the most eloquent manifestation of Parsi distinctiveness. "Our women wear a *sari* certainly," she wrote, "but it is of silk, and draped differently from the Hindu *sari* (over the right ear, behind the left)."[23]

In articulating her own hybrid identity, Cornelia attested to how inseparable its Parsi and Christian components were.[24] Christian values surfaced even in her expressions of Parsi pride: in rejecting caste, the Parsis, she argued, "are one body"; the Zoroastrian temple, she reminded, is dominated by an altar, a priest, and a prayerful congregation.[25] And she was certainly not alone among Indian reformers in emphasizing the commonalities between Indian religions and Christianity; much of the history of social reform in the nineteenth century is grounded in arguments about Hindu theism. If Sorabji cultivated a sense of difference from Hindu women, then, it was an equal mixture of Christian religious and Parsi cultural superiority—masked more or less successfully by a sentimentalized Victorian commitment to the improvement and uplift of Indian womanhood. Structuring this conviction of superiority at every turn was an unabashed admiration for things English and a sense of identification with the British civilizing mission in India. Her pride in her English upbringing has already been indicated. She took equal pleasure in detailing the full extent of her family's English customs: "The houses of our Parsee friends were furnished English (and early Victorian) like our own. We ate in the English manner off English plates, and with English adjuncts, and our diet included meat." "We were as cosmopolitan in our diet," she wrote, "as in our general upbringing."[26] Historians of the Parsi community in Bombay and in western India more generally have suggested that such anglophilia was part of how Parsis understood, and in turn invented, their role in colonial

India: as merchants, traders, and capitalist entrepreneurs they saw themselves as middlemen, both economically and culturally, between the British and a variety of Indian groups in the subcontinent.[27] Sorabji participated in this characterization when she wrote that "Parsees have shown no desire to compete with Hindus or Moslems for sovereignty in India. They have, like the British, helped the development of trade and, being, as a community, rich and prosperous, have been responsible for many public benefactions in the cities where they dwell; giving the lead, indeed, in these directions to native Indians themselves."[28] To take the lead in the reform of Hindu women's condition, in cooperation with the agents of Britain's civilizing mission, was an aspiration that emerged from Sorabji's location at the intersection of a variety of sociocultural identities (Parsi, Christian, Maharashtrian) even as it was forged in the crucible of family life in Poona. Ultimately, it was what took her to Britain in search of professional qualifications and that characteristically Victorian female moral obligation, "useful work."

Like Ramabai, Sorabji was a young woman who had gained a certain notoriety by challenging gender prescriptions in India even before she undertook the unconventional step of traveling to Britain to attend university. She had been the first girl student at Deccan College, where she encountered opposition and some hostility upon matriculation. Placing first in a degree examination entitled her to a government scholarship at a British university, but she was debarred from this opportunity on the grounds of sex — despite the fact that protestations over her disqualification were raised in the House of Commons by friends of Indian female education. Expressing sentiments similar to those held by individuals then fighting for the admission of women to British universities, Cornelia later noted ruefully that it was considered "impertinent of any woman to produce circumstances which were not in the mind of the Authorities as a possibility when they dangled a gilded prize before eyes that should have been male."[29] Soon thereafter she applied for and was appointed to the position of lecturer in English literature at a men's college at Ahmedabad in Gujerat. In an era when speaking in public (i.e., mixed company) was taboo for women not just in India but in Britain as well, this was an unprecedented step, and it brought tremendous criticism down on her head. She stuck with it because she thought "it would greatly benefit the cause of women generally, for a woman, even once, to have been entrusted with directing . . . men's intellects."[30]

Unlike Pandita Ramabai, who financed her travels in the 1880s to Britain and America through her writing, Sorabji had well-to-do patrons awaiting her when she disembarked at Liverpool. From at least 1888, Sorabji was in correspondence with Lady Mary Hobhouse, whose husband Lord Arthur Hobhouse had been the law member of the Governor General's Council in India from 1872 to 1877. Both of the Hobhouses had taken an interest in female education while they were in India, especially in the activities of the Brahmo school that Keshub Chunder Sen's daughter (later the Maharani of Cooch Behar) attended. One of Arthur Hobhouse's colleagues later remembered the couple's "desire to cultivate the society of Indians of the better class," and the Sorabjis of Poona may have been among those Indians with whom the English couple fraternized.[31] It was evidently Lady Mary Hobhouse who encouraged Cornelia to come and study in England. It was also she who took the lead in arranging to have the fund that she and her husband had established advertised in the columns of the *Queen* and in administering the money to Cornelia throughout her time at Somerville.[32] The *Queen* estimated that the total cost of Sorabji's expenses (for "outfit, journey, tuition, and vacation arrangements") would be £300, £160 of which had been collected by August 1889, and the magazine encouraged subscribers to send their contributions directly to Lady Hobhouse.[33] As with Ramabai, money was always a source of anxiety for Sorabji. She felt beholden to the Hobhouses during her fours years in Britain, perhaps especially since they insisted on calling the fund her "substituted scholarship," in compensation for the injustice she had experienced at being barred from the government grant. But while she worried over her expenses and justified nearly every penny to Lady Hobhouse, she did not reject their generosity — even when they steered her away from medicine into a teaching and then a legal career.

Because the Michaelmas term at Somerville did not begin until October, Sorabji spent her first month and a half in Britain in Maida Vale, living at the home of Elizabeth Adelaide Manning, whom she had met when Manning traveled to Bombay the previous January.[34] By then Manning had been the secretary of the National Indian Association for almost a decade, and her home was the center of its activities. Begun as an organization for promoting knowledge about India and understanding between its inhabitants and Britons, the NIA was a secular association, committed in principle, as its founder Mary Carpenter had been, to noninterference in Indian social and religious customs.[35] As Manning wrote in the association's journal, "[W]e do not seek so much to originate as to lend strength and support" to reform, and especially educational programs, in Britain and India.[36] Increasingly, however, the wide variety of schemes for the medical and general education of Indian girls that the NIA supported made this position untenable, even though it persisted as an ideal. As early as the late 1870s association branches throughout Britain and India were financing scholarships for teacher-training colleges and medical schools as well as a line of books called "The Mary Carpenter Series" for use in zenana teaching in India. One correspondent from India, a Mrs. Etherington, who was the inspectress of government schools in the North West Provinces, offered the discerning opinion that "the very attempt at improving the condition of women is an interfering with their social customs." For her, as for many who belonged to the NIA, it was neither possible nor desirable to avoid such intervention, especially when it came to issues like child marriage and widow remarriage.[37]

Promoting educational opportunities of all kinds was at the heart of the NIA's philosophical and practical commitments. As has been noted in chapter 1, by the mid-1880s chief among the association's schemes was an organized effort to oversee Indian students attending British institutions of higher education. The vast majority of these students were men who, according to a table published in the *Journal of the Indian National Association* of January 1885, came from all regions of India, mostly to study law and/or prepare for the Indian Civil Service examination. The author of the article (who may have been Manning herself) estimated that there were presently about 180 Indian "gentlemen" in Britain and that over the past two decades as many as 700 had come to live and study in Britain.[38] In response to these numbers, the NIA began actively to advertise itself as a clearinghouse for Indian students. It produced circulars publicizing what it could do for young men looking for lodging, for advice on what kind of clothing to bring, and for "exposure to English home life." One feature in the *Journal* even offered to help young Indian students with their money and to send a yearly report back to their parents.[39] It is difficult to know precisely how many Indians used the NIA services. We do know from the *Journal* (renamed the *Indian Magazine and Review* in January 1886) that Indians in residence at Cambridge and Oxford used the magazine — which had subscribers in India — as a space for discussing life at Britain's leading universities and for dispensing advice to their fellow Indians on what to expect at Oxbridge should they have the good fortune to attend.[40] Partly as a result of Sorabji's residence at Somerville, its principal collaborated with Lady Hobhouse on a piece about women's colleges in England for the journal, which was designed to attract more Indian women students to Oxford.[41]

Sorabji thus ended up at E. A. Manning's through a combination of circumstances: because of Manning's personal interest in her, because of the NIA's commitment to shepherding Indian students in England and, not least, because of Lord and Lady Hobhouse's active involvement in the association. She became something of a celebrity in missionary circles and was sought after by magazines for both her portrait and her opinions on Indian women's condition, but she turned up only occasionally in the pages of the NIA's journal, usually as part of the crowd at the association's annual soirees or special events. And although Lady Hobhouse and E. A. Manning considered her their personal responsibility, she was not in any sense sponsored by the NIA. Less straightforward was her relationship with the CMS and its representatives — to whom Sorabji referred in her correspondence home as "the Society." Even before she had gotten off the ship bringing her to England she was trying to keep invitations at bay from representatives of the CMS to speak about Indian mission work in London, though she had no official connection with the group except through her father's attachment in Poona. In the three years between Ramabai's departure and Sorabji's arrival in Britain, the quest for "native" missionaries had accelerated, making a Christian-born Indian like Sorabji of potentially critical use in the mission field, as well as good publicity for the work of the CMS in India.[42] Sorabji's activities and accomplishments had been broadcast in Britain via the *Indian Female Evangelist*, a women's mission magazine that chronicled a variety of "native" evangelization efforts; reports on Franscina Sorabji's projects at the VHS and elsewhere received regular attention throughout the 1880s, as did Cornelia's educational successes.[43] Indeed, well before she arrived at Oxford, Cornelia had to cope with competing claims on her person and her future, and to navigate her way through the expectations of the English philanthropists who were sponsoring her passage, her education at Somerville, and her professional aspirations.

During her first month in England Sorabji faced gentle and not-so-gentle pressure to follow the paths laid out for her mainly by well-meaning English women — women who had different and competing goals in mind for her and who fully expected that she would follow their direction. Throughout the long voyage to Britain, Cornelia fretted over her plans for a medical career. "My heart begins to fail me a bit about the Dr. scheme," she wrote on the voyage out. "Suppose no one will rise [to it], I will have to come back with my tail between my legs. Suppose also I fail — but I daresay these morbid broodings are another result of the sea."[44] As it turned out, she was quite prescient: during her very first meeting with Madeleine Shaw-Lefevre, the then outgoing principal of Somerville College, she was told that "medicine had better be given up." Shaw-Lefevre offered a series of good reasons for the decision: the course was very trying and it would have to be done in London since in her view, the Oxford Medical School was unsatisfactory.[45] Equally persuasive was the fact that Shaw-Lefevre had written to the Countess of Dufferin about getting Sorabji a scholarship from her Fund to Supply Female Medical Aid to the Women of India and was told that the countess "does not think Indian girls ought to study out of their own country, as the Grant Medical College is quite good enough for them."[46] Cornelia reported to her parents two even more compelling reasons to abandon medicine: both of her patrons, Elizabeth Adelaide Manning and Lady Hobhouse, "rather expect . . . me to keep to the Educational line." In fact, as Carol Dyhouse has noted, teaching was the major occupational outlet for women graduates from British universities in the nineteenth century.[47] "I have submitted," she told her parents, "not because I easily relinquish my plans, but if my health would not stand it and if the money cannot be procured — then the wisest thing is to give up."[48]

Fears about an Indian woman's health in the damp, cold climate of England were not totally unfounded. Several years earlier Anandibai Joshi had died of complications from a cold while studying to be a doctor at the Women's Medical College in Philadelphia, making her something of a martyr in Indian communities abroad.[49] It was a fate of which Cornelia was well aware (she "submitted" to flannel clothes because "of course I do not want to be a second Anandibai Joshi"), and she took extra precautions by dressing warmly and having colds and other minor health setbacks quickly seen to.[50] But she was also clearly influenced by Elizabeth Manning's long-term plans for her: "Miss Manning is so very kind to me. She thinks it is a pity to forsake Arts and Education, as she says I seem to have a special gift for that line, and there are really so many to devote themselves to medicine."[51] Manning may have been thinking of Kadambini Ganguly and Rukhmabai, both of whom were in Britain at the time studying medicine. Rukhmabai was the more well-known of the two, partly because she had been "the unwilling heroine" of a much-publicized legal case in which she, a child bride, contested her husband's conjugal rights in the later 1880s. She was attending medical school in London at this time under the patronage of Walter McLaren, member of Parliament, and his suffragist wife, Eva.[52] Manning was, however, also steering Sorabji away from medicine toward teaching because she had some specific plans in mind for her: she wanted Sorabji to head up "Mr. Bhownaggree's Institute." Bhownaggree was a Parsi merchant and philanthropist who had studied law in London and was called to the bar in 1885. He was known for his interest in women's issues, and he was eventually elected to the House of Commons in 1895 as a Tory member of Parliament.[53] Sorabji was not entirely averse to this idea ("this you know is just the position I should most like — teaching young Parsee girls"), but she told her parents not to broadcast it because "I have seen Mr. Bhownaggree's scheme and he wants an English lady as head; so that if I were appointed it would have to be after various plannings on the part of Miss Manning and her friends. Mr. B. is coming to England in the Winter, and I daresay the plan will then be fully discussed."[54] The question of English women being chosen over Indians for positions of administrative responsibility would arise again during Sorabji's time in England, but Sorabji had faith at this point in Manning's influence and connections. Manning's arguments also appealed to Sorabji's desire to stand out, to be considered unique and exceptional: "Miss Manning says she wants to save me for Education and for something new and special, like this future college in Bombay."[55]

Giving up medicine so soon after arriving must have been disappointing and, at particular moments, hard to live with. Shortly after settling in with Manning, Sorabji was taken on a tour of the "Ladies' Medical Halls" (presumably at University College, London), where she heard Elizabeth Blackwell read a paper and was introduced to both Elizabeth Garrett Anderson and Mary Scharlieb. All three of these women were pioneer "lady doctors" of the day, and Sorabji could barely contain her excitement: "The first London M.D. [Scharlieb] was actually close to me." Having chosen Somerville over medicine, Sorabji was fated to be reminded of her decision again and again while in England, largely because of her contact with Rukhmabai, whom she saw at Blackwell's talk. Although she wrote home that she was "very pleased to see an Indian face," she did not appreciate Rukhmabai telling her that Cornelia had had many more advantages than she, among them Sorabji's educational background and her flawless command of the English language. As time went on, Sorabji expressed more and more resentment toward Rukhmabai, quite possibly because Rukhmabai was pursuing the course of study Sorabji had herself desired. In fact, she speculated to her parents that Rukhmabai might not even end up reading medicine because Sorabji doubted she could pass the necessary exams. Such cattiness stemmed in part from fear about what her family would think of her having abandoned her plans for medicine. She insisted that "Mother will have her doctor in the fam[ily] after all in our little Ailsa [Alice]."[56] In order to ensure this, Sorabji wrote letters of inquiry on Alice's behalf to Lady Dufferin and to heads of medical colleges in Britain in order to try to get her sister matriculated and funded.[57]

In spite of the fact that Manning was pressing her to give up medicine and pursue teaching or educational administration, Sorabji had nothing but praise for her in these early days.

I feel it such a privilege to be with her. She is very busy all day and for others, interviewing Indian students . . . arranging for their work, sympathising in their troubles, throwing herself into their interests, supervising even their wardrobes, listening to all their plans, so kindly advising and helping. She is really wonderful.

She says I must look upon this [the house in Maida Vale] as one of my English homes, and come whenever I can. Is it not good of her? . . . I am quite sorry I shall be leaving her so soon.[58]

While Manning was full of admiration in return for Sorabji's parents and for the good work done by missionaries in India, she was also frank with Cornelia about her views on religion, declaring that she had some ideological difficulties with Christianity and was at present a theist. Sorabji, for her part, pronounced Manning "so tolerant," particularly in contrast to the women of the CMS with whom she had contact and some conflict during her first month in Britain. Cornelia recounted to her parents how Mrs. Gilmore (a member of the Society's London Committee who had also had contact with Ramabai) had criticized Manning's lack of religious principles and worried that she would try to "influence" Sorabji's faith. Even more galling to Sorabji was the criticism Gilmore and other Society women made of her having taught in a men's college. They thought it "not at all proper" and treated her, she felt, as something of a "moral leper." Her reaction was to let them know in no uncertain terms that she was "not Society"— that is, not under obligation to them — and that she would work to get them some subscriptions among the influential people she might meet but would not be their agent in England. This contretemps set Sorabji on the offensive against the Society and, privately at least, she made her position clear: "I have faced this righteous committee now, and am not afraid of it. I shall speak for them at holidays, as Mr. Lewis is wanting me to promise to do . . . [T]hey are under obligation to me, for the happy fact that I am Indian is an advertisement in itself." Prompted by the CMS's expectation that she would do as they wished, Sorabji discerned what capital there was to be made out of being "the native."

She soon discovered that she could exploit that capital in order to control her time and her studies (hence her insistence on speaking only during vacations). She began to realize how crucial her independence from organizational control would be: "I am glad I am not Society for I can say what I please." She knew too that her parents, who were dependent on grants from the Society for the running of the VHS, would worry that she was offending their benefactors. "Meanwhile dear Mother and Father do not think I am being rude or otherwise unpleasant to these good people. I am sweetness and gentleness itself as they will write and tell you, I have no doubt — and this is diplomacy . . . I have stood up for kind Miss M. when they question her faith . . . but otherwise I have kept my hair on."[59] Because she understood what might be at stake for the Sorabjis in Poona if she alienated the CMS people in London, Sorabji worked hard to remember that "they are good people" who had been kind to her mother when she visited England some years before. But this did not blunt her critique of the CMS members, who, in her view, "lose the interests of the individual in the desire for the good of the Society."[60]

Why Sorabji was more willing to take direction from Manning, a self-confessed Christian doubter, than from local ladies of the CMS, is a matter for speculation. Manning's connections with the NIA, and hence with her patrons the Hobhouses, may have had something to do with it; Sorabji's perception that the Society presumed to exploit her surely did. Just before she left for Oxford, Manning had another talk with Cornelia in which she pressed her to consider doing a course in teacher training after only one year at Somerville. Manning's reasoning was that this way, Sorabji would be likely to secure the position of in-spectress of a normal school in India — a post unusual for an Indian women to hold at this time. Sorabji was clearly ambivalent about this and agreed to relinquish doing a degree in Anglo-Saxon honors chiefly because she feared being accused of "striving after fame rather than useful work." "And besides," she wrote to the family, "I ought not to be spending too many years acquiring [knowledge] when there is work to be done . . . I shd not like to be too big for work at home in dear old

India."[61] If she was in danger of doubting the wisdom of this noble and self-sacrificing scheme, another meeting with Rukhmabai shored up her conviction about Manning's plans for her. "Rukhmabai came to see me yesterday. She is bent on some grand scheme for a Ladies Assn for which she wishes to raise funds. I wish all Indian women would work steadily and usefully instead of aiming at original schemes. I feel that about myself. There are too many unfinished projects extant in India. I told Rukhmabai she ought to help Ramabai, but that would be second fiddle, and she does not want that."[62] Rukhmabai was clearly becoming Sorabji's shadow — one might even say her double — with Cornelia constructing the career paths she was torn about acquiescing in as superior to those that her Bombay presidency sister seemed to be carving out for herself.[63]

In the end, very little was fixed about Sorabji's course of study when she arrived at Somerville. Lady Hobhouse advised Sorabji before her departure for Oxford that she should take one step at a time, suggesting that she might do two years at Somerville, take an examination, and *then* proceed to the training school in London that Manning had recommended. Although Sorabji did not comment on it, it seems quite likely that Hobhouse's and Manning's different perspectives are explicable at least in part in terms of class: given Hobhouse's aristocratic background it is hardly surprising that she would have emphasized Somerville over a training college. Manning too had her reasons: she had been actively involved in the whole training school movement since the 1870s, and it would have undoubtedly been a coup to get Sorabji, an Indian woman, enrolled in one of the metropolitan institutions she had been promoting for years.[64] What these differences indicate is that, among other things, several versions of "the right way of doing things" were made available to Sorabji, as Britons offered possibilities for a quintessentially "English" success story that were differently inflected by class and hence cultural concerns. Sorabji was probably unaware of these backstage details and, in any event, she was too dependent on Hobhouse's and Manning's financial and emotional support to have questioned their motives. She was determined to get to Oxford and her first glimpse of it prompted this response: "So at last I am here, in the town of my dreams."[65]

The Oxford that greeted Sorabji when she moved into Somerville Hall in mid-October of 1889 was to become famous as the nursery of imperial statesmen: between 1888 and 1905, three viceroys in succession were Balliol men and, over the whole period of British rule in India, fifteen viceroys or Governors General came from Oxford (versus five from Cambridge).⁶⁶ Home of the Oxford Mission, the university would also send out missionaries to all parts of the empire and dominions during the decades following Sorabji's time there. Although the transformation of undergraduates into semiprofessional proselytizers for the Christian faith coincided with the "new imperialism" and the "scramble for Africa" of the 1880s, this particular dimension of the civilizing mission had deep roots at Oxford. For Victorians interested in religion "saw the Empire as providing a framework within which the heirs to the Oxford move-ment could advance their work from the shores of Britain to India, Africa and the Pacific."⁶⁷ Teachers, civil servants, and lawyers were also among those educated at Oxford for imperial service. Although there were critics of imperial policy at Oxford in the nineteenth century — Goldwin Smith, Regius Professor of History, chief among them — few seriously entertained the notion that the empire should be dismantled or done away with. Most Oxonians were convinced that imperialism was a beneficent force, exporting what was most valuable in British civilization and culture. As the young Curzon (later chancellor at Ox-ford) confided to a fellow undergraduate, "[T]here has never been any-thing so great in the world's history as the British Empire, so great an instrument for the good of humanity. We must devote all our energies to maintaining it." And while he was not exactly a disinter-ested observer, Curzon was to say in later years that "he could not understand how anyone educated at Oxford in his time could fail to be an Imperialist."⁶⁸

Richard Symonds has argued that "the highest tide of Imperialism" reached Oxford between the Boer War and 1914, and that from the mid-1880s to mid-1890s there was but a "mild interest in Empire."⁶⁹ At the same time, evidence of Oxford's role in the empire, and more specifically of its connections with the colonial administration of India, was every-where to be found during Sorabji's residence there. This was largely because Oxford had been such a major force in reshaping the Indian Civil Service examinations in the 1850s.⁷⁰ Benjamin Jowett, later master of Balliol College (from 1870 to his death in 1893), was instrumental in opening recruitment to men from English universities, a campaign fa-cilitated by the events of 1857, which eventuated in the British Govern-ment dismantling the East India Company. Oxford men joined the ICS in large numbers in the wake of these changes, and, in response to de-mand for scholastic preparation that would help future colonial admin-istrators, Oxford appointed a teacher of Hindustani and a Reader in

Indian Law and History by the early 1860s.[71] Debates about the preparation for and administration of the ICS exam continued to enliven the Oxford community and to solidify its links to the India Office until the First World War, thus fulfilling Jowett's wish that Oxford's "true relation to the country" and the empire be recognized.[72]

Even before these institutional changes, however, Oxford had formal and semiformal connections with India that were as old as the empire itself. There had been an endowed chair in Sanskrit since 1832. Competition over who was to succeed to the post pitted the two Indianists at Oxford, Max Muller and Monier Williams — both of whom advised and tutored Sorabji — in a bitter rivalry that did not subside even after the loser, Max Muller, got a chair in comparative philology as a consolation prize.[73] Nineteenth-century Oxford was also home to the Indian Institute, conceived by Monier Williams as "a center for union and intercourse for all engaged in Indian and Oriental Studies."[74] As Chris Baldick has shown, not just the development of English studies at Oxford but the total university experience itself was bound up with imperial concerns. According to members of the ICS contributing to a symposium on "The Duties of the Universities towards Our Indian Empire" in 1884, "the culture that men got at Oxford or Cambridge was of the greatest importance in dealing with the natives."[75] Significantly, there were those at Oxford who did not approve of the university's cultivation of ICS appointments. This led Ruskin to oppose the Institute on the grounds that "Oxford, as I understand its position, has to educate English gentlemen in the elements of noble human knowledge — not to prepare them . . . [to be] clerks in foreign counting houses."[76]

Ruskin was perfectly right about the historic mission of Oxford: educating *English gentlemen* had been the university's raison d'être for five centuries by the time Sorabji graced its lawns and lecture halls. There *was* an Indian student presence at Oxford in the late-nineteenth century, albeit a small one. Technically, Indians could attend the university from 1871, when religious tests were no longer required for entrance. By 1893, the year after Sorabji left Oxford, forty-nine Indian students had matriculated — twenty-two of them at Balliol, one of those being Sorabji's brother, Richard (Dick), another the celebrated Indian poet Manmohan Ghose.[77] The tolerance for "native races" apparently exhibited by some colleges was not necessarily practiced by everyone at Oxford. Despite the interest he took in Cornelia Sorabji during her time at Oxford — despite even his conviction that India had as much to teach the West as vice versa — Max Muller had a reputation for disapproving of Indians who came to Oxford in the 1880s. He believed that they should be studying their own ancient literature so that they might produced new texts of their own, "impregnated with Western ideas, yet retaining [their] native spirit and character."[78] As Rhodes scholarships promised to bring more and more "natives" to Oxford in the early twentieth century, fears and fantasies about a colonial invasion grew apace. To wit, the anonymous *Lament of an Old Oxonian*:

> The married mussalman arrives
> With 37 moon-eyed wives
> And fills a quad at Oriel
> While Magdalen's classic avenues
> Are occupied by shy Yahoos
> Whose habits are arboreal.

> The Afghan hillsmen, knives in hands
> Pursue the Proctor in his bands
> From Folly Bridge to Johns
> And Dyak head collectors stalk
> Behind the elms of Christ Church walk
> Decapitating Dons.

> O — that such things should come to be
> In my old University
> But if some folk prefer 'em
> And like a Barnum-Bailey show
> Then Oxford's where they ought to go
> *My* son shall go to Durham.[79]

If colonials were considered interlopers at Oxford — the inevitable, if unwelcome, burden of imperial commitments — women seeking university education failed to provide the same kind of self-congratulatory confidence in Britain's civilizing mission that Macaulay's "little brown Englishmen" may have done for some Oxford dons. This, despite the fact that large numbers of women graduates took up the mantle of imperial service themselves during life "after Oxford."[80] By Michaelmas term in 1889, there had been women at Oxford officially for ten years — since 1879, that is, when two women's residence halls, Lady Margaret and Somerville, opened their doors. It is worth emphasizing "officially," since women had long been at Oxford as the sisters of heads and professors — and as domestic workers in those households as well. Wives were a phenomenon only after the 1870s, when fellows were allowed to marry for the first time.[81] Other women tried to get in via a more academic route. Annie M. A. H. Rogers headed the list of senior candidates

in 1873, hence technically gaining her entrance into Balliol. She was ultimately denied matriculation because she was female, a fact overlooked
when she sent in her exams because she used only her initials, not her
full name.[82] Reaction to the opening of Somerville and Lady Margaret
Halls was hostile. Edward Pusey, Regius Professor of Hebrew at Oxford, reckoned their establishment to be "one of the greatest misfortunes
that has happened ever in our own time at Oxford."[83] In an era when
education for women was considered unorthodox, potentially damaging
to their reproductive organs, and a harbinger of the end of civilization,
Pusey's observation seems almost benign. The dean of New College
conveyed more of the righteous indignation with which women at Oxford were greeted by some, if not many. "Inferior to us God made you,"
he intoned in a sermon at Oxford in 1884, "and inferior to the end of
time you will remain"— a fate the good bishop, one presumes, doubted
even an Oxford education could alter.[84] "The ordinary undergraduate
rarely saw ladies," Annie Rogers wrote in her memoirs, and when they
did, it was all the more rarely as equals, intellectual or otherwise.[85] As
late as 1896, when the battle for women to be able to sit examinations
for B.A. degrees was on, opponents of women's education at Oxford
persisted in seeing female students as "honoured guests." The resolution
was defeated 215–140 by the Oxford Congregation, and women did not
secure the right to a B.A. from Oxford until 1920.[86]

If Sorabji was aware of the struggles that had surrounded the history
of her beloved Somerville, she gave no indication of it. As Vera Brittain
has described it, Oxford women "lived, inevitably, a self-centered life
with few distractions, in which their hopes and aspirations created their
world."[87] In this sense, they were little different from Oxford men. According to Ved Mehta in Up at Oxford, his memoir of his time there as
a student in the 1950s, "most of us structured our lives around the Oxford year— short, concentrated terms for enjoying everything the university had to offer, and vacations for reading and travel."[88] The primary
space in Sorabji's Oxford world was undoubtedly Somerville Hall, then
presided over by its new principal, Agnes Maitland. She was known
fondly to students as "the Warden," a term Sorabji used frequently and
affectionately to describe her in her letters home.[89] As Janet Courtney
recounts in An Oxford Portrait Gallery, "Somerville, behind its high walls
at the beginning of Woodstock Road, kept a cloistered seclusion, though
[it was] a little more in the Oxford world [than Lady Margaret]. Its
undenominational character gave it rather a wider appeal amongst Oxford tutors and the friends of Higher Education for Women."[90]

Somerville in fact had a reputation for embodying "the life of an English family," whereas Lady Margaret Hall was thought to provide the life of a "Christian family."[91] Given Cornelia's own "English" up-bringing, Somerville suited her perfectly. When she visited Holloway College in the summer of 1890 she deplored its "painfully new red brick" and its lack of a common drawing room, which made it much "less natural and home like" than what she had grown used to at Somerville.[92] Her nickname in the hall quickly became "Myjee" (Gujerati for "mother") because she nursed several of her fellow students through an early-winter cold.[93] Sorabji was not the only Indian woman at Somerville in this period: the daughters of the Maharajah Duleep Singh arrived in the spring of 1890. Cornelia anticipated that they would be "snobbish," would demand to be called "princesses," and would offend the other Somerville girls by wearing "uninteresting English garb."[94] When they arrived she was more gracious, reporting home that the two newcomers were "very nice" and "I have taken them under my wing."[95] Nonetheless, she enjoyed being singled out as exceptional, the only Indian woman doing law — so much so that she worried that other Indian women she heard might be coming to Britain to study might upstage her.[96]

Cornelia's letters are full of the thrill and excitement many women in this generation experienced living away from home for the first time, surrounded by books, interesting people, and the chance to mix in a university community.[97] She decorated her rooms at the beginning of each term, hosted guests and had tea parties, pulled tricks on "freshers," took boat rides with college friends, and generally seemed to thrive in the socially active milieu of Somerville.[98] Partly because her brother Dick was at Balliol, and partly because of links between Somerville's governors and Jowett, Sorabji went often to concerts, lectures, and parties at Balliol. She became personally acquainted with Jowett, who took a special interest in her studies and her future. They met in her first few weeks there and she described him at the time as "a sweet old man" of the "courteous old school" who insisted: "Allow me, Madam, to conduct you across [the quad] in safety."[99] She later recalled that he told her she was smart and "original."[100] Sorabji gloried in Oxford life from the start and quickly joined in on the good-natured rivalry between Oxford and Cambridge in sports, academics, and achievement.[101] "You can't think what a lovely place Oxford is, and how perfect its academical life is," she wrote enthusiastically to Poona after less than a month at Somerville. "I think one's ideal of a happy life is nearer being realized here than anywhere else: in the way of gentle and intellectual intercourse, with something of happiness for the future, as one looks back in after life on this beautiful spot in one's memory."[102]

Almost immediately upon arrival at Somerville, Sorabji announced to her parents that she was to read for two years for the Literature Honors exam and do a course in teacher training, "if possible," in the third year.[103] She was soon busy attending lectures in her Anglo-Saxon course, writing papers on Spenser, and passing many happy hours in the Bodleian, reading and making notes "undisturbed for hours. Perfectly delightful."[104] Hilary term was hardly underway when she rather abruptly announced a change of plans: "I am to read Law and to have an extra year at Somerville." Her new curriculum was prompted by an advertisement Miss Maitland had seen announcing that the Nizam of Hyderabad was seeking to appoint two "lady legal commissioners for the purpose of taking evidence from zenana residents."[105] Among the qualifications required was law and three Indian languages besides English. Sorabji told her parents that Lady Hobhouse had connections with the Nizam and that while her appointment was not assured, she had a good chance once she had done her qualifications. "To think of [it] . . . jurisprudence!" She was soon visited by Sir William Markby, who suggested she read Persian and Sanskrit as well as Hindu law.[106] He offered to be her tutor and after consulting with him, she laid out her course of study as follows:

I find that neither the Honours *Jurisprudence* nor the Pass (sic) *Greats* is exactly what India needs — so Sir William suggests that I do a *Law Course* he will sketch parallel to that done by the Indian Civil servants when they come into residence — and submitting myself to the same exams — I shall then be sent out a certificated Indian Legal Practitioner and if I want a degree can easily earn one in Bombay. Anyway I shall have had as much training as an ICS judge — Sir William did think I might do the B.C.L. exam but that includes Roman Law which he says I do not want and he does not think it right I should waste precious time on what will not be useful: so "little me" had to choose between *Notoriety* and *Usefulness*, and "me's" been able to choose the latter, and "me's" heart is glad and for me too things look happy. Lady H. has written to Hyderabad about the post and if it is right I will get it and after all your "C.S." . . . will be a sort of real Indian Civil Servant — and some day, who knows she may even wear a wig and hold Court. One more thing about myself — I am to read *Hindu Law* and *Mohammedan Law*, and the *Penal and Criminal Code*, and the *Law of Contract and Property*. Ain't it scrumptious? I feel no longer as if I were brought up inside a Hottentot, and my heart is glad indeed.[107]

Sorabji's reference to the Hottentot is unclear; she may have been aware of the Hottentot Venus or she may have been mistaken for an African on the streets of London, as Indians in Western metropolises were and are.[108] This idiomatic expression was also no doubt evidence of her concern for status, suggesting the ways in which colonials in Britain understood and made use of taxonomies of colonial-racial difference as casually as some Britons "Othered" Indians.

In any event, Sorabji was ecstatic about this turn of events because she thought she could finish her course within twelve months. She had expressed the desire to return home from the moment her boat left India, perhaps because she knew that her funds were limited and she did not relish taking more money from the Hobhouses.[109] "I [feel] delicate about the money part . . . Indians have so often taken advantage of English people's kindness that I did not want [Lady Hobhouse] to imagine that I was going to do likewise."[110] Sorabji was also eager to be financially independent so that she could help her other siblings realize their educational goals, especially her sister Alice, whom she wanted to see obtain the medical education she herself had forsaken.[111] A sense of responsibility for and obligation to the family in Poona weighed on her heavily during her whole stay in Britain, and she was often visibly torn between enjoying Oxford life and feeling that she must hurry home to help her parents in their old age.

As W. W. Hunter wrote in *Bombay, 1885–1890: A Study of Indian Administration*, "[I]n Bombay as in other provinces of India, the keenest intellects are attracted . . . to the study and practice of law."[112] Law was certainly a more respectable choice than medicine at this particular historical moment: the medical profession was still in the process of constructing its own sociocultural identity even as the entrance of women was challenging its claims to a certain kind of status. The choice of law was a declaration of Sorabji's desire to move into a certain kind of elite male space as well.[113] Of all the motivations that drove her as she undertook this difficult and unprecedented course, however, the idea that she might be the first and only Indian woman of her time to do the law had special appeal for her, in the first instance because it would mortify her detractors in India.[114] Her belief, supported as it was by the Hobhouses, Sir Markby, and especially Jowett, that law would translate into "useful" work in India further pleased her, and allowed her during her time at Somerville to distinguish herself from women whose educational and reform pursuits she deemed more frivolous, less worthy of attention, and above all unwomanly.[115]

Serious female students were referred to in late-Victorian educational parlance as "women," while those in pursuit of "general culture" were deemed merely "ladies"— a distinction Sorabji herself was continually in the process of negotiating.[116] Doing serious work—"what India needs"— became her badge of honor, and it enabled her to carry on with her heavy course work, long hours in the library, and dread of examination, at moments when even the desire to be exceptional was not enough to sustain her. Once the decision for law had been taken, there was a tremendous amount of work to be done, some of it in trying circumstances peculiar to her status as an Indian and a woman. Until 1893, all women students at Oxford had to be accompanied to lectures; Sir William Markby was Cornelia's chaperone.[117] From a letter home in 1890 one has the impression that she was not allowed to call out questions in class like the men, but had to write them down so that she could ask them discreetly in private of her tutors.[118] While there is no reason to believe that her assignments were any different from those given to male students, her professors gave her tasks that required traveling to London during vacations to use the British Library at a moment when the whole question of "women in public" was extremely contested. Taking public transport was still not entirely respectable for middle-class British women, and it took Sorabji several trips from Manning's house in Maida Vale to the British Library to decide that "the underground is more convenient though less wholesome" than the bus.[119] Indeed, Sorabji's mobility is in striking contrasted to the kind of purdah Ramabai's benefactors tried to impose on her. Once at the British Library, it was incumbent upon Cornelia to prove herself as not just respectable, but as worthy of working in the public of the Reading Room. In 1886, three years before Sorabji came to England, the *Saturday Review* had featured an article on "Ladies in Libraries" that complained that "woman makes the Reading Room a place where study is impossible" because "she talks and whispers and giggles beneath the dome . . . [S]he flirts, and eats strawberries behind folios, in the society of some happy student of the opposite sex." The author went on to say that the Reading Room was "not the place for a fastidious scholar," in part because "the natives of our Oriental dependencies are thought to come here because it is the warmest place in London."[120]

Sorabji negotiated this situation (which may or may not have been her personal experience) by throwing herself into her work and criticizing the other women readers in the British Library as slovenly and unkempt and effectively "not her." She deliberately sat at the "Ladies' Tables," where "happily there is always room for me as most of the ladies prefer working at the men's Quarters." "One who sat near me yesterday," she wrote her parents during September of 1890, "was a caution. They many of them look dirty and dress badly (they think it is literary to do so — Girton started that filthy College Etiquette: but we at Oxford do not do so) but this dame beat them all. Her hair was matted and ragged, on her head she wore a black monstrosity meant for a hat. Her garb was what had once been a brocaded silk black robe — but was now green with dirt and age. The shape of it, how can I describe? . . . It was more-over short, and to remedy this, from underneath it peeped a rusty black ragged frill — she'd tacked that on her petticoat no doubt . . . but me! She was a specimen."[121] Sorabji, who viewed a neat personal appearance as a sign of respectability and who prided herself on her beautiful and distinctive saris, here invoked the woman reader's "bad" dress as a marker of cultural and even class inferiority. She was by no means un-usual in this regard: modesty of dress was a common theme among contemporary Indian women, as Ramabai's attention to dress codes in *Stree Dharma-Neeti* testifies.[122] Her disdain is evident not just in the detailed description she gave but in the language she used to represent this woman as having fallen from grace — that is, from fashion, finery, and propriety — so that Sorabji ended up representing her quite clini-cally ("she was a specimen"), as if she were looking at a bug under a microscope. If, as Inderpal Grewal has suggested, the Reading Room (like the British Museum which housed it) was an imperial project be-cause it represented a "love of order," Sorabji was clearly quite enamored of that order herself.[123]

Who knows exactly what kinds of scrutiny Sorabji was subject to in public and what impact it may have had on her reading of other women in the British Library. Years later she was to recall how she had to "un-deceive a proselytizing old [English] lady" who told her reproachfully, "but you *look* so very heathen!"[124] It may well be that the urban spaces of the British Library and of London more generally called her "native" body into question as a sexual subject in ways that Somerville did not, insofar as it was not a mixed-public space.[125] Sorabji's parting shot in the British Library affair was to differentiate her work as serious and above all respectable compared to what the woman next to her was doing. "She consulted huge volumes half my length — I found after-wards they were bound volumes of an old newspaper. I suppose she is a novelist and was getting material for a tragedy from the newspaper scandal . . . [T]he worst of the museum is that others, [for example,] newspaper writers and such, are admitted — not only students as at Oxford, so that one misses the 'rapport' one gets at one's own dear Bodleian."[126] Not only had Cornelia quickly made Oxford her own, she identified with its sense of superiority and adopted its snobbery. And significantly, in order to cope with her own exceptionalism — an exceptionalism that was both real and actively cultivated by her— she internalized some of its chauvinism as well.[127] In point of fact, the law digests Sorabji had to read were also "half her length." There was, in other words, little to distinguish her from this woman — or from what Sorabji read as her disrespectability — except physical appearance and dress. These differences were not inconsiderable, and they broadcast images on the streets and in the public spaces of Victorian London that Sorabji had little control over— as the comment "you *look* so very heathen" could not but have reminded her.

As if preparing for exams and all that that entailed were not stressful enough, there were a number of people and problems that threatened to distract Sorabji if she let them. The round of parties, the holiday trips, and the endless At Homes she attended were undoubtedly a welcome break from her work, but she also acquired social debts she felt obligated to reciprocate and these were always pressing into her study time. She kept abreast of everything that happened in Poona, especially the intrigues around her mother's school, Alice's attempts to get to England, and her sister Mary's struggle with Miss Hurford to be appointed head of the Poona Girls High School (a government school, as opposed to the VHS, which was mission-run).[128] News from home was a welcome and at times agitating weekly event, and Cornelia devoted large portions of her letters back to giving advice, asking for more details, and expressing concern over her mother's overwork. Her brother Dick had been in England since before her arrival but he leaned on her, in those first months especially, more than she did on him, chiefly because he was having trouble matriculating at Balliol. As the older sister she had responsibility for him: she worried over his fate and his finances and hastened to reassure her father that all would be well with Dick's future.[129] From November of 1890 her widowed sister Pheroze was also in England with her daughter Elsie — two more family members for Cornelia to worry about. Phiz, as she was called, could not make up her mind about what she wanted to do in Britain and her indecision was a source of anxiety and frustration for Cornelia, particularly once she had decided on her own path toward the law.[130] She was concerned too because Phiz lived in a boarding house, was allowing herself to be courted by an

English doctor whom Cornelia did not trust, and seemed on the verge of entering into a marriage that might throw the Sorabjis' respectability as a family into question.[131] Cornelia must have spent hours writing letters home on this subject alone, in addition to all the time she spent talking to Phiz and making sure that her niece was being well taken care of. All this while she was trying to go to lectures, absorb case after legal case, and stave off her terror at the prospect of the examinations, which always loomed large on her horizon. Through it all she remained committed to and enthusiastic about the intellectual challenges of her work. She copied questions handed out in lecture into letters home, commenting, "[T]hey look most interesting [and] I am looking forward with pleasure to writing them for next week."[132] Although she didn't lose weight, and actually warned her family that they would find her "stouter" on her return, she did suffer from bouts of "neuralgia"—back and head pain—that could lay her up for days at a time. Some indication of her constant busy-ness may be adduced from her offhand remark in a letter home that even "my minutes are full."[133]

In addition to her studying and socializing, Sorabji was in regular contact with the agents of the Church Missionary Society in Britain, chiefly because of her father's affiliations with the CMS in Poona. She spoke at their meetings and helped them to fund-raise, not just in Oxford but all over England. These commitments did not, however, preclude critiques of what she perceived as the Society's imperialist prejudices. She objected, for example, to some CMS members' characterizations of Indian women as "impure." "It is a side I have never seen, nor have most, I am sure. Why then present it as the only one, and let Missionary work in India seem [to be] rescue work[?]"[134] Perhaps Cornelia did not wish to be mistaken as the kind of Indian woman who qualified in missionaries' eyes as the right and proper subject of "rescue."[135] If Sorabji, like Ramabai, acted as the foil against which Britons could consolidate what was English (and hence superior) about their reform practices, she was nonetheless always subject to slippage—to characterization not just as the willful "heathen" but as the helpless one as well. Sorabji was clearly worried that the CMS was trying to turn her into a missionary, and she wrote to Lady Hobhouse somewhat anxiously to tell her that while she admired those who undertook it, "I do not feel every one is fitted for it—and that it is too sacred a calling, like holy orders, to be entered upon by those whose vocation it is not."[136] Nor was her willingness to rally publicly behind the CMS cause unconstrained by family obligations. The longer she was in England the more firmly she believed that the Society's support for her mother's school was contingent on her own cooperation with the CMS in England. She began to refer to one CMS lady, Mrs. Gilmore, in unflattering terms ("the Cat," "the Hag," "that grasping female") and to resent the hold the Society seemed to have on herself and through her, the Sorabjis in Poona. She was sure that the CMS continued to fund her mother's Victoria High School in large measure because they wished to control what was taught there and who taught it, rather than to alleviate the pressure on Franscina and her staff, as one committee woman, Mrs. Duncan, claimed.[137] If Sorabji was suspicious of their motives, she may have had good reason to be. Everywhere she turned she saw English women controlling the purse strings of, and with them the power of appointment in, educational institutions in India. She believed that her sister Mary had been cheated out of a headship, and, what was worse, that there were English women in high posts in schools in India who had had no training at all, in spite of the fact that people like E. A. Manning insisted Indian women could not hold such positions unless they had teacher college training, preferably in England.[138] She was equally upset when she heard that Ramabai was taking "an active part" in the Indian National Congress.[139] Sorabji also expressed chagrin at learning that Ramabai might be appointed head of a high school in Bombay presidency — partly because she believed that Miss Hurford was campaigning against her sister Mary. Given her attitude toward Hindu women, especially those in the public eye, Sorabji's reaction was more than the result of family feeling or personal jealousy, though these were clearly at work. It was the product of a triangular set of power relations among Hindu, Parsi Christian, and English women whose dynamics were dictated, if not fully determined, by the operations of colonial rule.

This state of affairs angered and disheartened Sorabji. In the end, it tested her relationship not with the CMS women or Ramabai, but with E. A. Manning, pushing their friendship to its breaking point. Manning and Sorabji had remained on good terms through Sorabji's first several terms at Somerville, with Manning coming down for tea and tours of the university and Cornelia spending the part of her vacation she was not traveling living at Manning's house in Maida Vale. She continued to write weekly to Manning at least until the winter of 1891.[140] But in April of 1891, when Cornelia was in London between terms, she had a conversation with Manning that altered their relationship permanently. Manning told her that she thought Sorabji was making a mistake by not going to the Maria Grey Training College.[141] Cornelia began relating her response in a letter home by patronizing Manning a bit: "I do not mean disrespect — but she is very faddy — dear old thing that she is — and thinks no one *Educational* who has not done the Maria Grey." As she warmed to her subject, she drew upon that Oxford snobbery she had used in the British Library Reading Room, describing the Maria Grey as "a stupid Training School which Miss Maitland disapproves of." Later, at dinner at the Max Müllers, she recounted Manning's criticism to her dinner companion, Sir Montstuart Elphinstone, who reassured her that she had chosen by far the more useful path for India's future, and suggested she ask the India Office to make her some kind of specially appointed lawyer in Bombay. She felt tremendously reassured by her conversation with him, even though in the end he said that should she be offered a lectureship or an inspectress-ship at an educational institution, she would be foolish to turn it down.[142]

In spite of the fact that what distinguished Elphinstone's advice from Manning's was not necessarily ends but means, things were never the same between Sorabji and Manning. In January of 1892 Sorabji wrote home that she had recently learned that before she had come to England, Manning had recommended an English woman over her for a teaching post in Mysore on the grounds that "an English lady would be best for so high a post." Sorabji offered the following explanation: "Miss M., though a good woman, . . . is still greedy for her own nationality to have the first place on all occasions. She is curiously unjust too — when there was talk of that Legal Commissionership in Hyderabad she said I would not do because I did not know the language — and yet none of these ladies she sends out know *anything* about India much less about *language*. I think she has unconsciously more than once wronged us . . . However, the best of women and men are but Imperfect . . . I am going to have it out with her some day."[143] Whether Sorabji ever did "have it out" with Manning, we do not know. She was not given to personal confrontation, and as her earlier conflict with the Society ladies suggests, she was able to transform the Victorian stereotype of the docile Indian woman into what Penelope Russell has called "the genteel performance" in the Australian colonial context.[144] Judging from her correspondence with the family in Poona, it was a strategy she made a habit of whenever she felt she was being interrogated by people who appeared to be questioning her career plans. After being asked at a garden party about the wisdom of doing law by a Miss Tammylander, who had the temerity to suggest that medicine might be more useful, Cornelia acted the perfect lady. She recorded that she "made up my mind at once. The old girl had no business to exercise her mind about me but sarcasm would be lost on her hardened nerves [so I decided] I'd amuse myself. I looked bright at once" and went on to lecture Miss Tammylander not about the value of law but, revealingly, about the fact that the woman had never even been to India. "It was such fun," Cornelia reported to her parents mischievously. "Miss Tammy prays no doubt that I may be shown the error of my ways."[145]

Sorabji had considerably less fun — and less patience — dealing with British women active in female emancipation whom she met on the party circuit in Oxford and around London. They were few in number, but Cornelia could not hide her contempt for them. She told her parents that she had little time for suffrage women. Even "bible women," whom in other circumstances Cornelia did not much care for, did more worthwhile work "than fighting Women's Rights battles and getting up Franchise meetings."[146] Sometime in the late autumn of 1890 she met Lady Sandhurst, who had run for the London County Council, and her daughter, whom Sorabji described as "a pale-faced insipid girl — not even feminine; a sort of neuter, most colourless." She called this "nature's revenge" on the daughter—"what comes of trying to appropriate a sex not one's own."[147] Of Mrs. Sheldon Amos she had this to say: "I like [her] partly and partly do not like [her]. She is a rather striking looking individual. I like her natural manners and she is devoted to her son and daughter but she is a *women's rights* person, a type I cannot appreciate. She also loves the franchise and would die for radicalism — so there are many points of argument between us. She also despises a woman with nerves — while to me a *platform* is like melons to our Ailsa. She turns me sour."[148]

Rukhmabai's attraction to the local women's rights community in southeast England was one of the things that further alienated Sorabji from her after Cornelia moved to Oxford. Rukhmabai visited her at Somerville and Sorabji felt that "her conversation was one long comparison between us." What made it worse for Sorabji was that "[Rukhmabai] has put aside her brown saree and wears red like me now."[149] Rarely did she encounter Rukhmabai, in fact, that she did not comment on her choice of sari.[150] As Madame Blavatsky wrote after a trip to India in 1892, "Parsee women could only be distinguished from their Hindu sisters by very slight differences"— their mode of sari-wearing being one of them.[151] Given Sorabji's investment in being the only Indian woman doing law, and given Rukhmabai's already "public" reputation in the wake of her trial, distinguishing herself from Rukhmabai through her saris may have seemed the only way to keep her identity, her plans, and her respectability distinct. In keeping with this concern, Sorabji always belittled Rukhmabai's schemes for women's education in India — which Rukhmabai put before important politicians in Britain, and in 1892, before the Lord Kimberley, then Secretary of State for India — as "vague" and "unformed."[152] Sorabji recounted to her parents that Rukhmabai had had an interview with Lord Harris, "and she most amusingly appeared as the champion of Female Education in India!! Did you ever?" Cornelia sounded her usual theme: "I suggested that a visit here brought responsibilities, and that we ought to seek usefulness not notoriety and fame. She is quite spoilt and thinks no end of herself."[153] For all her criticisms, Sorabji thought Rukhmabai "a nice girl at bottom." The problem was that she had fallen under bad influences. "The McLarens' . . . Women's Rights Women are not the best people to advise her: and it is really sad to see how much she is left to herself."[154]

Cornelia did not like to be reminded of her relatively privileged life at Oxford, a fact Rukhmabai was evidently keen to talk about.[155] "She came to see me and made disparaging comparisons of our respective lots — [lectur]ing me on the necessity of happiness since I was at Somerville while she toiled in a noisy street in Town and had no aids to work as I had [here]," Sorabji wrote in the spring of 1891. She talked "until I was sick of her jargon."[156] The two were thrown together during vacations and in the fall of 1890 they ended up at Manning's house together. Under duress, Sorabji went out and about with Rukhmabai in London and also to Hampton Court, where the two romped in the maze, much to the amusement of the guards there.[157] Sorabji had to admit that "Rukhmabai is tired by nothing" while "I was mad with despair and fatigue." What Sorabji could not countenance, however, was Rukhmabai's "wandering about most publicly alone" and worse, walking the streets with an Indian man she had taken up with.

She has taken a great fancy to a stuck-up fop from Kolapoor, the most despicable youth I've ever set eyes on — who is reading for the C.S. and spent a Vac in France, with the result that he dresses and talks [like a] "masher" now and wears his hair in furbellows [sic] around his head. I loathed him the first time I saw him, when at Miss Manning's he talked big about his attainments and expressed his indignation at being taken for an Abyssinian Prince — 'that black fellow' — as he said with the worst taste possible, seeing his complexion and his remarks were present at the same time. His name is Mutgatkar. And Miss Bailey told me that he and Rukhmabai wander about the streets together—most disgraceful I call it. That comes of opposing existing laws, and breaking loose from proper restraint.[158]

Sorabji was no doubt referring in those last two lines to Rukhmabai's suit against her husband in Bombay, which brought great publicity to her and great public attention in Britain to the question of Indian child marriage.[159] Once again, Sorabji's harsh reaction was refracted through a critique of clothing — this time, it was the "foppishness" of Rukhmabai's male friend that helped to make Rukhmabai the object of her scorn. Blackness also recurs as a trope of her superiority to other Indians in Britain, a significant maneuver here given both Parsis' light skin and Sorabji's own possible Toda ancestry.[160] As for Rukhmabai, the smugness of higher breeding and traces of Somervillian superiority combined as Sorabji constructed her countrywoman as decidedly disrespectable, both in absolute terms and in comparison to herself.

The strain of performing "the Indian woman student at Oxford" combined with the pressure of doing well academically was taking a toll on Cornelia — whether her audience was her family in Poona, her peers at Oxford, fellow travelers in the British Library, or Rukhmabai, whom she perceived as a rival for the attention of the colonial reform community in England. In the midst of all this, Sorabji's benefactors were trying to rearrange her course once again, this time so that she could sit for the Bachelor of Civil Law examination. This idea had originally been Cornelia's, and at first Sir William Markby had discouraged her, telling her it was "off [her] lines."[161] Over time he realized that she was moving more quickly through the Civil Service preparation than he anticipated and, together with Jowett and Maitland, he set the wheels in motion for a petition to let her sit the BCL. The stakes were again being raised, since Sorabji now had one year in which to prepare an exam that, when she had first come to Oxford almost two years earlier, Markby did not think she could have succeeded at in that time frame. But she was undaunted, except by the delay it meant in returning to her family in India. She was buoyed too by positive feedback from her tutors and an almost filial relationship with Jowett and Muller.[162] A. V. Dicey was another character altogether. While he assured her that her papers were better than those of many of the men, she thought his interactions with her strained. "I wish he would treat me like a man and not make gallant speeches about my 'intellect' and 'quickness of perception' . . . [H]e is so ugly, it offends the innocence of my eye to look at him while he deals me criminal precepts."[163] After returning from the Christmas vacation in 1891 she lamented, "Mr. Dicey is just as full of knowledge and as clear and as uncouth and badly dressed and unwashed as he was last term."[164] Ever frank and to the point, Cornelia Sorabji left us a portrait of Victorian Oxford not easily matched in its intimacy, its humor, and its utter lack of self-censorship.

Perhaps understandably, Sorabji's predisposition toward candor was more easily realized in private than in public, where she sensed that even well-meaning observers were apt to make rash and stereotypical judgments about her based on their presumptions of what an "Indian woman" was. She was not necessarily averse to doing public speaking but she was far more comfortable in the all-female debating club at Somerville, in which she participated with great enthusiasm and some success, than in her talks for the CMS.[165] Understanding that she was an "advertisement" for India and for the Christian mission there, and performing that role, were vastly different experiences. When she arrived at one CMS meeting in the spring of 1890 to speak, for example, she discovered that it was "a large public affair, and to my great annoyance I saw I had been placarded about. I hate this publicity."[166] She was furious whenever articles were written in the press about her because they inevitably recorded inaccuracies about her story — the *Times* misrepresented her as studying literature when she had been doing philology, while the *Graphic* had her down as doing education when she had told them she was decided for law. She even turned away two women photographers who came to visit her while she was staying in London, politely but firmly declining their offer to take her picture.[167] On another occasion, when she was apparently having second thoughts about allowing a picture of herself to be published, Lady Hobhouse advised her as follows: "[T]hough you may not desire thus to circulate your portrait, yet the objection on the score of taste is too slight . . . to counterbalance the publisher's wish."[168]

This was in an important sense exactly what Sorabji objected to. She was not against "being public" as much as she resisted being *made public* without any control over how she was represented. She was quite upset when Mrs. Chapman's *Sketches of Some Distinguished Indian Women* appeared in 1891: she called the book "largely fiction" and told her parents "I am annoyed to find myself in it. I hate my finances and everything to become public property — and there are some mistakes in the article."[169] These latter she blamed on Chapman's carelessness, on Manning having given the author inaccurate details, and on her own failure to have insisted that some of what she had shared with Chapman be kept private. She had a similar reaction to the essay on English women's colleges Lady Hobhouse and Miss Shaw-Lefevre had contributed to the NIA's journal: "I was so angry when I saw my plans in print."[170] When Phiz announced her intention to come to England, Sorabji warned her more than once in letters home to keep her plans to herself. "She must announce her intentions to no one — *first* she must make her friends — then use her voice, or else she will use it to no purpose."[171] Cornelia was no doubt remembering her own vexed attempts to maintain control over her course in Britain and she wanted to spare her sister the same fate.

And yet, Sorabji's relationship to publicity was not exactly as straightforward as this. To be sure, she was entitled to her privacy, especially over her financial arrangements; being a good sister was also important to her. But she was loathe to see her plans in print because she did not want any other Indian women coming to Oxford, to study law or anything else, while she was there.[172] Her desire to be "the" Indian woman at Oxford, and indeed, in England — a desire manifested in her response to the princesses, to Rukhmabai, and to the woman novelist in the British Library — was never more pronounced than in her reaction to the possibility that one of her countrywomen might come to Britain to study law. In response to her sister Lena's inquiry about whether she had heard of another Indian woman doing law, Sorabji replied that she knew nothing about it. "There is no one else at Oxford but myself . . . Happily I have my School to myself — and doubtless will to the end of my course unless a Bhore appears to compete with me."[173] She had heard rumors that the Bhore sisters (who were from an Indian family whom the Sorabjis knew) were thinking of coming to Britain to study. She admitted to her parents that her reluctance to see her plans made public was "only a petty monopoly of my ideas — lest the Bhores should get them. I am resigning myself to '*a shadow*' within the next year or so — Lily Bhore perhaps or even the fair Isabel."[174] One of the Bhores figures heavily in the family correspondence as a rival with Mary over a school superintendentship in Poona, so that Sorabji's jealousy of her uniqueness and of her family's interests was as complicated as it was intense.[175]

Perhaps because she was so invested in being the one and only Indian jewel in the crown of imperial Oxford, exercising control over her career and her public image was of the utmost importance to Sorabji throughout her time at Somerville.[176] She was less reticent about speaking her mind — and hence perhaps about being herself — in print than in person, even when her printed word entered the public arena. While she was in

Britain, Sorabji wrote several articles for the *Nineteenth Century*.[177] One of these, "Stray Thoughts of an Indian Girl" (which she had originally titled "Social India"),[178] was quite controversial for the position she took in it on the question of child marriage reform — a question very much in the public eye in Britain and India since the Age of Consent Act controversy the year before. "I fear I am very unorthodox," Sorabji wrote home in March of 1891, before her piece was in print, "for I do not see how any legislation can meet the difficulty. India lacks the moral courage to make her own social reforms and I think legislation would only be giving her a crutch which however I doubt whether she will use. The fault of our country has always been . . . talking and agitating too much and acting too little. I will refrain from corrupting your respectable ideas on the subject . . . It is sufficient if one of the family be heterodox."[179] If Sorabji reveled in being unorthodox with regard to her parents' views, she took even more pleasure in agitating "the Congress people" in India, some of whom had reacted strongly to Sorabji's remarks in the *Nineteenth Century*. The fact that Rukhmabai's legal case had been among the fillips for the age-of-consent legislation may have also motivated Sorabji's remarks, especially since Rukhmabai herself had written a piece for an English periodical on the subject in 1890.[180] In any event, the antinationalist stance for which Sorabji was later to become infamous was in the process of being articulated for the first time here. "All the Reformers talk big and act small," she wrote home in November of 1891, a month after the publication of her essay. "India has the [gift] of the *gab* and a painful inertia [in] action."[181]

Doing instead of talking was Sorabji's motto, and it must have been frustrating to find herself so ready for action while she still had the hurdle of the BCL exam to get over. As the exams approached, Sorabji went into virtual seclusion at Somerville, reading and revising, getting very little sleep and, because of the physical and mental strain, thinking she saw ghosts in the residence hall corridors at night.[182] Once again, the fact that she was Indian and a woman intruded upon her course. As late as a week before the BCL she learned that "owing to some mismanagement," the conditions under which she was to be allowed to sit the exam — that is, whether it was to be "in public," with the men, or privately — were still not settled. She was "driven nearly mad with distraction" until Jowett sent her word that she was to write her papers in the examination hall like everyone else.[183] Cornelia's description of the experience is worth reproducing at length, for it is a rare enough account of what women faced who sought university credentials from Oxbridge in the nineteenth century.

My Fellow-Candidates were very comic indeed. I went down to the Schools in company with Cherub [her nickname for a Somervillian friend] and one or two others who were in for History and Classics — pale anxious undergraduates in white ties thronged the Schools Entrance Hall. To the left stood my co-victims — 25 in number with . . . Graduates' gowns and furlined hoods — scared Barristers who had waited 50 years for a brief, Country Clergy (some of them M.A.s) and all in the style of Fathers of Families and Grandfathers and Paternal Relations of sorts — except for one or two aged 30 or thereabouts who were [closest to the] brother type, fresh from working in Chambers.
       I felt so small and humiliated in comparison. They treated me very kindly . . . I was conducted to a seat and taken care of till that awful electric bell went, and the clerk shouted — "Civil Law. BCL. East School, through the quad." Then one squeeze of Jackie's hand (she is a friend of mine here) and a "good-bye old fellow you're going to floor them" from her — and I followed the clerk to my place, in the wake of the ancient Father to the funeral pyre. I was not at all frightened, I was quite calm outwardly, but very curious as to what would happen, half-fearing I would have to scratch (i.e., retire because I knew nothing), half-despairing.
       . . . I clenched my left fist hard, and wrote for my very life. The Papers were *very* difficult — and they gave [the] stiffest things in my nicest subjects so that I felt I could *not* have done myself justice: but I know that a power outside mine was helping me for my pen wrote so many things that I did not think I knew. The standard is exceedingly high so don't expect more than *a third* even if I am through.[184]

When Sorabji spoke of the experience as a humiliation, she anticipated the characterization that other first generation university women would use to describe their collegiate experiences. Florence Rich, writing to Helen Darbishire, the principal of Somerville, in 1938, recounted that she had wanted to read zoology in the early days of the college but discovered that it was not open to her — though one of the professors she approached suggested that she apply anyway. "I shrank from having this fuss made for me. I dreaded the horrid publicity (!) of being the first woman to take the examination, and the awful humiliation that would ensue if I did not do well, so I begged to be allowed to take some branch of science that was already open."[185]
       Sorabji, for her part, may have been referring to the fact that she was the only woman in public in a crowd of older men; being the only Indian as well as the only woman was no doubt an added strain. Taking the

exam under these circumstances must have made it extremely difficult
to concentrate. Her description of the exam takers as "co-victims" and
her equation of approaching the exam site with mounting a "funeral
pyre" is, however, undoubtedly the most remarkable feature of this passage. Sorabji's nephew Richard has suggested that this is an instance of
classic Sorabji wit, as well as a subtle jibe at Oxford — a place that, for
all its civilizing pretensions, nonetheless required women to commit a
ritual sacrifice (exam taking) for the sake of an Oxford degree.[186]
Geraldine Forbes has suggested that Sorabji may also have been referring
to the Rajasthani ritual of Johur, when the wives of the defeated
mounted a pyre together to escape abduction and rape at the hands of
their enemies.[187] In addition, I think, Sorabji's choice of language signals
an identification with the Hindu sati that tells us how acutely aware she
was at this critical juncture of her Indianness as well as her femaleness —
and how dense the web of signification was around the self-sacrificing
Hindu woman in Victorian imperial culture.[188] And if, as Indira
Chowdhury-Sengupta has argued, satis represented chastity (as well as
conjugal devotion), Cornelia may have been attempting to prove her
sexual respectability in this particularly public mixed space.[189] To seek
to become "the Indian woman" at the heart of the empire meant, in
some profound if not ineluctable way, identifying with one of the most
available, and most stereotypical, behaviors of Indian womanhood: self-
sacrifice. Even though she was not a Hindu woman but a Parsi Christian,
and even though she had invested so much time and energy in differentiating herself from "the Hindu woman" in the person of Rukhmabai,
when she faced the judgment of the Oxford examination system, Sorabji
laid claim to the same powerful image that shaped much contemporary
opinion of Indian women.[190] In this particular theater of empire —
which is to say, playing to both Oxford and the audience of her family —
adopting the identity of the Parsi Christian could not finally match the
spectacle of performing as "the" Indian, if not "the Hindu," woman.[191]
There appears at this moment to have been little heroism in it for her.
For while she had enthusiastically embraced the BCL and its challenges,
she may have felt in the end that she had been maneuvered into this
close and terrible space by a set of systems — Oxford, philanthropy, imperial culture — that demanded submission, with consent, of the female
colonial subject.

Sorabji did not of course give up her will or relinquish control: she
wrote the exam and got a third. She was disappointed and upset, partly
as she felt that she had been bullied by a Professor Nelson in the viva

when she challenged some unspecified canonical interpretation of "private law." She was also embarrassed at not having got a first or even a second, no doubt because she understood that those were a direct avenue to important careers for men at Oxford, if not for women as well.[192] "The world in general seeks to console me," she wrote her parents in one of her most dejected letters home since arriving in Britain. "They say I ought to be proud of it and all the rest — but I am conceited enough to feel it."[193] To Lady Hobhouse she wrote, "I feel I have betrayed the faith which so many of my friends were kind enough to put in me. Write and tell me that you are not very ashamed of or disappointed in me though if you are it will be only what I deserve."[194] Later she expressed amazement at the "*enormous* amount of work I was able to get through in those two years" and wonder "that I did not go out of my mind as I had so much anxiety with it all: and it was audacious to attempt the highest Law School, straight away like that."[195] She hardly had time to digest everything that had happened since as soon as the exams were over she had to move out of her rooms at Somerville — a prospect that filled her with sadness and nostalgia. "All the College is nearly down. I am staying to dissolve and pack — [O]n Monday I turn my face forever on the happiest time life can have for me. I feel it intensely. Dear Oxford — no other place can ever be to me what thou art!"[196]

Sorabji remained another year in England after leaving Somerville. During this time she visited friends all over the British Isles, worked as a clerk in the London law offices of Lee and Pemberton (where her friend Alice Bruce's uncle was also employed), and tried to settle a more permanent position for herself consonant with her training and new qualifications in India. It was an uphill battle, in part because on the colonial no less than in the "domestic" British scene, patronage and connections were key to getting work.[197] She had well-placed contacts in London and indeed, throughout England, who gave her conflicting advice about what kind of work to seek and how to find it. Lord Reay thought she should aim for the Indian bar; Sir Ameer Ali recommended a post in a solicitor's office in Bombay; while Sir Raymond West counseled her to set up independent practice in Kattiawar after passing the pleaders' exam.[198] Nothing more was mentioned about the Nizam's advertisement for a "lady legal commissioner," but Sorabji continued to hope for a post that would enable her to work with women's property cases.[199] *Purdahnashin* were already uppermost in her mind. As she put it in a talk she gave in Chelsea in March of 1893, "[T]he man can do the pleading in the Courts of Law but none but a woman can put in train for him cases which come from behind the purdah."[200] In the meantime, her clerkship kept her very busy, as did her attempts to get her sister Alice settled in a medical course in Britain. Cornelia was reluctant to deliver her sister up to Mrs. Gilmore and the CMS, for she felt certain that the Society would bind Alice to missionary work in exchange for their financial support. "They will not scruple," she wrote of British missionary women, "to do anything . . . in the name of religion."[201] And, with her own schedule more flexible now that she was no longer a student, Cornelia had more time and energy to devote both to researching and worrying about Alice's future. It may well have distracted her from dwelling too much on her own. In the end, Alice qualified as a doctor in London in 1905.[202]

Sorabji continued to consider Dick and Phiz her responsibilities, but what she most worried about was money. Lady Hobhouse relieved of her the necessity of paying back the fund the Hobhouses had established and Lord Hobhouse provided the fifty guineas necessary to article her at Lee and Pemberton.[203] Meanwhile, she had few funds of her own with which to support herself and was forced, almost immediately upon leaving Somerville, to ask her father to loan her money for her eventual passage home. In keeping with what Reba Soffer has noted about other British university women of her generation, Sorabji discovered that independence ended rather than began with graduation.[204] This was not easy for her: "[Y]ou can't think *how* I feel having to come upon you like this, dear Father, but how can I help it? I have no one else to provide for me."[205] Her lack of economic independence and her dim prospects for work in India made her even more self-conscious about "being public," out of fear that those people who had questioned the wisdom of her pursuit of the law would feel vindicated in their criticism of her "impractical schemes."[206]

These were in the long run merely temporary setbacks. Upon her return to India she eventually qualified as a barrister of the High Court, Calcutta, worked as a legal adviser to women landholders under the Court of Wards, and served as consulting counsel to the government of Bengal. Sorabji traveled back and forth between Britain and India often during her lifetime. As she put it in 1908, "[I]f to feel in one's pulse the great axioms of two continents, if to love two worlds as different as East is from West, to vibrate with one set of susceptibilities to the griefs and joys, the folktales and literatures of both, be a privilege, then indeed I am blessed and privileged among women."[207] There were a variety of influences that shaped the woman she became, Oxford being only one of them. Her years at Somerville and in London are interesting and important not necessarily because they were formative, but because they reveal the complexity of the late nineteenth-century colonial encounter as it occurred on British soil, as well as the hybridity of colonial subjectivities, historically speaking. That Sorabji could see through what she called "the brutal oppression of [missionaries] which they label zeal for the cause";[208] that she analyzed and resisted her exploitation and that of her family by all manner of colonial reformers' schemes; that she succeeded in negotiating the chiefly male, white world of Victorian Oxford and, in the end, remained an anglophile, no less — all this is testament to what Ania Loomba calls the "torturous but dynamic movement" of identities under colonialism.[209] This "torturous but dynamic movement" — and the fixity it defies — is an index of the contingency of colonial hegemony, evidence of the possibility that it may be negotiated and resisted, that it is ultimately always transformed by those who encounter it, and not always in predictable ways. If Sorabji represents an unusual and even unique instance of this kind of transformation, one can only imagine that she would be delighted to hear it.

CHAPTER 4

A "Pilgrim Reformer" at the Heart of the Empire

Behramji Malabari in Late-Victorian London

In London, men must do as men do in London.
John Murray, *The World of London* (1844)

Toward the end of his account of his London sojourn, entitled *The Indian Eye on English Life: or, Rambles of a Pilgrim Reformer* (published in 1893) Behramji Malabari, a Bombay Parsi, narrated his experience of the following incident on the streets of the British Empire's capital city: "Next morning I go out to the Bank with my land-lady's daughter as a guide. Poor Annie pilots me through the rocks and shoals of street-arabism. I am dressed in a loose flannel suit, such as we often use in India on a rainy day. They do not seem to use flannel here, save for cricket or lawn-tennis. So, near Paddington, I am assailed with the sneering question — 'Yaw, gov'nor, foine day for cricket?' (It was drizzling)." Malabari's wordless response was apparently "not enough for my tormentor." Having momentarily disappeared, the jeering boy returned to the scene "with two or three other imps of mischief," and according to Malabari, cried out: " 'Jim, look at 'is 'at, Jim; hoo, look at 'is 'at, Googe.' Annie apologises and explains that Indian pugarees [turbans] are new to these boys, — 'though I am sure that we like them.' She is right. Scarcely have we come to a turning when three ladies walk up to me, and one of them asks if I'll let them look at my hat. These ladies are not street arabs. Annie suggests they may be photographers or artists. Very likely. But I would rather not give them a sitting."[1] The story that Malabari relates here, together with the entirety of his account of his visit to London in the summer of 1890 in *The Indian Eye on English Life*, is evidence of how another subject of empire — who was both similarly and differently colonial than Ramabai and Sorabji — went public in late-Victorian Britain. His travelogue provides an opportunity for examining some of the complex negotiations a colonial traveler who fashioned himself as a tourist and a flaneur might have to perform, as well as the shifting ground an Indian man might be required to occupy, in public in the imperial capital of the fin de siècle. Like his countrywomen, Malabari faced the scrutiny of a variety of English observers invested alternately in his authentic Indianness and his apparent pretensions to Englishness ("Yaw, gov'nor, foine day for cricket?"). And like so many colonial and former colonial travelers who have made their way to the metropole and to London in particular, Malabari was repeatedly hailed as "the" colonial — an interpolation that called attention to, and tried to contain, the spectacle of the native at home.[2] If, as James Winter has suggested, mastery of the streets constituted a claim to manhood, Englishness, and even subjecthood in Victorian cultural terms, *The Indian Eye* may be read as a display of Malabari's claim to all three.[3] It produces, in the process, a critique of the promise of "manly" sovereignty offered by colonial rule. Because Malabari's own locations in the political economy of colonial power were complex and multiple — and because he inhabited them in ways often, if not always, of his own making — *The Indian Eye* is, finally, a primer in the protocols of the patriarchal bargain between English men and elite male colonial subjects in late-Victorian imperial culture.[4]

The historical relationships between manhood, manliness, and colonial power relations that Marilyn Lake has drawn our attention to for the Australian context, Catherine Hall for Jamaica, Mrinalini Sinha for Bengal, and Gail Bederman for the United States are played out in equally culturally specific ways throughout the narrative of *The Indian Eye*.[5] Whether as the target of young street boys' taunts or as the object of the polite yet intrusive curiosity of strangers, Malabari was made into a colonial spectacle, a process that repeatedly called the legitimacy of his masculinity, as measured by Victorian standards, into question. As Mrinalini Sinha has argued, ideologies of masculinity were already a crucial component of justifications for imperialism in this period. Throughout official imperial policy and unofficial imperial mentalities, the very category of "Indian masculinity" — typically associated with physical weakness and uncontrolled sexuality, two characteristics also assigned to European women — was continually suspect, and such sus-

Figure 4 Behramji Malabari.

picion was used as grounds for forestalling Indian self-rule and political self-determination.[6] If Malabari was unnerved by assaults on his person in the streets of London, however, he was quick to neutralize challenges to his masculinity and, by implication, to his right as a citizen-subject of empire to walk the capital's thoroughfares unmolested. The Paddington boys' mockery — their insinuation that he did not look the part of the authentic Englishman — led him to "Other" them by labeling them street "arabs." He thus invoked a racialized hierarchy rooted in class markers, urban investigative traditions, and imperial referents that constructed the boys as not-men, commoners, and outcasts.[7] He also demonstrated that he was "streetwise" — that is, possessed of a certain kind of urban "knowingness" that was proof of his urbanity in the face of modernity's "primitive" underside.[8] Malabari, meanwhile, was momentarily stabilized as the bemused but still gentlemanly observer, especially since (though it is not self-evident from the excerpt above) he was accompanied by an Indian manservant. The English women's scrutiny provoked a somewhat different response. When they indicated that they might be interested in representing him — either by photograph or painting — Malabari recorded his staunch refusal: he would "rather not give them a sitting." If the gaze of the colonizer has the power to transfix the native, even if only to refract back to the colonizer his or her own distorted image, it is a technology Malabari rejected outright when it was directed at him. He rejected it in part because in this instance, it was being mobilized by women who, drawn to him by his Indian adornment (*pugaree*), threatened to effeminize him by making him the fetishized colonial subject upon which imperial rule depended. Anticipating what Homi Bhabha calls the characteristic maneuver of the resistant postcolonial subject, Malabari appeared to be questioning the very space, the very frame of representation, through which the colonizer manages the antagonism at the heart of the colonial relation.[9]

The above anecdotes suggest that performances of masculinity can be strategically mobilized according to specific, situational asymmetries of power, and that men subordinated by hegemonic gender norms are capable of deploying other forms of masculinity both to resist domination and to create subordinates of their own.[10] In the context of British imperialism, where Indian men competed with British men for terrain, legitimacy, and authority over colonized women, the performance of colonial masculinity varied enormously and was contingent on the ever-shifting ground of imperial hegemony and nationalist-indigenous challenges to it. This grid is particularly germane for the case of Malabari, whose interest in raising the age of consent for Hindu girls animated his reform commitments in the 1880s and occasioned his trip to London in the first place. Chapter 4 examines Malabari's movement to and movement through the imperial metropole in order to explore the spatial and cultural contingencies of one colonial subject's masculinity in the late-Victorian period. As a flaneur, a social reform crusader, and the apparently quintessential "Indian man" in London during the 1890 season, Malabari encountered challenge after challenge to his presumptions about how to operate as "the male colonial subject" at the heart of the empire, even while he produced a critical reading of English culture, Western sexual mores, and European modernity itself. His ethnography of local British culture and of native Britons participated in a domestic tradition of urban social investigation as well as an emergent literature that turned Indian male "eyes" on English life. Like the letters of Ramabai and Sorabji, then, Malabari's text is historical evidence of how the workings of imperial power may be analyzed in the everyday social relations of a variety of domestic urban spaces — particularly since the "man in the street" is one of the chief figures of the everyday in the modern Western cultural imagination.[11]

Behramji Malabari was no stranger to metropolitan culture: he spent most of his adolescence and his adult life in Bombay, a thriving colonial city that contemporaries referred to as "the metropolis of the Western Presidency" and the "imperial port of India." It was also undoubtedly one of the most cosmopolitan cities of the British Raj. Mrs. Postans, an early Victorian observer, was just one of many who noted the cultural vibrancy of Bombay. Its bazaars were "animated with the groups and costumes of various and many nations," among whom numbered "the proud Moslem, the stately Armenian, the crafty Jew, the daring Arab, and the cautious Hindoo, all mingled in her streets."[12] S. M. Edwardes, an Indian Civil Servant writing of Bombay in 1902, reproduced her orientalist taxonomies and, with them, an even fuller picture of Bombay's ethnic diversity:

Nowhere else probably in the world, not even in Alexandria, are so many and such striking varieties of race, nationality, and religion represented as in Bombay. Not only is there great diversity of type among the Hindoos, the Banias of Gujarat differing as widely in appearance and manners from the Maratha of the Deccan, as the Englishman differs from the Italian; not only do the Mohammodans include, besides Indian Musalmans, many Afghans, Persians, Arabs, Turks, Malays and Abyssinians; not only are colonies of Jews and Armenians to be found among this motley population; but the city is the head-quarters of the thriving and prolific race of Parsis, and contains many thousands of Indo-Portuguese inhabitants. To crown all, there are the European inhabitants, engaged either in the service of the Government, or in professional or mercantile pursuits — a class of the community not strong in numbers, but supreme in political and social power.[13]

By midcentury "an asylum for all,"[14] Bombay was also home to a carefully forged and institutionally variable political and social system that balanced the interests of the four main groups in the city: Europeans, Hindus, Parsis, and Muslims.

Although it has not been the focus of recent studies of either *The Indian Eye* or his role in the Age of Consent Act controversy, the fact that Malabari was a Parsi was crucial to the ways he was able to navigate Hindu and European communities in India, as well to the kind of gender politics he embraced before and during his sojourn in the United Kingdom.[15] Parsi wealth was founded on collaboration with European entrepreneurs, mostly in western India: in economic terms, they were the middlemen between British capital and indigenous materials (especially cotton). Leaders of the Parsi community in Bombay also saw themselves as cultural mediators between the English and the Hindus. By the 1870s Parsi identification with the British government and with European commercial enterprise in India generated an attitude of "aloofness" toward Hindu social customs and a concomitant identification with British reform initiatives that targeted them — a propensity we have already seen at work in Cornelia Sorabji's attitudes toward Rukhmabai.[16] Some of this aloofness may be attributed to a movement among a group of Parsis led by K. J. Readymoney to reclaim a more pure Zoroastrianism — the monotheistic religion to which the majority of Parsis subscribed and which some believed had become corrupted by contact with Hindu polytheism.[17] But the critique of Hinduism was also part of the larger embrace of the project of anglicization that many urban Parsis espoused. In their quest to align themselves with the economic prosperity of British rule in India — to demonstrate their "commercial honesty and capacity"[18] — Parsis sought to differentiate themselves from other "natives" by emphasizing their progressive sympathies and their support for the educational and social reforms of the British in the western presidency. They recognized, in other words, that the allegedly "sustaining structure of error in Hinduism" was the symbolic site of British claims to cultural superiority and that connection with or sympathy for contemporary Hindu traditions and communities threatened to associate other colonial subjects with the same pathologies, inferiority, and incapacity for rule that the British attributed to the totality of "the Hindu nation."[19] Sorabji's claim to Parsi "nationality" was thus not unique to her but indicative of broader sociocultural trends. Distancing themselves from Hinduism and its symbolic linkages to colonial subjection was, from midcentury onward, essential to the Parsis' project of accommodation with British power and prestige.

Accommodating the process of Westernization in Bombay entailed a social distancing from the Hindu way of life. It also required a rejection of what were perceived as regressive Hindu attitudes toward women — most notably in terms of child marriage, the seclusion of women, and the prohibition of widow remarriage. As a number of scholars have argued, such practices were considered to represent authentic Hinduism by British authorities and nationalist reformers alike — even though Dadhabai Naoroji, a leading Parsi and president of the Indian National Congress, had married a child bride himself.[20] Critiques of Hindu women's status or condition were generally held up as evidence of both a civilizing potential and a modernizing capacity on the part of those who articulated them.[21] Dosabhai Karaka, a Parsi writing in the 1880s, clearly understood what kind of cultural capital he wielded when he pointed with pride to the fact that benevolence and civic philanthropy in Bombay illustrated an affinity between Parsis and the British that no other group in the city could match. It was an affinity demonstrated, he believed, by the fact that the Parsis "have not followed the Hindus into the cruel custom of prohibiting their widows from re-marrying, a tyranny which is sometimes followed by so much sin and mischief."[22] Karaka was by no means alone either in articulating the rules of Hindu social practices or in using them to clarify and refine Parsi distinctiveness for the benefit of Western audiences. Parsis who came to Britain for a variety of business, educational, and political purposes took to platforms and produced pamphlets testifying to what they constructed as the cultural divide between themselves and "other" natives of India. Dadhabai Naoroji, perhaps the most well-known Parsi in the West, drew attention to such distinctions in more than one public lecture in the 1860s, arguing that whereas Hindus had fallen from a golden age where women's status had been higher (and by implication, their marital arrangements less coercive), Parsis had always been monogamous.[23]

Such hierarchies themselves were in part exacted by colonial rule. As Partha Chatterjee has noted, in order to shore up its own legitimacy, the colonial state was invested in enumerating diverse communities and in "bringing over to its side the 'natural leaders'" from some of those communities to join its rule over "the rest" of India.[24] In one of his lectures referred to above, Naoroji defended the progress of some communities in India over others in order to refute the claims of an ethnologist that the "Asiatic races" had been slower to evolve than Europeans. Thus the quest to represent the Hindus as the truly backward "race" must be read as a strategy for appropriating cultural and finally political power under colonial rule — and the connection between culture and politics is crucial here, since Naoroji was eventually to become president of the Indian National Congress. If this gesture appears to homogenize and differentiate communities with the same stroke, that is because Parsi nationalism, like all nationalisms, is "a phenomenon that registers difference even as it claims a unitary or unifying identity."[25] What Douglas Haynes has written of Parsis in Surat might thus be said of Parsis in Bombay as well: they exhibited an appreciation for things English not so much to merge with their rulers as to "maintain and enhance their control over community affairs and to preserve a distinct Parsi identity."[26] Doing so gave them distinct material advantages, and not just in terms of education or business; David Arnold has suggested that their receptivity to the smallpox vaccination, a markedly Western medical technology, may account for why they suffered "relatively lightly" as a community from the nineteenth-century plague epidemics.[27] Parsis' quest to preserve a discrete cultural identity — a quest that one historian has called Parsi "anglophilia" and that we have already seen at work in Sorabji's letters[28] — did not necessarily preclude a critique of Englishness, as will be evident in Malabari's London journal. And yet by downplaying the historical impact of Hindu customs on Parsis in Bombay, spokesmen for the community did more than articulate their ambivalence toward colonial rule. They worked to identify themselves with the civilizing mission of the British so that they could deflect the colonial reform gaze and become reformers of other "native" communities themselves. Parsis were certainly not unique among Indian reformers in pledging their loyalty to the British Empire in the nineteenth century. As Tanika Sarkar has written, "[T]he historian cannot afford to view the colonial past as an unproblematic retrospect where all power was on one side and all protest on another . . . [We have] to take into account a multi-faceted nationalism . . . all aspects of which were compliant with power and domination even when they critiqued western knowledge and challenged colonial power."[29] Parsis' attempts to articulate a reform authority that targeted Hindu custom and at the same time claimed to be authentically Indian suggest how mistaken are analyses that insist on the tension between "colonizer" and "colonized" while foreclosing the complex and fragmented struggle for power that was colonialism in situ.

Malabari was at the very center of these cultural politics in the Bombay of the 1880s. The son of a clerk, he was educated in mission schools and had a reputation as an established poet by the 1880s.[30] He was instrumental not just in refining the gendered dimensions of contests for cultural legitimacy and power in the western presidency, but in refiguring such contests for consumption by the British reform public at home as well. What propelled Malabari to prominence across India and prompted his visit to Britain in 1890 was what reformers in Victorian England and India called "the problem of Hindu women." In August of 1884 Malabari published a set of "notes" on infant marriage in India, in which he decried the practice as a "social evil" that warranted state intervention.[31] His "notes" also contained analyses of the prohibition against widow remarriage, a practice that he and other reformers conventionally linked to child marriage in their critiques of Hindu religious custom. By the next year, the celebrated case of Rukhmabai filled the Bombay newspapers. The tremendous publicity her case received, combined with the fact that the judge ordered her to return to her husband or go to jail, gave Malabari's campaign against what he sometimes called "baby marriages" a singular, popular focus. He used his own newspaper as well as other city papers in Bombay and all over India to condemn the practice, to call for state-sponsored reform and generally to feed the sociopolitical frenzy that surrounded the issue into the next decade. In so doing he helped to revive what had become a moribund social reform movement in Bombay, chiefly by using the Bombay press as his platform.[32]

Historians of late-Victorian Britain will recognize Malabari's use of the urban press corps to reflect and reproduce anxiety about the sexual activities of women and girls as strikingly parallel to W. T. Stead's agitation in the *Pall Mall Gazette* over the "Maiden Tribute of Modern Babylon."[33] That these two men should have exploited the emergent institutions of metropolitan journalism to foreground the question of female sexuality and its protection at precisely the same historical moment in two different cities in the British Empire lends credibility to recent claims that domestic and imperial politics ought to be brought

into the same field of debate.[34] Eighteen eighty-five was clearly the "an-
nus mirabilis" of sexual politics in locations beyond London, which Judith Walkowitz, Jeffrey Weeks, and others have identified as a primary
site for state-sanctioned sexual proscription. Marina Valverde's recent
work on the politics of social purity in English-speaking Canada in general and in Toronto in particular reinforces the dual conviction that such
coincidences were far-reaching and that a refiguration of "British imperial culture" and its politics is therefore required.[35] While it is tempting
to see campaigns like those of Malabari and Stead as evidence of a kind
of breakdown of masculinity in modernity, it is more important I think
to resist the characterization of "crisis," because there is little evidence
that fin-de-siècle men (or women) ever lost their faith in masculinity per
se. Moreover, as Gail Bederman so persuasively argues, neither manhood nor modernity are transhistorical categories with "good moments
as well as bad," but are rather ideological constructs and social practices
that "[were] constantly being remade" in the nineteenth century.[36] Malabari, for his part, was greatly interested in "the revelations of Mr.
Stead," and their campaigns eventuated in legislation regulating the age
of consent for females in Britain and India — the Criminal Law Amendment Act of 1885 and the Age of Consent Act of 1891.[37]

Since it was his claim to represent "native opinion" about the age-of-
consent issue, together with his search for British allies in his crusade
for the reform of Hindu women, that brought Malabari to London in
1890, I want to focus on three aspects of Malabari's involvement with
"the woman question" in Bombay during this period: (1) his attitude
toward Hinduism, (2) his critique of both English and Hindu masculinities in relation to child marriage, and (3) his sense of personal identification with Indian women, particularly widows. Malabari's attacks
on child marriage were rooted in a critique of contemporary Hindu
tradition, particularly its brahminical varieties. In his "notes" he blamed
the "priestly class" and the "social monopolists" with whom it had allied
for their "vulgar prejudices"— prejudices he claimed endorsed a reading
of the Shastras as advocating early marriage and the outcasting of widows.[38] In this respect, he echoed the sentiments of Victorian reformers
like Mary Carpenter and prominent Indologists like Max Muller, both
of whom had influenced his thinking on social questions in the decade
before the Rukhmabai case.[39] His views resonated more generally with
over a century of British claims to understand the Vedic texts more
accurately than the pundits themselves.[40] As a journalist at the heart of
Bombay city politics, Malabari understood what was at stake in these

controversies. He knew too that "the woman question" in India was not simply a matter of enlightened English critics versus Hindus blindly defending the Vedic tradition — even if this was sometimes how the controversy was replayed in the imperial metropole. Debates about the status, role, and reform of women in India divided secular reformers from orthodox ones, causing rifts inside progressive organizations and between liberal individuals, as the political crises over the passage of the Age of Consent Act testify.[41] Given this situation, Malabari could not but acknowledge that many educated Hindus deplored such customs and themselves approved of government intervention. At times he spoke of the problem as if it were an all-India question: "[G]overnment [*sic*] only do what we pray them to do — they save us from ourselves, from our clamorous wives and ignorant relatives." Despite his tendency to generalize the problem, however, he always returned for explanation to "the greedy priests" and to the operation of Hindu "superstition" that, he argued, insisted that " 'a girl after ten is a serpent in the parents' house.' "[42]

Malabari's "notes" echoed contemporary metropolitan attitudes and hence effectively made him as much of an outsider to "the problem of India's women" as British reformers. They also worked to question the viability of Hindu masculinity. In the context of Rukhmabai's case, Malabari had charged the English magistrate in question, Judge Pinhey, with being "un-English" in his determination to sentence her to prison for seeking release from an unwanted marriage. Chastising the judge for his "mode of hunting down an unwilling wife," he insinuated that Pinhey was betraying the chivalry of both his sex and of his English heritage.[43] He was much more direct about what he believed the persistence of child marriage among Hindus revealed about some Hindu men. He called orthodox opponents of age-of-consent measures "those effeminate fanatics" and claimed that when earlier reformers like Keshub Chunder Sen had pushed for changes in women's condition, they had been "set upon by an unmanly and unmannerly faction" from within the Hindu community.[44] Malabari warned that such behavior, though not necessarily representative of all Hindu opinion, was in danger of "very nearly discrediting a whole community." Somewhat paradoxically, Malabari argued that those who resisted colonial reform legislation did so because they were "unmanly" and that they further "unmanned" themselves in the process. One effect of his observations was to imply that some Hindu men put at risk the claims of all Hindu men to the protection, regulation, and guardianship of Hindu women.

Such a maneuver opened up a space for the British government to insert itself as the right and proper custodian of Hindu women's honor and, with it, of the reproduction of the bulk of the colonial population in India. It was an intervention that Malabari believed the imperial state in India had a moral obligation to perform.[45] Challenges to the legitimacy of Hindu reformers' masculinity also permitted Malabari to cast himself as the chivalrous representative of Hindu women to a British metropolitan public already alive, in the wake of the debates generated by Stead, to the problem of British girls' and women's protection — and in the Victorian feminist community at least, to the condition of Indian women as well.[46] Significantly, Malabari contended that it was Hindu men's neglect of their duty to Indian women that compelled him to move the battle from Bombay to London. He claimed to be reluctant to do this because it seemed to him "an experiment fraught with risk." For all his confidence in the moral righteousness of British imperial rule, Malabari thought that the British government in India was a "sleeping giant." He may have also been privately doubtful about the likelihood of being able to work up the kind of support he needed in Parliament. Although Indian reformers had traveled to England seeking support for their causes since the late 1820s, and Parsi entrepreneurs like Naoroji (later an member of Parliament for Finsbury) had been influential in Liverpool and London since the 1850s, Malabari's bid for reform in India through the agitation of the British public at home was virtually unprecedented. Finally, he understood that as a Parsi he would be perceived as an outsider to Hindu customs, though he justified his marginality by linking himself with the early-Victorian abolitionists, who, he argued, had also been outsiders to Afro-Caribbean culture.[47] In the end he decided to travel to England because "I am beginning to fear that there is scarcely [no] other way open."[48]

It would be a mistake, however, to imagine that Malābari developed a hypermasculinized chivalry with respect to Indian women in order to compensate for or show up what he characterized as the effeminacy of Hindu conservatives in and around Bombay. To the contrary. Malabari's stance was one of self-professed identification with Indian women, particularly with Hindu widows. This functioned in the first instance as a retort to Hindu critics who claimed that widows themselves were unwilling to remarry. "It is worth noting," he wrote in his article "Some Results of Infant Marriage," "that those who advance such excuses speak for themselves, not for the widows. I, on the other hand, speak *for* the widow and *as* the widow [emphasis his]."[49] If Rukhmabai's frequent contributions to both the Bombay and the London press made his claims about the necessity of "speaking for" Indian women less urgent, his desire to "speak as" a female victim marked Malabari as capable of understanding, indeed, capable of feeling the very pain and suffering of widows and of secluded women. In the words of his biographer, Day-aram Gidumal, "he felt vividly the sin" visited on Hindu women by religious custom; to which Malabari added, "Englishmen can have no idea of [its] bitterness."[50] As Sumanta Bannerjee has pointed out, the practice of indigenous male reformers adopting the widow's voice had a precedent in the 1850s, when I. C. Vidyasagar's campaign for widow remarriage found expression among writers in the Bengali vernacular press who frequently spoke "as women" of their pleasure at the prospect of escaping the "cold suttee" of the widow's life.[51] Nor was W. T. Stead averse to this kind of discursive ventriloquism: as Judith Walkowitz has noted, he performed a similar maneuver when he said, facing the task of writing his exposé on the Maiden Tribute, "[Y]ou know what a woman I am in these things."[52]

Rather than signifying gender confusion or even simply self-serving rhetorical manipulation, Malabari's shifting gender identification reflects the kinds of melodramatic innovations that could be produced by the challenges of negotiating a subaltern identity inside what Ania Loomba calls the "patriarchal racism" of empire.[53] He keenly understood that one of the ways in which British rule was justified was through the feminization of its colonial subjects. Because he wanted to control the colonizing project in order to secure his own exemption, he mimicked that process when he insisted on the effeminacy of Hindu conservatives who opposed the modernizing influence of the colonial state in India. But he also understood that he himself was, inescapably, a colonial subject. And because he recognized the fundamental truism of British claims to civilization — that is, that the self-sacrificing reform of "Others" by the ruling classes was the path to subjecthood, emancipation, and liberty — he affirmed the construction of the Hindu woman as Other and adopted the Hindu widow's suffering as his personal, pathetic burden. As Malabari mobilized that burden, it represented the kind of selfless imperial responsibility that was, theoretically, the precursor to Indian women's "uplift" and "improvement" and, not incidentally, to the recognition of his own claims to be a petitioning subject of the imperial nation. Forged in the crucible of colonial politics in Bombay, Malabari's quest for subjecthood was predicated on a masculinity that (1) was decidedly not-Hindu; (2) was protective of women, and (3) was identified

with the feminine, however unstably and selectively. It was with the
intention of portraying himself as the disinterested but "authentically"
Indian representative of female reform that Malabari came to London
in 1890 to make claims on both the imperial nation-state and the imperial
British public on behalf of his Indian "sisters."

Despite the fact that what occasioned Malabari's trip and the publication
of *The Indian Eye on English Life* was his search for parliamentary and
public support for an age-of-consent bill in India, those activities figure
hardly at all in the text. In fact, except for a page-and-a-half discussion
of how costly it was to print his tract, *An Appeal from India's Daughters*,
for circulation in London and environs, *The Indian Eye* scarcely alludes
to Malabari's political activities, and it mentions the London committee
he formed for the purposes of organizing metropolitan social reform
support for his cause just once. By his own admission, Malabari set out
to "vivisect" the British.[54] What results is a text that is part travelogue,
part ethnography, part investigative essay, and part laboratory report on
English civilization as observed primarily though not exclusively in the
city of London. Because there is no such thing as an innocent ethnography, *The Indian Eye* may be read as a text purposefully constructed to
serve Malabari's reform interests and to consolidate his position as *the*
authoritative, manly voice of Indian social reform.

   The majority of encounters with the "natives" of Britain that Malabari
recorded in *The Indian Eye* occurred on the streets of London. For almost two hundred pages the text describes the main thoroughfares, the
back alleys, the famous sights, and the less savory quarters of what Malabari called "the metropolis of the world."[55] "The best way of doing
London," according to Malabari, was to "tramp the streets and lanes, if
you can, in the company of a retired policeman, or a friendly clergyman."[56] He was often accompanied by his manservant (whom he refers
to as "Crocodile" throughout the account), or else by a Parsi doctor
friend named Bhabha, and, as in the opening excerpt, at least once by
the daughter of his landlady, Annie.[57] If he actually sought out the company of a retired policeman or clergyman, he did not record it — though
the friendliness and efficiency of the metropolitan police was something
that a number of Indian visitors to London commented on, suggesting
that they may have sought help from them as they wandered the streets
of the city.[58] Throughout *The Indian Eye* Malabari gives the impression
that he almost always walked out alone — the solitary "pilgrim rambler"
of the book's subtitle. This particular self-styling evoked an earlier genre

of male urban solitary writing in which city wandering had been the pretext for social criticism as well as the precursor to social reform — from Henry Mayhew's *London Labour and the London Poor* (1849–51) to Henry Gavin's *Sanitary Ramblings* (1848) to John Shaw's *Travels in England* (subtitled *A Ramble with the City and Town Missionaries*, 1861). It is quite likely that Malabari was familiar with this tradition because of the attention it received, through reviews in Anglo-Indian newspapers or other allusions to it gleaned either in India or on his first trip to Britain in 1870. Jhinda Ram, whose *My Trip to Europe* was published in the same year as the first edition of *The Indian Eye*, appeared to invoke the rhetoric of rambling quite self-consciously and even quoted from Mayhew's reportage in the course of his observation of the London docks.[59] The rash of travelogues produced in the 1890s by Indian men who had traveled to both Britain and the Continent suggests that Malabari was not the only colonial subject either experimenting with a "national" genre like the urban investigative report or, as we shall see, challenging the "rhetoric of walking" it had mapped.[60] Indeed, that rhetoric was in the process of changing even as Malabari strolled the streets of London. Almost exactly contemporary with *The Indian Eye* were those conspicuously "East End" travelogues that had begun to emerge in the 1860s and gained new ground, as it were, in the 1890s. These texts were invested in differentiating the East from the West End of London: William Booth's *In Darkest England and the Way Out* and Margaret Harkness's *In Darkest London*, for example, both mapped London itself as a colonial space and conjured the East End in particular as a site of colonial diaspora.[61] Even as Indians were on the move in Britain, producing their versions of what made the capital "imperial," late-Victorian observers were reimagining the metropole in colonial terms for consumption by an avid reading public. By the time Malabari wandered the streets of London as "the" colonial flaneur, in other words, London had already begun to be consolidated as both quintessentially English *and* indubitably (if unstably) modern because of the traces of colonialism that made it the "national-imperial" capital.

Several Indians "rambling" through London in this period (re)-produced the city's East-West divisions, mostly in order to emphasize the contrasts between rich and poor by leading a tour of the slum neighborhoods within the larger "tour" of London, Britain, or even Europe. Such excursions into working-class areas could be brief interludes, or they could take up a substantial portion of the travelogue; in either case the East End was held up as one of the "landmarks" of English civilization, no more to be missed than the British Museum or the Tower of London.[62] Unlike either his fellow countrymen or his English contemporaries, Malabari did not exploit the metaphor of East versus West to conjure up the two ends of London. But *The Indian Eye* nonetheless has several features in common with the kind of urban exploration literature that was produced by both natives and colonials and that was circulating at home and in the empire during this period. Malabari remarked on the city's size, its "perpetual motion," its crushing crowds, its transport system, its riches and its poverty, its street people and its street activity. For him as for other Victorian observers London was "our modern Babylon," the "stronghold of all that is best and worst in the national character."[63] Sudden and unanticipated encounters, such as his run-in with "street arabs," were also a common feature of this particular genre of travel writing. Recording such face-to-face contact was a strategy that, according to Deborah Nord, allowed "the labourers of London to speak for themselves" in the context of amassing the socioeconomic details of their lives.[64]

Although we may be skeptical of the ways in which such "speaking" was reenacted in ethnographic texts — Malabari was by no means alone among Victorian observers in ventriloquizing the Cockney accent — representing Britain's city dwellers "as they were" was a technique used frequently by the generations of urban explorers that preceded and followed after Malabari.[65] In addition to these features, *The Indian Eye* shares with other British urban investigative narratives the critique of secular materialism, albeit with a different twist than the standardized evangelical attack on the worshippers of Mammon and Self. Referring to the fact that in London men seemed only to run after money and pleasure, Malabari pronounced the following indictment of metropolitan life: "If this be your English culture of the nineteenth century, let us remain ignorant in India. I had much rather that India remained superstitious enough to worship her stone-god. That means something of self-sacrifice: it lifts the worshipper out of himself. The worship of self is the worst form of idolatry."[66] This rejection of the values of Western modernity is the first hint that what Malabari saw in the empire's capital caused him to rethink if not his anglophilia, then certainly his relatively uncritical view of the universal benefits of English civilization. Such a conversion was not uncommonly the result of urban wandering in the Victorian period, with social investigators sounding the doom of modern society even as they anatomized both the symptoms of and the cures for its ills.[67] Such was almost uniformly the case for colonial travelers to

Britain, for whom tourism blurred easily, and quite deliberately, not just into ethnography but into a full-fledged critique of the claim to social and cultural superiority that underwrote justifications for colonial rule. Some compared London to Paris and found the former wanting: too sooty, and not as monumental as its continental rival.[68] Others complained about the crammed streets, the impersonality of the hustle-bustle, and the dangers posed by the "criminal elements" especially to untutored foreigners. Commentary on the extremes between luxury and poverty was as common among Indian investigators as it was among native English observers; those who explored the East End as well as the West noted the pathetic faces of deprivation in great detail. If the critique they articulated was similar to those offered by Western contemporaries, it had special resonance for them as colonial subjects. As one Indian traveler put it, not only was poverty everywhere in Britain "at home," but poverty itself was the "all but inseparable concomitant . . . of civilized life."[69]

And yet it was not materialism, disembodied capitalist greed, or poverty alone that served as the cautionary tale. As had other male urbanites like W. T. Stead, Malabari equated the instabilities and pathologies of the social order with those of the sexual order, to such an extent that the narrative of *The Indian Eye* is driven by Malabari's preoccupation with English women — wives, elderly matrons, working-class girls, and prostitutes — "parading" in public. For Malabari the public was not simply the streets but "the crowd" and especially the various modes of public transport that were, by 1890, well-established and essential features of heavily trafficked London city life.[70] Although he was not unconcerned with lower-class women and working girls on the streets — whose "lupine" visages and consumptive appearances fascinated him — Malabari attended mainly to the rosy-cheeked types whom he saw rushing about London, negotiating their way through the urban landscape with apparent ease. "What strikes you most about Englishwomen," wrote Malabari, "is their look of health, strength, elasticity, all proclaiming — freedom of mind, to begin with. How they walk and talk and carry themselves generally!" What was fascinating about this freedom of movement could also be distasteful. "The crowds of women in the streets, walking rapidly past, pushing and elbowing every one who stands in the way, all intent on business or pleasure, are a sight not likely to be forgotten," Malabari wrote. "For me it is a sight more striking than attractive."[71] For what it tells us about how he negotiated those personal and cultural locations, Malabari's account of one experience on a London omnibus is worth quoting in full:

I am [sitting] in between two of the prettiest and quietest [of the women who have rushed onto the bus], feeling a strange discomfort. As the bus hobbles along I feel my fair neighbours knocking against me every moment. They do not seem to mind it at all: it is a matter of course . . . Evil to him who evil thinks. We are all too busy here, reading the paper, chatting about the weather, minding our packages and our toes . . . I have also noted that respectable Englishwomen rather avoid entering a carriage occupied by men. It is mainly through such experience that I am learning to take a charitable view of ladies sitting on the knees of gentlemen, gentlemen on the knees of ladies, when three of one family happen to be in one hansom or more than ten in a railway carriage. These sights, queer as they are, do not offend me, now. They would be an eyesore amongst our own people. I myself could hardly bear them at first; but that is no reason why I should judge others in such a matter, before I am well equipped to form a judgment.[72]

As Henry Mayhew had in *London Labour and the London Poor*, Malabari displaced the threat of his exposure to sexuality in public onto the public women into whose company he was thrown.[73]

If this is a strategy that did not entirely succeed — since the proximity of bodies and the attention he drew to them arguably works to eroticize this scene — it nonetheless represented Malabari as a gentleman who had accustomed himself to one of the necessary indelicacies of daily urban life in the West. His readers, whether English or Indian, were being instructed in the conditions facing an Indian man in a London omnibus. They were also being offered evidence that a colonial subject was engaged in trying to master a major challenge of modern English life — the sexual temptations of women in public. Indeed, for English as well as for Indian readers, Malabari's very proximity to the English girls on the bus may have been what made them so delectably "English." The spectacle of bodies he produces here may also have been calculated to deflect attention from Malabari's own spectacularity and to persuade his audience of the ordinariness of the event, thus securing another characteristic crucial to the manliness of the English gentleman: disinterestedness. If, as Meaghan Morris has argued, the founding narratives of European imperialism portray the modern as something that had already happened elsewhere, Malabari is clearly asserting that the native has come "here," to the heart of the empire, to meet modernity on its own terms and on its own turf.[74] That he should be staking his claim to

belonging, to subjecthood, through such a public display of manhood —
in this case, of manly restraint in the presence of so many English female
bodies — indicates his investment in proving a certain kind of gender-
specific claim to civilized behavior. That he could not fully manage his
own discomfort suggests that despite even his complicity with hegemonic masculinity, his status as colonial subject was not flexible enough
to enable him to transform himself into a stable British citizen. In this
sense, Malabari's representational crisis may be read as a political crisis
as well.[75] It also suggests that the meaning of the "public woman" in
the Western metropole was neither monolithic nor self-evident. Like the
fallen woman, she could stand "as an emblem of social suffering or
debasement, as a projection of or analog to the male stroller's alienated
self, an instrument of pleasure and a partner in urban sprees." In *The
Indian Eye* she figures additionally as evidence of the colonial male subject's capacity to negotiate, if not master, the kind of sexual encounter
endemic to the late-Victorian imperial metropole.[76]

Other encounters with English women in public were even more
discomfiting for Malabari, and they generated not just the performance
of a certain claim to masculinity but a critique of the whole phenomenon
of "women in public" that was often attendant upon it. To wit, this
second omnibus experience: "I have alluded to the modesty and candour
of my fellow-passengers of the other sex. That picture also needs shad-
ing. You have sometimes the misfortune of having women beside you,
with a trick of leaning on your arm or shoulder when they are quite
capable of supporting themselves; of giggling, of laughing a dry hollow
laugh or trying otherwise to draw you out of yourself. The conductor,
entering into your feelings, or reading them in your face, may announce,
'Room up top, sir!' or you may yourself get out before time. But why
recall such experiences amid so much that is beautiful and true? Let it
be forgotten, like an evil dream."[77] It is difficult to make out exactly
what is going on here, let alone what Malabari thought was going on.
One interpretation suggested by the passage is that Malabari is trying
to make humorous an embarrassing moment — inhabiting a jocular or
ironic discursive space in order underline his seeming innocence, and/
or to diffuse a tense situation. And yet, Malabari is, I think, quite serious
here — chiefly because, as Vera Kutzinski has speculated in another context, in order for a situation like this one to be comical, it would have
to have been socially, and sexually, safe.[78] Given the impropriety that
Victorians attached to public women, together with the possibilities for
sexualized encounters that public transport offered, Malabari no doubt

believed he was the object of solicitation.[79] His familiarity with Stead and with the drama of the Maiden Tribute may even indeed have primed him for this possibility.[80] His allusion to his experience being akin to an "evil dream" bears out this reading. Not all Indian men experienced the London bus as threatening, a "traveling incarceration" in this way, or if they did, they did not record it.[81] For many it was "a time-honoured institution" that they used as a tool for producing a map of the city that was quite traditionally touristic (Westminster Abbey, Hyde Park, etc.), though perhaps sanitized for a bourgeois readership.[82] And yet Malabari was not alone. Another Indian traveler to London, who was the chief justice of Hyderabad, described a similar experience in the *Indian Magazine and Review* in the late winter of 1890. Medhi Hasan Khan had been convinced that he was being solicited by a woman he met on a bus — until he confronted the lady in question and she, according to his account, expressed horror at the thought of being mistaken for a prostitute.[83]

Whether the fact that both Malabari and Khan were Indian meant that they were singled out for attention by certain women in public is virtually impossible to know with any certainty. In the chief justice's story, the woman whom he confronted told him that she spoke to him initially because her fiancé's cousin lived in India, and she was curious about his country.[84] As was suggested in chapter 1, in addition to lascars, domestic servants, and a community of South Asian urban poor, there was a small but culturally and politically active Indian middle class in Victorian London (as well as in other British cities), many of whom were connected with Oxford, Cambridge, and various medical schools and colleges or, after July 1889, with the British Committee of the Indian National Congress in Britain.[85] Among other things, these facts tell us that seeing Indians in particular and colonial peoples in general on the streets of London was not a completely unlikely or even an uncommon phenomenon, despite the fact that it has escaped the notice of all but the most astute British historians.[86] That late-Victorian London can be appropriately referred to as an "imperial" metropole does not, of course, preclude the probability that *all* nonwhite peoples were made exotic and erotic by the Victorian public gaze — which could be both personal and impersonal, passing and sustained. And Indian male travelers may have fetishized the English woman's "public body" precisely in order to manage and reorder transgressive desires that did not always begin with them: to warn that the bus or even the city of London was not an interior space undisturbed by historically colonial power relations, and that indulging in such fantasies in the social realm was taboo.[87] Jhinda Ram, for example, recalled in 1893 how he had been assaulted on a London street several years earlier by an English woman (her class was not specified or even hinted at) who declared she was in love with him — and that she had been watching him for two weeks.[88]

In any event, both Khan and Malabari recorded embarrassment not unmixed with pleasure as they reflected on their encounters with "native" women. "Why," Malabari asked his readers with resignation, "should I cry out against the inevitable?"[89] Not unlike a variety of cultural productions contemporary with it, *The Indian Eye on English Life* suggested that there was a thin line between women in public and "public women" in the capital city of the empire. Respectable women could slip quickly and almost imperceptibly into the category of dangerous and "evil." Meanwhile British men (the bus conductor) and the colonial "native" could just as easily collude, as in the excerpt above, to enjoy the pleasures of women in public even as they conspired to agree about how unsettling it was to share public space with them. If this configuration of men and women in public evokes Eve Sedgwick's "erotic triangle" — demonstrating how heterosexual patriarchy functions in terms of a traffic in women — it is not destabilized simply by asymmetries of gender; those very asymmetries are themselves constituted simultaneously by asymmetries of race and of class as well.[90] In the case of Ram, a policeman interrupted his encounter with the amorous young woman, an intervention Ram saw as benign but one that raises questions about what other kinds of surveillance colonial travelers might have been under in the metropole.[91]

There is also undoubtedly slippage in these particular homosocial relationships: it is quite possible, for example, that the conductor suggested that Malabari go to the top of the bus because he wished to segregate him, the brown man, from the same cramped space in which the English woman circulated. Malabari's representation of both his unease and his pleasure at these mixed encounters thus constitutes a performance of a specific kind of anxiety in relation to "the English woman in public." The implication, sustained throughout *The Indian Eye*, that this kind of mixed encounter was somehow characteristic of London and not of Bombay or India more generally may not, however, have been entirely accurate. European accounts of Bombay in the nineteenth century represent the city not just as extremely cosmopolitan, but as an urban space where Europeans and natives could be seen "in pretty close contact" with each other and where Indian and English women were to

be seen in the bazaar, on the streets, and in a variety of public conveyances.[92] "The carts are chiefly open, but there are a few covered *rhuts*,
the conveyances probably of rich Hindu or Muslim women . . . ," wrote
one observer. "Young Parsee women of the better class are frequently
to be seen in carriages with their male relations, nor do they object to
appear publicly in the streets following wedding processions."[93] For Indians traveling throughout the subcontinent, too, women in Bombay
seemed to have more freedom than elsewhere in India, possibly because
it was not either a sacred center or an "indigenous" Indian city, but a
magnet for migrants from many different communities from the subcontinent and beyond.[94] As N. Dasa put it in his *Reminiscences English
and Australasian*, in Bombay "women of all classes walked about in the
streets without reserve or veil"—an observation ratified by the latest
scholarship on Bombay, which cites the nineteenth century city's reputation for permissiveness on the issue of women in public.[95]

Nor was the Bombay of Malabari's time untouched by contests about
the propriety of women moving through the urban space of the public.
The case of Anandibai Joshi, who suffered public humiliation as she
made her way to school every day in Bombay, is perhaps one of the best
known incidents of the kind of harassment attendant on women seeking
out the public sphere. As she recalled in 1883, "Passers-by, whenever they
saw me going to school, gathered round me; some of them made fun
of me and convulsed themselves with laughter; others more respectable
in appearance made ridiculous remarks and did not feel ashamed to
throw pebbles at me. Banias [merchants] and Tambulies [betel leaf and
nut sellers] spitted [sic] at the sight of me and made gestures too obscene
to describe."[96] Padma Anagol has recently argued that the 1880s was an
important decade for public discussions and legal interventions about
Indian women's public movements — as in 1883, when Parsi "miscreants"
were charged with gibing at Parsi ladies on street corners, and in 1886,
when the Pachumba case brought attention to the harassment of Hindu
women by British soldiers on a steamer. In another case, at least one
Parsi woman's family succeeded in bringing a legal injunction against a
car driver for harassing her.[97]

Malabari — who, as a Bombay resident and newspaper proprietor,
must have been aware of these events — did not refer to them in *The
Indian Eye*, preferring instead to equate mixed urban "intercourse" with
English urbanity and by implication, to represent India as the irreducibly
simpler, unhurried society by contrast. The London of the 1880s had
also been a site of public contest over public women — as the contro-

versies over the Maiden Tribute of Modern Babylon, the Jack the Ripper murders, and the Contagious Diseases Acts agitation each, in different ways, represented — but this goes curiously unremarked by Malabari in his travelogue. Such omissions demonstrate Malabari's investment in overdetermining both the metropole/colony dichotomy and the apparently uniform and rational modernity of London — a modernity that thrived on a rather unstable heterogeneity.[98] Clearly what was in danger of being destabilized in these interactions was not the ideal English woman as much as Malabari's own carefully constructed identification with the ideal of "the Indian gentleman" — someone who was as capable as the European gentleman of walking the thoroughfares of the Western city unmolested. In fact, Malabari's pretensions to being a flaneur — a "new kind of public person with the leisure to wander, watch and browse," as Elizabeth Wilson has described him, the "archetypal occupant and observer of the public sphere" — were not as easily realized as those of his British or European contemporaries.[99]

Wilson and Pollock have remarked on the fact that both the social investigator and the flaneur were typically white males and had masculinized relationships to the city and to public space: that is to say, they enjoyed "the effects of power through a gaze signifying possession and familiarity, being at home on the streets, in the public realm."[100] Deborah Nord's recent work has extended their critique by detailing how difficult it was for middle-class English women to claim a similar kind of ease in public, in part because they themselves were often, if not always, subject to a sexualized urban gaze.[101] *The Indian Eye on English Life* does not display the sense of possession or the confident familiarity that was generally characteristic of English men ("bourgeois tourists") observing the English scene.[102] Malabari's quest to be a flaneur resonates more with the experience of Victorian bourgeois women who walked the streets as social investigators, insofar as it was impossible to see without also being seen, for them both. As Nord illustrates, the privilege of self-erasure accorded to the white male flaneur was not available to either Malabari or women like Helen Bosanquet — not just because they were conspicuous, but because the trauma of their public (sexualized) exposure (he by English women and she by English men) produced an anxiety about authority that was difficult to conceal.[103] Malabari's text, in contrast to those of English male ramblers, recounts a series of encounters in which he is thrown off balance, and in which his attempts to play the chivalrous colonial male end up in discomfort if not disaster. In this respect, *The Indian Eye* is as much a part of the tradition of Indian male visitors to London as it is of Western urban ethnographic conventions: the "London experience" manifested itself in the memoirs, autobiographies, and reminiscences of nationalist reformers from Rammohun Roy in the 1820s to Tagore in the 1870s to Gandhi in the 1880s — acting as a test of courage, tenacity, and, above all, of manhood.[104] The temptations that the streetwalkers posed to Gandhi when he attended a vegetarian convention in the late 1880s in Portsmouth are perhaps the best known of these tests, but hardly any colonial Indian's account of his time at the heart of the empire is without reference to the difficulties of navigating "mixed company," either on the streets or in the less public spaces of middle-class society (drawing rooms, At Homes, soirees, teas).[105]

That nearly all these men, Gandhi and Malabari included, had wives at home lent dramatic tension to their encounters, straining their sense of their own chivalry and manly honor to the breaking point. Nor were such tension-ridden encounters limited by any means to prominent Indians or even Congressmen. Practically every account of an English sojourn written by an Indian man in English in the 1880s and after chronicles his attempts to disentangle himself from either the gaze or the attentions of English women, if not on the street, then in some other kind of public, social setting. If, as David Morgan has suggested, masculinity — and in this case heterosexual subjecthood — is performed in response to the presence of "public" women, then control over women in public may well have been part of the display of belonging that was produced by Indian men's travels in nineteenth-century Britain.[106] After a page or so of describing the typical English (middle-class) beauty, Malabari ends with a paragraph's discussion of English women's eyes. "They are beautiful eyes," he writes, and "used to the languid, downcast look of the Eastern eye, one feels a strange sensation coming over him . . . [T]his is not at all a look of boldness, but of earnest sympathy and self-confidence." He goes on to anatomize teeth, hair, noses, and then he ends rather abruptly. "But hist!" he says, drawing himself up short; "whither are we wandering?"[107]

The kind of "wandering" that brought Malabari into contact with English women "in public" was by no means limited to the streets. As his accounts of his experiences in the omnibus reveal, the city itself was full of all kinds of interior spaces that could be more or less public, depending not just on the specificity of the space itself, but on who was watching the encounter. Arjun Appadurai's phrase, "the incarceration of the native," together with the historical connections that railway car experiences have had with the birth of nationalist-resistant consciousness (from South Africa to the Jim Crow South), speak powerfully to the kinds of power relations that might be produced and contested in such enclosures.[108] The first such space for Indian men and women on the voyage to Britain was usually the ship. Some travelers discovered themselves as "natives" for the first time as their steamers headed toward the West, not just because they ran into the infamous reserve of English travelers but also because, as in the case of Dasa, the lascars employed on the ship subjected him to the same kind of inquisitive scrutiny as his fellow passengers did.[109] Malabari recorded no such scrutiny, perhaps because there were mostly Germans on the steamer, perhaps because he chose not to dine at table but "in seclusion," as he put it, with Crocodile in his cabin. Significantly, however, the one awkward encounter he did relate has to do with a German woman on board. He had been told to approach her because she was the sister of an acquaintance, but "with my usual knack at blundering I go up to the wrong lady"— that is, he mistook her maid for the woman in question.[110] Like the omnibus of the anecdotes related above, the constricted, albeit public, space of the ship's deck heightened the stakes of such encounters and — unlike the rather quicker movement through the streets — put Malabari on display for a captive audience to see.

The Indian Eye offers a several enclosed spaces as ministages for the exhibition of Malabari's cosmopolitanism and for his claims to be not just a civilized colonial subject but an expressly English subject as well. Chief among these is the boardinghouse.[111] During his stay in London Malabari lived in a number of different arrangements but preferred, as did many long- and short-term Indian visitors to the capital city, the boardinghouse to most other options. This was the kind of lodging recommended both by Baedeker's guide, which targeted tourists in general, and by the National Indian Association, which published information in the 1880s on where students and visitors from the subcontinent could affordably live.[112] Indian men's travelogues of this period suggest that many who came to Britain went first to a hotel and then to boardinghouses that they found either through the help of friends or, if they were students, through the NIA. Advertisements for accommodation also ran in Indian newspapers.[113] Malabari warned his readers against choosing the "apartments" option, which he claimed was less genteel and more expensive than advertised; he recommended what he called "private family lodgings . . . maintained by respectable families."[114] Although its specific location is not given, Malabari's lodging might have been in South Kensington or possibly Bayswater, a part of London known to late-nineteenth-century Indian travelers and students as "Asia Minor," as so many of them lived there.[115]

Malabari had nothing but praise for his landlady, whom he referred to throughout *The Indian Eye* as "Mrs. M —." He was keen to emphasize the respectability of the family, in part because the undesirability of "low lodgings" was viewed as a deterrent by many Indians considering a trip to Britain.[116] Mrs. M's second husband was a florist and she had children from two marriages ranging from four to forty years old; Annie, her daughter, "was a quiet, self-contained little lady, with a very fine devotional nature, fond of music, and a total abstainer." To shore up her respectability — and his own — even further, Malabari speculated that she might even come to India as a "salvation lass" but concluded that she would not because "she is too quiet for that."[117] If the lodging house gave Malabari proximity to some respectable working women, it also threw him into close quarters with Maggie, Mrs. M's "maid-of-all-work." Malabari described Maggie as "a strapping Scotch lassie, who had come to 'Lunnun,' she said, for the fun of it," and he devoted several pages in *The Indian Eye* to a description of her physical energy, her work habits, and her love life. " 'Crocodile' stood in awe of her for the first few days," but "to me it was a sight to see her heaving up, like a steam-engine, with broom and mop and duster." Malabari was evidently fascinated with her menial tasks and uncomfortable when those tasks involved him. When she offered to take off his boots for him, he objected — "I told her in our country we never suffered girls to do that" — and though he tells us that she was puzzled at his reaction, he does not say whether he allowed this kind of "service" to continue.

Malabari's voyeurism, and his fascination with Maggie's household duties, recalls Arthur Munby's preoccupation with his scullery maid Hannah Cullwick, without the explicit sexual involvement or the same kind of master/servant dynamic that structured their relationship.[118] And yet the question of class as a subject position in a nexus of gendered — and here, colonial — power relations also operated in the boardinghouse scene. For Malabari's surveillance of Maggie in *The Indian Eye* allowed him to assume a class position superior to hers — a location afforded by the context of the lodging house, and one that could not perhaps have been sustained as easily when confronted by her "lupine"-visaged working-class sisters on the streets of London. At the same time, it was not a status Malabari inhabited comfortably: for when he saw her working "like a steam-engine," "I greeted her as My Lady Margarita Honoria

Montgomery Tibs, walking up in her court dress." Here Malabari attempted to deflect the possibilities of an intimate, sexualized encounter by resorting to and inverting class hierarchies — by forcing Maggie into a mock aristocratic position so that they both seemed to be respectable players in the enclosed theater of the boardinghouse, and perhaps too so that she seemed unreachable. In doing so, Malabari again demonstrated his desire to exhibit a kind of mastery over the domestic servant who might show up his pretensions to gentlemanliness, just as he had done with the potentially disrespectabilizing "street arabs."

His determination to display his control over Maggie becomes even more marked as the narrative continues and he explains how he advised her about her relationship with "her 'young man,' a Scotch sailor who had given up the sea for her sake and had followed her to London." Lest the propriety of this conversation be at issue, Malabari reassures his readers that he counseled her wisely: "I spoke to her seriously," he recounts, "urging [her] that it was far better to become the wife of an honest fellow, who loved her, than a 'lady' about town, and a servant-girl . . . ." Casting doubt on Maggie's respectability because she works in a lodging house threatens, of course, to undermine Malabari's respectability as well, but his mission to reform her working-class sexual habits is designed to redeem him in the eyes of Victorian bourgeois — and perhaps also Indian bourgeois — readers. This section of *The Indian Eye* ends with Malabari reporting that shortly after this encounter with Maggie she left Mrs. M's service "to make up with her young man. If this turns out so, it will be one of the matches of which I shall be very proud."[119] The wayward working-class girl had long been a defining trope of British urban investigative literature; in Malabari's own time it was being redeployed in new ways by feminists, Salvation Army soldiers, social surveyors, and others seeking to stake their claims to social reform authority in fin-de-siècle Britain. By offering Maggie's story as evidence of his civilizing capacities over "the lower orders," Malabari laid claim to one authoritative reform voice among many; and he proved his reform credentials by demonstrating that, like any British contenders for such authority, he could manfully guide the working-class girl onto the straight and narrow path. That he did so inside the confines of the lodging house demonstrated that he was capable of "putting his house in order," further proving that his aspirations to English gentlemanliness were not misplaced. Indeed, his encounters with Maggie and his intervention in the management of household affairs made the boardinghouse no longer exclusively Mrs. M's purview, but his very own domain as well. Not incidentally, Malabari reported that shortly after Maggie left, he and Crocodile also moved out. He claimed that their departure was prompted by the fact that Mrs. M did not approve of Crocodile, who ate more food than she felt Malabari was paying for. She also complained that Crocodile "went about half dressed"—an accusation that implies the sexual danger of such intimate shared interiors. One way of reading this charge is to see Mrs. M and Malabari locked in a contest for respectability that they conducted through accusations about the *un*respectability of each other's servants.[120] The question of whether or not Mrs. M felt that between them, the Indian men were presuming to make her house their home, is an interesting if ultimately unanswerable one. Malabari's departure from Mrs. M in the wake of these tensions suggests among other things that colonial encounters in Britain could and did occur at the intersection of the personal, the socioeconomic, the sexual, and the cultural—and that even such local relations had decidedly geopolitical resonances.

For Malabari the purity — and the sanctity — of the English home was a preoccupying interest. His residence in it, however temporary, and his attempts to master it, however unsuccessful, consolidated and valorized its "Englishness" as no mere view from the outside could have done. His exile from Mrs. M's produced a series of digressions on the instructive value of English life "as seen at home"— a home whose counter was inevitably India. "The home life of England is practically a sealed book to us," he lamented, and the most that might be obtained was "a few glimpses."[121] He was not alone in emphasizing how beneficial it was for Indian men to observe English family life in action, or how difficult it was for Indian men to gain access to that most interior, and in the context of Victorian domestic ideology, most ambiguously "private," of spaces. Other Indian travelers observing British culture in the context of travel guides of either the United Kingdom or Europe waxed enthusiastic about the opportunities their sojourns gave them to get glimpses of English home life, partly because they were eager to explain how differently English men behaved "by their firesides" than they did in India. There, as one traveler put it, "we see only one of the sides of the Englishman, and that is the official side — a stiff and unlovely side it is too."[122] There was no guarantee that Indian travelers were any more protected from interpolation as "the" colonial on the threshold of the "domestic" than on the streets of the capital. T. N. Mukharji recalled the astonishment of one little girl, the daughter of an acquaintance he was visiting in Liverpool, when he came to the house for the first time: seeing him at the door, she ran back into her mother's skirts and cried, "Ma! A black man."[123] *The Indian Eye*, for its part, moves chapter by chapter from "Bombay to London" to "In and about London" to "Life as Seen at Home." Malabari's particular voyage in is structured, in other words, so that the reader travels apparently ineluctably from colony to imperial capital to the very heart of the empire, the English household. Not surprisingly, at the center of the domestic empire is "the English mother." As he did with Mrs. M, Malabari heaps praise on her and by extension, on all mothers in Britain. "Being grown-up women, with useful knowledge at the back," he relates, "they know how to deal with children — to help the natural growth, to teach them self-reliance; in a word, to educate all their faculties comfortably to nature and their environments." They do not, he adds, "kill their children with kindness, as mothers sometimes do in India."[124] Unlike some of his Indian contemporaries, Malabari does not talk about the working-class home; nor is he particularly interested in how the house is physically laid out.[125] For him the source of both the English home and the English mother is middle-class English marriage; his ethnography therefore focuses almost exclusively on what he views as this peculiarly English cultural institution. The success of English civilization is to be found, Malabari argues, in the equality practiced between husband and wife: "[T]hey love, trust, serve each other as true partners, each contributing his or her share to the common stock of happiness." In articulating these claims, he again echoed the tradition of progressive, Western-minded Indian male visitors to Britain since the days of Rammohun Roy.[126]

Malabari was not unaware of the legal challenges to marriage that had been made in Britain in the 1880s, in part because of his involvement with Rukhmabai's trial. Nor was he oblivious to the threat that middle-class women's independence meant to the English marriage system. He criticized some mothers' "selfishness" and took particular umbrage at women who hired nurses to tend their children, especially those who "aired" them in prams in the biting chill of London streets while they stood "chatting at a corner, making purchases, or gaping at the shop windows."[127] The urban scene was not the proper place for mothers with children because it contributed to the corruption of maternal instincts; as evidence of this he reported seeing "baby toppling out of the perambulator, whilst the mother or nurse is engaged at a distance." But in spite of these instances (and perhaps precisely because of their publicness), Malabari maintained that of all the "sights" available for consumption by the Indian tourist, the interior of the English home was the most authentic and the most gratifying — a standard and the model for the kind of peaceful relations that might exist in all families. After describing the domestic bliss of a particularly happy couple of his acquaintance, Malabari reflected, "If this is not home, I say to myself . . . there can be no such thing as home on earth."

Although he made no direct mention of it, it is evident that Malabari's focus on English marital relations was prompted by his concerns about the age-of-consent issues that brought him to London in 1890. He praised monogamy, dwelt for some time on the evils of polygamy as practiced in "that much abused colony," Utah, and emphasized the benefits for family life and children's health in late marriages in Britain.[128] But the connections between Malabari's reform quest and his metropolitan adventures are quite complex, especially since one of his chief audiences was the Victorian female reform community, which had been galvanized by the Rukhmabai trial and was alive to the whole "cause" of Indian women by the 1890s.[129] His observations of aristocratic and middle-class English women, and especially of their engagement with charity work among or on behalf of the urban poor, made him not just appreciate, but above all identify with, their "earnest sympathy and self-confidence." He praised English wives and women for "know[ing] how to protest — if need be, to revolt," especially compared to Hindu women, who were for him as for many Indian male reformers of this period, synonymous with the whole female population of India and indeed with all categories of "woman" in India. Thus, "in India wives are taught to be patient and enduring . . . [T]hat is the supreme merit of the wife, according to some spurious shastra."[130] In this sense, he appropriated some of the same languages of masculinity he had adopted in Bombay: the discourses of anti-Hinduism, of identification with Indian women's suffering, of chivalrous protection. In the end, his brush with the ambiguously "public women" he encountered in Britain and especially on the streets of London changed the discourses through which he articulated his colonial gender identity. For what had been, in Bombay, a rather generically female-gendered posture became, in London, a decidedly maternal one. "Poor daughters of India! . . . [N]ever mind the trouble and pain to me. You are all the dearer to me for the suffering you cause. I love you with a mother's love."[131] Privileging himself as mother allowed Malabari to offer himself as the asexual, reliable, and above all *safe* carrier of the colonial reform message, on behalf of the daughters of India, to the sons and daughters of Britain in the very heartland of the empire — a family idiom that managed, by suppressing and refiguring, some of the sexual tensions that had arisen in the narrative of urban-imperial exploration. Though he did not finally dismantle the patriarchal racism that was at the heart of the imperial project, and in which he as a Parsi man at times participated, Malabari did succeed in deflecting its gaze from himself back to that recurrent site of late-Victorian social improvement and cultural uplift, "the Hindu woman." In this sense he was, like many English feminists of his generation, at once a critic of women's social position in India and a collaborator in the ideological work of empire.[132]

The movement from woman-identified to mother-identified was not the only shift Malabari performed as he navigated imperial culture in the "motherland." In a departure from the kind of political accommodation that had characterized his rhetoric in Bombay, he took every opportunity to berate the English government into paying more attention to Indian affairs and, in one particularly lengthy passage, to upbraid an anonymous English member of Parliament for failing to be as courteous to him as Malabari believed he should have been.[133] This contretemps is recounted in the chapter called "Life as Seen in Public Affairs" and follows directly on "Life as Seen at Home," so that we follow Malabari's movements from urban public to domestic private to the most important public house of all — the House of Parliament. After several unsuccessful attempts to meet with the parliamentarian in question (whom Malabari describes as "a prominent nobleman"), he finally gained a private hearing for his child marriage reform program. Throughout their meeting the member of Parliament "sits there talking, smoking, and glancing at letters just brought in. This, to an Oriental, is very bad form."[134] Malabari was put off by what he implied was ungentlemanly behavior. Significantly, Malabari was not able to extract a promise of public support for his reform project from the man even at the end of this encounter, but had to "pelt him with reminders every three weeks" until he obtained the unnamed gentleman's commitment to the London committee. For Malabari, the relationship between English gentlemen and colonial subjects was crucial, not just for ad hoc reform schemes like his, but in terms of the very destiny of imperial rule. "To friends in India, and moreso [sic] to those in England, who . . . , simply because we happen to be strangers, . . . stoop and bend in order to pat us on the back," he gave this advice in *The Indian Eye*: "[T]reat us more like fellow-subjects . . . [and give us] the same equal treatment we ask for in the case of the nation as in the case of individuals."[135] As Ramabai and Sorabji had done, Malabari revealed the cultural presumptions of English practices in order to critique colonial power relations in Britain. For not only was the personal political, but the protocols of English gentlemanliness were the standards by which Indian subjects might measure the success and indeed the civilizedness of imperial power. As models, they were also open to competing ideals and versions of proper masculinity themselves.[136] If English women were the allies of the civilizing mission in India, and Indian women's bodies its largely silent terrain, that mission was often, if not ultimately, grounded in the kind of patriarchal bargain struck here. Malabari's "Indian eye on English life" makes it clear that colonial masculinity was not always content to be rendered powerless, but could and did seek collaboration with Victorian ideals of manliness to secure the benefits of power for "gentlemen" white and brown.

It was nothing less than the experience of English life, from the streets to the parlor and back again, that enabled Malabari to make the most important shift of all — that is, to consolidate himself not merely as the Parsi reformer, at odds with Hindu masculinity, but as *the* "Indian" eye of the book's title. Indeed, what holds the travelogue together, both structurally and symbolically, is the twin conviction that the English home functions as the nursery of British subjecthood in the imperial nation and that the men of "India" had the capacity to observe and appreciate its civilizing function. Malabari insisted that exposure to the English "at home" was the Indian male student's best lesson in how to become a "proper" subject of British rule — that only by lodging with an English family could young Indian men fully benefit from the university educations many came to Britain to seek. Some Indian men writing accounts of English life in this period agreed, believing that what made Oxbridge (as opposed to London) the most acceptable place for Indian men was that its college life was equivalent to the culture of an English home.[137] Malabari blamed the Indian home for ill-preparing Indian men for what he viewed as the rough and tumble of English life; if they had been raised to consider themselves equals, they would not be so easily discomfited or thrown off balance by the often jarring sociability of English culture. He clearly understood firsthand some of the "temptations" to be found in the path of Indian men in the metropole, and his admonition refers directly back to his own adventures "in and about London." "The stranger keeps his own company or, in seven cases out of ten, is taken in hand by the worst set at college or in the neighborhood. He learns to smoke, drink, gamble, to bet, and to squander his substance in worse ways. The life in 'apartments,' that he often has to accept, does not offer any relief from this round of vulgar dissipation. He may contract debts and disease, and return home with or without his degree . . . [T]he question . . . is, how to offer the comforts and convenience of home to an Indian student in England; how to enable him to make the best of his brief sojourn in the land of his rulers."[138] The "internal 'discipline' "of the English home — what Dipesh Chakrabarty calls "the European imperial-modern"— is offered here as the key to Indian prosperity and, ultimately, to political power.[139] Perhaps most tellingly, it is being offered by a colonial subject whose sojourn in Britain allowed, and perhaps even required, him to arrogate to himself the regulatory technology of "the Indian" eye so that he could claim to speak on behalf of, and for the benefit, of all "Indian" men. Such a claim was contested by many Indians at home, particularly orthodox Hindus, whose attacks on Malabari persisted as he traveled in Britain identifying himself as the representative of all-India opinion on the age-of-consent question.[140]

If Malabari ended up satisfying none of his audiences, it must be clear that he neither did, nor could, occupy a space "in between" a colonial and a metropolitan constituency. His sojourn in the metropole reveals how "the establishment of colonial power in the figure of the 'native' " rarely produces an easily recognizable dichotomy, but results in a displacement and relocation of colonial oppositions themselves.[141] Malabari's hybridity is to be found not in his Parsiness, or even in his carefully articulated "Indianness" of *The Indian Eye*, but precisely in his navigation through the complexities of imperial cultural geography in Britain — which is to say, in the variety of "home" spaces it encompassed rather than simply the duality between empire and colony. In the end, *The Indian Eye on English Life* testifies to the contingency of gendered identities and cultural locations even and especially when cultures and peoples are on the move.[142] It speaks too to the agency — if not always the resistance — of migrant subjects in the critique of geopolitical power and in the determination of their complex relationships to it. *The Indian Eye* makes clear that if London life represented "English civilization," and if "English civilization" were in turn equivalent to modernity, then Malabari had, like many other late Victorians, a deeply ambivalent attitude toward the imperial metropole. "The noise and bustle — the everlasting clang of feet, the whistling of engines and smoking of chimneys" of London was music to his ears. But, he concluded, "it is music which . . . I should prefer hearing at a safe distance."[143]

Malabari may be counted among other variously "colonial" people —

M. K. Gandhi, Mary Seacole, Olaudah Equiano, Mary Prince, Frederick Douglass, Pandita Ramabai, Ida B. Wells, C. L. R. James, and Cornelia Sorabji, to name just a few — for whom travel to the imperial metropole yielded new insights, sharpened political commitments, and effected profoundly personal and historical transformations in the nineteenth century and after.[144] The particularity of his story should not obscure the ways in which fears about "black men," "the black peril," and lynching hysteria were escalating around the British Empire and its former colonial sites beginning in the late nineteenth century and after.[145] To be a brown man not just circulating among white women but also producing accounts of his close and clearly sexualized encounters was a risky maneuver. For even as it bordered on impropriety, it signaled that the emblematic marker of English civilization, the white "native" woman, could be the possession of the colonial subject. She was in fact the indubitable, if troubling and sexually dangerous, proof of his masculinity — evidence that "English" civilization was not antecedent to colonial masculinity, but in effect created in dialectic tension with it.[146] If, as Anne McClintock has argued, commodity capitalism helped to reorder metropolitan culture for the display of imperial power, London was one of the primary spaces in which, and sexuality one of the technologies through which, this refiguration occurred.[147] As Malabari's travelogue illustrates, colonial subjects were among those historical actors who worked to manage — and to challenge — the terms upon which the spectacle of empire was sexualized in the late-Victorian imperial metropolis. Like other Eastern travelers who produced Europe itself as an exhibitionary site, Indians in Britain made London into a theater where the psychosexual dramas of the colonial citizen-subject were played out for the benefit of rulers and ruled alike.[148]

Whether on its boulevards, in its theaters, or through its exhibitions, Malabari seized the opportunity to engage the spectacle of London and refashion it for his purposes precisely because it too was among the most recognizable symbols of English civilization. His "Indian eye" succeeded in making London the object of colonial scrutiny; in the process, it also transformed the Indian travel writer and his readers into civilized and discerning citizen-subjects capable of producing and consuming that quintessentially English commodity, London itself. This shift from being the cynosure *of* all eyes to possessing London *through* the colonial eye was not merely a rhetorical maneuver but, like all operations in the discursive domain, had political ramifications. In the first instance, the very act of walking the city was evidence of a certain claim to Englishness and civilization, and had been since the early nineteenth century.[149] Representing the Victorian city required another display of manliness and civilization: that is, the erasure of the self, or the "distillation of that self into an all-perceiving Eye."[150] For an Indian observer in fin de siècle London, this process required the representation of the Indian traveler as an "I," a *self*— as the subject or see-er, that is, rather than merely as the object of colonial rule. The capacity to represent the Western city conferred a certain kind of person- or subjecthood on Malabari; it also enabled him to claim authority over a kind of collective identity as well. For in an age when India was considered by most if not all Britons to be a set of centripetal communities and factions incapable of ever consolidating into a national whole (and hence unworthy of the gift of self-government), the "Indian" eye offered a persuasive challenge to that presumption by insisting that London, and with it, the United Kingdom, could be taken in and held by a centrifugal Indian "national" gaze. He was by no means alone. More than one late-nineteenth-century travel book written in English used the technology of the eye (*London and Paris through Indian Spectacles, England to an Indian Eye*) in its title, indicating the articulation of a desire to make a spectacle of London, its streets, and its imperial treasures — a desire coincident, significantly, with the emergence of an "Indian" "National" Congress.[151]

The fact that Malabari's trip to London was followed in *The Indian Eye* by a trip to Europe suggests too that he was keen to put Britain in its place on the larger geopolitical map, at the precise historical moment when Britain was experiencing a crisis of confidence over the future of its worldwide imperial dominion. This provincialization of Britain, made visible by the telescoping lens that Malabari and a variety of other Indian male travelers invariably turned on London, was both a deliberate strategy and an effect of the unfulfilled promise of national sovereignty at the heart of the imperial project, insofar as that promise required proof of Indians' ability to produce an urbane, national vision as evidence of their fitness for self-rule.[152] Not just the Indian National Congress but agitation in Ireland, trade wars with Germany and the United States, and, by the end of the century, the Boer War — all these combined to produce an unease about longevity of the Raj to which colonial men's travel writing such as Malabari's may have contributed, however subtly and imperceptibly. For there is some indication that the spectacle of empire being offered by these tours of London was not designed exclusively for Indian eyes. As the introduction to T. N. Mukharji's 1886 travelogue points out, the value of such guides was that "the European will learn to see himself as others see him."[153] It was an image not perhaps entirely flattering to metropolitan spectators, but one that nonetheless accurately reflected the availability of imperial London and of Victorian culture more generally for appropriation, challenge, and transformation by Britain's colonial subjects.

Epilogue

Presumptions about racism and the experience of colonialism often function as unelaborated givens in histories of the British Empire. The archive left behind by colonial travelers making "the voyage in" offers us a valuable opportunity to understand how they discovered themselves as both raced and colonial subjects through a variety of "encounters in social space and historical time" in Victorian Britain itself. It also furnishes us with an ethnography of social relations at the heart of the empire, where colonialism was not just commodified for worldwide markets but was made, contested, and remade in the more local spaces of the everyday — suggesting that the global and the local are mutually dependent in any given historical moment.[1] Despite the asymmetries of power that structure the colonial encounter, it is and has historically been dynamic and dialogic, just as it is and has historically been constituted by gender, sexuality, religion, caste, and class, as well as by race. If these categories have become axiomatic in recent scholarly discussions about identity, postcolonialism, and feminism, and if the nature of the colonial encounter appears (therefore) to be self-evident, it behooves us to remember how unstable and, finally, how unpredictable the intersection of history with cultural forms and human agency must invariably be. As the accounts of the three colonial travelers featured in this book suggest, cultural identities are negotiable, contingent, and ever shifting, largely because they are the product not of inheritance or origins alone but of *politics* at the micro- and the macrolevels, and in the most elastic sense of the word.[2]

Their variously politicized locations in the metropole meant that, to borrow from Regenia Gagnier, colonial travelers became both participants and antagonists as they encountered imperial culture in Victorian Britain — even while, significantly, their maneuvers often exceeded even that flexible frame of performance.[3] Though they thwarted and recast them through small acts and with localized gestures, Ramabai, Sorabji, and Malabari did not succeed in dismantling the colonial reform projects of which they were the targets or in which they were, at times, the collaborators. The burdens of representation that they bore reflect how readily "the Indian traveler" might be commodified in the late-nineteenth-century metropole, as well as how readily Sorabji and Malabari, at least, sought identification with a certain kind of bourgeois modernity. Unlike that of Ramabai, whose identification was with Indian women in India rather than with British imperial culture, their stories may be read as an attempt to articulate a liberal imperialist position inside the empire — one that resonated with the impulse toward federation that was gaining currency in high imperial politics toward the end of the century.[4] In an important sense, however, none of them could ever completely elude the power of empire to construct them as colonial. Moreover, the density of their ethnic, religious, and cultural affiliations, together with the scorn heaped on the very idea of an "Indian nation" in the Great Britain of the 1880s and 1890s, meant that even their identification as "Indian" was itself partly produced by travel to England. Nor could they escape the possibility that movement across the imperial landscape would shape the terms through which they spoke and were spoken about. Someone like Sorabji, who wished to be seen as an "authentic Indian woman" of her own making, ultimately relied upon the discursive frameworks provided by colonialism and its technologies as she both claimed and refused identification with a certain kind of "Hindu woman." Neither could Malabari, or Pandita Ramabai for that matter, circulate at the heart of the empire without reference to the abiding, signing presence of that particular trope.

That image, along with the more generic term "native," was both "historically sedimented" and "unevenly entrenched across social space" — which is to say that neither one had the same resonance in Victorian England as in nineteenth-century India; nor of course, do they have the same meanings today.[5] And yet as vestiges of the stock of culturally loaded terms left by Victorian imperialism, concepts like "the native" continue to do their work among displaced South Asian subjects in the present. As Radhika Mohanram, an "Indian national" who has lived in North America and New Zealand has noted with respect to her diasporic condition in the late twentieth century, "I had to be dislocated from the United States to become an American just as I had to leave India to become an Indian."[6] When the native becomes a traveler, a tourist, a student, or even a "resident," is that person still a native? The answer is contingent, of course, on circumstance and relations of power. For Ramabai, Sorabji, and Malabari, as for many contemporary former colonial peoples laboring under the "new world order" of the modern West, the answer was often, if not always, yes. This is perhaps especially true for anglophiles like Malabari and Sorabji since, as Homi Bhabha has observed, to be anglicized is, in the eyes of many Britons, emphatically *not* to be English.[7] The quest for fixed identities and the sanctification of "national" borders is, of course, part of the crisis of nationhood itself, a crisis set in motion by the border crossings characteristic of colonialism and postcolonialism as well. One effect of that crisis is that people on the move are under surveillance and their access to unmarked identities — which are most often apparently unfragmented national identities — is regulated. As Enoch Powell reminded Britons at the height of the immigration "problem" in the 1960s, "[T]he West Indian or Asian does not, by being born in England, become an Englishman. In law he becomes a United Kingdom citizen by birth; in fact he is a West Indian or Asian still."[8]

Powell's certainties notwithstanding, the ethnographies of Britain that these Indian travelers produced as they walked the streets of London, the halls of Somerville, and the corridors of Cheltenham and Wantage do not and indeed cannot leave the nation either untouched or at center stage. Travel is undoubtedly an enunciative act, producing a here and a there as the basis for identity.[9] For Indian travelers the trip to Britain may have mapped a home and an away but it also revealed the plurality, rather than simply the duality, of terrains available for appropriation by colonial subjects — making those terrains visible not just to the travelers themselves but to their English audiences and their Indian compatriots alike. Indians who transgressed the boundaries of empire mapped "domestic" culture as a component of, rather than as an antecedent to, the colonial enterprise, in part because they took that already imperialized territory to be their own. In fact, if travel to Britain defined them as "Indian," Indians making their way across British landscapes helped to define Britain as Britain — especially when "Britain" is seen not as a coherent, originary "national body" but rather as a site of struggle produced in part by contests over the meanings of imperial rule.[10]

Travel to Britain enabled colonial subjects like Ramabai, Sorabji, and Malabari to lay claim to a kind of imperial citizenship: to insist that they were mobile subjects at least partly of their own making rather than fixed as the objects of colonial reform projects to which a variety of English patrons tried to harness their futures. In the process, they revealed just how pervasive imperial assumptions were among Britons in Britain, and how readily colonial subjects could provincialize the heart of the empire as well.[11] While the exhibitionary effect produced by ethnographies is perhaps most visible in the kinds of displacements that are peculiar to colonial encounters, it is of course also characteristic of the terrain of culture more generally. Given the possibility that the very concept of culture qua culture emerged historically in conjunction with the fact of European colonialism itself, this is no mere historical accident.[12] If "culture" is in fact the outsiders' invention — a map made by others — colonial subjects must be counted among the makers of imperial culture in and beyond the parameters of late-nineteenth-century "Britain." Their perambulations troubled the complacency of a comfortably national people like the Victorians, just as their narratives offer modest but nonetheless remarkable challenges to the enduring fiction of Britain's historical insularity from empire.

Notes

Introduction

1. See Pratt, *Imperial Eyes*, 1–4.
2. Said, *Culture and Imperialism*, 6.
3. Hulme, "Subversive Archipelagos," 3.
4. John M. Mackenzie's editorship of the multivolume series, Studies in Imperialism, is responsible for much of the wealth of historical material now available on the impact of empire on domestic British culture. See for example his *Imperialism and Popular Culture* and *Propaganda and Empire*. Other relevant monographs include Sharpe, *Allegories of Empire*; Azim, *Colonial Rise of the Novel*; Hall, *White, Male and Middle Class*; Ware, *Beyond the Pale*; Burton, *Burdens of History*; Coombes, *Reinventing Africa*; Sinha, *Colonial Masculinity*; and Mc-Clintock, *Imperial Leather*.
5. For a trenchant rejection of empire's constitutive impact on home, see Mackenzie, *Orientalism*. For a less toxic but equally powerful refusal, see Marshall, "No Fatal Impact?" 8–10. For a more moderate articulation, see his "Imperial Britain" and his edited collection, *Cambridge Illustrated History*.
6. The phrase "cultures of movement" is Barnor Hesse's. See his "Black to Front and Black Again," 162–82. A recent exception to this trend is Gerzina, *Black London*.
7. See Gandhi, *Autobiography*; and James D. Hunt, *Gandhi in London*.
8. Stanley, "British Feminist Histories," 3.
9. See Catherine Hall, "Rethinking Imperial Histories," 3–29; Gerzina, *Black London*; Tabili, *"We Ask for British Justice"*; and Anna Marie Smith, *New Right Discourse on Race and Sexuality*.
10. Visram, *Ayahs*.
11. See John Osmond in Walter, "Irishness, Gender and Place," 43. For an attempt to work out what it meant to be Jewish in nineteenth- and twentieth-

century London at the level of the everyday, see Kushner, "Jew and Non-Jew in the East End of London," 32–52.

12. For a discussion of a different context in which the pedagogic is ethnographic, see Romero, "Vanishing Americans," 385–404, reprinted in Moon and Davidson, *Subjects and Citizens*, 87–105. I am grateful to Darlene Hantzis for this reference.

13. See the *Times* (London), November 2, 1922, p. 5, where Sorabji is listed as a class II under "Constitutional Law (English and Colonial) and legal History," and Office of Indian and Oriental Collections, MSS EUR F 165/116. The first English woman to qualify for the bar in Britain was Eliza Orme. See Howsam, " 'Sound-Minded Women,' "44–55. I am grateful to Jane Rendall for sharing this reference with me. Mitham Tata (née Lam) was also among the first crop of Indian women barristers according to her memoir, *Autumn Leaves: Some Memories of Yesteryear* (held privately and provided courtesy of Geraldine Forbes).

14. See Sinha, "Gender in the Critiques of Colonialism and Nationalism," 246–75.

15. This included the consummation of child marriages when the bride was under the age of twelve. According to Dagmar Engels, "[S]uch illegal sex was defined as rape and was punishable by a maximum of ten years imprisonment or transportation for life." See her "Age of Consent Act of 1891," 107; and Kosambi, "Girl-Brides and Socio-Legal Change," 1857–68. For the most recent and most skillful examination of Malabari's campaign to date, see Sinha, *Colonial Masculinity*, especially chapter 4; Nair also deals briefly with age-of-consent debates in *Women and Law*, 71–79.

16. Ortner, "Resistance and the Problem of Ethnographic Refusal," 173.

17. Janaki Agnes Penelope Majumdar, "Family History," 7. Unpublished manuscript provided courtesy of Amar Singh.

18. Gerzina, *Black London*, 204. Hesse, "Black to Front and Black Again," 162–82, challenges what he considers to be the dominant narrative of the history of black Britain. See also Fryer, *Staying Power*; Visram, *Ayahs*; and Holmes, *John Bull's Island*, 1–85.

19. I am borrowing the term "critical geography" here from Morrison, *Playing in the Dark*, especially chapter 1. For Victorian London as an imperial city, see Port, *Imperial London*; for the call to remap British history, see Marks, "History, the Nation and the Empire," 111–19; Stanley, "British Feminist Histories," 3–7; Antoinette Burton, " 'Rules of Thumb,' "483–500. For an assessment of empire's impact on Europe more generally, see Stoler, *Race and the Education of Desire*.

20. See Bill Schwarz, introduction to *The Expansion of England*, 1–8. For a discussion of how cultures express their will through the mapping of urban space, see Harvey, *Condition of Postmodernity*. The persistent disaggregation of Home and Away seems as tenacious as the "dialectical polarity" of separate spheres. See Vickery, "Golden Age to Separate Spheres?" 383–414.

21. Fryer, *Black People in the British Empire*, 7.

22. See Mackenzie, *Orientalism*. The quote is from Benita Parry, "Overlapping Territories and Intertwined Histories," 24.

23. I am grateful to Catherine Hall for pressing this point in conversation; see her *White, Male and Middle Class*, 1, and her essay, "Histories, Empires."

24. See MacDonald, *Language of Empire*, esp. chapter 2, entitled "Island Stories," as well as Glendenning, "School History Textbooks," 33; Said, *Culture and Imperialism*, 209; and Holmes, *Immigrants and Minorities in British Society*. See also Ware, "Island Racism," 65–86.

25. Gilroy, *Black Atlantic*, 7.

26. Quote is from Kureishi, *London Kills Me*, x; see also Fryer, *Black People in the British Empire*, especially xi–xv and 73–77.

27. Olaudah Equiano was a slave from Benin who purchased his freedom in 1766 and wrote his life story (*The Interesting Narrative of the Life of Olaudah Equiano*) in 1789; Mary Seacole was a Jamaican nurse who served in the Crimean War and wrote an account of it (*The Wonderful Adventures of Mrs. Seacole in Many Lands*); see Edwards and Dabydeen, *Black Writers in Britain, 1760–1890*. For newspaper coverage of the Major government's response to their inclusion in British history texts, see "The 'Betrayal' of Britain's History," *Daily Telegraph* (London), September 19, 1995; "Heroic Virtues" and "History Fit for (Politically Correct) Heroes," *The Sunday Telegraph* (London), September 24, 1995. I am grateful to Audrey Matkins for these references.

28. Dabydeen, "On Not Being Milton," 12. Kobena Mercer, for his part, calls Britain "a green and not-always-so-pleasant Third World Albion." See his *Welcome to the Jungle*, 8.

29. In 1888 Sir John Strachey assured Cambridge undergraduates, "[T]here is not, and never was an India, or even any country of India . . . no nation, no 'people of India' of which we hear so much . . . [T]hat the men of the Punjab, Bengal, the North-west Provinces, and Madras, should ever feel that they belong to one great Indian nation, is impossible." Quoted in Sumit Sarkar, *Modern India 1885–1947*, 2.

30. Sorabji, *India Calling*, ix. Harish Trivedi suggests that Rabindranath Tagore felt the same way. See *Colonial Transactions*, 56.

31. For an example of the latter see Killingray, *Africans in Britain*.

32. Gilroy, *Black Atlantic*, 10.

33. This was true both inside Maharashtra as well as outside it. See Kosambi, "Meeting of the Twain," 1–22. As Madhu Kishwar has noted, as early as the mid-1890s, the names of Pandita Ramabai, Cornelia Sorabji, and Rukhmabai were well-known among educated Punjabis and especially in the Arya Samaj, which was dedicated to the education of women and girls. See her "Daughters of Aryavarta," 103.

34. Lindeborg, " 'Asiatic' and the Boundaries of Victorian Englishness," 401; see also Catherine Hall, "Rethinking Imperial Histories."

35. Sinha, *Colonial Masculinity*, 9.

36. See Kaviraj, "Imaginary Institution of India," 33; and Sangari, "Relating Histories," 32–34.

37. See for example Bholanath Chandra's *Travels of a Hindoo* (1869) as discussed in Grewal's *Home and Harem*, 155–59.

38. See for example Baijnath, *England and India*; and Pillai, *London and Paris through Indian Spectacles*.

39. I am indebted to Sumathi Ramaswamy for this point. For a discussion of the production of ethnographies in travel literature to the New World in the early modern period, see Schwartz's introduction in *Implicit Understandings*, 3–5.

40. I am grateful to Laura Tabili for urging me to clarify this point.

41. I am aided in this conceptualization by Greg Dening's "P 905. A512 x 100," 864; see also his *Performances*; and Ross, "Grand Narrative in American Historical Writing," 676. For recent examples of this in British history see Vernon, *Politics and the People*; Walkowitz, *City of Dreadful Delight*; Joyce, *Democratic Subjects*; and Mayhall, "Creating the 'Suffragette Spirit,'" 319–44.

42. From the handlist, Oriental and India Office Collections, MSS. EUR. F. 165, p. 1. Thanks to Philippa Levine for securing me a photocopy of the handlist.

43. *Pandita Ramabai yancha Englandcha Pravas* (1883). See Kosambi, *Pandita Ramabai's Feminist and Christian Conversions*.

44. See Adrienne Rich, "Notes towards a Politics of Location," where she compels feminists to ask "[W]here, when and under what conditions has the statement been true?" (214).

45. Indeed, with critics like James Clifford arguing that expatriate Indians have not and do not constitute a "true" diaspora, boundary keeping is at work even as diasporic movements are being historicized. See his "Diasporas," 302–38. For a counterargument, see Women of South Asian Descent Collective, *Our Feet Walk the Sky*.

46. Harvey, *Condition of Postmodernity*, 238.

47. Said, *Culture and Imperialism*, 7.

48. See Carr, "Crossing the First World/Third World Divides," 154.

49. Breckenridge, "Aesthetics and Politics of Colonial Collecting," 197. I am grateful to Barbara Ramusack for this reference.

50. See Boyce Davies's discussion of how Latinos/Latinas have reconceptualized America in her *Black Women, Writing, and Identity*, 10; Appadurai, "Heart of Whiteness," 796; and Linebaugh, "All the Atlantic Mountains Shook," 87–121.

51. This is a paraphrase of Kobena Mercer's "why the need for nation?" See *Welcome to the Jungle*, 5 and 31.

52. Sangari, "Relating Histories," 32.

53. See Catherine Hall, "Histories, Empires," 76. For an extended reflection on this theme see Chow, *Writing Diaspora*, 15 and ff. Vera Kutzinski argues that Cuban nationalism has historically been an exception. See her *Sugar's Secrets*.

54. See Dirks's introduction to *Colonialism and Culture*, 6.

55. Bannerji, *Thinking Through*, 23; and Robb, introduction to *Concept of Race*, 40. See also di Leonardo, "White Ethnicities, Identity Politics, and Baby Bear's Chair," 165–91.

56. While this idea is a commonplace of feminist and postcolonial theories, it has been less enthusiastically embraced by historians of Western metropolitan cultures. For an interesting exception, see Joyce, *Democratic Subjects*.

57. Loomba, "Dead Women Tell No Tales," 223.

58. Quote is from Ahmad, *In Theory*, 6; see also Walkowitz, *City of Dreadful*

Delight, 9–10. These are borrowings from and transformations of Karl Marx's claim that "men make their own history, but they do not make it just as they please; they do not make it under circumstances chosen by themselves, but under circumstances directly found, given and transmitted from the past." *The Eighteenth Brumaire of Louis Bonaparte* (1852; New York: International Publishers, 1963).

59. See Niranjana, Sudhir, and Dhareshwar, *Interrogating Modernity*, 7.

60. I am borrowing here from Mankekar's "Reflections on Diasporic Identities," 350. I am grateful to Madhavi Kale for sharing this reference with me.

61. Susan Stanford Friedman calls this "relational positionality," a strategy for reading that she offers as a counter to the polarities of "white versus other" in contemporary popular discourse. See her "Beyond White and Other," 1–49. I am grateful to Philippa Levine, Laura Tabili, and Susan Thorne for insisting on this point.

62. Sangari, "Politics of the Possible," 264.

63. See Kosambi, *At the Intersection of Gender Reform and Religious Belief*, 38–45. For a discussion of the complex and dangerous social locations of the Christian convert, though one that does not make gender a focus, see Viswanathan, "Coping with (Civil) Death," 183–210. For the most recent discussion of Ramabai's engagements with Indian nationalists after her return to India, see Grewal, *Home and Harem*, 203–208.

64. See Cooper and Stoler, "Tensions of Empire," 610; and Tanika Sarkar, "Rhetoric against Age of Consent: Resisting Colonial Reason in the Death of a Child-Wife," 1869–78.

65. Loomba, "Dead Women Tell No Tales," 209–27; and Sinha, "Gender in the Critiques of Colonialism and Nationalism," 246–75.

66. Chow, *Writing Diaspora*, 26; and Mani, "Female Subject," 274 and ff. See also Alcoff, "Problem of Speaking for Others," 5–32; and Griffiths, "Myth of Authenticity," 70–71.

67. For a critique of the normative impulses of some identity politics, see Butler, "Imitation and Gender Subordination," 13–31. The quote is from Dening, "P 905.A512 x 100," 861. Patrick Joyce calls this maneuver an "anthropological intervention." See his *Democratic Subjects*, 14.

68. See Fraser, "Reply to Zylan," 531.

69. I am drawing here for the latter point on R. Radhakrishnan's critiques of identity in his "Postcolonialism and the Boundaries of Identity," 759.

70. Brown, "Polyrhythms and Improvisation," 85–90; and Boyce Davies, *Black Women, Writing, and Identity*, 8.

71. Leslie Flemming treats Ramabai and Sorabji together on the grounds that they were converts, along with a third Indian Christian woman who was their contemporary, Krupabai Satthianadhan. See "Between Two Worlds," 81–107. See also Tuson, *Queen's Daughters*; Kosambi, "Indian Response to Christianity, Church and Colonialism," WS 61–71 and "Gender Reform and Competing State Controls over Women," 265–90; Sinha, *Colonial Masculinity*, chapter 4; and Burton, *Burdens of History*.

72. Vinay Lal, "Incident of the 'Crawling Lane,' "37.

73. See Stuart Hall, "Cultural Identity and Cinematic Representation," 68.

74. See Gouda, *Dutch Culture Overseas*, 6. For an elaboration of this point in another context, see Blunt, "Mapping Authorship and Authority," 53; and Fraser, "Reply," 532.

75. The term "identity project" is Amina Mama's. See her *Beyond the Masks*, 156.

76. According to John R. Hinnells, Parsis in the nineteenth century believed that they were "the most British-like of all the races." See his "Parsi Zoroastrians in London," 258.

77. Sorabji, *India Calling*, 52.

78. See Cornwall and Lindisfarne, *Dislocating Masculinity*, 1–8.

79. Bhabha, *Location of Culture*, 2.

80. Thanks to Alison Fletcher for helping me to articulate this point.

81. Santha Rama Rau experienced this phenomenon on her return to India after living in Britain as a girl; see her chapter "On Learning to Be an Indian," in *Home to India*, 13–25.

82. See Grewal and Kaplan, *Scattered Hegemonies*, esp. chapter 1.

83. For a similar approach to historical "subjects," see Kutzinski, *Sugar's Secrets*; Bederman, *Manliness and Civilization*; and Scott, *"Only Paradoxes to Offer."*

84. Code, *Rhetorical Spaces*, ix. Elsewhere Code labels these the speaker's or knower's "necessary and sufficient conditions" and calls for a "new *geography* of the epistemic terrain." See her "Taking Subjectivity into Account," 15 and 39. Emphasis in the original. Faith L. Smith describes how Sandra Pouchet-Pacquet reads the differences between Mary Seacole's and Mary Prince's narratives as evidence of their various social locations. See Smith's "Coming Home to the Real Thing," 901.

85. Walter, "Irishness, Gender and Place," 35; see also Blunt and Rose's introduction to *Women Writing and Space*, 5.

86. See for example Kelly, "Diaspora and World War," 476, 482. Kelly calls on scholars to banish the "identity fetish" from their vocabularies (487).

87. The idea of gender as performance, from which I derive much of this analysis, is from Butler's *Gender Trouble*. The quote is from Kutzinski, *Sugar's Secrets*, xiii; see also Faith Smith, "Coming Home," 902.

88. This is Bill Schwarz, "Memories of Empire," quoting Stuart Hall in Bammer, *Displacements*, 157.

89. See Scott, "Evidence of Experience," 773–97.

90. De Certeau, *Practice of Everyday Life*, xxiv.

91. This is Caren Kaplan quoting Chandra Mohanty in "Reconfigurations of Geography and Historical Narrative," 26. For a similar sentiment see Adrienne Rich, *Atlas of the Difficult World*, 6.

92. Boyce Davies, *Black Women, Writing, and Identity*, 22. See also Blunt and Rose's introduction to *Women Writing and Space*, 1.

93. I am borrowing from the insight of Eleni Varikas here, who suggests that late-twentieth-century feminist historians are working in diaspora, between social history on the one hand and "deconstruction" on the other. I am not embracing the dichotomous in-between that she maps, nor am I satisfied with the particular polarity she sets up; but I have found her use of the concept helpful

nonetheless. See "Gender, Experience and Subjectivity," 101. See also Kaplan, "Deterritorialization," 187–98.

94. Bhabha, *Location of Culture*, 9.

95. Painter, "Three Southern Women and Freud," 212; Cohen, *Combing of History*, 13. I am grateful to Joan Scott for pressing me on this point as well.

96. For an important example of the critique of the discursive turn in feminist theory, see Ebert's *Ludic Feminism and After*.

97. O'Connell et al., "Editorial," 787–96; Mbilinyi, "Research Methodologies in Gender Issues," 35; Connolly et al., "Editorial," 1–4; and Boyce Davies, *Black Women, Writing, and Identity*.

98. Meaghan Morris, "Man in the Mirror," 257. Many thanks to Saloni Mathur for this reference.

99. Kaminsky, "Gender, Race, *Raza*," 7–31. Thanks to Maria Lima for this reference. See also Brown, "Polyrhythms," 85–90.

100. Thorne, " 'Conversion of Englishmen,' " 238–62; and Kale, "Casting Labor in the Imperial Mold," provided courtesy of the author. For other examples of this claim at work, see Martinez-Alier, *Marriage, Class and Colour in Nineteenth-Century Cuba*, 82 and passim; and Frankenberg and Mani, "Crosscurrents, Crosstalk," 292–310.

101. See for example Tanika Sarkar, "Rhetoric against Age of Consent," 1869–78.

102. Feierman, "Africa in History," 50. For an interesting example of this in practice, see Demos, *Unredeemed Captive*.

103. Stoler, " 'Mixed-Bloods,' "145.

Chapter 1. The Voyage In

1. Quoted in Holmes, *John Bull's Island*, 31.

2. For a complex and shrewd analysis of the role of the British Museum in national-imperial culture, see Grewal, "The Guidebook and the Museum: Imperialism, Education and Nationalism in the British Museum," *Bucknell Review* 34 (1990): 195–217, recast in her recent *Home and Harem* as chapter 3.

3. Visram, *Ayahs*, 178.

4. Banerjea, *Nation in Making*, 12; Sanyal, *General Biography*, 17.

5. See Gandhi, *Autobiography*, 3–70.

6. Fryer, *Staying Power*, xi.

7. Shyllon, *Black People in Britain, 1555–1833*, 3.

8. In Hugh Kearney's *British Isles*, for example, the two chapters entitled "The Britannic Melting Pot" and "The Rise of Ethnic Politics" turn out to refer to the cultural mix and political aspirations of the Celtic fringe against "Englishness." Richard Price, who opens his 1996 essay on "Historiography, Narrative and the Nineteenth Century" with the claim that "the narrative stories of nineteenth-century British history have been pulled seriously out of joint," scarcely mentions empire (220–56).

9. Kim F. Hall, *Things of Darkness*, 133.

10. Ballard, *Desh Pardesh*, 8.

11. Williams, *Capitalism and Slavery*, 44, 142, 190; Walvin, *Slavery and the Slave Trade*, especially chapter 8; Hecht, "Continental and Colonial Servants," 37; McCalman, *Radical Underworld*, chapter 3; Gerzina, *Black London*.

12. See Fletcher, " 'God Shall Wipe All Tears from Their Eyes,' " provided courtesy of the author. See also Mackrell, *Hariru Wikitoria!*

13. Stock, *History*, 382; see also Collins, *Moonstone*, esp. FN. 3, p. 526.

14. Bolt, *Victorian Attitudes towards Race*, ix. Emphasis added.

15. Lorimer, *Colour, Class and the Victorians*; Paul Rich, *Race and Empire in British Politics* and "Black Diaspora in Britain," 151–73; File and Power, *Black Settlers in Britain, 1555–1958*; Walvin, *Black and White*. See also Scobie, *Black Britannia*; Lotz and Pegg, *Under the Imperial Carpet*; Tabili, *"We Ask for British Justice"*; Killingray, *Africans in Britain*; Gundara and Duffield, *Essays on the History of Blacks*; and McClintock, *Imperial Leather*.

16. For primary texts, see for example Edwards and Dabydeen, *Black Writers in Britain, 1760–1890*; Alexander and Dewjee, *Wonderful Adventures of Mrs. Seacole in Many Lands*; and Moira Ferguson, *History of Mary Prince, a West Indian Slave*.

17. Kathleen Wilson, "Citizenship, Empire and Modernity," 82.

18. George, *London Life in the Eighteenth Century*, 134.

19. Fryer, *Staying Power*, 235; Killingray, *Africans in Britain*, 2; Visram, *Ayahs*, 53; see also Gilroy, *Black Atlantic*; and Braidwood, *Black Poor and White Philanthropists*.

20. Fryer, *Staying Power*, 236; Nicholson, *Strangers to England*, 80; Walvin, *Black and White*, 189–201; Stedman Jones, *Outcast London*. The 1921 Census for the county of London documented that there were slightly more than twenty thousand "presumptively black" inhabitants (including people from the Indian Empire, Ceylon, Egypt, West African colonies, and the West Indies). See Tabili, "Reconstructing Black Migration in the Imperial Metropolis, 1900–1939."

21. The same racialism applied to "blacks" in the British Empire could be turned on the Irish as well. Two essays that are particularly thoughtful about the historical relations between the Irish and "Indians" are Gibbon, "Race against Time," 95–117; and Muldoon, "Indian as Irishman," 267–89. Thanks to Angela Woollacott for urging me to emphasize this point. For a history of Jewish communities in Britain, see Feldman, *Englishmen and Jews*; for the racialization of one of Victorian Britain's most public Jewish men, see Wohl, "Dizzi-Ben-Dizzi," 375–411.

22. Winter, *London's Teeming Streets, 1830–1914*; and Walkowitz, "Daughter of Empire."

23. See Henry Mayhew, *London Labour and the London Poor*; Doré and Blanchard, *London*, 146; "A Walk Round the Colonies," *Pall Mall Gazette*, May 4, 1886, p. 1; Collins, *Moonstone*. For a recent study of the representation of empire in Victorian fiction, see David, *Rule Britannia*.

24. Deakin, Cohen, and MacNeal, *Colour, Citizenship and British Society*, 31.

25. Among such representations is George Sims's *Edwardian London*, first published in three volumes in 1902 by Cassell and Co., Ltd., under the title *Living London*. I consulted volume 1 of the reprint. Individual "others" could interrupt the field of vision of the reader-consumer in brief but revealing con-

texts; see for example, Doré and Blanchard *London*. The term "scopic feast" is Coombes's. See her "Inventing the 'Postcolonial,' "43.

26. Henry Thompson, "Indian and Colonial London," 306–11. Thanks to Angela Woollacott for this reference.

27. Gilroy, *Black Atlantic*, 122.

28. Morrison, *Playing in the Dark*, 5, 9, and 14.

29. Frankenberg and Mani, "Crosscurrents, Crosstalk," 298.

30. See Said, *Culture and Imperialism*, xi–xxviii; and Bhabha, "Other Question," 71–87, esp. p. 72.

31. Women of South Asian Descent Collective, *Our Feet Walk the Sky*.

32. For an insightful discussion of the Aryan myth and its consequences for racism among South Asians, see Mazumdar, "Racist Responses to Racism," 47–55.

33. For an examination of the Indian lobby's various radical connections, see Morrow, "Origins and Early Years of the British Committee of the Indian National Congress, 1885–1907"; and S. B. Cook, *Imperial Affinities*.

34. Duffield, "Dusé Mohammed Ali," 124–49.

35. Visram, *Ayahs*, 24–25, 56–57.

36. As John R. Hinnells points out, though they were political opponents (Bhownaggree was a critic of the Indian National Congress), the two collaborated nonetheless — as, for example, in the Parsi Association, founded in London in 1861. See his "Parsi Zoroastrians in London," 258–59.

37. Salter, *Asiatic in England*, 182. I am grateful to Philippa Levine for introducing me to this source. Perhaps this was what Henry James referred to when he wrote that "the edge of Westminster evokes as many associations of misery as of empire. The neighbourhood has been much purified of late, but it still contains a collection of specimens . . . of the low, black element." See his "London," in Henry James, *Collected Travel Writings*, 30 (original essay first published in 1888).

38. Salter, *East in the West*.

39. Biswanath Das, *Autobiography of an Indian Princess*, esp., chapters 9 and 10.

40. See above, notes 6 and 7. For an example of the persistence of this investigative tradition into the twentieth century, see J. Parry, "New Britons," 17–25; December 5, 1971, 14–18 and 21–22; and December 12, 1971, 38–41, 43–44 — all of which peer into the urban and local spaces of Britain to observe "colonial immigrants" at work.

41. For reproductions of photographs and engravings of the exhibition, see Vadgama, *India in Britain*; for an example of coverage by newspapers, see *The Saturday Review* for May 8, May 22, June 5, June 19, July 17, and July 24, 1886.

42. See Kale, "Casting Labor in the Imperial Mold," unpublished paper provided courtesy of the author.

43. Gupta, *Indians Abroad*, 27; and Rajkumar, *Indians outside India*.

44. Jain, *Indian Communities Abroad*, 1; Tinker, *Banyan Tree*, 8.

45. "The Ameer Abdurrahman," *Times*, May 7, 1884, p. 6.

46. Kim F. Hall, *Things of Darkness*, 11.

47. "Ram Mohun Roy," *The Saturday Review*, July 7, 1888, p. 21.

48. Ibid., 22.

49. He stayed with John and Joseph Hare, brothers of David Hare, whom Roy knew from Calcutta. He landed in Liverpool in April of 1831 and made his way to London from there; he also traveled to France on this trip, though he experienced some difficulty in obtaining the necessary papers to cross the channel. See Brajendra Nath Banerji, "Last Days of Rajah Rammohun Roy," *The Modern Review*, 381–83.

50. Carpenter, *Last Days in England of the Rajah Rammohun Roy*, 80. For an account of Hill's career and reform interests, see Gorham, "Victorian Reform as a Family Business," 119–47. Thanks to Philippa Levine for bringing this reference to my attention.

51. See Brajendra Nath Banerji, "Sutherland's Reminiscences of Rammohun Roy," 65.

52. Carpenter, *Last Days*, p. 81.

53. Brajendra Nath Banerji, "Sutherland's Reminiscences of Rammohun Roy," 70. Many years later Edward Thompson, in an interesting parallel, insisted that Tagore's "feminine contradictoriness" was a crucial part of his character. See E. P. Thompson, *Alien Homage*, 49.

54. Carpenter, *Last Days*, 21.

55. Ibid., 61.

56. Ibid., 60.

57. See Brajendra Nath Banerji, "Rajah Rammohun Roy's Mission to England," 391–97, 561–65; "Rammohun Roy's Political Mission to England," 18–21, 160–65; "Rammohun Roy in the Service of the East India Company," 570–76; "Rammohun Roy's Embassy to England," 49–61.

58. See Manton, *Mary Carpenter and the Children of the Streets*; Barbara Ramusack, "Cultural Missionaries, Maternal Imperialists, Feminist Allies," 119–36; and Antoinette Burton, "Fearful Bodies into Disciplined Subjects," 545–74.

59. For a fuller discussion of the impact of India on female reform and feminist circles in Victorian Britain, see Burton, *Burdens of History*.

60. Brown, *Origins of an Asian Democracy*, 161–62.

61. See Borthwick, *Keshub Chunder Sen*, chapter 3.

62. Keshub Chunder Sen to Frances Power Cobbe, 10 September, 1869; Frances Power Cobbe Papers, Huntingdon Library Archives, Los Angeles, California. I am grateful to George Robb for this citation. See also Borthwick, *Keshub Chunder Sen*, 95–96.

63. P. C. Majumdar, *Life and Teachings of Keshub Chunder Sen*, 142.

64. Burton, *Burdens of History*. See also Burton, "Fearful Bodies into Disciplined Subjects," 545–74.

65. P. C. Majumdar, *Life and Teachings*, 144

66. Ibid.

67. Cobbe, *Life*, vol. 2, 452.

68. *Keshub Chunder Sen in England: Diaries, Sermons, Addresses and Epistles*, 26.

69. Borthwick, *Keshub Chunder Sen*, 100; F. Max Muller, *Biographical Essays*, 72.

70. P. C. Majumdar, *Life and Teachings*, 143.

71. Quoted in Borthwick, *Keshub Chunder Sen*, 108 and 132.

72. Borthwick, *Keshub Chunder Sen*, 101.

73. Cobbe, *Life*, 451. For a similar reading by an English woman of an Indian man in Britain at about the same time, see Captain Edward C. West, *Diary of the Late Rajah of Kolhapoor*, 136–40.

74. Cobbe, *Life*, 451.

75. *Keshub Chunder Sen in England*, 37.

76. P. C. Majumdar, *Life and Teachings*, 144–45.

77. Borthwick, *Keshub Chunder Sen*, 120.

78. Ibid., 46–47.

79. Ibid., 142. Sen gave no public explanation for his decision and, as Borthwick recounts, was extremely concerned about its impact on his international reputation. See *Keshub Chunder Sen*, 182 and ff. She suggests that pressure from the British administration of Cooch Behar was a factor. In fact, Keshub objected to the fact that the Maharaja was a minor (15) and his daughter was not yet 14; that the marriage was not performed with Brahmo rites; and that Keshub was excluded from the ceremony because he had lost his caste. I am grateful to Geraldine Forbes for these details.

80. *Keshub Chunder Sen in England*, 462.

81. Borthwick, *Keshub Chunder Sen*, 174. See also the *Times*'s obituary on Sen, Jan 10, 1884, p. 7.

82. "Ram Mohun Roy," *The Saturday Review*, July 7, 1888, pp. 21–22.

83. Nowrojee and Merwanjee, *Residence of Two Years and a Half in Great Britain*, 28.

84. Ibid., 31.

85. Ibid., 299.

86. Ibid., 24.

87. See for example Koolee Meerza, *Journal of a Residence in England*, 258–62. I am grateful to David Pike for this reference. See also Ragaviah, *Pictures*, 44; Dasa, *Reminiscences*, 37; and Ram, *My Trip*, 10 and 28.

88. Meerza, *Journal of a Residence*, 260. See also Tarakoli-Targhi, "Orientalism's Genesis Amnesia," 1–14.

89. See Malabari, *Indian Eye*, 33–34; and Mary Hobhouse, "Further Sketches by an Indian Pen," *Indian Magazine and Review* (March 1890): 145. The "Indian Pen" was M. Hasan Khan, who visited England in the spring and summer of 1888. Jhinda Ram recounted that the first person to "welcome" him when he got off the boat in Liverpool was a woman hailing him as follows: " 'Why don't you take me with you!' " It was "Horrible, horrible indeed," he recalled, "to get such a welcome when one goes to a country to seek enlightenment! I heeded her not, and proceeded on my way." *My Trip*, 8.

90. Sorabji, *India Calling*, 52.

91. This is an idea put forward by Michael Levenson in his National Endowment for the Humanities Summer Seminar, "The Culture of London, 1850–1925," 1995.

92. Levenson, "Culture of London, 1850–1925"; Mukharji, *Visit*, 105. For a fuller account of Indian men in London, see Burton, "Making a Spectacle of Empire," 96–117.

93. See for example Onwhyn, *Mr. and Mrs. Brown's Visit to London*; and Henry Sutherland Edwards, *Official Account of the Chinese Commission*.

94. Coombes, *Reinventing Africa*.

95. Desmond, *India Museum; Empire of India: Special Catalog of Exhibits*; and Cundall, *Reminiscences*.

96. Rakhal Haldar Das, *Diary*, 57. According to David Kopf, Das was a Brahmo. See *Brahmo Samaj and the Shaping of the Modern Indian Mind*, 30.

97. See Donna Haraway, "Teddy Bear Patriarchy: Taxidermy in the Garden of Eden, New York City, 1908–36," in her *Primate Visions*, 28.

98. Ibid. For an echo of Das's critical melancholia, see Boon, "Why Museums Make Me Sad," 255–77.

99. Ragaviah, *Pictures*, 68.

100. Dutt, *Three Years in Europe*, 123.

101. See Grewal's *Home and Harem*, 91 and chapter 3.

102. Ram, *My Trip*, 34–38.

103. Not only was Ceylon disaggregated from India in both the Great Exhibition of 1851 and the Colonial and Indian Exhibition of 1886, but more than one Indian traveler included the island in his grand tour. See *Great Exhibition of the Works of Industry of All Nations*, vol. 2, "British Possessions in Asia: India and Ceylon"), 857–938. The text breaks down the distinction further between the "East Indies" (857–937) and "Ceylon" (937–38); note the proportional difference in coverage (fifty pages versus two pages). See also Cundall, *Reminiscences*, "Plan" (n.p.), which shows Ceylon's one court dwarfed by the plethora of Indian display sites. For examples of Indian men who constructed Ceylon as a tourist site, see Dasa, *Reminiscences*; and Baijnath, *England and India*.

104. Mukharji, *Visit*, 100–107. For another virtually contemporary example of this taxonomic racism on the part of a Bengali, see Sinha, *Colonial Masculinity*, 92.

105. Ram, *My Trip*, 11.

106. Dutt, *Three Years in Europe*, iii.

107. See, for example, *The Mahratta*, February 28, 1886, p. 8.

108. Among the institutions devoted to "superintending" Indians in Britain in this period were the Asiatics' Home, the Oriental Institute at Woking, the Northbrook Indian Club, and the National Indian Association.

109. Dutt, *Three Years in Europe*, 153.

110. Emphasis in the original.

111. Dutt, *Three Years in Europe*, 144–45.

112. Tagore, *Reminiscences*, 157–77.

113. See the *Journal of the National Indian Association* (later the *Indian Magazine and Review [IMR]*]) for 1871–1895.

114. Rakhal Haldar Das, *Diary*, 50.

115. Malabari, *Indian Eye*, 188.

116. Janaki Agnes Penelope Majumdar, "Family History," 46.

117. Tagore, *Reminiscences*, 159.

118. Ibid., 169–74.

119. Wasti, *Memoirs and Other Writings*, 22–23. Alexander Crummell, an African American arriving in Britain in the 1840s, agreed, recalling, "My black

complexion is a great advantage and a real possession here, connected with other real qualities I am supposed to possess." See Wilson Jeremiah Jones, *Alexander Crummell*, 53. Thanks to Herman Bennett for this reference.

120. Rakhal Haldar Das, *Diary*, 88; Albion Rajkumar Banerji, *Indian Pathfinder*, 25.

121. Salter, *East in the West*, 19.

122. Duff, *Queen Victoria's Highland Journals*, 360. See also Vadgama, *India in Britain*.

123. For a discussion of this phenomenon in general terms, see Grewal, *Home and Harem*, 139–41.

124. Gandhi, *Autobiography*, 30–34; Sanyal, *General Biography*, 20.

125. Janaki Agnes Penelope Majumdar, "Family History," 12.

126. Albion Rajkumar Banerji, *Indian Pathfinder*, 24.

127. Banerjea, *Nation in Making*, 16.

128. See Dutt, *Romesh Chunder Dutt*, 12–14. Monmohun Ghose's father also died while he was in Britain, and because he had broken caste by crossing the "black waters," he could not perform the religious ceremonies connected with his father's passing when he did return to India. Quoted in Radford, *Indian Journal*, 171–72.

129. Wasti, *Memoirs*, 22 and 24–29. For an account by another Muslim traveler, see Sayyid Ahmad Khan's trip to England in 1869–70; see also Lelyveld, *Aligarh's First Generation*, 104–18.

130. Albion Rajkumar Banerji, *Indian Pathfinder*, 22–23.

131. Ibid., 31.

132. Gandhi, *Autobiography*, 54–60. He publicly announced his marital status in a vegetarian magazine in 1891 (after more than two years in London), as part of an interview about why he had come to Britain and how he experienced life there. See *Collected Works*, 57. For a discussion that contextualizes Gandhi's relationship to celibacy, see Alter, "Celibacy", 45–66.

133. Gosse, *Ancient Ballads*, 12–28; see also Harihar Das, *Life and Letters of Toru Dutt*; and Grewal, *Home and Harem*, 163–65.

134. Janaki Agnes Penelope Majumdar, "Family History."

135. See Tharu and Lalita, *Women Writing*, vol. 1, 329.

136. For a brief account of Joshi's time in the United States, see Rachel Bodley's introduction to Pandita Ramabai's *High-Caste Hindu Woman*, i–xxiv (Bodley was the dean of the Philadelphia College of Medicine for Women); and Dall, *Life of Dr. Anandabai Joshee*. I am grateful to Geraldine Forbes for the latter reference.

137. Shah, *Letters and Correspondence of Pandita Ramabai*; Sorabji, *India Calling*.

138. She was the paternal aunt of Mridula Sarabhai. See Basu, "Nationalist Feminist," 3.

139. Gandhi, *Autobiography*, 31.

140. As did other metropolitan commentators at the time, Kipling saved his contempt for Western-educated Indian men whom he believed did not exhibit a sufficiently chivalrous attitude toward Rukhmabai: "Graduate reformers with an English Education — / Lights of Aryavata take our heartiest applause, / For

the spectacle you offer of an 'educated' nation / Working out its freedom under 'educated' laws . . . / You can lecture government, draught a resolution . . . / Never such an opening for touching elocution / As the text of Rukhmibai [*sic*], jailed by Hindu law. / What? No word of protest? Not a sign of pity? / Not a hand to help the girl, but, in black and white / Writes the leading oracle of the leading city: / 'We the Indian nation, *we* hold it served her right.' " Rutherford, *Early Verse by Rudyard Kipling*, 373–74.

141. Rukhmabai trained at the LSMW; Ganguli, at Bengal Medical College and later at Edinburgh. For details of Rukhmabai's medical career, see letter from S. Bhatia, president of the Association for Medical Women in India, April 17, 1967 (Wellcome Institute for the History of Medicine, SFA/MWF/c. 144); *Report of the Cama Hospital's Jubilee Fund* (where she had been a house surgeon in 1895) (Wellcome Institute for the History of Medicine, SFA/MWF/ c. 146, 1936), pp. 14–17; Lutzker, *Edith Pechey-Phipson, M.D.*, 199–208; and Kosambi, "Meeting of the Twain", esp. 7–12. For Ganguli, see Karlekar, *Voices from Within*, 173–78. A Miss Jagannadhan also studied at the LSMW; see *IMR* (February 1891): 89.

142. See Maneesha Lal, "Politics of Gender and Medicine in Colonial India," 29–66; and Forbes, "Medical Careers and Health Care for Indian Women," 515–30.

143. Visram, *Ayahs*, 49.

144. Ibid., 49.

145. Ibid., 25

146. Salter, *East in the West*, 150.

147. Ibid., v–vi.

148. Ibid., 24.

149. Visram, *Ayahs*, 24–25.

150. Stock, *History*, vol. 2, 383. For an analysis of Salter's writings, see Lindeborg, " 'Asiatic,' "381–404.

151. *Times*, May 15, 1883, p. 5.

152. Ibid.

153. *Times*, May 22, 1883, p. 10.

154. *Times*, May 16, 1883, p. 9.

155. *Times*, May 22, 1883, p. 10.

156. *Times*, May 15, 1883, p. 5.

157. Anstey, *Baboo Hurry Bungsho Jabberjee, M.A.* Babus were also a figure of ridicule in India because of their anglicized manners and alleged pretensions. See for example Mokshodayani Mukhopadhyay (sister of W. C. Bonnerjee), from "Bangalir Babu" ("the Bengali Babu"), in Tharu and Lalita, *Women Writing*, vol. 1, 21–221. For a discussion of miscegenation fears in Britain in the interwar years, see Tabili, *"We Ask for British Justice,"* especially chapter 7.

158. Sir Gerald Fitzgerald, ADC, was one personal link between the two establishments. See Visram, *Ayahs*, 24 and 180 and the *Times* for May 15, 16 and 22, 1883.

159. Visram, *Ayahs*, 172 and 180.

160. See for example Sorabji to her parents, February 2, 1890, Oriental and India Office Collections, MSS EUR F 165/2; and the *Indian Magazine and Re-*

view (December 1892): 622, where she and Rukhmabai are reported as having attended the same NIA soiree.

161. Gandhi, *Autobiography*, 61–64.

162. Janaki Agnes Penelope Majumdar, "Family History," 59.

163. "Objects of the Association," *Journal of the National Indian Association* (October 1874): 240–42.

164. "Medical Women for India," *JNIA* (December 1882): 681–84. For a more detailed account of the NIA's relationship to the emergent community of British women doctors, see Burton, "Contesting the Zenana," 368–97.

165. "Ourselves," *IMR* (January 1892): 2.

166. "Objects," *JNIA*, 240–41.

167. *Keshub Chunder Sen in England*, 160; Wasti, *Memoirs*, 31.

168. Cornelia Sorabji to her parents, Jan 17, 1892, OIOC, MSS EUR F 165/6.

169. See for example S. Satthianadhan, "Indian Students and English Universities," *JNIA* (November 1880): 603–16.

170. 'Piyarilal,' "The Hindus in England," *JNIA* (June 1884): 281.

171. See for example *Handbook of Information Relating to University and Professional Studies*. For an exception to the male-oriented literature, see Lady Mary Hobhouse and Madeleine Shaw-Lefevre, "Colleges for Women in England," *IMR* (March 1891): 141–47; and Sorabji's reaction to it, OIOC, MSS EUR F 165/4, April 5, 1891.

172. See "The Natives of India," *The Times of India*, Overland Weekly Edition, November 20, 1876, pp. 12–13. I am grateful to Dane Kennedy for providing me with the text of this article. For an example of how this kind of "commonplace" made its way into late-Victorian popular fiction, see Cumberland, *Fatal Affinity*.

173. "Publications of the Oriental University Institute, with a Short Account of the Adjoining Mosque and Museum," *The Imperial, Asiatic Quarterly Review and Oriental and Colonial Record*, n.s. 2 (July 1891), p. 222.

174. The phrase "hopeful travelers" is Manab Thakur's and Roger Wilson's; see their "Hopeful Travelers," 476–92.

175. "Superintendence of Indian Students in England," *JNIA* (September 1885): 407. For an extended discussion of clothing as both a technology of colonial rule and a site for "native" contestation, see Tarlo, *Clothing Matters*, 23–61; and Timothy Burke, *Lifebuoy Men, Lux Women*, esp. chapter 4.

176. See Bannerji, "Textile Prison," 27–45, reprinted in Ray, *From the Seams of History: Essays on Indian Women*, 67–106.

177. Janaki Agnes Penelope Majumdar, "Family History," 119.

178. See Cornelia Sorabji to her parents, OIOC, MSS EUR F 165/1, December 12, 1889 and MSS EUR F 165/2, January 26, 1890.

179. See for example Satthianadhan, "Indian Students," 603–16; and (anon.) "Struggles of a Hindu Student Who Comes to England," *IMR* (August 1891): 386–91. Gandhi also wrote home expressing concern about the cost of living in England. See *Collected Works*, 23 and 55–56.

180. "The Superintendence Committee of the National Indian Association," *IMR* (April 1891): 203.

181. Mary Pinhey, "England as a Training Ground for Young India," *IMR* (May 1891): 228–29. Pinhey may have been the sister or wife of Justice Pinhey, who had presided over Rukhmabai's trial in Bombay a few years earlier.

182. Ibid., 230.

183. Ibid.

184. For an account of the Ilbert Bill agitation, see Sinha, " 'Chathams, Pitts, and Gladstone in Petticoats,' " 98–118.

185. Janaki Agnes Penelope Majumdar, "Family History," 21.

186. Radford, *Indian Journal*, 73–74.

187. Responses to Pinhey's article can be found in the *IMR* (June 1891): 304–8.

188. Syed A. M. Shah, "A Visit to the Tower of London," *IMR* (April 1893): 209.

189. Visram, *Ayahs*, 177–78.

190. Banerjea, *Nation in Making*, 10–12; and Sanyal, *General Biography*, 35–38.

191. Banerjea, *Nation in Making*, 10.

192. Ibid., 11–16.

193. Ibid., 19.

194. Ibid.

195. *Times*, May 14, 1884, p. 4.

196. Visram, *Ayahs*, 78; *Times*, February 1, 1884, p. 10 and January 29, 1885, p. 7.

197. "Ram Mohun Roy," *The Saturday Review*, July 7, 1888, pp. 1–22.

198. "Mr. Bright on India," *The Saturday Review*, July 16, 1887, p. 67.

199. *The Saturday Review* for March 21, 1885, p. 386 and January 5, 1889, p. 12. The trope of "vapour and gas" was commonly used for describing Indian "babus' " rhetoric in the 1880s; see Bamford, *Turbans and Tales*, chapter 2.

200. For suffrage women, see Burton, *Burdens of History*, chapters 5 and 6. Thanks to Laura Tabili for pressing this point.

201. "India Past and Present," *The Saturday Review*, February 15, 1890, p. 203.

202. "Report of the Indian National Congress," *The Saturday Review*, October 5, 1889, p. 382.

203. Sinha, *Colonial Masculinity*.

204. Quoted in Sanyal, *General Biography*, 39; for Naoroji, see his *Admission of Educated Natives*; Rawal, *Dadabhai Naoroji*, 15–22; and Parekh, *Essays*, 26–45 and 75–96.

205. *The Indian Appeal*, 1 (September 1889): 1. It was edited from Oxford by its proprietor, Hira Lal Kumar.

206. The best discussion of the British Committee is Morrow, "Origins and Early Years."

207. This was an issue debated at some length in the pages of the *Journal of the National Indian Association*. See for example Ellen Etherington, "Education in the North-west of India" *JNIA* (December 1875): 267–73; and Arabella Shore, "English Indifference toward India," *JNIA* (September 1882): 506–15.

208. Rutherford, *Early Verse by Rudyard Kipling*, 296.

209. Ibid., 293.

210. Quoted in Visram, *Ayahs*, 83.

211. Ibid., 171.

212. Ibid., 85.

213. See Desmond, *India Museum*.

214. See *English Opinion on India*, 1887–1894. This journal, subtitled "a monthly magazine containing extracts from English newspapers on Indian subjects," was founded in 1887 and published in Poona by Y. N. Ranade, in order "to place within the reach of our native readers what English papers, published in England, have to say relating to the most important Indian questions." See 1, no. 1 (February 1887): 2.

215. Visram, *Ayahs*, 108–109; see also James D. Hunt, *Gandhi in London*, especially pp. 127–32.

216. Geraldine Forbes has kindly allowed me to rely upon her unpublished paper, "Child-Marriage and Reform in India," which details the attention that the *Times* paid to the age-of-consent agitation in Indian in this period. In a review of Ramabai's *The High-Caste Hindu Woman*, *The Saturday Review* opened with a lament that "the extravagances of professional agitators and charlatans" like "the chorus of Bengali Baboos who fill the air with noisy declamation" divert attention from "the more modest claims of classes whose grievances are real and serious, and whose calm and sensible efforts at amelioration appeal forcibly to our sympathy and respect." "The High-Caste Hindu Woman," *The Saturday Review*, February 23, 1889, p. 223.

217. Bhor, *Some Impressions of England*, 26.

218. Rajkumar, *Indians outside India*, 7.

219. Said, *Culture and Imperialism*, xx.

220. Stoler, " 'Mixed-Bloods,' " 145.

221. Cooper and Stoler, "Tensions of Empire," 615.

222. Stoler, "Mixed-Bloods"; see also Stoler, *Race and the Education of Desire*, 97 and passim. An important exception to this is Sinha, *Colonial Masculinity*, and Blakely, *Blacks in the Dutch World*.

223. Salecl, "Fantasy Structure of Nationalist Discourse," 213–23.

Chapter 2. Pandita Ramabai

1. Ramabai's obituary is reprinted in her *Testimony*, 42–46; see also Shah, *Letters and Correspondence of Pandita Ramabai*, xi (all references to Shah are hereafter cited as *PRLC*); and Adhav, *Pandita Ramabai*, n.p. (preface).

2. Tharu and Lalita, *Women Writing*, vol. 1, 243.

3. See Kosambi, *At the Intersection of Gender Reform and Religious Belief*, 5. I am grateful to Meera Kosambi for sharing her work and her insights with me.

4. Bapat argues that she contested "the Orientalist discourses set up by colonialists of all species and nationalists of all hues." See his "Pandita Ramabai," 229. See also Chatterjee, "Nationalist Resolution of the Women's Question," 233–53; Tanika Sarkar, "Hindu Wife and the Hindu Nation," 213–35; Sinha, "Reading Mother India," 6–44; Chowdhury-Sengupta, "Mother India and

Mother Victoria," 20–37; and Anagol-McGinn, "Age of Consent Act (1891) Reconsidered," 100–118.

5. I am grateful to Meera Kosambi for pressing this point. For accounts of Ramabai in America, see Jayawardena, *White Woman's Other Burden*, chapter 3; Bapat, "Pandita Ramabai," 224–52; and Grewal, *Home and Harem*, chapters 4 and 5, published as this manuscript was being revised.

6. Kosambi, *At the Intersection*, 8–9 and 68.

7. For objections raised against Ramabai's proposed travel to England, see Kosambi, *Pandita Ramabai's Feminist and Christian Conversions*, 146–47.

8. Radha Kumar, *History of Doing*.

9. Kosambi, *Pandita Ramabai's Feminist and Christian Conversions*; see also her "Indian Response," WS 61–71.

10. "Notes of Conversations with Ramabai," *The Cheltenham College Ladies Magazine* 3, no. 10 (September 1884): 122–23; Adhav, *Pandita Ramabai*, 8. Eugene Stock called Father Goreh one of the most "zealous and faithful evangelists" among native converts in India. See *History*, vol. 2, 167.

11. Chakravarti, "Whatever Happened," 66. I am grateful to Uma Chakravarti for reading early versions of this chapter.

12. See Kosambi, *Pandita Ramabai's Feminist and Christian Conversions*, 13.

13. Ramabai, *Testimony*, 7.

14. Ramabai, *Testimony*, 6. Also quoted in Kosambi, *Pandita Ramabai*, 19.

15. See Adhav, *Pandita Ramabai*, 5.

16. According to Tanika Sarkar, "Orthodox Hindus of these times believed that a literate woman was destined to be a widow." "Book of Her Own," 36.

17. Ramabai, *Testimony*, 5.

18. Ibid., 9.

19. Ibid., 10; see also Kosambi, *Pandita Ramabai*, 31–35.

20. Ramabai, *Testimony*, 17, 20, 28.

21. Quoted in Adhav, *Pandita Ramabai*, 75.

22. *PRLC*, 17.

23. Kosambi, *Pandita Ramabai*, 26; *PRLC*, 17; Ramabai, *Testimony*, 10; and Adhav, *Pandita Ramabai*, 78–79.

24. Kosambi, "Meeting of the Twain," 2–4; see also Cornelia Sorabji's account of her father's persecution upon conversion in *Therefore*.

25. Ramabai, *Testimony*, 11–12.

26. Ibid., 12.

27. Tharu and Lalita, *Women Writing*, 244; see also Chakravarti, "Whatever Happened," 66; and Kosambi, *Pandita Ramabai*, 22.

28. Ramabai, *Testimony*, 13.

29. Ibid., 13–14.

30. Ibid., 15. Phule is also known as Jyotiba. See Tharu and Lalita, *Women Writing*, 211–12; and Omvedt, *Cultural Revolt in a Colonial Society*.

31. Ramabai, *Testimony*, 15.

32. *PRLC*, 17.

33. Ramabai, *Testimony*, 16; and *PRLC*, 18.

34. Ramabai, *High-Caste Hindu Woman*, 12–14 and chapter 3.

35. Chakravarti, "Whatever Happened," 66–67.

36. Kosambi, *Pandita Ramabai*, 45.

37. *PRLC*, 18; Adhav, *Pandita Ramabai*, 6. The significance of this ceremony should not be underestimated since, as Meera Kosambi has noted, marriage is the only religious sacrament to which a Hindu woman is entitled. See her introduction in Kosambi, *Women's Oppression in the Public Gaze*, 5.

38. Ramabai, *Testimony*, 17.

39. David Arnold estimates that "in the last quarter of the nineteenth century, an average of 1.75 out of every 1,000 of the population of British India died of cholera annually," with a fairly significant peak in the late 1870s. See *Colonizing the Body*, 164 and table, 165.

40. Ramabai, *Testimony*, 18. For a discussion of the Prarthana Samaj in its local religious reform context, see Kenneth W. Jones, *Socio-Religious Reform Movements in British India*, 141–44.

41. O'Hanlon, *Comparison*, 15; Padma Anagol-McGinn points out that Ranade's wife lamented his failure to support her when relatives abused her for attempts to become educated. See her "Age of Consent Act (1891) Reconsidered," 108.

42. "Ramabai Sanskrita," reprinted from the *Times of India* in *The Cheltenham College Ladies' Magazine* 3, no. 10 (September 1884): 116. For *Stree Dharma-Neeti*'s reception in Maharashtra, see Kosambi, *Pandita Ramabai*, 125–35 and 138–42.

43. Chakravarti, "Social Pariahs and Domestic Drudges," 138.

44. O'Hanlon, *Comparison*, 17.

45. See Kosambi's review of O'Hanlon's translation of Shinde in *The Indian Economic and Social History Review*, 276–78. One of these Maharashtrian women was Anandabai Joshi. "When I think over the sufferings of women in India in all ages," she wrote, "I am impatient to see the Western light dawn as the harbinger of emancipation." See Dall, *Life of Anandabai Joshee*, 38.

46. See Chakravarti, "Whatever Happened," 73–74; Anagol-McGinn, "Age of Consent Act (1891) Reconsidered," 100–118; Charles Heimsath, "Origin and Enactment of the Indian Age of Consent Bill, 1891," 502; and Chandra, "Whose Laws?" 187–211.

47. O'Hanlon, *Comparison*, 1. Her sentence was later commuted to transportation.

48. Dyer, *Pandita Ramabai*, chapter 2; *PRLC*, xii.

49. Karve, *Looking Back*; Athvale, *Hindu Widow*; and Kumar, *History of Doing*, 43–44. Karve's Hindu Sharada Sadan at Poona was begun as an alternative to Ramabai's Sharada Sahan, which was then being boycotted. For details see Kosambi, *Pandita Ramabai*.

50. For a discussion of Saraswati, see David Kinsley, *Hindu Goddesses*, chapter 4.

51. "The Education Commission," *JNIA* (November 1882): 639–40.

52. Ibid.

53. Dorothea Beale, "The Marchioness of Dufferin's Report," *EWR* April 15, 1889, pp. 145–52; "The Countess Dufferin Fund," *EWR* January 17, 1894, pp. 140–41. It was a claim that also guaranteed work for English women in India

and elsewhere in the "East." See Nair, "Uncovering the Zenana," 8–24; and Jane Hunter, *Gospel of Gentility*.

54. *IMR*, Nov. 1882, 640–41.

55. *PRLC*, p. 18.

56. Ibid., xii. Calcutta Medical College was the first in Bengal to admit female students in 1883; women were admitted to Campbell Medical School as hospital assistants in 1887 and for a three-year course in 1888. See Forbes, "Medical Careers and Health Care for Indian Women," 519, and *From Child Widow to Lady Doctor*. Possibly Ramabai did not want to return to Madras because of trouble she had experienced there over her views on female education. See *PRLC*, 17–18. Rukhmabai, a child wife who had taken her husband to court, came to England in the late 1880s and eventually got her medical degree from Glasgow. See *Women's Penny Paper*, May 18, 1889, p. 5; *Englishwomen's Review*, January 15, 1889, p. 47; and Rukhmabai's "Indian Child-Marriages," 263–69.

57. *PRLC*, 7, and Ramabai to Canon Butler, July 3, 1885, 73–74.

58. *PRLC*, xii; Tharu and Lalita, *Women Writing*, 243.

59. Shah translates this as "The Duties of Woman," while Lalita and Tharu translate it as "Morals for Women." As Meera Kosambi points out, the latter was the English title under which the book was first registered, in keeping with government regulations. See her translation in *Pandita Ramabai*, 54 and ff. Kosambi also questions how connected the book was with an intention to come to Britain, since it was advertised well before Ramabai had contact with the sisters of the CSMV (private correspondence).

60. Sister Geraldine to the dean of Lincoln, *PRLC*, July 1, 1885, 71–72.

61. *PRLC*, xx.

62. Kosambi, *Pandita Ramabai*, 146.

63. Tharu and Lalita, *Women Writing*, 243. Another such Indian woman was Rassundari Devi, who published her autobiography, *Amar Jiban*, in 1876. See Tanika Sarkar, "Book of Her Own," 55.

64. *PRLC*, xv–vi; Dyer, *Pandita Ramabai*, 35. Mano was also baptized at the same time; see Adhav, *Pandita Ramabai*, 106.

65. This in any event was Ramabai's narrative of it in 1907. See *Testimony*, 19–20. See also *PRLC*, 11. Meera Kosambi suggests that "possibly there was some hidden dimension to her conversion, born out of personal loneliness and social isolation." *At the Intersection*, 73. Elsewhere Kosambi argues that "the awakening of a feminist consciousness seemed to have played a major role in Ramabai's conversion." See *Pandita Ramabai*, 184.

66. I am grateful to Alison Fletcher for encouraging me to specify this point.

67. Tharu and Lalita, *Women Writing*, 245–46; *PRLC*, xxiii–iv; Kosambi, *At the Intersection*, 92. Ironically, as Kosambi notes, there was much in Ramabai's early writings that echoed Tilak's socially conservative views; see *Pandita Ramabai*, 117.

68. Tharu and Lalita, *Women Writing*, 246.

69. *PRLC*, 7. Sister Geraldine had been the sister-in-charge at St. Mary's School, Poona, but she was "invalided home" in 1883. She had met Ramabai while in India. See Adhav, *Pandita Ramabai*, n.p. (dedication).

70. This remained the case even at the height of their disputes. Sister Geraldine to Ramabai, *PRLC*, June 21, 1885, 65.

71. Ramabai kept in fairly regular contact with the sisters at Wantage until 1898 — the first year "that we received no tidings from her," according to Sister Geraldine. She visited England in 1898 but did not stop to visit either the CSMV women or Dorothea Beale. *PRLC*, 355.

72. Pandita Ramabai to Sister Geraldine, *PRLC*, October 1884, 27–28.

73. Ibid.

74. Ibid.

75. Ibid.

76. Ibid., 29.

77. Ibid.

78. Ramabai to Sister Geraldine, *PRLC*, 22 September night, 1885, 88–89.

79. Among them was Canon Westcott, whose *Historic Faith* Ramabai asked Sister Geraldine to read. Sister Geraldine to Ramabai, *PRLC*, Bath, October 1885, 101–2. Westcott was Regius Professor of Divinity at Cambridge and a New Testament scholar, whom Ramabai had met while in England (*PRLC*, 20). He rejected the more orthodox Protestant view that Hinduism and Islam were depraved, and "encouraged potential missionaries at Cambridge to listen for things of value from people in other cultures rather than merely preaching at them." It is not surprising that he appealed to Ramabai. Jeffrey Cox, "Independent Englishwomen, 166–84. My thanks to Jeff Cox for sharing a prepublication draft of his essay with me."

80. Ramabai to Sister Geraldine, *PRLC*, 22 September night, 1885, 88.

81. Ramabai, *Testimony*, 21.

82. Sister Geraldine to Ramabai, *PRLC*, Bath, October 1885, 103.

83. Adhav, *Pandita Ramabai*, 172.

84. Ibid., 176–77.

85. Sister Geraldine to Ramabai, *PRLC*, Bath, October 1885, 104.

86. Sister Geraldine, who had been in India, may have suspected the Unitarian women because they were known to be sympathetic to Brahmoism. See Kopf, *Brahmo Samaj and the Shaping of the Modern Indian Mind*.

87. Beale to Sister Geraldine, *PRLC*, April 22, 1885, 32.

88. See for example Beale to Sister Geraldine, *PRLC*, June 16, 1885, 62–63; and Raikes, *Dorothea Beale of Cheltenham*, 179–81 and 192–93.

89. Beale to Sister Geraldine, *PRLC*, June 16, 1885, 63.

90. Ibid., 62–63.

91. Ramabai to Sister Geraldine, *PRLC*, June (Monday), 1885, 70: "For if we were to become *like* or *as* equally perfect with the Father, we should undoubtedly be so many supreme Gods, as the Vedantists say."

92. Sister Geraldine to the Bishop of Lincoln, *PRLC*, July 1, 1885, 72.

93. Ramabai to Sister Geraldine, *PRLC*, June 24, 1885, 66; Beale to the Rev. Canon William Butler, July 1885, 77–8; Ramabai to Beale, June 1885, 125–26.

94. Sister Geraldine to Ramabai, *PRLC*, June 21, 1885, 64–65.

95. Beale to Canon Butler, *PRLC*, July 1885, 77–78.

96. For a discussion of women's communities in Britain in this period, see

Vicinus, *Independent Women*. Chapter 3 is devoted to "Church Communities: Sisterhoods and Deaconesses' Houses."

97. Beale to Sister Geraldine, *PRLC*, August 27, 1885, 35.

98. Ramabai to Sister Geraldine, *PRLC*, May 8, 1885, 50.

99. Beale to the Bishop of Bombay in England, *PRLC*, May 22, 1884, 40.

100. Hobsbawm, *The Age of Empire*, 71.

101. Cox, "Independent Englishwomen."

102. See Stock, *History*, vol. 2, 74, and vol. 3, 460–64.

103. Bishop of Lahore to Beale, *PRLC*, May 9, 1884, 38; Rt. Rev. Dr. Mylne, Bishop of Bombay, to Beale, May 21, 1884, 39. See also Kosambi, "Indian Response," WS-67.

104. Bishop of Lahore to Beale, *PRLC*, May 9, 1884, 38.

105. Rt. Rev. Dr. Mylne, Bishop of Bombay, to Beale, *PRLC*, May 21, 1884, 39.

106. Ibid.

107. Bishop of Lahore to Beale, *PRLC*, May 9, 1884, 38.

108. Rt. Rev. Dr. Mylne, Bishop of Bombay in England, to Beale, *PRLC*, May 26, 1884, 44.

109. Canon William Butler to Beale, *PRLC*, June 15, 1884, 45. For an interesting parallel discussion of the contradictions of nineteenth-century African American women lecturing in public, see Carby, *Reconstructing Womanhood*, 6 and 63.

110. Beale to the Bishop of Bombay in England, *PRLC*, May 22, 1884, 40–42.

111. Ibid.

112. Ramabai to Sister Geraldine, *PRLC*, May 8, 1885, 50.

113. Ramabai to Sister Geraldine, *PRLC*, May 12, 1885, 58–61.

114. Ibid., 60.

115. Ibid., 61.

116. Ibid., 60.

117. Ramabai to Beale, *PRLC*, May 8, 1885, 124.

118. Tyrrell, *Woman's World, Woman's Empire*, 102, 110.

119. *PRLC*, 8.

120. See "A School Treat in India," *The Indian Female Evangelist* 6, no. 39 (July 1881): 143–44; and chapter 3 on Sorabji, below.

121. Pandita Ramabai to Sister Geraldine, *PRLC*, March 9, 1885, 34

122. According to Sister Geraldine, "[T]he Society of St. John the Evangelist came to our relief and invited . . . [him] to their Mission House. There he was instructed, and eventually baptised and confirmed, after which he went back to India, and attached himself to some Mission." *PRLC*, 20.

123. See Kosambi, *Pandita Ramabai*, 70–75

124. Pandita Ramabai to Sister Geraldine, *PRLC*, May 12, 1885, 60.

125. Ibid., 59.

126. As Kosambi points out, widowhood was also equivalent to civil death in nineteenth-century India. See "Meeting of the Twain," 3.

127. Viswanathan, "Coping with (Civil) Death," 187.

128. Canon William Butler to Dorothea Beale, *PRLC*, July 5, 1885, 76. Emphasis in the original.

129. However, there is no evidence to suggest that the sisters at CSMV were trying to bypass or circumvent the proper ecclesiastical authorities.

130. Bishop of Lahore in England, to Beale, *PRLC*, May 25, 1884, 42–3.

131. Ibid.

132. Hunter is quoted in Rev. Canon William Butler to Beale, *PRLC*, June 15, 1884, 45.

133. Rev. Canon William Butler to Beale, *PRLC*, June 17, 1884, 45. Butler told Beale in the same letter (46) that he wanted to keep Ramabai in England until she was thirty (she was then 26).

134. Rt. Rev. Dr. Mylne, Bishop of Bombay in England, to Beale, *PRLC*, 26 May, 1884, 43.

135. Sister Geraldine to Beale, *PRLC*, May 6, 1885, 47.

136. Beale to the Rev. Canon William Butler, *PRLC*, July 1885, 78. According to Mary Fuller (1882–1965), who worked with Ramabai at Mukti Mission in Kedgaon, Ramabai became deaf "as a result of sleeping on damp earth during her pilgrimages before she became a Christian." Quoted in Adhav, *Pandita Ramabai*, 45.

137. Beale to the Rev. Canon William Butler, *PRLC*, July 1885, 78.

138. Beale to Ramabai, *PRLC*, July 5, 1885, 130.

139. Ramabai to Beale, *PRLC*, Friday [*sic*], 1885, 135.

140. Beale to Sister Geraldine, *PRLC*, January 3, 1885, 31.

141. Ibid.; Beale to the Bishop of Bombay in England, May 22, 1884, 40–42.

142. Beale to Sister Geraldine, *PRLC*, January 3, 1885, 30–31. For a discussion of the Queen's often unusual interest in India and Indians, see St. Aubyn, *Queen Victoria*, esp. chapter 9, "Indian Summer, 1887–1901."

143. Kamm, *How Different from Us*, 207.

144. Beale to Sister Geraldine, *PRLC*, April 1885, 33.

145. Beale to the Rev. Canon William Butler, *PRLC*, July 1885, 78.

146. Sister Geraldine to Rev. C. Gore, *PRLC*, 82. This was most likely the spring of 1885, though no date is attributed.

147. *PRLC*, 404.

148. Stock, *History*, vol. 3, 501.

149. For an elaboration of this imagery as it was constructed by Victorian feminists and female reformers, see Burton, *Burdens of History*.

150. Sister Geraldine to Beale, *PRLC*, December 18, 1883, 21–22.

151. Sister Geraldine to Beale, *PRLC*, May 10, 1885, 54.

152. *PRLC*, 4.

153. *PRLC*, 343.

154. *PRLC*, xxix.

155. *PRLC*, 4.

156. Sister Geraldine to Rev. C. Gore, *PRLC*, July 3, 1885, 83–84.

157. *PRLC*, 398–99.

158. Sister Geraldine to Beale, *PRLC*, May 25, 1885, 62.

159. Sister Geraldine to Ramabai, *PRLC*, October 1885, 103–4.

160. Ramabai to Beale, *PRLC*, January 12, 1886, 166.

161. *PRLC*, 343.

162. Pandita Ramabai to Canon Butler, *PRLC*, July 3, 1885, 72.

163. Ramabai to Dorothea Beale, *PRLC*, September 1, 1885, 134

164. I am thinking here particularly of Lily in Shula Marks, *Not Either an Experimental Doll*.

165. She laid down similar conditions for Beale: "[Y]ou are sorry because I do not accept the Church doctrine without proving it; please say it quite openly, and I will tear to pieces the letter containing seventy-six pages, and which I have just finished writing, and never say to you one word about my difficulties." See Adhav, *Pandita Ramabai*, 155.

166. Sister Geraldine to Ramabai, *PRLC*, October 1885, 107.

167. Ibid., 106.

168. Emphasis mine.

169. I am grateful to Leila J. Rupp for the idea of sisterhood as process, which she develops in both "Constructing Internationalism," 1571–1600 and "Challenging Imperialism," 9–27.

170. Ramabai to Beale, *PRLC*, May 31, 1885, 155.

171. Ibid.

172. Ramabai to Sister Geraldine, *PRLC*, June 25, 1885, 68–69.

173. Ramabai to Sister Geraldine, *PRLC*, October 1884, 28.

174. Ibid.

175. Ramabai to Beale, *PRLC*, Friday [*sic*], 1885, 135.

176. "Other people may call me an infidel if they like, but I trust in Him alone who is my God, Father and Guide, and [Who] will surely show me His ways." Ramabai to Dorothea Beale, *PRLC*, August 15, 1885, 134.

177. Ramabai to Beale, *PRLC*, no date except "St. Hilda's: Sunday," 151.

178. Ramabai to Beale, *PRLC*, Friday [*sic*], 1885, 135.

179. The letters on pages 150–54 are not dated.

180. This is where Manorama was boarded while Ramabai attended Cheltenham.

181. Ramabai to Sister Geraldine, *PRLC*, September 20, 1885, 84–86.

182. Ibid.

183. See Adhav, *Pandita Ramabai*, 147. This letter is from Sister Geraldine to Dorothea Beale, January 1886.

184. Ramabai to Sister Geraldine, *PRLC*, September 2, 1885, 89.

185. Sister Geraldine to Ramabai, *PRLC*, October 5, 1885, 93.

186. Ramabai to Sister Geraldine, *PRLC*, May 20, 1887, 199.

187. Mano was instrumental in helping her mother with her work in India in the 1890s and after. See Dyer, *Pandita Ramabai*; and *PRLC*, 365–424, passim.

188. Kosambi, *Pandita Ramabai*, 97–104 (section entitled "The Nurturance and Upbringing of Children"); for Ramabai's invitation to the United States, see 151–52.

189. I am grateful to Uma Chakravarti and Meera Kosambi both for helping me to clarify this point. As Sister Geraldine recounted in her introduction to the Shah volume (8), Ramabai had left Mano in the care of the sisters at Poona very briefly before she came to England in 1883. For Ramabai's fund-raising

efforts in the United States, see Jayawardena, *White Woman's Other Burden*, chapter 3.

190. This is a variation of Tyrrell's claim that Western temperance women "did battle for Christ and personal authority at the same time." *Woman's World, Woman's Empire*, 212.

191. Ramabai to Beale, "at sea," *PRLC*, February–March 1886, 169.

192. Ibid., 170.

193. See Adhav, *Pandita Ramabai*, 19 and 216.

194. Ramabai to Miss Noble, *PRLC*, July 6, 1886, 196.

195. Ramabai to Sister Geraldine, *PRLC*, May 12, 1885, 59.

196. See Visweswaran, *Fictions of Feminist Ethnography*; and Ortner, "Resistance and the Problem of Ethnographic Refusal," 184–85.

197. Kosambi, *At the Intersection*, 47. See also Kosambi's translation of *Stree Dharma-Neeti* (1882) (*Pandita Ramabai*, 59), which reads: "Self-reliance, that is, dependence on oneself, is the unparalleled way to progress."

198. See Rachel L. Bodley's introduction to Ramabai, *High-Caste Hindu Woman*, i–xxiv; *PRLC*, 171–224; Dyer, *Pandita Ramabai*, chapter 3. Grewal's *Home and Harem* begins to do some of this work in chapter 5; see also Bapat, "Pandita Ramabai," 224–52; and Kosambi, *Pandita Ramabai*.

Chapter 3. Cornelia Sorabji

1. Significantly, an English contemporary of Sorabji's who knew her in Bombay described her as "only half Parsee; her father is Parsee and her mother Hindu." See Radford, *Indian Journal*, 184.

2. For discussion of a virtually contemporary instance of the quest for the "pure Asiatic," see Sinha, *Colonial Masculinity*, 86.

3. See Sinha, "Gender in the Critiques," esp. 249.

4. Cornelia Sorabji to her family, MSS EUR F 165/5, October 19, 1891. All subsequent references are to letters from Sorabji to the family in Poona, unless otherwise specified.

5. Tharu and Lalita, *Women Writing*, vol. 1, 299; Brittain, *Women at Oxford*, 85.

6. Sorabji is certainly not alone in this. As Helen Lefkowitz Horowitz remarks in her biography of M. Carey Thomas, "[A]s a subject [she] cannot fulfill all feminist hopes." *The Passion and the Power: The Life of M. Carey Thomas* (New York: Alfred K. Knopf, 1994), xvi. For an account of Sorabji's life, see Gooptu, "Cornelia Sorabji."

7. The term is Horowitz's, as applied to the project of the biography of M. Carey Thomas, a contemporary of Sorabji's with a similarly vexed relationship to feminism and the women's movement. She also wanted to study medicine, though in the end she did not. *Passion and the Power*, xiv.

8. Here I am drawing on Faith L. Smith's arguments about Afro-Trinidadians of a similar and later period. See her "Coming Home to the Real Thing," 906.

9. Her sister Susie enjoyed telling the following story: "[A] missionary once

saw Susie and Cornelia playing the garden and asked the latter—'Are you saved?' 'No!' was the prompt reply, 'but my sister Susie is.' " Quoted in Sen Gupta, *Pioneer Women of India*, 75.

10. Cornelia's nephew Richard Sorabji speculates that she might have been a Toda. Private conversation, Oxford, June 21, 1995. Sumit Sarkar warns that the term "tribe" is misleading, as it conveys a sense of complete isolation from Indian life when in fact tribal peoples "are very much a part of Indian society." *Modern India*, 44. Thanks to Geraldine Forbes for insisting on this point. According to Dane Kennedy, the Todas prompted the largest ethnographic corpus in nineteenth-century Britain, in part because they were constructed as the most "primitive and pristine" tribal group in the Raj. They were also represented as being the closest to Christians. See his "Guardians of Edenic Sanctuaries: Paharis, Lepchas, and Todas in the British Mind," *South Asia* 14, 2 (1991): 57–77 and his *Magic Mountains*, chapter 4, especially the illustration, 75.

11. See Sorabji, *"Therefore,"* 41–45 and 23–39. There are a few of Lady Cornelia Ford's letters to Cornelia and to her mother from the 1880s in the India Office Library. See MSS EUR F 165/203. Cornelia's father's autobiography, as dictated to her sister Mary, which recounts the trauma of his conversion, is to be found in MSS EUR F 165/205. Cornelia's father's conversion story was the stuff of legend in Bombay down to the 1880s. See Radford, *Indian Journal*, 184. Nora Scott was the wife of Mr. Justice John Scott, who was appointed to the High Court of Bombay in 1882.

12. See for example, "Poona: The Victoria High School," *The Indian Female Evangelist* (publication of the Indian Female Normal School and Instruction Society, or, Zenana, Bible and Medical Mission), 9, no. 67 (July 1888): 344–48. The IFNSIS Society was founded by Lady Kinnaird and was theoretically interdenominational. In 1880–81 the Church Missionary Society broke from the IFNSIS to form the Church of England Zenana Missionary Society. See Stock, *History*, vol. 3, 258.

13. Sorabji, *India Calling*, 7.

14. I am grateful to Richard Sorabji, Dick's son, for confirmation of these details.

15. Sorabji, *India Calling*, 14.

16. Cornelia, Lena, Mary, Pheroze, Susie, Ailsa, and Zuleika (referred to as "Biggie" in Cornelia's correspondence). I am grateful to Richard Sorabji for information on Zuleika. There was another boy, Framroze, who died in infancy. See Sorabji, *Susie Sorabji*, 6.

17. Quoted in the obituary for "Miss Susie Sorabji: A Great Indian Educationalist," *Times*, June 4, 1931.

18. Sorabji, *India Calling*, 13.

19. Ibid., 17.

20. Ibid., 3.

21. Ibid., 2, 4.

22. Ibid., 3.

23. Ibid. For a discussion of traditions for Parsi women, see Rose, "Traditional Role of Women," 1–103.

24. For another interpretation of Sorabji's conversion and identity as a Christian Indian woman, see Flemming, "Between Two Worlds," 81–107.

25. Sorabji, *India Calling*, 4.

26. Ibid., 8–9. For another example of how a young colonial female subject might embrace "English modes of living and thinking," see Gooneratne, "Family Histories as Post-Colonial Texts," 95.

27. Kulke, *Parsis in India*; Dobbin, *Urban Leadership in Western India*.

28. Sorabji, *India Calling*, 4.

29. Ibid., 20.

30. Cornelia Sorabji to Lady Hobhouse, MSS EUR F 165/16, May 10, 1888. For an example of how women speaking in public were received at about the same time in Britain, see Lonsdale, "Platform Women," 409–15. According to an English woman who knew her in Bombay, Sorabji lectured and assisted at examinations, for which she was paid Rs. 100 a month. From Radford, *Indian Journal*, 185.

31. Hobhouse and Hammond, *Lord Hobhouse*, 107–9. See also Hobhouse, *Letters from India, 1872–1877*.

32. "Cornelia Sorabji," *The Queen: The Lady's Newspaper*, August 24, 1889, pp. 247 (engraving of Sorabji in cap and gown) and 276 (feature story). Among the contributors were Miss Manning, Miss Shaw-Lefevre, Sir William Wedderburn, Florence Nightingale, the Marchioness of Ripon, and Lord and Lady Hobhouse. See leaflet, "Miss Cornelia Sorabji," MSS EUR F 165/17, item 250.

33. Ibid., 276. *The Queen* reported that Sorabji contributed £60 of this from her personal savings.

34. "Reception of Miss Manning at Bombay," *Indian Magazine and Review* (January 1889): 33.

35. For the association's statements of purpose, see the *Journal of the National Indian Association*, October 1874, September 1877, and November 1880.

36. "The Future of the National Indian Association," *JNIA* (September 1877): 228.

37. Mrs. Etherington, "Education in the North-West of India," *JNIA* (December 1875): 268.

38. "Indian Students in England," *JNIA* (January 1885): 1–9.

39. "Superintendence of Indian Students in England," *JNIA* (September 1885): 406.

40. See for example S. Satthianadhan, "Indian Students and English Universities," *JNIA* (November 1880): 603–608; Ali Hamid, "The Cost of Living in London," *JNIA* (February 1882): 88–92; and "M. B.," "Suggestions to Indian Medical Students," *IMR* (November 1889): 567–69. The NIA also published a *Handbook of Information Relating to University and Professional Studies for Indian Students in the United Kingdom*, which was in its seventh edition in 1893.

41. [Lady Mary Hobhouse and Madeleine Shaw-Lefevre,] "Colleges for Women in England," *IMR* (March 1891): 141–47.

42. In 1886 a special committee was formed aimed specifically at the development and training of "native" missionaries. See Stock, *History*, vol. 3, 491–93; "On Native Antagonism to Christianity in India," *Church Missionary Intelligencer* 13 (May 1888): 281–96; "Are Missions a Great Failure?" *Church Mission-*

ary Intelligencer 13 (November 1888): 681–99; "Our Native Catechists," *Church Missionary Intelligencer* 16 (May 1891): 324–28. For an interesting comparison with the CMS in Africa at about this time, see Andrew Porter, "Cambridge," 5–34 and "Evangelical Enthusiasm," 23–46. I am grateful to Susan Thorne and Doug Peers for these references.

43. For Franscina's first annual report, see *The Indian Female Evangelist* 7, no. 47 (July 1883): 138–44; for an account of Cornelia's graduation from the Deccan College, see *The Indian Female Evangelist* 9, no. 67 (July 1888): 346.

44. MSS EUR F 165/1, August 29, 1889. For another articulation of a woman's sea-voyage broodings contemporary with Sorabji's, see Hoy and MacCurtain, *From Dublin to New Orleans*, 62.

45. Shaw-Lefevre's brother-in-law was Sir George Ryan, governor general of Ceylon. One former student remembered her as "an ardent Liberal, though never wishful to appear a partisan among the students." See Faithfull, *In the House of My Pilgrimage*, 53.

46. For a history of the Dufferin Fund, see Maneesha Lal, "Politics of Gender and Medicine in Colonial India," 29–66; for a discussion of Indian women's relationship to it, see Forbes, "Medical Careers and Health Care for Indian Women," 515–30 and *From Child Widow to Lady Doctor*.

47. Dyhouse, *No Distinction of Sex?* 18. Margaret Tuke, principal of Bedford College, complained that universities "were apt to be regarded, as far as women were concerned, as institutions for the training of teachers." Ibid.

48. MSS EUR F 165/1, September 26, 1889.

49. Sengupta, *Pioneer Women*, 15–19; Dall, *Life of Mrs. Anandabai Joshee*; Karlekar, *Voices from Within*, 177; and Rachel Bodley's introduction to Ramabai's *High-Caste Hindu Woman*, i–vii.

50. MSS EUR F 165/1, October 10, 1889.

51. MSS EUR F 165/1, September 26, 1889.

52. Kosambi, "Gender Reform," 265–90. The *Indian Female Evangelist* reported in 1889 that Rukhmabai was living with friends in London "and is much perplexed as to what her course shall be. She came over to this country, in the hope that she might qualify as a lady doctor, and devote herself to the relief of her country women but she finds the study of medicine extremely difficult and is much disheartened." 9, no. 72 (October 1889): 185. A copy of Rukhmabai's registration for the London School of Medicine for Women, signed by both herself and E. A. Manning, is in the Royal Free Hospital archives, London. See also Anagol-McGinn, "Age of Consent Act (1891) Reconsidered," 100–118; and Lutzker, *Edith Pechey-Phipson, M.D.*, esp. 199–209 (for details on Rukhmabai).

53. Visram, *Ayahs*, 92.

54. MSS EUR F 165/1, September 26, 1889.

55. Ibid.

56. MSS EUR F 165/1, October 1, 1889.

57. MSS EUR F 165/5, July 14 and 25, 1891.

58. MSS EUR F 165/1, October 1 and 8, 1889.

59. MSS EUR F 165/1, October 1, 1889.

60. MSS EUR F 165/1, October 8, 1889.

61. Ibid.

62. Ibid.

63. In her study of "black" British women of African and Afro-Caribbean descent, Mama calls this maneuver an expression of "competitive identity politics." See *Beyond the Masks*, 156.

64. Ellsworth, *Liberators of the Female Mind*, especially chapter 8; see also the *Journal of the Women's Education Union*, January 1873–October 1877.

65. MSS EUR F 165/1, October 16, 1889.

66. The three from Balliol were Lords Curzon and Elgin and the Fifth Marquess of Lansdowne. Symonds, *Oxford and Empire*, 2. Reba Soffer argues that Benjamin Jowett, who came to Balliol on an scholarship in 1836 and died as master in 1893, was married to the college and that the imperial statesmen Balliol produced were "the progeny" of his union with it. See her, "Authority in the University," 194.

67. Symonds, *Oxford and Empire*, 1.

68. Ibid., 36. See also Soffer, *Discipline and Power*.

69. Symonds, 16 and 9.

70. Ibid., 185.

71. Ibid., 186.

72. Ibid. One example of Jowett's ongoing involvement with Balliol graduates who became India men can be seen in Bennett, *Ilberts in India*. C. P. Ilbert was legal member of the Viceroy's Council. For debates on the ICS exams during Sorabji's residence in Oxford, see "Oxford and the Indian Civil Service," *The Oxford Magazine* (February 24, 1892): 187–88 and "Oxford and the Indian Civil Service," *The Oxford Magazine* (March 2, 1892): 207–208.

73. Symonds, 104–106.

74. Ibid., 109.

75. Baldick, *Social Mission of English Criticism, 1848–1932*, 71. See also Viswanathan, *Masks of Conquest*.

76. Symonds, 110. One Somervillian recalled that Ruskin had visited the college in the 1880s "in rather an Uncle-y spirit" and asked some of the women at teatime: "Do any of you study *nasty* Philosophy?" Florence Rich to Helen Darbishire, August 31, 1938, Somerville College Library Archives.

77. Symonds, 257; Lotika Ghose, *Manmohan Ghose*, 18. Ghose was at Christ Church, which he dubbed "the most expensive place on earth."

78. Quoted in Symonds, *Oxford and Empire*, 107.

79. Ibid., 15–16.

80. Ibid., 253–56.

81. Courtney, *Oxford Portrait Gallery*, 209. See also Dyhouse, *No Distinction of Sex?* chapters 1 and 2.

82. Rogers, *Degrees by Degrees*, 3. She was a tutor for Somerville girls in the 1880s. See Mary Teresa Skues to Helen Darbishire, March 26, 1941, p. 4, Somerville College Library Archives.

83. Ibid., 21.

84. Quoted in Jan Morris, *Oxford*, 99.

85. Rogers, *Degrees by Degrees*, 9. "Higher education has done much for woman. It has not taught [her] how to understand cricket." *The Oxford Magazine* (May 28, 1890): 341.

86. Leonardi, *Dangerous by Degrees*, 17.

87. Brittain, *Women at Oxford*, 95.

88. Mehta, *Up at Oxford*, 185.

89. Brittain, *Women at Oxford*, 87.

90. Courtney, *Oxford Portrait Gallery*, 228.

91. Rogers, *Degrees by Degrees*, 152. According to the College Log Book, "for the first few years two Cows and a Pig formed part of the establishment but these were later replaced by a Pony and Donkey which might be seen disporting themselves in the field, adding to the picturesque and homely look of the place." By the time the West Buildings were erected in 1885, however, "the rural character of Somerville finally disappeared." *Somerville College Log Book, 1879–1907*, Somerville College Library Archives, pp. 14 and 16.

92. MSS EUR F 165/3, July 2, 1890.

93. MSS EUR F 165/1, December 1(?), 1889.

94. MSS EUR F 165/2, March 4, 1890. For more on the princesses, see Alexander and Anand, *Queen Victoria's Maharajah*.

95. MSS EUR F 165/2, April 30, 1890.

96. See below, pp. 145–46.

97. For an account of other English university women's reactions at the time, see Dyhouse, *No Distinction of Sex?* chapter 3.

98. The college acquired a boat the year that Cornelia arrived, which was called, "in commemoration of Indian students in the College, the 'Urmila,' the Sanskrit name for the sacred Lotus Flower, one letter of each word being inscribed on each of the six skulls in English and in Gujerati character." See *Somerville College Log Book, 1879–1907*, Somerville College Library Archives, p. 54.

99. MSS EUR F 165/1, November 14(?), 1889. See also her "Benjamin Jowett," 297–305. In a handwritten recollection dated November 7, 1893, shortly after Jowett's death, Sorabji recalled that she was first introduced to Jowett by the Warden, Miss Maitland, and "I fell in love with the dear old gentleman at once." MSS EUR F 165/194.

100. MSS EUR F 165/194.

101. "*Oxford* you must remember— is as we pride ourselves, '*The University of Life*,' while Cambridge is '*The University of Work*,' and generally poorer work than ours." MSS EUR F 165/4, March 26, 1891.

102. MSS EUR F 165/1, November 10, 1889.

103. MSS EUR F 165/1, October 16, 1889.

104. MSS EUR F 165/1, October 31, and November 3, 1889.

105. The Nizam later sponsored Sarojini Naidu on a scholarship to Britain when she was fifteen (1894). See Meena Alexander, "Sarojini Naidu," 68. Sorabji was not the only woman to receive conflicting advice about which educational course to pursue; see also Oakly, *My Adventures in Education*. 58–59.

106. MSS EUR F 165/2, March 4, 1890.

107. MSS EUR F 165/2, March 9, 1890. Emphases in the original.

108. See for example Mukharji, *Visit to Europe*, 105, quoted above in chapter 2. Also of relevance is Mazumdar, "Race and Racism," 25–38, esp. the anecdote about Bharati Mukherjee, 31; and Robb, introduction to *Concept of Race*, 7, 9, 27–35.

109. MSS EUR F 165/3, September 3, 1890.

110. MSS EUR F 165/3, September 3, 1890.

111. MSS EUR F 165/5, July 25, 1891; and 165/7, August 4, 1892.

112. W. W. Hunter, *Bombay 1885–1890*, 156.

113. I am grateful to Judith Walkowitz for this latter observation.

114. EUR MSS F 165/2, February 25, 1890. She stuck with it because she thought "it would greatly benefit the cause of women generally, for a woman, even once, to have been entrusted with directing . . . men's intellects." Cornelia Sorabji to Lady Hobhouse, MSS EUR F 165/16, May 10, 1888.

115. See below. For a discussion of the relationship between utility and pleasure in Victorian women's work, see Antoinette Burton, "Fearful Bodies into Disciplined Subjects," 545–74.

116. Dyhouse, *No Distinction of Sex?* 23–24.

117. Brittain, *Women at Oxford*, 92; Dyhouse, *No Distinction of Sex?* chapter 2. "Kind Sir William chaperones me to my All Souls Lectures —*Hindu Law* and *The Contract Act*— I chaperone myself to Oriel, i.e., Bentham." MSS EUR F 165/2, May 8, 1890. At the age of 90, Emma Catherine Childs (née Pollard) recalled that when she was at Somerville in the late 1880s, "a list of ladies was kept who were glad for a small fee to sit placidly — often knitting, to the annoyance of the lecturer . . . — listening, and more often, probably playing the part of the deaf adder." Somerville College Library Archives. Florence Rich, who was at Somerville just before Sorabji's time there, recalled that "Somervillians were not allowed to visit the men's Colleges unless accompanied by the Head or the Vice, and we could not go to dances during term time." Florence Rich to Helen Darbishire, August 31, 1938, Somerville College Library Archives. See also Lodge, *Terms and Vacations*, 49.

118. MSS EUR F 165/2, May 10, 1890 (quotation from section dated internally May 15).

119. MSS EUR F 165/3, September 4, 1890.

120. "Ladies in Libraries," *The Saturday Review*, August 14, 1886, 213. The invasion of the Reading Room by women from "the bohemian set" had also been the subject of complaint earlier in the 1880s; see Walkowitz, *City of Dreadful Delight*, 69. See also Anand, *Conversations in Bloomsbury*, which details the author's experiences in the British Library and environs in the 1920s and 1930s.

121. MSS EUR F 165/3, September 14, 1890. Oxford women, despite Sorabji's remark about Girton, were not known for their fashion sense in the nineteenth century either. See Courtney, *Oxford Portrait Gallery*, 218–19.

122. See Kosambi, *Pandita Ramabai's Feminist and Christian Conversions*, 121–22; and Bannerji, "Textile Prison," 27–45, reprinted in Bharati Ray, *From the Seams of History*, 67–106.

123. Grewal, *Home and Harem*, 129.

124. Sorabji, *India Calling*, 52.

125. See Grosz, "Bodies-Cities," 242. I am grateful to Paul Walker Clarke for this reference.

126. MSS EUR F 165/3, September 14, 1890.

127. For two interesting parallel phenomena, see Faith L. Smith, "Coming

Home to the Real Thing," 908; and E. P. Thompson on Tagore in *Alien Homage*, 9.

128. This according to Sorabji, MSS EUR F 165/2, April 18, 1890. Hurford, who had also tutored Ramabai in English in Poona before her trip to England, was appointed the lady superintendent; see *Thacker's Indian Directory*, 1061. See also Radford, *Indian Journal*, 119.

129. See for example MSS EUR F 165/1, November 14(?), 1889; 165/2, March 9, and April 29, 1890; 165/3, October 12, 1890; and 165/4, April 2, 1891.

130. During Sorabji's time in Britain Elsie had already appeared as evidence of the success of the mission cause among Parsis. "Elsie is a dear little missionary already — and how she loves a meeting!" See "Elsie's Vow; or, I Promise," *Indian Female Evangelist* 10, no. 75 (July 1890): 345–47 (and photo).

131. Pheroze did a number of singing performances in and around London while Sorabji was in London. There is also evidence that by the later 1890s she was attached to a teacher training college. See the Countess of Warwick, *Progress in Women's Education*, 273–76.

132. MSS EUR F 165/2, May 10, 1890.

133. MSS EUR F 165/4, February 1, 1891.

134. MSS EUR F 165/2, April 2, 1890.

135. I am grateful to Susan Thorne for this observation.

136. Cornelia Sorabji to Lady Hobhouse, MSS EUR F 165/16, March 31, 1890.

137. MSS EUR F 165/(?), April 5, 1891.

138. She was referring here to Manning's friend Isabel Brander, an inspectress of government schools then visiting London from Madras. See MSS EUR F 165/3, December 3, 1890, and April 11, 1891. This was not an uncommon sentiment among Indian nationalists contemporary with Sorabji. Surendranath Banerjea, for example, was quite explicit in his conviction that Indians were excluded from civil service appointments because "our color is our disqualification." Quoted in Ghosh, " 'English in Taste,' " 193. Thanks to Alison Fletcher for this reference.

139. MSS EUR F 165/1, January 20, 1890.

140. MSS EUR F 165/4, February 8, 1891.

141. The Maria Grey Training College foundered in the 1870s — by 1881 it had only 32 students — and Manning may have been as concerned about numbers as she was about securing an Indian woman. For details see Ellsworth, *Liberators of the Female Mind*, 220–21.

142. MSS EUR F 165/4, May 25, 1891.

143. MSS EUR F 165/6, January 17, 1892.

144. Russell, *Wish of Distinction*, chapter 2.

145. MSS EUR F 165/3, September 7, 1890.

146. MSS EUR F 165/4, January 7, 1891.

147. MSS EUR F 165/3 (no date, first letter in 165/3).

148. MSS EUR F 165/5, August 9, 1891.

149. MSS EUR F 165/1, December 12, 1889. See also Meera Kosambi's claim that Rukhmabai "dressed like a Hindu married woman until [her husband's] death in 1904, after which she considered herself a widow." "Meeting of the

Twain," 7. It is possible that Rukhmabai wore saris in shades of red and brown while in London (what Marathi widows wore, as opposed to the white of Bengali widows). I am grateful to Geraldine Forbes for suggesting this possibility. According to C. A. Bayly, these color codings were from Hindu traditions, stemming from the laws of Manu. See his "Origins of *Swadeshi*," 291.

150. MSS EUR F 165/2, January 26, 1890. Cornelia's nephew Richard remembers that during the Second World War, the four Sorabji sisters then living in London wore "brilliant" saris that stood out against the dark and gray metropolitan landscape, especially when no lights were allowed. Private conversation, Oxford, June 21, 1995. For a discussion of clothes and nineteenth century social reform in India, see Bannerji, "Textile Prison," 27–45.

151. Madame Blavatsky, *From the Caves and Jungles of Hindustan* (1892), quoted in Karkaria, *Charm of Bombay*, 338.

152. See OIOC Judicial and Political Papers 6/333/1968 for details of the 1892 memorial. I am grateful to both Sudipta Sen and Philippa Levine for aiding me in my search for these documents.

153. MSS EUR F 165/2, February 2, 1890.

154. Ibid.

155. Rukhmabai had support from the Walter McLarens for her medical course, but she had left a life where child care was expected of her in her natal family, despite the fact that her stepfather was a well-established university botanist with a large medical practice in Bombay. See Radford, *Indian Journal*, 40, 42–43, 87.

156. MSS EUR F 165/4, March 30, 1891.

157. MSS EUR F 165/3, September 24(?), 1890.

158. MSS EUR F 165/2, February 2, 1890. One of Sorabji's Indian contemporaries thought the Rajah of Kolapore was "a jovial, honest, friendly fellow." See Radcliffe, *Indian Journal*, 80. Given the fact that Nora Scott met both Rukhmabai and the Rajah in Bombay, it may well be that Rukhmabai knew him before she saw him in London.

159. See for example Max Muller's letter to the *Times*, reprinted as "Rukhmabai and Ramabai" in the *Indian Magazine and Review* (1887–1888): 530–40. I am grateful to Emary Aronson for providing me with this reference.

160. As Dane Kennedy notes, Todas were constructed by the Victorians as the "aristocrats" of India's tribal peoples, with the nobility of their women primary among their "superior" qualities. See Kennedy, *Magic Hills*, 71–75.

161. MSS EUR F 165/3, July 2, 1890.

162. See Jowett to Sorabji, MSS EUR F 165/18, September 21, 1892, and August 6, 1893. Although she spent more time by far with Max Muller, she appears nowhere in his collected letters or memoirs, where his encounters in England with Ramabai, Rukhmabai, and Behramji Malabari dominate. See Mrs. M. Muller, *Life and Letters of the Right Honorable Max Muller*, vol. 2; Max Muller, *Auld Lang Syne*.

163. MSS EUR F 165/6, February 14, 1892.

164. MSS EUR F 165/4, January 18, 1891. An Oxford don with a tremendous legal reputation, Dicey admitted that, like most barristers, he could not have survived by practicing law alone. "The Bar was never anything but a loss to me,"

he said; "I should have long ago starved had I depended upon my briefs for food." Quoted in Collini, *Public Moralists*, 45.

165. MSS EUR F 165/5, November 28, 1891.

166. MSS EUR F 165/(?), April 2, 1890.

167. MSS EUR F 165/1, March 4, 1889; and 165/8, January 7, 1893.

168. Lady Hobhouse to Cornelia Sorabji, MSS EUR F 165/54, September 26, 1891(?).

169. Mrs. Chapman, *Sketches of Some Distinguished Indian Women*; MSS EUR F 165/4, April 11, 1891, and June 18, 1891.

170. MSS EUR F 165/4, April 5, 1891.

171. MSS EUR F 165/3, October 24, 1890.

172. Later in her life, she kept a running count of women in India holding legal qualifications; see the appendix to *India Calling*, where she actually put her statistics into table form, with herself as the baseline (301). The first African American woman to enter an American university law school got her J.D. in 1930. See Etter-Lewis, *My Soul Is My Own*, 23.

173. MSS EUR F 165/4, March 21, 1891.

174. MSS EUR F 165/4, April 12, 1891.

175. MSS EUR F 165/3, December 23, 1890. This was probably Mary Bhore, who was in residence at Somerville between 1898 and 1900, but who does not appear to have done exams there. She later became "directress of female education" in Baroda and head of the Female Training College at Poona. *Somerville College Calendars* (Oxford: Baxter's Press, n.d.), 27; *Somerville College Register 1879–1959* (Oxford: Oxford University Press, 1961), 24; and Bhor, *Some Impressions of England*.

176. I am grateful to Seth Koven for this point.

177. According to Stefan Collini, when the *Nineteenth Century* was begun in 1877, "it deliberately set out to capture big names with big fees." Contributors in Sorabji's day might expect as much as £50 an article (Collini, 40). She was not paid by the magazine's editor, James Knowles, for "Stray Thoughts by an Indian Girl," though he did commission at least one other piece from her for which he paid her a sum considerably less than the going rate.

178. MSS EUR F 165/5, September 23, 1891.

179. MSS EUR F 165/4, March 26, 1891.

180. Rukhmabai, "Indian Child Marriages," 263–69.

181. MSS EUR F 165/5, November 22, 1891.

182. MSS EUR F 165/6, February 21, 1892.

183. MSS EUR F 165/6, May 26, 1892.

184. MSS EUR F 165/6, June 15, 1892.

185. She chose chemistry, where other girls had gone before, but recalled: "[S]o I gave up my great love." Florence Rich to Helen Darbishire, Somerville College Archives, August 31, 1939. For a discussion of other contemporary women's entrances into science and medical courses, see Dyhouse, *No Distinction of Sex?*

186. Private conversation with Richard Sorabji, June 21, 1995. In his words the family "loved wit—[and it was often] not very well thought out, but graphic."

187. This was on the occasion of the Berkshire Conference of Women Historians, June 9, 1996, Chapel Hill North Carolina, where Forbes chaired a session in which I presented "Dress and the Colonial Female Subject: Cornelia Sorabji at Oxford."

188. For an interesting parallel, see Meena Alexander on Sarojini Naidu's use of sati, "Sarojini Naidu," 69.

189. Chowdhury-Sengupta, "Return of the Sati," 41–44.

190. For a discussion of the circulation of images of Indian women in Victorian culture, see Nair, "Uncovering the Zenana," 8–34; and Burton, *Burdens of History*.

191. I am indebted to Peterson's "What to Wear?" See Schwartz, *Implicit Understandings*, 403–21.

192. See Soffer, *Discipline and Power*, 157. According to Mary Stocks, Eleanor Rathbone (also a Somervillian) thought her Greats exam was a terrible ordeal; her right hand cramped, making her writing so poor that her examiners refused to decipher it. She eventually had to dictate the exam to a typist. In the end she got a second. See *Eleanor Rathbone*, 47. Florence Rich remembered her viva as an "ordeal" as well. When she and her friend Miss Seward entered the schools for the exam, a porter angrily called out, "What do you ladies want here?" Florence Rich to Helen Darbishire, Somerville College Library Archives, August 31, 1938. According to Eleanor Lodge, "I never did get a first class and whatever people say as to how little that matters in after life I cannot agree with them. My second class has always remained as a source of acute discomfort and self-distrust." *Terms and Vacations*, 55.

193. MSS EUR F 165/6, June 23, 1892.

194. Cornelia Sorabji to Lady Hobhouse, MSS EUR F 165/16, June 22, 1892. One of her tutors, Thomas Raleigh, wrote to Miss Maitland just before this, reassuring her of how challenging Sorabji's course was. "I mention this," he wrote " . . . because I know that Miss Sorabji was bent on doing credit to the Hall, and . . . proving that her time at Oxford has been turned to good account." Thomas Raleigh to Miss Maitland, MSS EUR F 165/116, item 4, June 18, 1892.

195. MSS EUR F 165/6, July 15, 1892.

196. MSS EUR F 165/6, June 23, 1892.

197. See Joyce, *Democratic Subjects*, 39. For an extended discussion of the dilemmas facing American women wage earners in Sorabji's time, see Meyerowitz, *Women Adrift*.

198. MSS EUR F 165/7, August 4, 1892; October 27, 1892; November 11, 1892 (respectively). West was the vice-chancellor of the University of Bombay during the early part of Lord Reay's administration and a frequent presider at the VHS's prize distribution days. See Hunter, *Bombay*, 141.

199. MSS EUR F 165/6, July 8, 1892.

200. Sorabji, "Law of Women's Property"; MSS EUR F 165/117.

201. MSS EUR F 165/7, September 29, 1892; and 165/8, January 18, 1893.

202. Alice Sorabji to the Sorabjis in Poona, MSS EUR F 165/207, June 1, 1905.

203. MSS EUR F 165/7, August 31, 1892.

204. Soffer, "Authority in the University," 192.

205. MSS EUR F 165/6, July 8, 1892.

206. MSS EUR F 165/7, September 29, 1892.

207. Sorabji, "Social Relations," 1.

208. MSS EUR F 165/7, December 13, 1892.

209. Loomba, *Gender, Race and Renaissance Drama*, 94.

Chapter 4. Behramji Malabari

1. Malabari, *Indian Eye*, 188.

2. For contemporary examples of men of color being "hailed" on the streets of the modern urban West, see Nirad C. Chaudhuri, *Passage to England*, 118; Stuart Hall, "Signification, Representation, Ideology," 108; Phillips, *European Tribe*, passim; Cornel West, *Race Matters*, ix–xi; and Appadurai, "Heart of Whiteness," 801–2.

3. Winter, *London's Teeming Streets, 1830–1914*, 9–10. He traces this sentiment back to the Putney debates of 1648, where General Ireton declared that among the basic birthrights of English men was "the freedom of the highways." An 1851 commentator put it this way: "[A]ll who consign themselves to the chances of the pavement are *equal*"(emphasis in the original).

4. I am grateful here to Lara Kriegel, who first suggested to me that *The Indian Eye* functioned as a kind of conduct guide. Ania Loomba's succinct comment is also appropriate: "Colonialism is manifestly the history of the intersection of various and color-coded patriarchies." See her "Color of Patriarchy," 33. For a discussion of a different but related kind of patriarchal bargain, see Laura Tabili's analysis of Indian nationalists' expectations of citizenship in exchange for support of the British Empire in World War I, *"We Ask for British Justice"*, 19.

5. Lake, "Politics of Respectability," 116–31; Hall, *White, Male and Middle Class*; Sinha, *Colonial Masculinity*; and Bederman, *Manliness and Civilization*. See also Adams, *Dandies and Desert Saints*.

6. Sinha, *Colonial Masculinity*; and Chowdhury-Sengupta, "Effeminate and the Masculine," 284–303. See also Sinha, "Gender and Imperialism," 217–31 and "Age of Consent Act," 99–127. Laura Tabili's 1994 book, *"We Ask for British Justice,"* argues that by the twentieth century, "British imperial identity was increasingly constituted around class-specific and gendered images of a predatory masculinity that was also race-specific — 'imperial manhood' " (10).

7. Malabari was certainly not alone among Indians in producing "racial prejudices" about the working class; the Bengali *bhadralok* adopted much the same attitude toward the indigenous proletariat in nineteenth-century India, with Sasipada Bannerjee a notable exception. See Chakrabarty, *Rethinking Working-Class History*, 146–48.

8. I am borrowing here from Jukes, *Shout in the Street*, xiv. I am grateful to Joe McLaughlin for this reference.

9. Bhabha, "Interrogating Identity," 184 and ff.

10. See Cornwall and Lindisfarne, *Dislocating Masculinity*, 1–8.

11. For relevant discussions of the everyday as a site of historical value, see

Sumit Sarkar, "Popular Culture, Community, Power," 309–23; Raychaudhuri, *Europe Reconsidered*; and Langebauer, "City, the Everyday and Boredom," 80–120.

12. Mrs. Postans (Marianne Young), *Western India in 1838*, vol. 2, 205.

13. Edwardes, *Rise of Bombay*, 299.

14. Douglas, *Book of Bombay*, 18.

15. I am thinking here particularly of Inderpal Grewal's *Home and Harem*, 143–55; and Sinha, *Colonial Masculinity*, chapter 4. Unfortunately, T. M. Lu-rhmann's *The Good Parsi* appeared only as this book was going to press; it addresses many of the questions of Parsi cultural location articulated by both Sorabji and Malabari.

16. Kulke, *Parsis in India*, 136. For a discussion of Parsis before the nineteenth century, see White, *Competition and Collaboration*.

17. Dobbin, *Urban Leadership in Western India*, 63.

18. Karaka, *History of the Parsis*, vol. 1, xx.

19. See Viswanathan, *Masks of Conquest*, 37; and Tanika Sarkar, "Hindu Wife and the Hindu Nation," 214–35.

20. She was seven and he, eleven. See Masani, *Dadhabai Naoroji*, 30.

21. See Chatterjee, "Nationalist Resolution of the Women's Question," 233–54.

22. Karaka, *History of the Parsis*, 191.

23. Naoroji, "European and Asiatic Races," 21. See also his *Manners and Customs of the Parsees* (Bombay: Union Press, 1864), a paper read before the Liverpool Philomatic Society, March 1861.

24. Chatterjee, *Nation and Its Fragments*, 223.

25. Thanks to Philippa Levine for encouraging me to pursue this point. Quote is from Duara, *Rescuing History from the Nation*, 7.

26. Haynes, *Rhetoric and Ritual in Colonial India*, 79.

27. Arnold, *Colonizing the Body*, 272. Kathryn Hansen also observes that Parsi theaters were most imitative of English-style playhouses in nineteenth-century Bombay and Calcutta. See her "Birth of Hindi Drama in Banaras, 1868–1885," 75 and 77.

28. Kulke, *Parsis*, 186–87.

29. Tanika Sarkar, "Rhetoric against Age of Consent," 1870.

30. See Karkaria, *India*, especially chapter 5.

31. The notes were published as *Infant Marriage and Enforced Widowhood in India: Being a Collection of Opinions for and against Received by B. M. Malabari from Representative Hindu Gentlemen and Officials and Other Authorities* (Bombay: Voice of India Printing Press, 1887). See also Gidumal, *Life*, 1–5.

32. Dobbin, *Urban Leadership*, chapter 10, esp. 247; see also Kosambi, "Gender Reform," 265–90.

33. See Gorham, " 'Maiden Tribute,' "353–79; and Walkowitz, *City of Dreadful Delight*, chapters 3 and 4.

34. Bayly, *Imperial Meridian*, 111; Marks, "History, the Nation and the Empire," 111–19; Stanley, "British Feminist Histories," 3–7; Burton, " 'Rules of Thumb,' "483–500; and Stoler, *Race and the Education of Desire*.

35. Valverde discusses the impact of Stead's "Maiden Tribute of Modern Bab-

ylon Campaign" in Toronto, in *The Age of Light, Soap and Water*, 90–92. See also Weeks, *Sex, Politics and Society*; Hearn, *Men in the Public Eye*; and Mort, *Dangerous Sexualities*.

36. Bederman, *Manliness and Civilization*, 11.

37. Gidumal, *Life*, 214; Gorham "Maiden Tribute," 353–79; and Anagol-McGinn, "Age of Consent Act (1891) Reconsidered," 110–118.

38. Gidumal, *B. Malabari: A Biographical Sketch*, 6.

39. For evidence of their influence on him, see B. M. Malabari, "Three Hours with Miss Carpenter in Bombay," *Indian Magazine and Review* 91 (July 1878): 300–304; and Gidumal, *Life*, 199–200 and 201–04.

40. Mani, "Contentious Traditions," 88–126.

41. See Kopf, *Brahmo Samaj and the Shaping of the Modern Indian Mind*; and Engels, "Age of Consent Act of 1891," 107–34.

42. Gidumal, *Life*, 137 and 143.

43. Ibid., 131. Sudhir Chandra points out that there was some debate over Malabari's use of the term "un-English" itself. See Chandra's "Whose Laws?" 202 (F. 25).

44. Ibid., 200.

45. Ibid., 1–5.

46. See Burton, "White Woman's Burden," 137–57, and *Burdens of History*.

47. Gidumal, *Life*, 206.

48. Gidumal, *Life*, 201.

49. Ibid.

50. Gidumal, *Life*, 205 and 199.

51. Quoted in Radha Kumar, *History of Doing*, 16–17. See also Tanika Sarkar, "Book of Her Own," 37. I am grateful to Mrinalini Sinha for urging me to seek out historical evidence that this practice predated Malabari's "speaking as" an Indian woman.

52. Walkowitz, *City of Dreadful Delight*, 96.

53. Loomba is quoted in Sinha, " 'Chathams, Pitts and Gladstone in Petti-coats,' " 105.

54. This is his term. See Gidumal, *Life*, 228 (subtext). For a discussion of Malabari's activities in London around the committee he formed, see Sinha, *Colonial Masculinity*, chapter 4.

55. Malabari, *Indian Eye*, 2.

56. Ibid., 144.

57. At least one other Indian visitor knew Dr. Bhabha. See Nadkarni, *Journal*, 10 and 57.

58. See for example, Ram, *My Trip*, 75–76; and Nadkarni, *Journal*, 26.

59. Ram, *My Trip*, 81. V. S. Naipaul admitted in *The Enigma of Arrival* that "the London I knew or imaginatively possessed was the London I had got from Dickens." Conversely, Jeremy Seabrook writing on Bombay in the twentieth century, could only see that Indian city as Mayhew's London. See Jukes, *Shout in the Street*, 10 and 39. For another take on England as the imaginary property of the colonial subject, see Gooneratne, "Family Histories as Post-Colonial Texts," 96.

60. The phrase "rhetoric of walking" is Michel de Certeau's. See *Practice of Everyday Life*, 100.

61. Booth, *In Darkest England and the Way Out*; and Margaret Harkness, *In Darkest London*, especially 3; Nord, "Social Explorer as Anthropologist," 122–34. George Sims's *How the Poor Live* (1883) suggests that the literature of the 1890s was the acceleration of a well-established Victorian trend; see Jukes, *Shout in the Street*, 22. See also Keating, *Into Unknown England, 1866–1913*; Arata, "Occidental Tourist," 621–45; and McLaughlin, *Writing the Urban Jungle*. I am also grateful to Michael Levenson and my colleagues in the NEH summer seminar, "The Culture of London, 1850–1925," for enabling me to appreciate this point.

62. See Baijnath, *England and India*, 30; and Pandian, *England to an Indian Eye*. For a fuller discussion of Indian male travelers in the metropole, see Antoinette Burton, "Making a Spectacle of Empire," 96–117.

63. Malabari, *Indian Eye*, 94, 1, 87, respectively.

64. Nord, "City as Theater," 186.

65. The Anglo-Indian photojournalist Olive Christian Malvery ventriloquized the Cockney visually rather than verbally in her investigative reports for the early twentieth-century London periodical press. See Walkowitz, "Daughter of Empire."

66. Malabari, *Indian Eye*, 70.

67. See for example Shaw, *Travels in England*.

68. Baijnath, *England and India*, 22; Satthianadhan, *Holiday Trip to Europe and America*, 99. For a contemporary contrast, see Phillips, *European Tribe*: "In the rain Paris looks suspiciously like London. This is one of the reasons I dislike France. It reminds me of Britain" (56).

69. Pandian, *England to an Indian Eye*, 91.

70. Pollin, "Transport Lines and Social Divisions," 29–61.

71. Malabari, *Indian Eye*, 27.

72. Ibid., 32.

73. See Pollock, "Dangers of Proximity," esp. 11. Alejo Carpentier uses a bus scene to stage another kind of colonial encounter in an interior space in *The Lost Steps* (1953). For an analysis of this text, see Kutzinski, *Sugar's Secrets*, 2–4.

74. Quoted in Chakrabarty, "Difference-Deferral of (a) Colonial Modernity," 1.

75. I am grateful here to Kutzinski, *Sugar's Secrets*, 32.

76. I am drawing heavily here from Nord's *Walking the Victorian Streets*, 2–3.

77. Malabari, *Indian Eye*, 33–34.

78. See *Sugar's Secrets*, 41. For my arguments about humor and seriousness, I am also drawing on Paul Edwards's helpful essay, "Unreconciled Strivings and Ironic Strategies," 32; and Henry Louis Gates Jr.'s *Figures in Black*, 85. I am grateful to Harry Marks for encouraging me to consider Malabari's irony in the first place.

79. Murray's 1875 *Handbook to London as It Is* warned about the "heat and crowding" of the omnibus and about the difficulty, if not the unsuitability, of climbing upon the "knife-board," or roof, for women (36). For a fuller description, see Clunn, *Face of London*, 6.

80. I am grateful to Judith Walkowitz for this suggestion.

81. The expression is de Certeau's. See his *Practice of Everyday Life*, 111.

82. Jhinda Ram knew the fleshpots, however: he named the Royal Aquarium as a site for profligate women, in *My Trip*, 49. See also Baijnath, *England and India*, 26; and Nadkarni, *Journal*, 7.

83. Mary Hobhouse, "London Sketches by an Indian Pen," *Indian Magazine and Review* (February 1890): 61–73 and "Further Sketches by an Indian Pen" (March 1890): 139–58. The incident described above is related in the second installment by M. Hasan Khan, who visited England in the spring and summer of 1888.

84. Hobhouse, "Further Sketches," 145.

85. Visram, *Ayahs*, 81–82 and 169–89.

86. M. Dorothy George was one of the earliest historians of London to note the presence of Afro-Caribbean and South Asian peoples. See her *London Life in the Eighteenth Century*, 134–44. See also Visram, *Ayahs*, esp. chapter 4 and appendices; Salter, *Asiatic in England*; Augustus Mayhew, *Paved with Gold*, 1–4; Duffield and Gundara, *Essays on the History of Blacks in Britain*.

87. See Kutzinski, *Sugar's Secrets*, 3 and 32.

88. Ram, *My Trip*, 77.

89. Malabari, *Indian Eye*, 31.

90. See Sedgwick, *Between Men*, especially chapters 1 and 10; and Brown, "Polyrhythms and Improvisation," 85–90. Thanks to Robert Reid-Pharr for helping me to make this connection.

91. Ram, *My Trip*, 76.

92. Karkaria, *Charm of Bombay*, 292 and 297.

93. Ibid., 319.

94. Dwivedi and Mehrotta, *Bombay*. Thanks to Rob Gregg for the reference and to Barbara Ramusack for the gift.

95. Dasa, *Reminiscences*, 237; Thorner, "Bombay," xv; and Kosambi, "British Bombay and Marathi Mumbai", 3–24.

96. Anandibai Joshi, *Speech by a Hindu Lady*, 7–8, quoted in Anagol, "Sexual Harassment in India," 228. See also Dall, *Life of Dr. Anandabai Joshee*, 40. Kadambini Ganguli suffered similar humiliations in Bengal, suggesting that the woman doctor was among the most threatening public women of all. Karlekar, *Voices from Within*, 177–79.

97. Anagol, "Sexual Harassment," 225.

98. I am grateful to Judith Walkowitz for pressing this point.

99. Elizabeth Wilson, "Invisible Flaneur," 93.

100. Pollock, "Vicarious Excitements," 38; Elizabeth Wilson, "Invisible Flaneur," 90–93; and for the American context, see Ryan, *Women in Public*.

101. Nord, *Walking the Victorian Streets*.

102. As an American, Jack London apparently didn't feel much at home either as he did his investigative slumming in London disguised as a stoker—dressed, in his words, "in the clothes of the other and unimaginable men." See his "People of the Abyss" (1903) in Keating, *Into Darkest England*, 226–38.

103. Nord, *Walking the Victorian Streets*, 145 and 240.

104. Gandhi, *Autobiography*; Rakhal Haldar Das, *English Diary of an Indian*

Student, 1861–62; Meredith Borthwick, *The Life and Teachings of Keshub Chunder Sen* (Calcutta: Minerva Associates, 1977); Tagore, *My Reminiscences*.

105. Or of "black men" in spaces where contact with white women might be unregulated. For three examples, see Fanon, *Black Skin, White Masks*, 72; Anant, "Three Faces of an Indian," 87–88; and Kureishi, "London and Karachi," 270–288

106. David Morgan, *Discovering Men*, 202. Significantly perhaps, Morgan makes this observation in connection with the challenges to masculinity posed by the women's suffrage movement.

107. Malabari, *Indian Eye*, 87.

108. Quoted in Mohanram, "Postcolonial Maori Sovereignty," 64. I am grateful to Devoney Looser for pointing me toward this reference. According to W. E. B. Du Bois, "[T]he black man is a person who must ride 'Jim Crow' in Georgia." Quoted in Appiah, *In My Father's House*, 40.

109. Dasa, *Reminiscences*, 1–5.

110. Malabari, *Indian Eye*, 12.

111. Restaurants and theaters are two other such spaces.

112. Baedeker, *London and Its Environs*, 12–13; Hamid Ali, "The Cost of Living in London," *Indian Magazine and Review* 134 (February 1882): 88–92.

113. See for example *The Indian Spectator*, December 17, 1893, p. 1004.

114. Malabari, *Indian Eye*, 152.

115. Baijnath, *England and India*, 29. See also Mrs. E. T. Cook, *Highways and Byways of London*, 295. I am grateful to Heidi Holder for this latter reference.

116. See Ragaviah, *Pictures of England*, 58.

117. Malabari, *Indian Eye*, 155. See also Walker, "Men and Masculinity in the Salvation Army, 1865–1890," 92–112.

118. See Davidoff, "Class and Gender in Victorian England," 17–71; Pollock, "Dangers of Proximity;" and McClintock, *Imperial Leather*, part II.

119. Malabari, *Indian Eye*, 156.

120. Ibid., 154. I am grateful to Angela Woollacott for suggesting this particular reading to me.

121. Malabari, *Indian Eye*, 59

122. Satthianadhan, *Holiday*, 98.

123. Mukharji, *Visit to Europe*, 87.

124. Malabari, *Indian Eye*, 75–76.

125. See Baijnath, *England and India*, 40; Pandian, *England to an Indian Eye*, 16–17; and Dutt, *Three Years in Europe*, 28.

126. See Kopf, *Brahmo Samaj*, 13–15.

127. Malabari, *Indian Eye*, 76.

128. Ibid., 74

129. See for example, "The Hindoo Marriage Law," *Englishwomen's Review*, April 15, 1887, p. 182; Behramji Malabari's *Appeal from the Daughters of India*; and Sinha, *Colonial Masculinity*.

130. Malabari, *Indian Eye*, 73.

131. Ibid., 159. Significantly perhaps, one of Malabari's biographers believed that Malabari had inherited his concern for Hindu women from his own mother,

a Parsi woman with "an almost incredible attachment for Hindus." Karkaria, *India*, 123.

132. Burton, *Burdens of History*. To borrow from Chakrabarty's analysis of the working class in nineteenth-century Bengal, the nature of Malabari's defiance may also be said to have mirrored the nature of the colonial authority to which he was responding. See *Rethinking Working-Class History*, 185.

133. Malabari, *Indian Eye*, esp., 59–66.

134. Ibid., 121–22. T. B. Pandian recounted a similar resistance on the part of English officials when he tried to meet with some on a trip to London in 1893. See his *Slaves of the Soul in Southern India* (Madras, 1899), 193. The official in question was G. W. E. Russell, undersecretary of state for India. See also John Bright's brief account of one of his visits with Lalmohun Ghose (1879) in Walling, *Diaries of John Bright*, 424.

135. Malabari, *Indian Eye*, 60–62.

136. See Lake, "Politics of Respectability," 117.

137. Satthianadhan, *Four Years in an English University*, 21.

138. Malabari, *Indian Eye*, 60.

139. Chakrabarty, "Difference-Deferral," 5.

140. See for example *The Mahratta*, August 17, 1890, p. 4 and August 24, 1890, p. 5.

141. See Prakash's introduction to his *After Colonialism*, 3.

142. I intend this as a critical reading of recent tendencies to speak of "trans" national practices and "globalized" cultural formations. See Grewal and Kaplan, *Scattered Hegemonies*. Robert Carr's essay in the volume, *Crossing the First World/ Third World Divides*, 153–72, offers an important and useful critical appraisal of these tendencies in his reading of how *I, Rigoberta Menchu* has been put to use in Western-feminist classrooms; see also Gyan Prakash in his introduction to *After Colonialism*.

143. Malabari, *Indian Eye*, 192.

144. Hay, "Making of a Late-Victorian Hindu," 74–98; Moira Ferguson, *History of Mary Prince*; Alexander and Dewjee, *Wonderful Adventures of Mrs. Seacole in Many Lands*; C. L. R. James, *Beyond a Boundary*; Equiano, *Interesting Narrative of the Life of Olaudah Equiano, Written by Himself*; Murphy, "Olaudah Equiano, Accidental Tourist," 551–68; Western, *Passage to England*; Foner, *Life and Writings of Frederick Douglass*, 62–75; and David H. Burton, *Anglo-American Plutarch*, chapter 4; and Gilroy, *Black Atlantic*.

145. Bederman, *Manliness and Civilization*, chapter 5. I am grateful to Herman Bennett and Susan Thorne for urging me to engage this point.

146. See Sinha, *Colonial Masculinity*, chapter 1.

147. Anne McClintock, *Imperial Leather*, 16.

148. See Mitchell, *Colonising Egypt*, chapter 1.

149. See Wallace, *Walking, Literature and English Culture*, esp. chapter 4, "Walking as Ideology"; and Grewal's *Home and Harem*, esp. 171–77.

150. Nord, *Walking the Victorian Streets*, 238.

151. Pandian, *England to an Indian Eye*; and Pillai, *London and Paris through Indian Spectacles*.

152. For a discussion of postcolonial history as a quest to provincialize Europe, see Chakrabarty, "Postcoloniality and the Artifice of History," 20.

153. Mukharji, *Visit to Europe*, xi. See also Nagendra Nath Ghose, *Indian Views of England*.

Epilogue

1. For a fuller discussion of relating the global to the everyday, see Holt's "Marking," 1–20.

2. See Clifford, "Traveling Cultures," 116.

3. Gagnier, *Subjectivities*, 6.

4. I am grateful to Mrinalini Sinha for making this connection at our Berkshire Conference of Women Historians Panel, June 9, 1996.

5. Fraser, "Reply to Zylan," 532.

6. Mohanram, "Postcolonial Maori Sovereignty," 63. See also Radhakrishnan, "Is the Ethnic 'Authentic' in the Diaspora?" 219–33.

7. Bhabha, "Of Mimicry and Man," 128.

8. This is from Powell's speech at Eastbourne, November 16, 1968, quoted in Gilroy, *"There Ain't No Black in the Union Jack,"* 46. See also Waters, "The Pink and the Black," 210–21.

9. See de Certeau, *Practice of Everyday Life*, xii and 99–100, and Robertson et al., *Travelers' Tales*, 2.

10. I am grateful here to Saskia Sassen's observation that "throughout history people have moved and through these movements [have] constituted places." See "Whose City Is It?" 219. See also Clifford, "Notes on Travel and Theory," 179.

11. Here I am self-consciously echoing Dipesh Chakrabarty's call for "the provincialization of Europe" as one method of challenging orientalism in history-writing. See his "Postcoloniality and the Artifice of History," 1–26, and Prakash's discussion of this tack in "Subaltern Studies as Postcolonial Criticism," 1484.

12. Dirks, *Colonialism and Culture*; Thomas, *Colonialism's Culture*.

Bibliography

Primary Sources

MANUSCRIPTS AND COLLECTIONS

Janaki Agnes Penelope Majumdar, "Family History". Unpublished manuscript provided courtesy of Amar Singh. Private Collection.
Office of Indian and Oriental Collections (OIOC). Cornelia Sorabji Papers, MSS EUR F 165.
Somerville College Library Archives, Oxford College, Oxford.
The Wellcome Institute for the History of Medicine, Medical Women's Federation Archives, London.

NEWSPAPERS AND PERIODICALS

The Bombay Gazette, 1884–87
The Cheltenham College Ladies' Magazine, 1884–85
Church Missionary Intelligencer, 1888–94
English Opinion on India, 1887–94
The Englishwoman's Review, 1880–90
The Imperial, Asiatic Quarterly Review and Oriental and Colonial Record, 1886–91
The Indian Appeal, 1889–90
The Indian Female Evangelist, 1878–95
The Indian Magazine and Review, 1886–1910
The Indian Spectator, 1890–94
The Journal of the National Indian Association, 1871–85
Journal of the Women's Education Union, 1873–77
The Mahratta, 1885–93
The Oxford Magazine, 1885–95

The Pall Mall Gazette, 1880–95
The Saturday Review, 1880–95
Times (London), 1880–95

PRINTED AND PAMPHLET MATERIAL

Anand, Mulk Raj. *Conversations in Bloomsbury*. 2nd ed. Delhi: Oxford India Paperbacks, 1995.

Anstey, F. (Pseudonym for Thomas Anstey Guthrie). *Baboo Hurry Bungsho Jabberjee, M.A.* New York: D. Appleton, 1897.

Athvale, Parvati. *Hindu Widow: An Autobiography*. New Delhi: Reliance Publishing House, 1986.

Baedeker, Karl. *London and Its Environs*. 11th ed. London: Dulau, 1898.

Baijnath, Lala. *England and India: Being Impressions of Persons, Things, English and Indian, and Brief Notes of Visits to France, Switzerland, Italy and Ceylon*. Bombay: Jehangir B. Karani, 1893.

Bamford, Alfred J. *Turbans and Tales; or, Sketches in the Unromantic East*. London: Sampson, Low, Marston, Searle, and Rivington, 1888.

Banerjea, Surendranath. *A Nation in Making: Being the Reminiscences of Fifty Years of Public Life*. 1925. Reprint, Calcutta: Oxford University Press, 1963.

Banerji, Brajendra Nath. "The Last Days of Rajah Rammohun Roy". *The Modern Review* 46 (October 1919): 381–83.

———. "Rajah Rammohun Roy's Mission to England". *The Modern Review* 39 (April–May 1926): 391–97, 561–65.

———. "Rammohun Roy in the Service of the East India Company". *The Modern Review* 47 (May 1930): 570–76.

———. "Rammohun Roy's Embassy to England". *The Modern Review* 55 (January 1934): 49–61.

———. "Rammohun Roy's Political Mission to England". *The Modern Review* 45 (January–February 1929): 18–21, 160–65.

———. "Sutherland's Reminiscences of Rammohun Roy". *Calcutta Review* 56 (October 1935): 58–70.

Bhor, Marie. *Some Impressions of England: A Lecture Delivered under the Auspices of the Friends Liberal Association, Poona*. Poona: Duyan Chakshu, 1900.

Booth, William. *In Darkest England and the Way Out*. London: International Headquarters of the Salvation Army, 1890.

Brittain, Vera. *The Women at Oxford: A Fragment of History*. London: George G. Harap, 1960.

Carpenter, Mary. *The Last Days in England of the Rajah Rammohun Roy*. 1866. Reprint, Calcutta: Riddhi, 1976.

Chapman, Mrs. E. F. *Sketches of Some Distinguished Indian Women*. London: Longman's, 1891.

Cobbe, Frances Power. *Life of Frances Power Cobbe by Herself*. 2 vols. Cambridge: Riverside, 1894.

Collins, Wilkie. *The Moonstone*. 1868. Reprint, New York: Oxford University Press, 1982.

Cook, Mrs. E. T. *Highways and Byways of London*. London: Macmillan, 1902.

Courtney, Janet E. *An Oxford Portrait Gallery*. London: Chapman and Hall, 1931.

Creighton, Mandell. *Historical Lectures and Addresses*. London: Longman's, 1903.

Cumberland, Stuart. *A Fatal Affinity: A Weird Story*. London: Spencer Blackett, 1889.

Cundall, Frank, ed. *Reminiscences of the Colonial and Indian Exhibition*. London: William Clowes and Sons, 1886.

Dall, Caroline Healey. *The Life of Dr. Anandabai Joshee*. Boston: Roberts Brothers, 1888.

Das, Harihar. *Life and Letters of Toru Dutt*. London: Oxford University Press, 1921.

Das, Rakhal Haldar. *The English Diary of an Indian Student, 1861–62*. Dacca: Asutosh Library, 1903.

Dasa, N. *Reminiscences English and Australasian; Being an Account of a Visit to England, Australia, New Zealand, Tasmania, and Ceylon*. Calcutta: Herald, 1893.

Doré, Gustave, and Jerrold Blanchard. *London: A Pilgrimage*. London: Dover Publications, 1970.

Douglas, James. *Book of Bombay*. Bombay: Bombay Gazette Steam Press, 1883.

Dutt, R. C. *Three Years in Europe, 1868–71, with an Account of a Second Visit to Europe in 1886*. Calcutta: S. K. Lahiri, 1890.

Dyer, Helen. *Pandita Ramabai: A Great Life in Indian Missions*. London: Pickering and Inglis, 1923.

———. *Pandita Ramabai: The Story of Her Life*. New York: Fleming H. Revell, n.d.

Edwardes, S. M. *The Rise of Bombay: A Retrospect*. Bombay: Times of India Press, 1901.

Edwards, Henry Sutherland. *An Official Account of the Chinese Commission, Which Was Sent to Report on the Great Exhibition*. London: H. Vizitelly, n.d.

Empire of India: Special Catalog of Exhibits by the Government of India and Private Exhibitors. London: William Clowes and Sons, 1886.

Equiano, Olaudah. *The Interesting Narrative of the Life of Olaudah Equiano, Written by Himself*. Edited with an introduction by Robert J. Allen. New York: St. Martin's, 1995.

Faithfull, Lillian M. *In the House of My Pilgrimage*. London: Chatto and Windus, 1924.

Gandhi, Mohandas K. *An Autobiography; or, the Story of My Experiments with Truth*. 1927. Reprint, Ahmedabad: Navajivan Publishing House, 1990.

———. *The Collected Works of Mahatma Gandhi*. Vol. 1. 1884–1896. Reprint, New Delhi: Government of India, 1958.

Gedge, Evelyn C., and Mithan Choksi, eds. *Women in Modern India: Fifteen Papers by Indian Writers*. Bombay: D. P. Taraporevala Sons, 1929.

Ghose, Nagendra Nath. *Indian Views of England: The Effects of Observation of England upon Indian Ideas and Institutions*. Calcutta: Thacker, Spink, 1877.

Gidumal, Dayaram. *The Life and Life-Work of Behramji M. Malabari*. Byculla: Bombay Education Society Press, 1888.

———. *The Status of Women in India; or, a Handbook for Indian Social Reformers*. Bombay: Fort Printing Press, 1889.

Gosse, Edmund, ed. *Ancient Ballads and Legends of Hindustan by Toru Dutt*. London: Kegan Paul, Trench, 1885.

Great Exhibition of the Works of Industry of All Nations, 1851: Official Descriptive and Illustrated Catalog Guide. 3 vols. London: William Clowes and Sons, 1851.

Handbook of Information Relating to University and Professional Studies for Indian Students in the United Kingdom. 7th ed. London: Archibald and Constable, 1893.

Harkness, Margaret. *In Darkest London*. London: William Reeves, 1891.

Hobhouse, L. T., and J. L. Hammond. *Lord Hobhouse: A Memoir*. London: Edwin Arnold, 1905.

Hobhouse, Mary. *Letters from India, 1872–1877*. Printed for private circulation, 1906, British Library.

Hunter, W. W. *Bombay 1885–1890: A Study in Indian Administration*. London: Henry Frowde, 1892.

———. *The Hindu Child-Widow*. Bombay: Voice of India Printing Press, 1887.

James, Henry. *Collected Travel Writings: Great Britain and America*. New York: Library of America, 1993.

Joshi, Anandibai. *A Speech by a Hindu Lady*. Bombay, n.p., 1883.

Karaka, Dosabhai Framji. *History of the Parsis; Including Their Manners, Customs, Religion and Present Position*. 2 vols. 1884. Reprint, Delhi: Discovery Publishing House, 1986.

Karkaria, R. P. *The Charm of Bombay: An Anthology*. Bombay: D. B. Taraporevala, Sons, 1915.

———. *India: Forty Years of Progress and Reform: Being a Sketch of the Life and Times of Behramji M. Malabari*. London: Henry Frowde, 1896.

Karve, D. K. *Looking Back*. Poona: Hindu Widows' Home Association, 1936.

Keshub Chunder Sen in England: Diaries, Sermons, Addresses and Epistles. 1871. Reprint, Calcutta: P. Lal for the Writers' Workshop, 1980.

Koolee, Meerza Najaf. *Journal of a Residence in England, and of a Journey from Syria*. 2 vols. London: William Tyler, 1839.

Lodge, Eleanor C. *Terms and Vacations*. London: Oxford University Press, 1938.

Lonsdale, Margaret. "Platform Women". *Nineteenth Century* 85 (March 1884): 409–15.

Majumdar, P. C. *The Life and Teachings of Keshub Chunder Sen*. Calcutta: Nababidhan Trust, 1931.

Malabari, Behramji M. *An Appeal from the Daughters of India*. London: Farmer and Sons, 1890.

———. *The Indian Eye on English Life; or, Rambles of a Pilgrim Reformer*. Westminster: Archibald Constable, 1893.

Mayhew, Augustus. *Paved with Gold: Or, the Romance and the Reality of London Streets*. 1858. Reprint, London: Frank Cass, 1978.

Mayhew, Henry. *London Labour and the London Poor*. London: G. Woodfall and Son, 1851.

Mukharji, T. N. *A Visit to Europe*. Calcutta: W. Newman; London: Edward Stanford, 1889.

Muller, F. Max. *Auld Lang Syne (Second Series): My Indian Friends*. London: Longman's Green, 1899.

———. *Biographical Essays*. London: Longman's Green, 1884.

Muller, Mrs. M. *Life and Letters of the Right Honorable Max Muller*. 2 vols. London: Longman's Green, 1901.

Murray, John. *Handbook to London as It Is*. London: John Murray, 1874.

———. *The World of London*. London: Thomas Tegg, 1844.

Nadkarni, G. N. *Journal of a Visit to Europe in 1896*. Bombay: D. B. Taraporevala, 1903.

Naoroji, Dadhabai. *Admission of Educated Natives into the Indian Civil Service*. London: Macmillan, 1868.

———. *The European and Asiatic Races: Observations on the Paper Read by John Crawfurd before the Ethnographical Society*. London: Trubner, 1866.

Natesan, G. A. *Famous Parsis: Biographical and Critical Sketches*. Madras: G. A. Natesan, 1930.

Nehru, S. K., ed. *Our Cause: A Symposium by Indian Women*. Allahabad: Allahabad Law Journal Press, 1936.

Nowrojee, Jehangeer, and Hirjeebhoy Merwanjee. *A Residence of Two Years and a Half in Great Britain*. London: William H. Allen, 1841.

Oakly, Hilda D. *My Adventures in Education*. London: Williams and Norgate, 1939.

Onwhyn, Thomas. *Mr. and Mrs. Brown's Visit to London to See the Great Exhibition of All Nations*. London: Ackerman, 1851.

Pandian, T. B. *England to an Indian Eye; or, English Pictures from an Indian Camera*. London: Elliot Stock, 1897.

———. *Slaves of the Soul in Southern India*. Madras, n.p., 1899.

Pandita Ramabai yancha Englandcha Pravas. 1883. Reprint, Bombay: Maharashtra State Board of Literature and Culture, 1988.

Parekh, Chunilal Lallubhai. *Essays, Speeches, Addresses and Writings on Indian Politics by the Honorable Dadabhai Naoroji*. Bombay: Caxton Printing Works, 1887.

Pillai, G. P. *London and Paris through Indian Spectacles*. Madras: Vaijayanti, 1897.

Postans, Mrs. (Marianne Young). *Western India in 1838*. 2 vols. London: Saunders and Otley, 1839.

Radford, John, ed. *An Indian Journal: Nora Scott*. London: Radcliffe Press, 1994.

Ragaviah, P. J. *Pictures of England*. Madras: Gantz Brothers, 1876.

Raikes, Elizabeth. *Dorothea Beale of Cheltenham*. London: Archibald Constable, 1909.

Ram, Jhinda. *My Trip to Europe*. Lahore: Mufid-I-Am, 1893.

Ramabai, Pandita. *The High-Caste Hindu Woman*. 1884. Reprint, New Delhi: Inter-India Publications, 1984.

——. *A Testimony*. 1907. Reprint, Kedgaon: Ramabai Mukti Mission, 1968.

Rogers, Annie M. A. H. *Degrees by Degrees: The Story of the Admission of Oxford Women Students to Membership of the University*. Oxford: Oxford University Press, 1938.

Rukhmabai. "Indian Child-Marriages: An Appeal to the British Government". *The New Review* 16 (September 1890): 263–69.

Salter, Joseph. *The Asiatic in England: Sketches of Sixteen Years' Work among Orientals*. London: Seeley, Jackson, and Halliday, 1873.

——. *The East in the West, or Work among the Asiatics and Africans in London*. London: S. W. Partridge, 1895.

Satthianadhan, S. *Four Years in an English University*. Madras: Lawrence Asylum, 1890.

——. *A Holiday Trip to Europe and America*. Madras: Srinivasa, Varadachari, 1897.

Shah, A. B. *The Letters and Correspondence of Pandita Ramabai*. Bombay: Maharashtra State Board for Literature and Culture, 1977.

Shaw, John. *Travels in England: A Ramble with the City and Town Missionaries*. London: William Johnson, 1861.

Sims, George. *Living London*. 3 vols. 1901. Reprint, London: Village, 1990.

"Somerville College Log Book, 1879–1907". Somerville College Library Archives, Oxford College, Oxford.

Sorabji, Cornelia. "Benjamin Jowett—Master of Balliol College: Some Recollections". *The Nineteenth Century and After* (August 1903): 297–305.

——. *India Calling: The Memories of Cornelia Sorabji*. London: Nisbet, 1934.

——. *India Recalled*. London: Nisbet, 1936.

——. "The Law of Woman's Property in India in Relation to Her Social Position". A paper read at Queen's House, Chelsea, by invitation of the Reverend R. Haweis, March 19, 1893. OIOC MSS EUR F 165/117.

——. "The Position of Hindu Widows Fifty Years Ago". In *Our Cause: A Symposium by Indian Women*, edited by S. K. Nehru, 3–21. Allahabad: Allahabad Law Journal Press, 1936.

——. "Social Relations—England and India". In *Pan-Anglican Papers: Being Problems for Consideration at the Pan-Anglican Congress, 1908*. London: Society for Promoting Christian Knowledge, 1908.

——. *Susie Sorabji, Christian-Parsee Educationalist of Western India: A Memoir by Her Sister*. London: Oxford University Press, 1932.

——. *Therefore: An Impression of Sorabji Kharsedji Langrana and His Wife, Franscina*. Oxford: Oxford University Press, 1934.

Stock, Eugene. *The History of the Church Missionary Society*. 3 vols. London: Church Missionary Society, 1899.

Tagore, Rabindranath. *My Reminiscences*. New York: Macmillan, 1917.

Thacker's Indian Directory. Calcutta: Thacker, Spink, 1892.

Thompson, Henry. "Indian and Colonial London". In *Living London*, edited by George Sims, 306–11. Vol. 3. London: Village, 1990.

Walling, R. A. J., ed. *The Diaries of John Bright*. New York: William Morrow, 1931.

Warwick, Countess of, ed. *Progress in Women's Education in the British Empire. Being a Report of the Education Section, Victorian Era Exhibition, 1897*. London: Longman's, Green, 1898.

Wasti, Syed Razi, ed. *Memoirs and Other Writings of Syed Ameer Ali*. Lahore: People's Publishing House, 1968.

West, Captain Edward C. *Diary of the Late Rajah of Kolhapoor during His Visit to Europe in 1870*. London: Smith, Elder, 1872.

Secondary Sources

Adams, James Eli. *Dandies and Desert Saints: Styles of Victorian Masculinity*. Ithaca: Cornell University Press, 1995.

Adhav, S. M. *Pandita Ramabai*. Madras: Christian Literature Society, 1979.

Aguilar-San Juan, Karin, ed. *The State of Asian America*. Boston: South End, 1994.

Ahmad, Aijaz. *In Theory: Nations, Classes, Literatures*. London: Verso, 1992.

Alcoff, Linda. "The Problem of Speaking for Others". *Cultural Critique* 17 (winter 1991): 5–32.

Alcoff, Linda, and Elizabeth Potter, eds. *Feminist Epistemologies*. New York: Routledge, 1993.

Alderman, Geoffrey, and Colin Holmes, eds. *Outsiders and Outcasts: Essays in Honour of William J. Fishman*. London: Duckworth, 1993.

Alexander, Meena. "Sarojini Naidu: Romanticism and Resistance". *Economic and Political Weekly* 20, no. 43 (Review of Women's Studies: October 26, 1985): WS 68–71.

Alexander, Michael and Sushila Anand, *Queen Victoria's Maharajah: Duleep Singh, 1838–93*. New York: Tapling Publishing, 1980.

Alexander, Ziggi, and Audrey Dewjee, eds. *The Wonderful Adventures of Mrs. Seacole in Many Lands*. Bristol: Falling Wall, 1984.

Alter, Joseph S. "Celibacy, Sexuality, and the Transformation of Gender into Nationalism in India". *Journal of Asian Studies* 53, no. 1 (February 1994): 45–66.

Anagol, Padma. "Sexual Harassment in India: A Case Study of Eve-Teasing in Historical Perspective". In *Rethinking Sexual Harassment*, edited by Clare Brant and Yun Lee Too, 220–34. London: Pluto, 1994.

Anagol-McGinn, Padma. "The Age of Consent Act (1891) Reconsidered: Women's Perspectives and Participation in the Child-Marriage Controversy in India". *South Asia Research* 12, no. 2 (November 1992): 100–118.

Anant, Victor. "The Three Faces of an Indian". In *Alienation*, edited by Timothy O'Keefe, 79–92. London: MacGibbon and Kee, 1960.

Appadurai, Arjun. "The Heart of Whiteness". *Callaloo* 16, no. 4 (1993): 796–807.

———, ed. *The Social Life of Things: Commodities in Cultural Perspective*. Cambridge: Cambridge University Press, 1986.

Appiah, Kwame Anthony. *In My Father's House: Africa in the Philosophy of Culture*. Oxford: Oxford University Press, 1992.

Arata, Stephen D. "The Occidental Tourist: *Dracula* and the Anxiety of Reverse Colonization". *Victorian Studies* 33 (summer 1990): 621–45.

Arnold, David. *Colonizing the Body: State Medicine and Epidemic Disease in Nineteenth-Century India*. Berkeley and Los Angeles: University of California Press, 1993.

Azim, Firdous. *The Colonial Rise of the Novel*. London: Routledge, 1993.

Baldick, Chris. *The Social Mission of English Criticism, 1848–1932*. Oxford: Clarendon, 1987.

Ballard, Roger, ed. *Desh Pardesh: The South Asian Presence in Britain*. London: C. Hurst, 1994.

Bammer, Angelika, ed. *Displacements: Cultural Identities in Question*. Bloomington: Indiana University Press, 1994.

Banerji, Albion Rajkumar. *An Indian Pathfinder: Being the Memoirs of Sevabrata Sasipada Banerji, 1840–1924*. Oxford: Kemp Hall Press Printers, n.d.

Bannerji, Himani. "Textile Prison: The Discourse on Shame (*Lajja*) in the Attire of the Gentlewoman (*Bhadramahila*) in Colonial Bengal". In *From the Seams of History: Essays on Indian Women*, edited by Bharati Ray, 67–106. Delhi: Oxford University Press, 1995. First published in *South Asia Research* 13, no. 1 (May 1993): 27–45.

———. *Thinking Through: Essays on Feminism, Marxism and Anti-Racism*. Toronto: Women's Press, 1995.

Bapat, Ram. "Pandita Ramabai: Faith and Reason in the Shadow of the East and West". In *Representing Hinduism: The Construction of Religious Traditions and National Identity*, edited by Vasudha Dalmia and H. von Stietencron, 224–52. New Delhi: Sage, 1995.

Basu, Aparna. "A Nationalist Feminist: Mridula Sarabhai [1911–1974]". *The Indian Journal of Gender Studies* 2, no. 1 (1995): 1–24.

Bayly, C. A. *Imperial Meridian: The British Empire and the World 1780–1830*. London: Longman's, 1989.

———. "The Origins of *Swadeshi* (Home Industry): Cloth and Indian Society, 1700–1930". In *The Social Life of Things: Commodities in Cultural Perspective*, edited by Arjun Appadurai, 285–322. Cambridge: Cambridge University Press, 1986.

Bederman, Gail. *Manliness and Civilization: A Cultural History of Gender and Race in the United States, 1880–1917*. Chicago: University of Chicago Press, 1995.

Bennett, Mary. *The Ilberts in India, 1882–1886: An Imperial Miniature*. London: British Association for Cemeteries in South Asia, 1995.

Bhabha, Homi K. "Interrogating Identity: The Postcolonial Prerogative". In *The Anatomy of Racism*, edited by David Theo Goldberg, 183–209. Minneapolis: University of Minnesota Press, 1990.

———. *The Location of Culture*. New York: Routledge, 1994.

———. "Of Mimicry and Man: The Ambivalence of Colonial Discourse". *October* 28 (spring 1984): 125–33.

———. "The Other Question: Difference, Discrimination and the Discourse of Colonialism". In *Out There: Marginalization and Contemporary Cultures*, edited by Russell Ferguson, Martha Gever, Trinh T. Minh-ha, and Cornel West, 71–87. New York: New Museum of Contemporary Art; Cambridge: MIT Press, 1990.

Blakely, Allison. *Blacks in the Dutch World: The Evolution of Racial Imagery in a Modern Society*. Bloomington: Indiana University Press, 1993.

Blunt, Alison. "Mapping Authorship and Authority: Reading Mary Kingsley's Landscape Descriptions". In *Women Writing and Space: Colonial and Post-colonial Geographies*, edited by Alison Blunt and Gillian Rose, 51–72. London: Guilford, 1994.

Blunt, Alison, and Gillian Rose, eds. *Women Writing and Space: Colonial and Postcolonial Geographies*. London: Guilford, 1994.

Bolt, Christine. *Victorian Attitudes towards Race*. London: Routledge, Kegan, Paul, 1971.

Boon, James A. "Why Museums Make Me Sad". In *Exhibiting Cultures: The Poetics and Politics of Museum Display*, edited by Ivan Karp and Steven D. Lavine, 255–77. Washington, D.C.: Smithsonian Institution Press, 1991.

Borthwick, Meredith. *Keshub Chunder Sen: A Search for Cultural Synthesis*. Calcutta: Minerva Associates, 1977.

Boyce Davies, Carole. *Black Women, Writing, and Identity: Migratory Subjects*. London: Routledge, 1994.

Braidwood, Stephen J. *Black Poor and White Philanthropists: London's Blacks and the Foundation of the Sierra Leone Settlement, 1786–1791*. Liverpool: Liverpool University Press, 1994.

Brant, Clare, and Yun Lee Too, eds. *Rethinking Sexual Harassment*. London: Pluto, 1994.

Breckenridge, Carol A. "The Aesthetics and Politics of Colonial Collecting: India at World Fairs". *Contemporary Studies in Society and History* 31 (spring 1989): 195–216.

———, ed. *Consuming Modernity: Public Culture in a South Asian World*. Minneapolis: University of Minnesota Press, 1995.

Breckenridge, Carol A., and Peter van der Veer, eds. *Orientalism and the Post-colonial Predicament: Perspectives on South Asia*. Philadelphia: University of Pennsylvania Press, 1993.

Brown, Elsa Barkley. "Polyrhythms and Improvisation: Lessons for Women's History". *History Workshop Journal* 31 (spring 1991): 85–90.

Brown, Judith M. *The Origins of an Asian Democracy*. Oxford: Oxford University Press, 1994.

Burke, Timothy. *Lifebuoy Men, Lux Women: Commodification, Consumption, and Cleanliness in Modern Zimbabwe*. Durham: Duke University Press, 1996.

Burton, Antoinette. *Burdens of History: British Feminists, Indian Women, and Imperial Culture, 1865–1915*. Chapel Hill: University of North Carolina Press, 1994.

———. "Contesting the Zenana: The Mission to Make "Lady Doctors for India," 1874–1885". *Journal of British Studies* 35 (July 1996): 368–97.

———. "Fearful Bodies into Disciplined Subjects: Pleasure, Romance and the

Family Drama of Colonial Reform in Mary Carpenter's *Six Months in India*. *Signs*, 20, no. 3 (spring 1995): 545–574.

———. "Making a Spectacle of Empire: Indian Travelers in Fin-de-Siècle London". *History Workshop Journal* 42 (1996): 96–117.

———. "'Rules of Thumb': Remapping Imperial Culture in Nineteenth- and Twentieth-Century Britain". *Women's History Review* 3, no. 4 (December 1994): 483–500.

———. "The White Woman's Burden: British Feminists and 'The Indian Woman,' 1865–1915". In *Western Women and Imperialism: Complicity and Resistance*, edited by Nupur Chaudhuri and Margaret Strobel, 137–57. Bloomington: Indiana University Press, 1991.

Burton, David H., ed. *An Anglo-American Plutarch*. New York: University Press of America, 1990.

Butler, Judith. *Gender Trouble: Feminism and the Subversion of Identity*. New York: Routledge, 1990.

———. "Imitation and Gender Subordination". In *Inside/Out: Lesbian Theories, Gay Theories*, edited by Diana Fuss, 13–31. New York: Routledge, 1991.

Buzard, James. *The Beaten Track: European Tourism, Literature, and the Ways to 'Culture,' 1800–1918*. Oxford: Clarendon, 1993.

Carby, Hazel. *Reconstructing Womanhood: The Emergence of the African-American Woman Novelist*. New York: Oxford University Press, 1987.

Carr, Robert. "Crossing the First World/Third World Divides: Testimonial, Transnational Feminisms, and the Postmodern Condition". In *Scattered Hegemonies: Postmodernity and Transnational Feminist Practices*, edited by Inderpal Grewal and Caren Kaplan, 153–72. Minneapolis: University of Minnesota Press, 1994.

Centre for Urban Studies, ed. *London: Aspects of Change*. London: MacGibbon and Kee, 1969.

Chakrabarty, Dipesh. "The Difference-Deferral of (A) Colonial Modernity: Public Debates on Domesticity in British Bengal". *History Workshop Journal* 36 (autumn 1993): 1–34.

———. "Postcoloniality and the Artifice of History: Who Speaks for 'Indian' Pasts?" *Representations* 37 (winter 1992): 1–26.

———. *Rethinking Working-Class History: Bengal, 1890–1940*. Princeton: Princeton University Press, 1989.

Chakravarti, Uma. "Social Pariahs and Domestic Drudges: Widowhood among Nineteenth-Century Poona Brahmins". *Social Scientist*, 21, no. 9–11 (September–November 1993): 130–58.

———. "Whatever Happened to the Vedic *Dasi*?" In *Recasting Women: Essays in Colonial History*, edited by Kumkum Sangari and Sudesh Vaid, 27–87. New Delhi: Kali for Women, 1989.

Chambers, Iain, and Lidia Curti, eds. *The Post-Colonial Question: Common Skies, Divided Horizons*. New York: Routledge, 1996.

Chandra, Sudhir. "Whose Laws? Notes on a Legitimising Myth of the Colonial Indian State". *Studies in History* 8, no. 2 n.s. (1992): 187–211.

Chatterjee, Partha. *The Nation and Its Fragments: Colonial and Postcolonial Histories*. Princeton: Princeton University Press, 1993.

———. "The Nationalist Resolution of the Women's Question". In *Recasting Women: Essays in Colonial History*, edited by Kumkum Sangari and Sudesh Vaid, 233–53. New Delhi: Kali for Women, 1989.

Chatterjee, Partha, and Gyanendra Pandey, eds. *Subaltern Studies VII: Writings on South Asian History and Society*. Delhi: Oxford University Press, 1992.

Chaudhuri, Nirad C. *A Passage to England*. Delhi: Orient Paperbacks, 1972.

Chaudhuri, Nupur, and Margaret Strobel, eds. *Western Women and Imperialism: Complicity and Resistance*. Bloomington: Indiana University Press, 1992.

Chew, Shirley, and Anna Rutherford, eds. *Unbecoming Daughters of the Empire*. Sydney: Dangaroo, 1993.

Chow, Rey. *Writing Diaspora: Tactics of Intervention in Contemporary Cultural Studies*. Bloomington: Indiana University Press, 1993.

Chowdhury-Sengupta, Indira. "The Effeminate and the Masculine: Nationalism and the Concept of Race in Colonial Bengal". In *The Concept of Race in South Asia*, edited by in Peter Robb, 284–303. Delhi: Oxford University Press, 1995.

———. "Mother India and Mother Victoria: Motherhood and Nationalism in Nineteenth-Century Bengal". *South Asia Research* 12, no. 1 (May 1992): 20–37.

———. "The Return of the Sati: A Note on Heroism and Domesticity in Colonial Bengal". *Resources for Feminist Research/Documentation sur la recherche féministe* 22, no. 3–4 (1993): 41–44.

Clifford, James. "Diasporas". *Cultural Anthropology* 9, no. 3 (1994): 302–38.

———. "Notes on Travel and Theory". *Inscriptions* 5 (1989): 177–88.

———. "Traveling Cultures". In *Cultural Studies*, edited by Lawrence Grossberg, Cary Nelson, and Paula Treichler, 96–112. New York: Routledge, 1992.

Clunn, Harold P. *The Face of London*. London: Phoenix House, 1951.

Code, Lorraine. *Rhetorical Spaces: Essays on Gendered Locations*. New York: Routledge, 1995.

———. "Taking Subjectivity into Account". In *Feminist Epistemologies*, edited by Linda Alcoff and Elizabeth Potter, 15–48. New York: Routledge, 1993.

Cohen, David William. *The Combing of History*. Chicago: University of Chicago Press, 1994.

Cohn, Bernard S. "Cloth, Clothes and Colonialism". In *Cloth and the Human Experience*, edited by Annette B. Weiner and Jane Schneider, 303–53. Washington, D.C.: Smithsonian Institution Press, 1989.

———. *Colonialism and Its Forms of Knowledge: The British in India*. Princeton: Princeton University Press, 1996.

Collini, Stefan. *Public Moralists: Political Thought and Intellectual Life in Britain, 1850–1930*. Oxford: Clarendon, 1991.

Colomina, Beatriz, ed. *Sexuality and Space*. New York: Princeton Architectural Press, 1992.

Conlon, Frank F. "Dining Out in Bombay". In *Consuming Modernity: Public*

Culture in a South Asian World, edited by Carol A. Breckenridge, 90–130. Minneapolis: University of Minnesota Press, 1995.

———. "Hindu Revival and Indian Womanhood: The Image and Status of Women in the Writings of Vishnubawa Brahmachari". *South Asia* 17, no. 2 (1994): 1–19.

Connolly, Clara, Catherine Hall, Mary Hickman, Gail Lewis, Ann Phoenix, and Ailbhye Smith. "The Irish Issue: The British Question" [editorial]. *Feminist Review* 50 (summer 1995): 1–4.

Conway, Jill Ker, and Susan C. Bourque, eds. *The Politics of Women's Education: Perspectives from Asia, Africa, and Latin America*. Ann Arbor: University of Michigan Press, 1993.

Cook, S. B. *Imperial Affinities: Nineteenth-Century Analogies and Exchanges between India and Ireland*. New Delhi: Sage Publications, 1993.

Coombes, Annie E. "Inventing the 'Postcolonial': Hybridity and Constituency in Contemporary Curating". *New Formations* 18 (Winter 1992): 39–54.

———. *Reinventing Africa: Museums, Imperial Culture, and Popular Imagination*. New Haven: Yale University Press, 1994.

Cooper, Frederick, and Ann Stoler. "Tensions of Empire: Colonial Control and Visions of Rule". *American Ethnologist* 16 (1989): 609–21.

———. eds. *Tensions of Empire: Colonial Cultures in a Bourgeois World*. Berkeley and Los Angeles: University of California Press, 1996.

Cornwall, Andrea, and Nancy Lindisfarne, eds. *Dislocating Masculinity: Comparative Ethnographies*. New York: Routledge, 1994.

Cox, Jeffrey. "Independent Englishwomen in Lahore, 1860–1947". In *Religion and Irreligion in Victorian England*, edited by R. W. Davis, 166–84. New York: HarperCollins, 1994.

Curtis, Lionel. *Apes and Angels: The Irishman in Victorian Caricature*. Washington, D.C.: Smithsonian Institution Press, 1971.

Dabydeen, David. "On Not Being Milton: Nigger Talk in England Today". In *The State of the Language*, edited by Christopher Ricks and Leonard Michaels, 3–14. Berkeley and Los Angeles: University of California Press, 1990.

Dalmia, Vasudha, and H. von Stietencron, eds. *Representing Hinduism: The Construction of Religious Traditions and National Identity*. New Delhi: Sage, 1995.

Das, Biswanath, ed. *Autobiography of an Indian Princess: Memoirs of Maharani Sunity Devi of Cooch Behar*. New Delhi: Tarang Paperbacks, 1995.

David, Deirdre. *Rule Britannia: Women, Empire and Victorian Writing*. Ithaca: Cornell University Press, 1995.

Davidoff, Leonore. "Class and Gender in Victorian England". In *Sex and Class in Women's History*, edited by Judith L. Newton, Mary P. Ryan, and Judith R. Walkowitz, 17–71. New York: Routledge, 1983.

Davis, R. W., ed. *Religion and Irreligion in Victorian England*. New York: HarperCollins, 1994.

Deakin, Nicholas, Brian Cohen, and Julia MacNeal. *Colour, Citizenship and British Society*. London: Panther Modern Society for the Institute of Race Relations, 1970.

de Certeau, Michel. *The Practice of Everyday Life*. Berkeley and Los Angeles: University of California Press, 1984.

Demos, John. *The Unredeemed Captive: A Family Story from Early America*. New York: Vintage Books, 1994.

Dening, Greg. "P 905.A512 x 100: An Ethnographic Essay". *American Historical Review* 100, no. 3 (June 1995): 854–64.

———. *Performances*. Melbourne: Melbourne University Press, 1996.

Desai, Neera. "Women's Education in India". In *The Politics of Women's Education: Perspectives from Asia, Africa, and Latin America*, edited by Jill Ker Conway and Susan C. Bourque, 23–43. Ann Arbor: University of Michigan Press, 1993.

Desmond, Ray. *The India Museum, 1801–1879*. London: Her Majesty's Stationery Office, 1982.

di Leonardo, Micaela. "White Ethnicities, Identity Politics, and Baby Bear's Chair", *Social Text* 41 (winter 1994): 165–91.

Dirks, Nicholas, ed. *Colonialism and Culture*. Ann Arbor: University of Michigan Press, 1992.

Dobbin, Christine. *Urban Leadership in Western India: Politics and Communities in Bombay City, 1840–1885*. London: Oxford University Press, 1972.

Dossal, Miriam. *Imperial Designs and Indian Realities: The Planning of Bombay City, 1845–1875*. Bombay: Oxford University Press, 1991.

Driver, Felix. "Geography's Empire: Histories of Geographical Knowledge". *Environment and Planning D: Society and Space* 10 (1992): 23–40.

Duara, Prasenjit. *Rescuing History from the Nation: Questioning Narratives of Modern China*. Chicago: University of Chicago Press, 1995.

Dubinsky, Karen. "'The Pleasure Is Exquisite but Violent': The Imaginary Geography of Niagara Falls in the Nineteenth Century". *Revue des études canadiennes/Journal of Canadian Studies* 29, no. 2 (1994): 64–88.

Duff, David, ed. *Queen Victoria's Highland Journals*. London: Webb and Bower, 1980.

Duffield, Ian. "Dusé Mohammed Ali, Afro-Asian Solidarity and Pan-Africanism in Early Twentieth-Century London". In *Essays on the History of Blacks in Britain*, edited by J. Gundara and I. Duffield, 129–49. London: Avebury, 1992.

Dutt, R. C. *Romesh Chunder Dutt*. New Delhi: Government of India, 1968.

Dwivedi, Sharada, and Rahul Mehrotta. *Bombay: The Cities Within*. Bombay: India Book House PVT, 1995.

Dyhouse, Carol. "Miss Buss and Miss Beale: Authority in the History of Education". In *Lessons for Life: The Schooling of Girls and Women, 1850–1950*, edited by Felicity Hunt, 22–36. Oxford: Basil Blackwell, 1987.

———. *No Distinction of Sex? Women in British Universities, 1870–1939*. London: UCL Press, 1995.

Ebert, Teresa L. *Ludic Feminism and After: Postmodernism, Desire and Labor in Late Capitalism*. Ann Arbor: University of Michigan Press, 1996.

Edwards, Paul. "Unreconciled Strivings and Ironic Strategies: Three Afro-British Authors of the Late Georgian Period". In *Africans in Britain*, edited by David Killingray, 28–48. London: Frank Cass, 1994.

Edwards, Paul, and David Dabydeen, eds. *Black Writers in Britain, 1760–1890*. Edinburgh: Edinburgh University Press, 1991.

Ellsworth, Edward. *Liberators of the Female Mind: The Shirreff Sisters, Educational Reform and the Women's Movement*. Westport, Conn.: Greenwood, 1979.

Engels, Dagmar. "The Age of Consent Act of 1891: Colonial Ideology in Bengal". *South Asia Research* 3 (1983): 107–34.

Engels, Dagmar, and Shula Marks, ed. *Contesting Colonial Hegemony: State and Society in Africa and India*. New York: I. B. Tauris, 1994.

Etter-Lewis, Gwendolyn. *My Soul Is My Own: Oral Narratives of African-American Women in the Professions*. New York: Routledge, 1993.

Fanon, Frantz. *Black Skin, White Masks*. New York: Grove and Weidenfeld, 1967.

Feierman, Steven. "Africa in History: The End of Universal Narratives". In *After Colonialism: Imperial Histories and Postcolonial Displacements*, edited by Gyan Prakash, 40–65. Princeton: Princeton University Press, 1994.

Feldman, David. *Englishmen and Jews: Social Relations and Political Culture, 1840–1914*. New Haven: Yale University Press, 1994.

Ferguson, Moira, ed. *The History of Mary Prince, a West Indian Slave*. Ann Arbor: University of Michigan Press, 1993.

Ferguson, Russell, Martha Gever, Trinh T. Minh-ha, and Cornel West, eds. *Out There: Marginalization and Contemporary Cultures*. New York: New Museum of Contemporary Art; Cambridge, Mass.: MIT Press, 1990.

File, Nigel, and Chris Power. *Black Settlers in Britain, 1555–1958*. London: Heinemann Educational Books, 1981.

Flemming, Leslie. "Between Two Worlds: Self-Construction and Self-Identity in the Writings of Three Nineteenth-Century Indian Christian Women". In *Women as Subjects: South Asian Histories*, edited by Nita Kumar, 81–107. Charlottesville: University of Virginia Press, 1994.

Fletcher, Alison. " 'God Shall Wipe All Tears from Their Eyes': Refugees from Madagascar in Britain 1839–1842". Paper presented at the Global Studies Seminar, Johns Hopkins University, April 1996.

Foner, Philip S. *The Life and Writings of Frederick Douglass: Early Years, 1817–1849*. New York: International, 1950.

Forbes, Geraldine. "Child-Marriage and Reform in India". Unpublished paper.

———. *From Child Widow to Lady Doctor: The Intimate Memoir of Haimavati Sen*. Forthcoming.

———. "Managing Midwifery in India". In *Contesting Colonial Hegemony: State and Society in Africa and India*, edited by Dagmar Engels and Shula Marks, 152–72. New York: I. B. Tauris, 1994.

———. "Medical Careers and Health Care for Indian Women: Patterns of Control". *Women's History Review* 3, no. 4 (1994): 515–30.

Fox, Celina, ed. *London — World City: 1800–1840*. New Haven: Yale University Press, 1992.

Frankenberg, Ruth, and Lata Mani, "Crosscurrents, Crosstalk: Race, 'Postcoloniality' and the Politics of Location". *Cultural Studies* 7 (spring 1993): 292–310.

Fraser, Nancy. "Reply to Zylan". *Signs* 21, no. 2 (winter 1996): 531–36.

Freitag, Sandria B., ed. *Culture and Power in Banaras: Community, Performance and Environment, 1800–1980*. Berkeley: University of California Press, 1989.

Friedman, Susan Stanford. "Beyond White and Other: Relationality and Narratives of Race in Feminist Discourse". *Signs* 21, no. 1 (autumn 1995): 1–49.

Fryer, Peter. *Black People in the British Empire*. London: Pluto, 1988.

———. *Staying Power: The History of Black People in Britain*. London: Pluto, 1987.

Fuss, Diana, ed. *Inside/Out: Lesbian Theories, Gay Theories*. New York: Routledge, 1991.

Gagnier, Regenia. *Subjectivities: A History of Self-Representation in Britain, 1832–1920*. New York: Oxford University Press, 1991.

Gates, Henry Louis, Jr. *Figures in Black: Words, Signs and the 'Racial' Self*. New York: Oxford: Oxford University Press, 1987.

George, M. Dorothy. *London Life in the Eighteenth Century*. New York: Capricorn Books, 1965.

Gerzina, Gretchen. *Black London: Life before Emancipation*. New Brunswick: Rutgers University Press, 1995.

Ghose, Lotika. *Manmohan Ghose*. New Delhi: Sahitya Akademi, 1975.

Ghosh, Suresh Chandra. " 'English in Taste, Opinions, in Words and in Intellect': Indoctrinating the Indian through Textbook, Curriculum and Education". In *The Imperial Curriculum: Racial Images and Education in the British Colonial Experience*, edited by J. A. Mangan, 175–93. London: Routledge, 1993.

Gibbon, Luke. "Race against Time: Racial Discourse and Irish History". *Oxford Literary Review* 13 (spring 1991): 95–117.

Gilroy, Paul. *The Black Atlantic: Modernity and Double Consciousness*. Cambridge, Mass.: Harvard University Press, 1993.

———. *Small Acts: Thoughts on the Politics of Black Cultures*. London: Serpent's Tail, 1993.

———. *'There Ain't No Black in the Union Jack': The Cultural Politics of Race and Nation*. Chicago: University of Chicago, 1991.

Glendenning, F. A. "School History Textbooks and Racial Attitudes, 1804–1911". *Journal of Educational and Administrative History* 5, no. 2 (July 1973): 31–45.

Goldberg, David Theo, ed. *Anatomy of Racism*. Minneapolis: University of Minnesota Press, 1990.

Gooneratne, Yasmine. "Family Histories as Post-Colonial Texts". In *Unbecoming Daughters of the Empire*, edited by Shirley Chew and Anna Rutherford, 93–100. Sydney: Dangaroo, 1993.

Gooptu, Suparna. "Cornelia Sorabji, 1866–1954: Imperialism, Nationalism and Gender in the Making of an Early Indian Feminist". Ph.D. diss., St. Antony's College, Oxford, in progress.

Gorham, Deborah. "The 'Maiden Tribute of Modern Babylon' Re-Visited". *Victorian Studies* 19 (spring 1976): 353–79.

———. "Victorian Reform as a Family Business: The Hill Family". In *The Victorian Family: Structure and Stress*, edited by Anthony S. Wohl, 119–47. New York: St. Martin's, 1978.

Gouda, Frances. *Dutch Culture Overseas: Colonial Practices in the Netherlands Indies, 1900–1942*. Amsterdam: Amsterdam University Press, 1995.

Grewal, Inderpal. *Home and Harem: Nation, Gender, Empire and Cultures of Travel*. Durham: Duke University Press, 1996.

Grewal, Inderpal, and Caren Kaplan, eds. *Scattered Hegemonies: Postmodernity and Transnational Feminist Practices*. Minneapolis: University of Minnesota Press, 1994.

Griffiths, Gareth. "The Myth of Authenticity". In *De-Scribing Empire: Post-Colonialism and Textuality*, edited by Chris Tiffin and Alan Lawson, 70–85. London: Routledge, 1994.

Grimshaw, Patricia, Marilyn Lake, Ann McGrath, and Marian Quartly. *Creating a Nation, 1788–1990*. Ringwood, Australia: Penguin Books Australia, 1994.

Grossberg, Lawrence, Cary Nelson, and Paula Treichler, eds. *Cultural Studies*. New York: Routledge, 1992.

Grosz, Elizabeth. "Bodies-Cities". In *Sexuality and Space*, edited by Beatriz Colomina, 241–54. New York: Princeton Architectural Press, 1992.

Guha, Ranajit. *An Indian Historiography of India: A Nineteenth-Century Agenda and Its Implications*. Calcutta: K. P. Bagchi, 1988.

Guha, Ranajit, and Gayatri Spivak, eds. *Selected Subaltern Studies*. New York: Oxford University Press, 1988.

Gundara, Jagdish S., and Ian Duffield, eds. *Essays on the History of Blacks in Britain from Roman Times to the Mid-Twentieth Century*. London: Avebury, 1992.

Gupta, Anirudha, ed. *Indians Abroad: Asia and Africa*. Delhi: Orient Longman, 1969.

Hall, Catherine. "Histories, Empires and the Post-Colonial Moment.". In *The Post-Colonial Question: Common Skies, Divided Horizons*, edited by Iain Chambers and Lidia Curti, 65–77. New York: Routledge, 1996.

———. *White, Male and Middle Class: Explorations in Feminist History*. London: Routledge, 1992.

Hall, Kim F. *Things of Darkness: Economies of Race and Gender in Early Modern England*. Ithaca: Cornell University Press, 1995.

Hall, Stuart. "Cultural Identity and Cinematic Representation". *Framework* 36 (1989): 68–81.

———. "Signification, Representation, Ideology: Althusser and the Post-Structuralist Debate". *Critical Studies in Mass Communication* 2, no. 2 (June 1985): 91–114.

Hansen, Kathryn. "The Birth of Hindi Drama in Banaras, 1868–1885". In *Culture and Power in Banaras: Community, Performance and Environment, 1800–1980*, edited by Sandria B. Freitag, 62–92. Berkeley and Los Angeles: University of California Press, 1989.

Haraway, Donna. *Primate Visions: Gender, Race and Nature in the World of Modern Science*. New York: Routledge, 1989.

Harvey, David. *The Condition of Postmodernity*. Oxford: Blackwell, 1990.

Hay, Stephen. "The Making of a Late-Victorian Hindu: M. K. Gandhi in London, 1888–1891". *Victorian Studies*, 33, no. 1 (1989): 74–98.

Haynes, Douglas. *Rhetoric and Ritual in Colonial India: The Shaping of a Public Culture in Surat City, 1852–1928*. Berkeley and Los Angeles: University of California Press, 1991.

Haynes, Douglas, and Gyan Prakash, eds. *Contesting Power: Resistance and Everyday Social Relations in South Asia*. Berkeley and Los Angeles: University of California Press, 1991.

Hearn, Jeff. *Men in the Public Eye: The Construction and Deconstruction of Public Men and Public Patriarchies*. London: Routledge, 1991.

Hecht, J. J. "Continental and Colonial Servants in Eighteenth-Century England". *Smith College Studies in History* 40 (1954): 1–61.

Heimsath, Charles. "The Origin and Enactment of the Indian Age of Consent Bill, 1891". *Journal of Asian Studies* 21, no. 4 (1962): 491–504.

Hendricks, Margo, and Patricia Parker, eds. *Women, 'Race,' and Writing in the Early Modern Period*. London: Routledge, 1994.

Hesse, Barnor. "Black to Front and Black Again". In *Place and the Politics of Identity*, edited by Michael Keith and Steve Pile, 162–82. London: Routledge, 1993.

Hinnells, John R. "Parsi Zoroastrians in London". In *Desh Pardesh: The South Asian Presence in Britain*, edited by Roger Ballard, 251–71. London: C. Hurst, 1994.

Hobsbawm, Eric. *The Age of Empire, 1875–1914*. New York: Pantheon, 1987.

Holmes, Colin. *John Bull's Island: Immigration and British Society, 1871–1971*. London: Macmillan, 1988.

———, ed. *Immigrants and Minorities in British Society*. London: George Allen Unwin, 1978.

Holt, Thomas C. "Marking: Race, Race-Making, and the Writing of History". *American Historical Review* 100, no. 1 (February 1995): 1–20.

———. *The Problem of Freedom: Race, Labor, and Politics in Jamaica and Britain, 1832–1938*. Baltimore: Johns Hopkins University Press, 1992.

Horowitz, Helen Lefkowitz. *The Passion and the Power: The Life of M. Carey Thomas*. New York: Alfred K. Knopf, 1994.

Howsam, Leslie. " 'Sound-Minded Women': Eliza Orme and the Study and Practice of Law in Late-Victorian England". *Atlantis* 15, no. 1 (fall 1989): 44–55.

Hoy, Sue Ellen, and Margaret MacCurtain. *From Dublin to New Orleans: Nora and Alice's Journey to America, 1889*. Dublin: Attic, 1994.

Hulme, Peter. "Subversive Archipelagos: Colonial Discourse and the Break-Up of Continental Theory". *Dispositio* 14, no. 36–38 (1989): 1–23.

Hunt, Felicity. *Lessons for Life: The Schooling of Girls and Women, 1850–1950*. Oxford: Basil Blackwell, 1987.

Hunt, James. *Gandhi in London*. Springfield, Virginia: Nataraj Books, 1994.

Hunt, Margaret. "Racism, Imperialism and the Traveler's Gaze in Eighteenth-Century England". *Journal of British Studies* 32 (October 1993): 333–57.

Hunter, Jane. *The Gospel of Gentility: American Women Missionaries in Turn-of-the-Century China*. New Haven: Yale University Press, 1984.

Jain, Ravindra K. *Indian Communities Abroad: Themes and Literature*. New Delhi: Manohar, 1993.

James, C. L. R. *Beyond a Boundary*. 1958. Reprint, Durham: Duke University Press, 1993.

Jayawardena, Kumari. *The White Woman's Other Burden: Western Women and South Asia During British Rule*. New York: Routledge, 1995.

Jones, Kenneth W. *Socio-Religious Reform Movements in British India*. Cambridge: Cambridge University Press, 1989.

———, ed. *Religious Controversy in British India: Dialogues in South Asian Languages*. Albany: State University of New York Press, 1992.

Jones, Wilson Jeremiah. *Alexander Crummell: A Study of Civilization and Discontent*. New York: Oxford University Press, 1989.

Joshi, Svati, ed. *Rethinking English: Essays in Literature, Language and History*. New Delhi: Trianka, 1991.

Joyce, Patrick. *Democratic Subjects: The Self and the Social in the Nineteenth Century*. Cambridge: Cambridge University Press, 1994.

Jukes, Peter. *A Shout in the Street: An Excursion into the Modern City*. New York: Farrar, Straus, and Giroux, 1990.

Kale, Madhavi. "Casting Labor in the Imperial Mold: Indian Indentured Migration to the British Caribbean, 1837–1912". Unpublished paper.

———. "Projecting Identities: Empire and Indentured Labor Migration from India to Trinidad and British Guiana, 1836–1885". In *Nation and Migration: The Politics of Space in the South Asian Diaspora*, edited by Peter van der Veer, 73–92. Philadelphia: University of Pennsylvania Press, 1995.

Kaminsky, Amy. "Gender, Race, *Raza*". *Feminist Studies* 20, no. 1 (spring 1994): 7–31.

Kamm, Josephine. *How Different from Us*. London: Bodley Head, 1958.

Kaplan, Caren. "Deterritorialization: The Rewriting of Home and Exile in Western Feminist Discourse". *Cultural Critique* (1992): 187–98.

———. "Reconfigurations of Geography and Historical Narrative: A Review Essay". *Public Culture* 3, no. 1 (fall 1990): 25–32.

Karlekar, Malavika. *Voices from Within: Early Personal Narratives of Bengali Women*. Delhi: Oxford University Press, 1993.

Karp, Ivan, and Steven D. Lavine, eds. *Exhibiting Cultures: The Poetics and Politics of Museum Display*. Washington, D.C.: Smithsonian Institution Press, 1991.

Kaviraj, Sudipta. "The Imaginary Institution of India". In *Subaltern Studies VII: Writings on South Asian History and Society*, edited by Partha Chatterjee and Gyanendra Pandey, 1–39. Delhi: Oxford University Press, 1993.

Kearney, Hugh. *The British Isles: A History of Four Nations*. Cambridge: Cambridge University Press, 1989.

Keating, Peter, ed. *Into Unknown England, 1866–1913: Selections from the Social Explorers*. Manchester: Manchester University Press, 1976.

Keith, Michael, and Steve Pile, eds. *Place and the Politics of Identity*. London: Routledge, 1993.

Kelly, John. "Diaspora and World War, Blood and Nation in Fiji and Hawaii". *Public Culture* 7, no. 3 (1995): 475–97.

———. *A Politics of Virtue: Hinduism, Sexuality and Countercolonial Discourse in Fiji*. Chicago: University of Chicago Press, 1991.

Kennedy, Dane. "Guardians of Edenic Sanctuaries: Paharis, Lepchas, and Todas in the British Mind". *South Asia* 14, no. 2 (1991): 57–77.

———. *The Magic Mountains: Hill Stations and the British Raj*. Berkeley and Los Angeles: University of California Press, 1996.

Killingray, David., ed. *Africans in Britain*. London: Frank Cass, 1994.

Kimmel, Michael S., ed. *Changing Men: New Directions in Research on Men and Masculinity*. London: Sage, 1987.

Kinsley, David. *Hindu Goddesses: Visions of the Divine Feminine in the Hindu Religious Tradition*. Berkeley and Los Angeles: University of California Press, 1988.

Kishwar, Madhu. "The Daughters of Aryavarta". In *Women in Colonial India: Essays on Survival, Work and the State*, edited by J. Krishnamurty, 78–98. Delhi: Oxford University Press, 1989.

Kopf, David. *The Brahmo Samaj and the Shaping of the Modern Indian Mind*. Princeton: Princeton University Press, 1979.

Kosambi, Meera. *At the Intersection of Gender Reform and Religious Belief*. Bombay: S.N.D.T. Women's University, Research Centre for Women's Studies, 1993.

———. "British Bombay and Marathi Mumbai: Some Nineteenth-Century Perceptions". In *Bombay: Mosaic of Modern Culture*, edited by Alice Thorner and Sujata Patel, 3–24. Bombay: Oxford University Press, 1995.

———. "Gender Reform and Competing State Controls over Women: The Rakhmabai Case [1884–1888]". *Contributions to Indian Sociology* (n.s.) 9, no. 1–2 (1995): 265–90.

———. "Girl-Brides and Socio-Legal Change: Age of Consent Bill [1891] Controversy". *Economic and Political Weekly* 26 (August 3–10, 1991): 1857–68.

———. "Indian Response to Christianity, Church and Colonialism: The Case of Pandita Ramabai". *Economic and Political Weekly* 27, no. 43–44 (October 24–31, 1992): WS 61–71.

———. "The Meeting of the Twain: The Cultural Confrontation of Three Women in Nineteenth-Century Maharashtra". *Indian Journal of Gender Studies* 1, no. 1 (1994): 1–22.

———. *Pandita Ramabai's Feminist and Christian Conversions: Focus on Stree Dharma-Neeti*. Bombay: S.N.D.T. Women's University, Research Centre for Women's Studies, 1995.

———. Review of *A Comparison between Men and Women*, by Rosalind O'Hanlon. *The Indian Economic and Social History Review* 32, no. 2 (1995): 276–78.

————, ed. *Women's Oppression in the Public Gaze*. Bombay: S.N.D.T. Women's University, Research Centre for Women's Studies, 1994.

Krishnamurty, J., ed. *Women in Colonial India: Essays on Survival, Work and the State*. Delhi: Oxford University Press, 1989.

Kulke, Eckehard. *The Parsis in India: A Minority as Agent of Social Change*. New Delhi: Vikas Publishing House, Bell Books, 1978.

Kumar, Nita, ed. *Women as Subjects: South Asian Histories*. Charlottesville: University of Virginia Press, 1994.

Kumar, Radha. *The History of Doing: An Illustrated Account of Movements for Women's Rights and Feminism in India, 1800–1990*. London: Verso, 1994.

Kureishi, Hanif. "London and Karachi". In *Patriotism: The Making and Unmaking of British National Identity*, edited by Raphael Samuel, 270–88. Vol. 2. London: Routledge, 1989.

————. *London Kills Me: Three Screenplays and Four Essays*. London: Penguin, 1992.

Kushner, Tony. "Jew and Non-Jew in the East End of London: Towards an Anthropology of 'Everyday' Relations". In *Outsiders and Outcasts: Essays in Honour of William J. Fishman*, edited by Geoffrey Alderman and Colin Holmes, 32–52. London: Duckworth, 1993.

Kutzinski, Vera. *Sugar's Secrets: Race and the Erotics of Cuban Nationalism*. Charlottesville: University of Virginia Press, 1993.

Lake, Marilyn. "The Politics of Respectability: Identifying the Masculinist Context". *Historical Studies* 22 (April 1986): 116–31.

Lal, Maneesha. "The Politics of Gender and Medicine in Colonial India: The Countess of Dufferin's Fund, 1885–1888". *Bulletin of the History of Medicine* 68, no. 1 (1994): 29–66.

Lal, Vinay. "The Incident of the 'Crawling Lane': Women in the Punjab Disturbances of 1919". *Genders* 16 (spring 1993): 35–60.

Langebauer, Laurie. "The City, the Everyday and Boredom: The Case of Sherlock Holmes". *differences* 5, no. 3 (fall 1993): 80–120.

Lelyveld, David. *Aligarh's First Generation: Muslim Solidarity in British India*. New Delhi: Oxford University Press, 1996.

Lemelle, Sidney, and Robin D. G. Kelley, eds. *Imagining Home: Class, Culture and Nationalism in the African Diaspora*. London: Verso, 1994.

Leonardi, Susan. *Dangerous by Degrees: Women at Oxford and the Somerville College Novelists*. New Brunswick: Rutgers University Press, 1989.

Levine, Philippa. "Re-reading the 1890s: Venereal Disease as 'Constitutional Crisis' in Britain and British India". *Journal of Asian Studies* 55, no. 3 (1996): 585–612.

————. "Venereal Disease, Prostitution, and the Politics of Empire: The Case of British India". *Journal of the History of Sexuality* 4, no. 4 (1994): 579–602.

————. *Victorian Feminism, 1850–1900*. Tallahassee: Florida State University Press, 1987.

————. " 'Walking the Streets in a Way No Decent Woman Should': Women Police in World War One". *Journal of Modern History* 66 (1994): 34–78.

————. "The White Slave Trade and the British Empire". *Criminal Justice History*. Forthcoming.

Lewis, Reina. *Gendering Orientalism: Race, Femininity and Representation*. London: Routledge, 1996.

Lindeborg, Ruth H. "The 'Asiatic' and the Boundaries of Victorian Englishness". *Victorian Studies* 37 (spring 1994): 381–404.

Linebaugh, Peter. "All the Atlantic Mountains Shook". *Labour/Le Travailleur* 10 (autumn 1982): 87–121.

Loomba, Ania. "The Color of Patriarchy: Critical Difference, Cultural Difference, and Renaissance Drama". In *Women, 'Race,' and Writing in the Early Modern Period*, edited by Margo Hendricks and Patricia Parker, 17–34. London: Routledge, 1994.

————. "Dead Women Tell No Tales: Issues of Female Subjectivity, Subaltern Agency and Tradition in Colonial and Postcolonial Writings on Widow Immolation in India". *History Workshop Journal* 36 (1993): 209–27.

————. *Gender, Race and Renaissance Drama*. Manchester: Manchester University Press, 1989.

Lorimer, Douglas. *Colour, Class and the Victorians*. New York: Holmes and Meier, 1978.

Lotz, Rainer, and Ian Pegg, eds. *Under the Imperial Carpet: Essays in Black History, 1780–1950*. Crawley, England: Rabbit, 1986.

Luhrmann, T. M. *The Good Parsi: The Fate of a Colonial Elite in a Postcolonial Society*. Cambridge: Harvard University Press, 1996.

Lutzker, Edith. *Edith Pechey-Phipson, M.D.: The Story of England's Foremost Pioneering Woman Doctor*. New York: Exposition, 1973.

MacDonald, Robert H. *The Language of Empire: Myths and Metaphors of Popular Imperialism, 1880–1918*. Manchester: Manchester University Press, 1994.

Mackenzie, John M. *Imperialism and Popular Culture*. Manchester: Manchester University Press, 1986.

————. *Orientalism: History, Theory and the Arts*. Manchester: Manchester University Press, 1995.

————. *Propaganda and Empire*. Manchester: Manchester University Press, 1984.

Mackrell, Brian. *Hariru Wikitoria! An Illustrated History of the Maori Tour of England, 1863*. Auckland: Oxford University Press, 1985.

Mama, Amina. *Beyond the Masks: Race, Gender and Subjectivity*. New York: Routledge, 1995.

Mangan, J. A., ed. *The Imperial Curriculum: Racial Images and Education in the British Colonial Experience*. London: Routledge, 1993.

Mani, Lata. "Contentious Traditions: The Debate on *Sati* in Colonial India". In *Recasting Women: Essays in Colonial History*, edited by Kumkum Sangari and Sudesh Vaid, 88–126. New Delhi: Kali for Women, 1989.

————. "The Female Subject, the Colonial Gaze". In *Interrogating Modernity: Culture and Colonialism in India*, edited by T. Niranjana et al., 273–91. Calcutta: Seagull, 1993.

Mankekar, Purnima. "Reflections on Diasporic Identities: A Prolegomena to an Analysis of Political Bifocality". *Diaspora* 3, no. 3 (winter 1994): 49–70.

Manton, Jo. *Mary Carpenter and the Children of the Streets*. London: Heinemann, 1976.

Marks, Shula. "History, the Nation and the Empire: Sniping at the Periphery". *History Workshop Journal* 29 (1990): 111–19.

———, ed. *Not Either an Experimental Doll: The Separate Worlds of Three South African Women*. London: Women's Press, 1987.

Marshall, Peter J. *Imperial Britain*. The Creighton Lecture. London: University of London, 1994.

———. "No Fatal Impact? The Elusive History of Imperial Britain". *Times Literary Supplement*, March 12, 1993, pp. 8–10.

———, ed. *The Cambridge Illustrated History of the British Empire*. Cambridge: Cambridge University Press, 1996.

Martinez-Alier, Verena. *Marriage, Class and Colour in Nineteenth-Century Cuba: A Study of Racial Attitudes and Sexual Values in a Slave Society*. Ann Arbor: University of Michigan Press, 1974.

Masani, R. P. *Dadhabai Naoroji*. Delhi: Ministry of Information and Broadcasting, 1960.

Mayhall, Laura. "Creating the 'Suffragette Spirit': British Feminism and the Historical Imagination". *Women's History Review* 4, no. 3 (1995): 319–344.

Mazumdar, Sucheta. "Race and Racism: South Asians in the United States". In *Frontiers of Asian American Studies: Writing, Research and Commentary*, edited by Gail M. Nomura, Russell Endo, Stephen Sumida, and Russell C. Leong, 25–38. Pullman, Washington: Washington State University Press, 1989.

———. "Racist Responses to Racism: The Aryan Myth and South Asians in the United States". *South Asia Bulletin* 9, no. 1 (1989): 47–55.

Mbilinyi, Marjorie. "Research Methodologies in Gender Issues". In *Gender in Southern Africa: Conceptual and Theoretical Issues*, edited by Ruth Meena, 31–70. Harare: SAPES Books, 1992.

McCalman, Iain. *Radical Underworld: Prophets, Revolutionaries and Pornographers in London, 1795–1840*. Oxford: Clarendon, 1988.

McClintock, Anne. *Imperial Leather: Race, Gender and Sexuality in the Colonial Contest*. New York: Routledge, 1995.

McLaughlin, Joseph. *Writing the Urban Jungle / Reading Imperial London*. Charlottesville: University of Virginia Press, forthcoming.

Meena, Ruth, ed. *Gender in Southern Africa: Conceptual and Theoretical Issues*. Harare: SAPES Books, 1992.

Mehta, Ved. *Up at Oxford: Continents of Exile*. New York: W. W. Norton, 1993.

Mercer, Kobena. *Welcome to the Jungle: New Positions in Black Cultural Studies*. New York: Routledge, 1994.

Metcalf, Thomas R. *Ideologies of the Raj*. Cambridge: Cambridge University Press, 1994.

Meyerowitz, Joanne J. *Women Adrift: Independent Wage Earners in Chicago, 1880–1930*. Chicago: University of Chicago Press, 1988.

Mitchell, Timothy. *Colonising Egypt*. Berkeley and Los Angeles: University of California Press, 1988.

Mohanram, Radhika. "Postcolonial Maori Sovereignty". *Women's Studies Journal* (special issue: *Aotearoa/New Zealand and their Others: Feminist and Postcoloniality*) 11, no. 1–2 (1995): 63–94.

Moon, Michael, and Cathy N. Davidson, eds. *Subjects and Citizens: Nation, Race, and Gender from Oroonoko to Anita Hill*. Durham: Duke University Press, 1995.

Morgan, Cecilia. " 'Of Slender Frame and Delicate Appearance': the Placing of Laura Secord in the Narratives of Canadian Loyalist History". *Journal of the Canadian Historical Association* 5 (1994): 195–212.

Morgan, David. *Discovering Men*. New York: Routledge, 1992.

Morris, Jan. *Oxford*. Oxford: Oxford University Press, 1978.

Morris, Meaghan. "The Man in the Mirror: David Harvey's 'Condition' of Postmodernity". *Theory, Culture and Society* 9 (1992): 253–79.

Morrison, Toni. *Playing in the Dark: Whiteness and the Literary Imagination*. New York: Vintage, 1993.

Morrow, Margot D. "The Origins and Early Years of the British Committee of the Indian National Congress, 1885–1907". Ph.D. diss., University of London, 1977.

Mort, Frank. *Dangerous Sexualities: Medico-Moral Politics in England since 1830*. London: Routledge, 1987.

Muldoon, James. "The Indian as Irishman". *Historical Collections* (Essex Institute) 3 (1975): 267–89.

Murphy, Geraldine. "Olaudah Equiano, Accidental Tourist". *Eighteenth Century Studies* 27 (1994): 551–68.

Nair, Janaki. "Uncovering the Zenana: Visions of Indian Womanhood in Englishwomen's Writings, 1813–1940". *Journal of Women's History* 2 (spring 1990): 8–24.

———. *Women and Law in Colonial India: A Social History*. New Delhi: Kali for Women, 1996.

Newton, Judith L., Mary P. Ryan, and Judith R. Walkowitz, eds. *Sex and Class in Women's History*. New York: Routledge, 1983.

Nicholson, Colin. *Strangers to England: Immigration to England, 1100–1952*. London: Wayland Publishers, 1974.

Niranjana, T., P. Sudhir, and V. Dhareshwar, eds. *Interrogating Modernity: Culture and Colonialism in India*. Calcutta: Seagull Books, 1993.

Nomura, Gail M., Russell Endo, Stephen Sumida, and Russell C. Leong, eds. *Frontiers of Asian American Studies: Writing, Research and Commentary*. Pullman, Washington: Washington State University Press, 1989.

Nord, Deborah Epstein. "The City as Theater: From Early Georgian to Victorian London". *Victorian Studies* 31 (winter 1988): 158–88.

———. "The Social Explorer as Anthropologist: Victorian Travellers among the Urban Poor". In *Visions of the Modern City: Essays in History, Art, and Literature*, edited by William Sharpe and Leonard Wallock, 122–34. Baltimore: Johns Hopkins University Press, 1987.

———. *Walking the Victorian Streets: Women, Representation and the City*. Ithaca: Cornell University Press, 1995.

Nussbaum, Felicity A. *Torrid Zones: Maternity, Sexuality and Empire in*

Eighteenth-Century English Narratives. Baltimore: Johns Hopkins University Press, 1995.

O'Connell, Joanna, Angela Reyes, Iris Berger, Elsa M. Chaney, Veve A. Clark, Francoise Lionnet, and Mrinalini Sinha. "Editorial". *Signs* (special issue: *Postcolonial, Emergent, and Indigenous Feminisms*) 20, no. 4 (summer 1995): 787–96.

O'Hanlon, Rosalind. *A Comparison between Men and Women: Tarabai Shinde and the Critique of Gender Relations in Colonial India*. Madras: Oxford University Press, 1994.

———. "Issues of Widowhood: Gender and Resistance in Colonial Western India". In *Contesting Power: Resistance and Everyday Social Relations in South Asia*, edited by Douglas Haynes and Gyan Prakash, 62–108. Oxford: Oxford University Press, 1991.

O'Keefe, Timothy, ed. *Alienation*. London: MacGibbon and Kee, 1960.

Omvedt, Gail. *Cultural Revolt in a Colonial Society: The Non-Brahman Movement in Western India, 1873–1930*. Bombay: Scientific Socialist Education Trust, 1976.

Ong, Aihwa. "On the Edges of Empires: Flexible Citizenship among Chinese in Diaspora". *positions* 1, no. 3 (1993): 745–78.

Ortner, Sherry. "Resistance and the Problem of Ethnographic Refusal". *Studies in Comparative Society and History* 37, no. 1 (January 1995): 173–93.

Painter, Nell Irvin. "Three Southern Women and Freud: A Non-exceptionalist Approach to Race, Class, and Gender in the Slave South". In *Feminists Revision History*, edited by Ann-Louise Shapiro, 195–216. New Brunswick: Rutgers University Press, 1994.

Parry, Benita. "Overlapping Territories and Intertwined Histories: Edward Said's Postcolonial Cosmopolitanism". In *Edward Said: A Critical Reader*, edited by Michael Sprinker, 19–47. Oxford: Blackwell, 1993.

Parry, J. "The New Britons". *The Observer*. November 28, 1971, pp. 17–25.

Peterson, Willard J. "What to Wear? Observation and Participation by Jesuit Missionaries in Late Ming Society". In *Implicit Understandings: Observing, Reporting, and Reflecting on the Encounters between Europeans and Other Peoples in the Early Modern Era*, edited by Stuart B. Schwartz, 403–21. Cambridge: Cambridge University Press, 1994.

Phadke, Y. D. *Social Reformers of Maharashtra*. New Delhi: Maharashtra Information Centre, 1975.

Phillips, Caryl. *The European Tribe*. London: Faber and Faber, 1987.

Pieterse, Jan Nederveen. *The Decolonization of Imagination: Culture Knowledge, Power*. London: Zed Books, 1995.

Pollin, Harold. "Transport Lines and Social Divisions". In *London: Aspects of Change*, edited by the Centre for Urban Studies, 29–61. London: MacGibbon and Kee, 1969.

Pollock, Griselda. "The Dangers of Proximity: The Spaces of Sexuality and Surveillance in Word and Image". *Discourse* 16, no. 2 (winter 1993–94): 3–50.

———. "Vicarious Excitements: *London: A Pilgrimage* by Gustave Doré and Blanchard Jerrold 1872. *New Formations* 4 (spring 1988): 25–49.

Pooncha, Veena. "Redefining Gender Relationships: The Imprint of the Colonial State on the Coorg/Kodava Norms of Marriage and Sexuality". *Contributions to Indian Sociology* (n.s) 29, no. 1–2 (1995): 39–64.

Poovey, Mary. *Making a Social Body: British Cultural Formation, 1830–1864.* Chicago: University of Chicago Press, 1995.

Port, M. H. *Imperial London: Civil Government Building in London, 1850–1915.* New Haven: Yale University Press, 1995.

Porter, Andrew N. "Cambridge, Keswick and Late 19th-Century Attitudes toward Africa". *Journal of Imperial and Commonwealth History* 5 (1976): 5–34.

———. "Evangelical Enthusiasm, Missionary Motivation and West Africa in the late 19th-Century: The Career of G. W. Brooke". *Journal of Imperial and Commonwealth History* 6 (1977): 23–46.

Porter, Roy, ed. *Myths of the English.* Cambridge, England: Polity, 1992.

Prakash, Gyan, ed. *After Colonialism: Imperial Histories and Postcolonial Displacements.* Princeton: Princeton University Press, 1994.

———. "Subaltern Studies as Postcolonial Criticism". *American Historical Review* 99, no. 5 (December 1994):1475–90.

Pratt, Mary Louise. *Imperial Eyes: Travel Writing and Transculturation.* London: Routledge, 1992.

Price, Richard. "Historiography, Narrative and the Nineteenth Century". *Journal of British Studies* 35 (April 1996): 220–56.

Radhakrishnan, R. "Is the Ethnic 'Authentic' in the Diaspora?" In *The State of Asian America*, edited by Karin Aguilar-San Juan, 219–33. Boston: South End, 1994.

———. "Postcolonialism and the Boundaries of Identity". *Callaloo* 16, no. 4 (1993): 750–71.

Rajkumar, N. V. *Indians outside India: A General Survey.* Madras: Commercial Printing and Publishing House, for All-India Congress Committee, n.d (1949 or after).

Ramusack, Barbara. "Cultural Missionaries, Maternal Imperialists, Feminist Allies: British Women Activists in India, 1865–1945". In *Western Women and Imperialism: Complicity and Resistance*, edited by Nupur Chaudhuri and Margaret Strobel, 119–36. Bloomington: Indiana University Press, 1992.

———. "The Indian Princes as Fantasy: Palace Hotels, Palace Museums, and Palace on Wheels". In *Consuming Modernity: Public Culture in a South Asian World*, edited by Carol A. Breckenridge, 66–89. Minneapolis: University of Minnesota Press, 1995.

Rau, Santha Rama. *Home to India.* London: Harper Brothers, 1945.

Rawal, Munni. *Dadabhai Naoroji: A Prophet of Indian Nationalism.* New Delhi: Anmol Publications, 1989.

Ray, Bharati, ed. *From the Seams of History: Essays on Indian Women.* Delhi: Oxford University Press, 1995.

Raychaudhuri, Tapan. *Europe Reconsidered: Perceptions of the West in Nineteenth-Century Bengal.* Delhi: Oxford University Press, 1988.

Rhys, Jean. *Wide Sargasso Sea.* New York: W. W. Norton, 1982.

Rich, Adrienne. *An Atlas of the Difficult World.* New York: W. W. Norton, 1991.

————. *Blood, Bread and Poetry: Selected Prose, 1979–1985*. New York: W. W. Norton, 1986.

Rich, Paul. "The Black Diaspora in Britain: Afro-Caribbean Students and the Struggle for Political Identity, 1900–1950". *Immigrants and Minorities* 3, no. 1 (1984): 151–73.

————. *Race and Empire in British Politics*. Cambridge: Cambridge University Press, 1986.

Richards, Thomas. *The Commodity Culture of Victorian England: Advertising and Spectacle, 1851–1914*. London: Verso, 1990.

Ricks, Christopher, and Leonard Michaels, eds. *The State of the Language*. Berkeley and Los Angeles: University of California Press, 1990.

Robb, Peter, ed. *The Concept of Race in South Asia*. Delhi: Oxford University Press, 1995.

Robertson, George, Melinda Mash, Lisa Tickner, Jon Bird, Barry Curtis, and Tim Putnam, eds. *Travelers' Tales: Narratives of Home and Displacement*. London: Routledge, 1994.

Romero, Lora. "Vanishing Americans: Gender, Empire, and New Historicism". *American Literature* 63, no. 3 (1991): 385–404.

Roper, Michael, and John Tosh, eds. *Manful Assertions: Masculinities in Britain since 1800*. London: Routledge, 1991.

Rose, Jennifer. "The Traditional Role of Women in Iranian and Indian (Parsi) Zoroastrian Communities from the Nineteenth to the Twentieth Century". *Journal of the K. R. Cama Institute* 56 (1989): 1–103.

Ross, Dorothy. "Grand Narrative in American Historical Writing". *American Historical Review* 110, no. 3 (June 1995): 651–77.

Rupp, Leila J. "Challenging Imperialism in International Women's Organizations, 1888–1945". *National Women's Studies Association Journal* 8 (spring 1996): 9–27.

————. "Constructing Internationalism: The Case of Transnational Women's Organizations, 1888–1945". *American Historical Review* 99 (1994): 1571–1600.

Russell, Penelope. *A Wish of Distinction: Colonial Gentility and Femininity*. Melbourne: Melbourne University Press, 1994.

Rutherford, Andrew, ed. *Early Verse by Rudyard Kipling, 1879–1889*. Oxford: Clarendon, 1986.

Ryan, Mary. *Women in Public: Between Banners and Ballots, 1825–1880*. Baltimore: Johns Hopkins University Press, 1990.

Said, Edward. *Culture and Imperialism*. New York: Vintage Books, 1993.

St. Aubyn, Giles. *Queen Victoria: A Portrait*. New York: Atheneum, 1992.

Salecl, Renata. "The Fantasy Structure of Nationalist Discourse". *Praxis International* 13, no. 3 (October 1993): 213–23.

Samuel, Raphael, ed. *Patriotism: The Making and Unmaking of British National Identity*, Vol. 2. London: Routledge, 1989.

Sangari, Kumkum. "The Politics of the Possible". In *Interrogating Modernity: Culture and Colonialism in India*, edited by T. Niranjana et al., 242–272. Calcutta: Seagull Books, 1993.

————. "Relating Histories: Definitions of Literacy, Literature, Gender in

Early Nineteenth-Century Calcutta and England". In *Rethinking English: Essays in Literature, Language, History*, edited by Svati Joshi, 32–123. New Delhi: Trianka, 1991.

Sangari, Kumkum, and Sudesh Vaid, eds. *Recasting Women: Essays in Colonial History*. New Delhi: Kali for Women, 1989.

———, eds. *Women and Culture*. 1985. Reprint, Bombay: S.N.D.T. University, Research Centre for Women's Studies, 1994.

Sanyal, Ram Gopal. *A General Biography of Bengal Celebrities Both Living and Dead*. Calcutta: Riddhi, 1976.

Sarkar, Sumit. *Modern India, 1885–1947*. Madras: Macmillan India, 1983.

———. "Popular Culture, Community, Power: Three Studies of Modern Indian Social History". *Studies in History* 8, no. 2, n.s. (1992): 309–23.

Sarkar, Tanika. "A Book of Her Own. A Life of Her Own: Autobiography of a Nineteenth-Century Woman". *History Workshop Journal* 36 (1993): 35–65.

———. "The Hindu Wife and the Hindu Nation: Domesticity and Nationalism in Nineteenth-Century Bengal". *Studies in History* 8, no. 2, n.s. (1992): 213–35.

———. "Rhetoric against Age of Consent: Resisting Colonial Reason in the Death of a Child-Wife". *Economic and Political Weekly* 28, no. 36 (September 4, 1993): 1869–78.

Sassen, Saskia. "Whose City Is It? Globalization and the Formation of New Cities". *Public Culture* 8, no. 2 (1996): 205–224.

Schwarz, Bill. "Memories of Empire". In *Displacements: Cultural Identities in Question*, edited by Angelika Bammer, 156–71. Bloomington: Indiana University Press, 1994.

Schwarz, Bill, ed. *The Expansion of England: Race, Ethnicity, and Cultural History*. London: Routledge, 1996.

Schwartz, Stuart B., ed. *Implicit Understandings: Observing, Reporting, and Reflecting on Encounters between Europeans and Other Peoples in the Early Modern Era*. Cambridge: Cambridge University Press, 1994.

Scobie, Edward. *Black Britannia: A History of Blacks in Britain*. Chicago: Johnson Publishing, 1972.

Scott, Joan. "The Evidence of Experience". *Critical Inquiry* 17 (summer 1991): 773–97.

———. *'Only Paradoxes to Offer': French Feminists and the Rights of Man*. Cambridge: Harvard University Press, 1996.

Sedgwick, Eve Kosofsky. *Between Men: English Literature and Male Homosocial Desire*. New York: Columbia University Press, 1985.

Sen Gupta, Padmini. *Pioneer Women of India*. Bombay: Thacker, 1944.

Seton, Rosemary, and Emily Nash. *A Preliminary Guide to the Archives of the British Missionary Societies*. London: School of Oriental and African Studies, 1992.

Shapiro, Ann-Louise, ed. *Feminists Revision History*. New Brunswick: Rutgers University Press, 1994.

Sharpe, Jenny. *Allegories of Empire: The Figure of Woman in the Colonial Text*. Minneapolis: University of Minnesota Press, 1993.

Sharpe, William, and Leonard Wallock, eds. *Visions of the Modern City: Essays in History, Art, and Literature*. Baltimore: Johns Hopkins University Press, 1987.

Shyllon, Folarin. *Black People in Britain, 1555–1833*. London: Oxford University Press for the Institute of Race Relations, 1977.

Sinha, Mrinalini. "The Age of Consent Act: The Ideal of Masculinity in Nineteenth-Century Bengal". In *Shaping Bengali Worlds, Public and Private*, edited by T. K. Stewart, 99–127. Ann Arbor: University of Michigan, 1989.

———. " 'Chathams, Pitts, and Gladstone in Petticoats': The Politics of Gender and Race in the Ilbert Bill Controversy, 1883–84". In *Western Women and Imperialism*, edited by Nupur Chaudhuri and Margaret Strobel, 98–118. Bloomington: Indiana University Press, 1992.

———. *Colonial Masculinity: The 'Manly Englishman' and the 'Effeminate Bengali' in the Late Nineteenth Century*. Manchester: Manchester University Press, 1995.

———. "Gender and Imperialism: Colonial Policy and the Ideology of Moral Imperialism in Late Nineteenth-Century Bengal". In *Changing Men: New Directions in Research on Men and Masculinity*, edited by Michael S. Kimmel, 217–31. London: Sage, 1987.

———. "Gender in the Critiques of Colonialism and Nationalism: Locating the 'Indian Woman'". In *Feminists Revision History*, edited by Ann-Louise Shapiro, 246–75. New Brunswick: Rutgers University Press, 1994.

———. "Reading Mother India: Empire, Nation and the Female Voice". *Journal of Women's History* 6, no. 2 (summer 1994): 6–44.

Smith, Anna Marie. *New Right Discourse on Race and Sexuality: Britain, 1968–1990*. Cambridge: Cambridge University Press, 1995.

Smith, Faith. "Coming Home to the Real Thing: Gender and Intellectual Life in the Anglophone Caribbean". *South Atlantic Quarterly* 93, no. 34 (fall 1994): 895–922.

Soffer, Reba. "Authority in the University: Balliol, Newnham and the New Mythology". In *Myths of the English*, edited by Roy Porter, 192–215. Cambridge, England: Polity, 1992.

———. *Discipline and Power: The University, History, and the Making of an English Elite, 1870–1930*. Palo Alto: Stanford University Press, 1994.

Sprinker, Michael, ed. *Edward Said: A Critical Reader*. Oxford: Blackwell, 1993.

Stanley, Liz. "British Feminist Histories: An Editorial Introduction". *Women's Studies International Forum* 13 (1990): 1–7.

Stedman Jones, Gareth. *Outcast London*. Oxford: Oxford University Press, 1971.

Stewart, T. K., ed. *Shaping Bengali Worlds, Public and Private*. Ann Arbor: University of Michigan, 1989.

Stocks, Mary. *Eleanor Rathbone: A Biography*. London: Victor Gollancz, 1949.

Stoler, Ann Laura. " 'Mixed-Bloods' in Colonial Southeast Asia". In *The Decolonization of Imagination: Culture, Knowledge, Power*, edited by Jan Nederveen Pieterse, 128–48. London: Zed Books, 1995.

———. *Race and the Education of Desire: Foucault's History of Sexuality and the Colonial Order of Things*. Durham: Duke University Press, 1995.

Strobel, Margaret. *European Women and the Second British Empire*. Bloomington: Indiana University Press, 1991.

Sunder Rajan, Rajeswari. *Real and Imagined Women: Gender, Culture and Postcolonialism*. New York: Routledge, 1993.

Symonds, Richard. *Oxford and Empire: The Last Lost Cause?* New York: St.
Martin's, 1986.

Tabili, Laura. "Reconstructing Black Migration in the Imperial Metropolis,
1900–1939". Paper given at the North American Conference of British
Studies, Washington D.C., October 1995.

———. *'We Ask for British Justice': Workers and Racial Difference in Late Imperial Britain*. Ithaca: Cornell University Press, 1994.

Tarakoli-Targhi, Mohamed. "Orientalism's Genesis Amnesia". *Comparative
Studies of South Asia, Africa, and the Middle East* 16, no. 1 (1996): 1–14.

Tarlo, Emma. *Clothing Matters: Dress and Identity in India*. Chicago: University of Chicago Press, 1996.

Thakur, Manab, and Roger Wilson. "Hopeful Travelers: A Study of Asian
Graduates Working in Britain". *New Community* 4, no. 4 (1975–76): 476–
92.

Tharu, Susie, and K. Lalita, eds. *Women Writing in India*. 2 vols. New York:
Feminist, 1991.

Thomas, Nicholas. *Colonialism's Culture: Anthropology, Travel and Government*.
Cambridge, England: Polity, 1994.

Thompson, E. P. *Alien Homage: Edward Thompson and Rabindranath Tagore*.
Delhi: Oxford University Press, 1993.

Thorne, Susan. " 'The Conversion of Englishmen and the Conversion of the
World Inseparable': Missionary Imperialism and the Language of Class,
1750–1850". In *Tensions of Empire: Colonial Cultures in a Bourgeois World*, edited by Frederick Cooper and Ann Stoler, 238–62. Berkeley and Los Angeles: University of California Press, 1996.

Thorner, Alice. "Bombay: Diversity and Exchange". In *Bombay: Mosaic of
Modern Culture*, edited by Thorner and Sujata Patel, xi-xxxiii. Bombay:
Oxford University Press, 1995.

Thorner, Alice, and Sujata Patel, eds. *Bombay: Mosaic of Modern Culture*. Bombay: Oxford University Press, 1995.

Tiffin, Chris, and Alan Lawson, eds. *De-Scribing Empire: Post-colonialism and
Textuality*. London: Routledge, 1994.

Tinker, Hugh. *The Banyan Tree: Overseas Immigrants from India, Pakistan, and
Bangladesh*. Oxford: Oxford University Press, 1977.

Trivedi, Harish. *Colonial Transactions: English Literature and India*. New York:
St. Martin's, 1995.

Tuson, Penelope, ed. *The Queen's Daughters: An Anthology of Victorian Feminist
Writings on India, 1857–1900*. Reading: Ithaca Press, 1996.

Tyrrell, Ian. *Woman's World, Woman's Empire: The Women's Christian Temperance Union in International Perspective, 1880–1930*. Chapel Hill: University of
North Carolina Press, 1991.

Vadgama, Kusoom. *India in Britain: The Indian Contribution to the British
Way of Life*. London: Robert Royce, 1984.

Valverde, Marina. *The Age of Light, Soap and Water: Moral Reform in English Canada, 1885–1925.* Toronto: McClelland and Stewart, 1991.

Van der Veer, Peter, ed. *Nation and Migration: The Politics of Space in the South Asian Diaspora.* Philadelphia: University of Pennsylvania Press, 1995.

Varikas, Eleni. "Gender, Experience and Subjectivity: The Tilly-Scott Disagreement". *New Left Review* 21 (May–June 1995): 89–104.

Vernon, James. *Politics and the People: A Study in English Political Culture, c. 1815–1867.* Cambridge: Cambridge University Press, 1993.

Vicinus, Martha. *Independent Women: Work and Community for Single Women, 1850–1920.* Chicago: University of Chicago Press, 1985.

Vickery, Amanda. "Golden Age to Separate Spheres? A Review of the Categories and Chronology of English Women's History". *The Historical Journal* 36, no. 2 (1993): 383–414.

Visram, Rozina. *Ayahs, Lascars and Princes: The History of Indians in Britain, 1700–1947.* London: Pluto, 1986.

Viswanathan, Gauri. "Coping with (Civil) Death: The Christian Convert's Rights of Passage in Colonial India". In *After Colonialism: Imperial Histories and Postcolonial Displacements*, edited by Gyan Prakash, 183–210. Princeton: Princeton University Press, 1994.

———. *Masks of Conquest: Literary Study and British Rule in India.* New York: Columbia University Press, 1989.

Visweswaran, Kamala. *Fictions of Feminist Ethnography.* Minneapolis: University of Minnesota Press, 1993.

Walker, Pamela J. "Men and Masculinity in the Salvation Army, 1865–1890". In *Manful Assertions: Masculinities in Britain since 1800*, edited by Michael Roper and John Tosh, 92–112. London: Routledge, 1991.

Walkowitz, Judith R. *City of Dreadful Delight: Narratives of Sexual Danger in Late-Victorian London.* Chicago: Chicago University Press, 1992.

———. "Daughter of Empire: Olive Christian Malvery, Photojournalism and the Fashioning of Imperial Citizenship". Paper delivered at the Berkshire Conference of Women Historians, Chapel Hill, North Carolina, June 9, 1996.

Wallace, Anne D. *Walking, Literature and English Culture: The Origins and Uses of the Peripatetic in the Nineteenth Century.* Oxford: Clarendon, 1993.

Walter, Bronwen. "Irishness, Gender and Place". *Environmental and Planning D: Society and Space* 13 (1995): 35–50.

Walvin, James. *Black and White: The Negro and English Society, 1555–1945.* London: Allen Lane for the Penguin Press, 1973.

———. *Slavery and the Slave Trade: A Short Illustrated History.* Jackson: University of Mississippi Press, 1983.

Ware, Vron. *Beyond the Pale: White Women, Racism and History.* London: Verso, 1992.

———. "Island Racism: Gender, Place, and White Power". *Feminist Review* 54 (Autumn 1996): 65–86.

Waters, Christopher M. "The Pink and the Black: Race and Sex in Postwar Britain". *Transition* 69 (1996): 210–21.

Weeks, Jeffrey. *Sex, Politics and Society: The Regulation of Sexuality since 1800*. Essex: Longman, 1981.

Weiner, Annette B., and Jane Schneider, eds. *Cloth and the Human Experience*. Washington, D.C.: Smithsonian Institution Press, 1989.

West, Cornel. *Race Matters*. Boston: Beacon, 1993.

Western, John. *A Passage to England: Barbadian Londoners Speak of Home*. Minneapolis: University of Minnesota Press, 1992.

White, David L. *Competition and Collaboration: Parsi Merchants and the East India Company in 18th-Century India*. New Delhi: Munshiram Manoharlal Publishers, 1995.

Williams, Eric. *Capitalism and Slavery*. 1944. Reprint, Chapel Hill: University of North Carolina Press, 1994.

Wilson, Elizabeth. "The Invisible Flaneur". *New Left Review* 191 (1992):90–110.

Wilson, Kathleen. "Citizenship, Empire and Modernity in the English Provinces, c. 1720–1790". *Eighteenth-Century Studies* 29, no. 1 (1995): 69–96.

Winter, James. *London's Teeming Streets, 1830–1914*. London: Routledge, 1993.

Wohl, Anthony S. " 'Dizzi-Ben-Dizzi': Disraeli as Alien". *Journal of British Studies* 34, no. 3 (July 1995): 375–411.

———, ed. *The Victorian Family: Structure and Stress*. New York: St. Martin's, 1978.

Women of South Asian Descent Collective. *Our Feet Walk the Sky: Women of the South Asian Diaspora*. San Francisco: Aunt Lute, 1993.

Index

Composition:	Impressions Book and Journal Services, Inc.
Text:	10/13 Galliard
Display:	Galliard
Printing and binding:	Thomson-Shore, Inc.